CW01163228

EVERGREENING PATENT EXCLUSIVITY IN PHARMACEUTICAL PRODUCTS

This book analyses four central pieces of EU pharmaceutical regulation: the Orphan Drugs Regulation, the Paediatric Regulation, the Supplementary Protection Certificate Regulation, and the ATMP (Advanced Therapy Medicinal Products) Regulation. These four regulatory instruments constitute focal points in the pharmaceutical industry's approach to modern business and legal strategy. Their central role is justified by the way these regulatory instruments interact with each other and with the patent system, and by the considerable impact they (as a whole) have for the evergreening of exclusive rights on pharmaceutical products.

The book guides the reader through the latest case law and legislative developments and discusses how these influence strategic legal and business choices in the pharmaceutical industry. It brings to the forefront the often-overlooked significance of the legislative architecture of the EU pharmaceutical regulatory framework, and evaluates its results through the lens of the efficiency test.

The book is an important resource for academics and practitioners interested in updated case law and an in-depth analysis of these four regulations. It is also important for those interested in legislative studies, evaluation of legislation and a critical approach to legislative architecture.

Evergreening Patent Exclusivity in Pharmaceutical Products

Supplementary Protection Certificates, Orphan Drugs, Paediatric Extensions and ATMPs

Frantzeska Papadopoulou

·HART·
OXFORD · LONDON · NEW YORK · NEW DELHI · SYDNEY

HART PUBLISHING

Bloomsbury Publishing Plc

Kemp House, Chawley Park, Cumnor Hill, Oxford, OX2 9PH, UK

1385 Broadway, New York, NY 10018, USA

29 Earlsfort Terrace, Dublin 2, Ireland

HART PUBLISHING, the Hart/Stag logo, BLOOMSBURY and the Diana logo are trademarks of Bloomsbury Publishing Plc

First published in Great Britain 2021

Copyright © Frantzeska Papadopoulou, 2021

Frantzeska Papadopoulou has asserted her right under the Copyright, Designs and Patents Act 1988 to be identified as Author of this work.

All rights reserved. No part of this publication may be reproduced or transmitted in any form or by any means, electronic or mechanical, including photocopying, recording, or any information storage or retrieval system, without prior permission in writing from the publishers.

While every care has been taken to ensure the accuracy of this work, no responsibility for loss or damage occasioned to any person acting or refraining from action as a result of any statement in it can be accepted by the authors, editors or publishers.

All UK Government legislation and other public sector information used in the work is Crown Copyright ©. All House of Lords and House of Commons information used in the work is Parliamentary Copyright ©. This information is reused under the terms of the Open Government Licence v3.0 (http://www.nationalarchives.gov.uk/doc/open-government-licence/version/3) except where otherwise stated.

All Eur-lex material used in the work is © European Union, http://eur-lex.europa.eu/, 1998–2021.

A catalogue record for this book is available from the British Library.

Library of Congress Cataloging-in-Publication data

Names: Papadopoulou, Frantzeska, author.
Title: Evergreening patent exclusivity in pharmaceutical products : supplementary protection certificates, orphan drugs, paediatric extensions and ATMPs / Frantzeska Papadopoulou.
Description: Oxford ; New York : Hart, 2021. | Includes bibliographical references and index.
Identifiers: LCCN 2021024006 (print) | LCCN 2021024007 (ebook) | ISBN 9781509950287 (hardback) | ISBN 9781509950324 (paperback) | ISBN 9781509950300 (pdf) | ISBN 9781509950294 (Epub)
Subjects: LCSH: Drugs—European Union countries—Patents. | Patent extensions—European Union countries. | Patent medicines—Law and legislation—European Union countries. | Patent laws and legislation—European Union countries.
Classification: LCC KJE2751.M44 P37 2021 (print) | LCC KJE2751.M44 (ebook) | DDC 346.2404/86—dc23
LC record available at https://lccn.loc.gov/2021024006
LC ebook record available at https://lccn.loc.gov/2021024007

ISBN: HB: 978-1-50995-028-7
ePDF: 978-1-50995-030-0
ePub: 978-1-50995-029-4

Typeset by Compuscript Ltd, Shannon

To find out more about our authors and books visit www.hartpublishing.co.uk. Here you will find extracts, author information, details of forthcoming events and the option to sign up for our newsletters.

PREFACE

A book evaluating the regulatory rights system and how it interacts with patent rights is timely when we are experiencing the worst pandemic of the past century; when immediate access to large quantities of safe vaccines and medicines becomes a concern for everyone, irrespective of geographical, political or financial circumstances. The concerns and multilayered considerations that have arisen during the Covid-19 pandemic are expected to leave traces even after the pandemic is over, both because more pandemics are expected to come, and because Covid-19 has uncovered pathologies that make the system unreliable when it is needed the most. While solutions have been found and vaccines have made it to the market in a timely manner, this is only thanks to immense political support and the willingness of relevant authorities, such as the European Medicines Agency (EMA), to pave the way forward with admirable speed (for obvious reasons).

However, it is clear that this political willingness to remedy gaps and weaknesses in the system is not a long-term solution.

The pharmaceutical industry operates within a multilayered system of rights and obligations where national and EU competences intertwine, providing for hybrid solutions. The interpretation and application of EU regulations is based on requirements and key terms stipulated in EU Directives, while Member States strive to keep as much independence as possible in public health matters in order to preserve control over their national public health budgets. Furthermore, the system is to a considerable extent dependent on the role and legitimacy of a unique EU agency, the EMA. Criticism of the efficiency and transparency of the EMA's operations, as well as its relations to national agencies, is expressed to this day.

The European system of regulatory rights is the result of a quasi-successful legal transplant, through which the US approach has been transplanted only partially to the European pharmaceutical industry. Needless to say, attempting this could never have been an uncomplicated endeavour. The differences in the legislative architecture between the United States and the EU are characteristic examples of the practical limitations that had to be considered. At the same time, the regulatory framework has to accommodate diverging and conflicting interests. On the one hand, there is a need to protect innovators (the traditional pharmaceutical industry); on the other hand, there is a need to support those market stakeholders that contribute to decreased public health costs (ie the generic drugs industry). During the past few years, these two categories – originators and generics – have started to merge more and more. Technological advancements, political objectives and the eternal battle of competences in the field of public health between the EU and Member States are some additional components of what seems to be a thousand-piece puzzle.

The patent system, which remains of central importance for the pharmaceutical industry and the operation of the regulatory system, is only partly harmonised at an EU level; there are notable diversities in national patent legislations, and in the way these are interpreted and applied, while there is still no unitary patent right. Supplementary protection certificates are rights whose legal source is an EU regulation, while the rights as such are granted by national patent offices, which make their own interpretations and whose administrative systems will have an impact on how the patent system works in practice.

This book looks into and analyses four central regulations of the modern regulatory rights regime in Europe, namely: the Supplementary Protection Regulation (Regulation (EC) No 469/2009), the Paediatric Regulation (Regulation (EC) 1902/2006), the Orphan Drugs Regulation (Regulation (EC) No 141/2000), and the Advanced Treatments Regulation (Regulation (EC) 1394/2007). These four regulations, their drafting histories, their objectives and – above all – their effects are investigated and discussed through the lens of legislative studies and, notably, of the effectiveness test.

By offering the first in-depth analysis of these regulations, which are examined both on their own and in their interactions with one another, the book provides insights into how modern pharmaceutical regulations are drafted and applied, and discusses the weaknesses in their drafting that also haunt their application. The book further explores the relation between the regulatory system and intellectual property (IP) rights, and submits that modern IP law making in the pharmaceutical sector takes place under the radar of public attention and within the framework of regulatory rights.

However, the book does not perceive these as isolated elements of relevance for the pharmaceutical market, but as interrelated components of one and the same context. Not only are these respective regulations interrelated, but they are also related to other key components that interfere, directly or indirectly, with the way the regulations are interpreted and applied – such as the EMA and the data and market protection regulations.

The Commission has recently identified gaps and weaknesses in the system, which can found on two different axes: that of the IP rights system and that of pharmaceutical regulatory rights system as such. The Commission Communication concerning the intellectual property action plan (COM(2020) 760 final) identified the need for further building upon existing innovation capital by reviewing and, if needed, re-modelling key aspects of the IP rights system. This is not just a way of advancing European research and development, but also a necessary route in order to address social and environmental challenges. The Commission identified five IP-related challenges that need to be addressed in the future intellectual property action plan. Two of them are of central importance for the analysis in this book: the fragmented character of the patent system and the need to provide a well-developed mechanism for access to IP. In order to address these two challenges, there is a need to unify practices in patent law as well as in the supplementary protection certificates system. Further, there must be more streamlined forms of cooperation, both voluntary and mandatory, in order to address needs that require access, in an immediate and uncomplicated manner, to materials protected by IP rights.

On the other hand, in the new pharmaceutical strategy for Europe proposed in the Commission Communication (COM(2020) 761 final), the following were identified as 'flagship initiatives on unmet needs': to revise legislation on medicines for children and rare diseases, and to investigate the relation between incentives and obligations in the pharmaceutical legislation and how this interacts with the intellectual property rights system. Although this communication addressed the need to review existing legislation and introduce new legislation, in order to take into account new needs of the pharmaceutical sector and patients' rights to access medicines and therapies at affordable prices, one echoing absence remains. The same absence can be noted in the communication on the intellectual property action plan. What is missing in these two communications is also the main message of this book: the need to proceed in a holistic manner when legislating.

Efficiency in the regulation of the pharmaceutical market presupposes interaction between the IP system, regulatory rights and factors that influence how IP rights and other forms of exclusivities and obligations are conferred on the pharmaceutical sector. Seeing them as bits and pieces of a bigger picture, is a difficult and demanding endeavour. However, it is necessary. IP rights and regulatory rights of different sorts will interact in the ways that they exclude competitors from the market. They will be part of the pharmaceutical companies' business strategies and will, at times, prevent or delay access to medicines. Thus, even if we create efficient legislative acts as such, they will never work in isolation. There will always be a context to relate to; a context in which even a balanced and efficient piece of legislation can become a legislative catastrophe.

This perspective is unfortunately missing in both the current system and the changes proposed by the Commission. The question is why. Is it because it is not yet obvious that interactions on such an innovation- and regulation-intensive market as the pharmaceutical one require a comprehensive approach? Or is it because such a holistic, all-encompassing perspective is not a quick fix? Or maybe, because 'fixing' would require tackling some very sensitive issues: the EU/Member State division of competence and the EU legislative architecture as such, where central concepts for the application of a certain regulation are based on definitions in an EU Directive, which is in practice interpreted and applied in differing ways by Member States' agencies and courts? The answer is unclear. What this book will give you is an illustration of why addressing these issues is of key importance, and an explanation of why efficiency in legislation may not be achieved when the context in which legislative acts are to operate is not perceived through a shared and systematic lens.

In this respect, legislative efficiency is not a matter of bits and pieces, but of an entirety.

Frantzeska Papadopoulou

ACKNOWLEDGEMENTS

The process of writing this book has considerably benefited from the research environment at the Law Faculty of Stockholm University and the possibility to converse with colleagues in the field and outside. A separate thank you to my colleague Mauro Zamboni for introducing me to the fascinating world of legislative studies and to Helen Xanthaki and Maria Mousmouti for discussing theoretical models and the possibility to apply efficiency in legislation in the field of regulatory rights. This book has benefited very much from the discussions with my mentor and good friend Panos Iosifidis who is an endless source of inspiration for all intellectual endeavours.

A warm thank you to my husband Björn for his untiring support, without which this book would never come into being and to Manos, Nicole, Amalia and Ariadne, well, for everything.

CONTENTS

Preface v
Acknowledgements ix
Table of Cases xvii
Table of Legislation xxiii

1. Regulating the EU Pharmaceutical Sector: A Multilayered Challenge 1
   1. The Pharmaceutical Sector: A Need for Regulation 1
   2. The Structure of the Pharmaceutical Industry in Europe 8
   3. EU Competence in the Field of Public Health 10
      3.1. EU Public Health Competence in Theory 10
      3.2. EU Public Health Competence in Practice 14
      3.3. The Public Health Programmes 19
         3.3.1. The First Public Health Programme 19
         3.3.2. The EU Health Strategy 20
         3.3.3. The Third Health Programme (2014–20) 20
         3.3.4. Health 2020 21
   4. Effective Legislation and Regulatory Rights 22
      4.1. The Impact Assessment 26
      4.2. The Public Consultation 28
      4.3. Regulatory Rights and why the Effectiveness Test is Not Straightforward 29
   5. The Structure of the Book 34

2. Setting the Stage for Regulatory Rights: The Regulatory Agencies and the Marketing Authorisation Procedure 36
   1. Regulatory Authorities 37
      1.1. The European Medicines Agency 37
         1.1.1. Background 37
         1.1.2. The Legal Basis for the Establishment of the EMA 41
         1.1.3. The Mandate and Role of the EMA 45
         1.1.4. Committees under the EMA 47
            1.1.4.1. The Committee for Medicinal Products for Human Use 47
            1.1.4.2. The Committee for Medicinal Products for Veterinary Use 48

		1.1.4.3.	The Committee for Orphan Medicinal Products...48
		1.1.4.4.	The Paediatric Committee 49
		1.1.4.5.	The Committee for Advanced Therapies 50
		1.1.4.6.	The Committee on Herbal Medicinal Products (HMPC)..50
		1.1.4.7.	The Pharmacovigilance Risk Assessment Committee 51
	1.1.5.	Other Working Groups of Interest for the EMA 51	
		1.1.5.1.	The Heads of Medicines Agencies 51
		1.1.5.2.	The National Competent Authorities of European Member States..................................51
		1.1.5.3.	The Coordination Group for Mutual Recognition and Decentralised Procedures: Human (CMDh) 52
		1.1.5.4.	The European Directorate for the Quality of Medicines..52
		1.1.5.5.	The International Conference on Harmonisation of Technical Requirements for Registration of Pharmaceuticals for Human Use (ICH) 52
2.	The Marketing Authorisation Procedure 53		
	2.1.	The Legal Framework 54	
	2.2.	The Application Dossier..55	
	2.3.	Alternative Marketing Authorisation Procedures 57	
		2.3.1.	The Centralised Procedure 58
		2.3.2.	The Mutual Recognition Procedure (MRP) 60
		2.3.3.	The Decentralised Procedure (DCP) 61
		2.3.4.	The National Procedure 61
		2.3.5.	The Name of the Product..61
		2.3.6.	Validity, Renewal and Termination 61
		2.3.7.	Transparency of the MA Procedure 62
3.	Concluding Remarks... 63		

3. Data Exclusivity...65
   1. The Legal Framework.. 65
   2. Clinical Data... 67
   3. The Marketing Authorisation Procedure and Directive 2001/83 – Original Pharmaceuticals... 68
   4. Marketing Authorisation for Generic Products 69
      4.1. What Constitutes a Generic Product?..69
      4.2. Data Exclusivity and Generics..70
      4.3. The Nature of the Protection Granted..76

		4.4. Improvements to Already Existing Pharmaceuticals 77
		4.4.1. New Therapeutic Indications with Significant Clinical Benefits 77
		4.4.2. Separate Data Exclusivity for Significant Pre-clinical or Clinical Studies for New Therapeutic Indications 78
		4.4.3. Data Exclusivity for Derivatives, New Dosages and Other Variations of the Original Pharmaceutical.......78
		4.4.4. Extension of Data Exclusivity for Rx-to-OTC Switches...79
	5.	The Weaknesses of the System.. 80
	6.	Data Exclusivity for Paediatric Medicines that are Not Patent-Protected 81
	7.	Concluding Remarks... 81
4.	The Supplementary Protection Certificate 83
	1.	Background to the Legal Framework.. 83
	2.	The Legal Framework.. 86
		2.1. Requirements for Protection 86
		2.2. The SPC Application..89
		2.3. The Relation between the SPC Application and the MA 91
		2.4. Procedural Rules: A Case for National Accommodation 92
	3.	The Subject of Protection 93
		3.1. Complex Pharmaceuticals 93
		3.2. Is the Product Part of the Patent and how is the Scope of Article 3(a) of the Regulation Defined?...96
		3.3. New Use, Old Substance: What Constitutes a New Active Ingredient in View of the SPC Regulation?.....................................100
		3.4. One Product, One SPC, One Patent? 106
		3.5. The Excluded Subject Matter...113
		3.5.1. The Case of Medical Devices..114
	4.	The Rights Granted 117
		4.1. The Term of Protection 117
		4.2. The Nature of the Rights Granted and their Enforcement 119
		4.3. The SPC Manufacturing Waiver...124
	5.	The SPC Beneficiary..128
		5.1. Several Patent Holders for the same Product? 128
		5.2. Making Use of a Third-party MA 129
	6.	Concluding Remarks.. 131
5.	The Paediatric Extension 137
	1.	Background 137
	2.	The General Legal Framework.. 138

3. A New Committee to Implement the Legal Framework:
      The Role of the Paediatric Committee (PDCO) 140
   4. The PIP 141
   5. PIP Compliance Control 142
   6. Exemptions and Waivers 144
   7. The Incentives of the Regulation 145
   8. Rewards for Orphan Medicinal Products under Regulation
      1901/2006 148
   9. Other Incentives in the System 149
      9.1. Free Scientific Advice 150
      9.2. Paediatric Use Marketing Authorisation (PUMA) 150
   10. Post-approval Obligations 151
      10.1. Putting the Product on the Market 151
      10.2. Pharmacovigilance 151
      10.3. Paediatric Product Discontinuation 151
      10.4. The Paediatric Symbol 152
      10.5. Penalties for Breach of Regulation (EC) No 1901/2006 ... 152
      10.6. Transparency 152
      10.7. Cooperation on the Basis of the Regulation 153
   11. Concluding Remarks 153

6. Orphan Drugs 155
   1. Background to the Legal Framework 155
   2. Procedural Aspects 158
      2.1. The Designation Process 158
         2.1.1. The Pre-application Meeting 160
         2.1.2. The Review of the Application 160
         2.1.3. Market Exclusivity Review 161
   3. The Criteria for Orphan Drugs Designation 162
      3.1. Article 3(1)(a): The Prevalence Criterion 162
      3.2. The Insufficient Return on Investment Criterion 164
      3.3. Medical Plausibility 165
      3.4. Article 3(1)(b) Requirements 166
         3.4.1. Existing Satisfactory Method 166
         3.4.2. Significant Benefit 167
      3.5. Timing of the Application 171
   4. Marketing Authorisation of Orphan Drugs 172
   5. The Incentives of the Orphan Drug Designation 173
      5.1. Market Exclusivity 173
      5.2. Exceptions to Market Exclusivity 175
      5.3. Technical Assistance/Fee Reductions 176
   6. Post-grant Obligations of the Sponsor 176
   7. Difficulties in the Interpretation of Orphan Drugs Regulation
      Case Law 177
   8. Concluding Remarks 181

7. Advanced Therapy Medicinal Products 183
   1. The Legal Framework... 183
   2. Definitions of Key Terms in the ATMP Regulation............................... 185
      2.1. Gene Therapy..185
      2.2. Somatic Cell Therapy Medicinal Products 186
      2.3. Tissue-engineered Products (Article 2(b)
           of the ATMP Regulation)..187
      2.4. Combined ATMPs 187
      2.5. Rules of Classification..188
   3. The ATMP Regulation and Other European Legislation 189
   4. Marketing Authorisation for ATMPs..191
      4.1. The Main Procedure: The Centralised MA.........................191
      4.2. The Hospital Exemption..191
      4.3. The Marketing Authorisation Procedure for ATMPs..........192
      4.4. Incentives for Small- and Medium-sized Enterprises 193
      4.5. Other Requirements Related to ATMPs 193
   5. Post-authorisation Requirements.. 194
   6. Concluding Remarks.. 195

8. How Effective is the Effectiveness Test in the Field of Regulatory Rights?........ 196
   1. The Objectives... 196
      1.1. The SPC Regulation 200
           1.1.1. The Objectives through the Lens
                  of Negotiating History..200
           1.1.2. The Objectives of the SPC Regulation in its Text 206
      1.2. The Orphan Drugs Regulation 211
           1.2.1. The Objectives through the Lens of the Negotiation
                  History 211
           1.2.2. The Objectives of the Orphan Drugs Regulation
                  in its Text..214
      1.3. The Paediatric Regulation 216
           1.3.1. The Objectives through the Lens of the History
                  of the Negotiations..216
           1.3.2. The Objectives of the Paediatric Regulation
                  in its Text..218
      1.4. The ATMP Regulation...219
           1.4.1. The Objectives through the Lens of the History
                  of the Negotiations..219
           1.4.2. The Objectives of the ATMP Regulation in its Text.........221
   2. The Contents 222
      2.1. The SPC Regulation 222
      2.2. The Orphan Drugs Regulation 223
      2.3. The Paediatric Regulation 223
      2.4. The ATMP Regulation...224

3. The Context 225
   3.1. Other Regulatory Rights 226
        3.1.1. Combination of Protection 226
        3.1.2. The Protection of the One is the Basis for the Other 228
               3.1.2.1. Negative SPCs 228
               3.1.2.2. Orphan Drugs/Paediatric Extension 228
   3.2. The Patent System 230
   3.3. The MA System 232
4. The Results 233
   4.1. The SPC Regulation 233
        4.1.1. From Objectives to Results? 233
        4.1.2. Objectives and Results in a State of Flux? 237
   4.2. The Orphan Drugs Regulation 241
   4.3. The Paediatric Regulation 245
   4.4. The ATMP Regulation 247
5. General Conclusions 249

Bibliography 258
Index 269

TABLE OF CASES

Canadian Cases

Bristol-Myers Squibb Pharma EEIG v European Commission and European Medicines Agency, T-329/16, EU:T:2018:878 .... 49, 169
Canada – Patent Protection of Pharmaceutical Products – Arbitration under Article 21.3(c) of the Understanding on Rules and Procedures Governing the Settlement of Disputes – Award of the Arbitrator, WT/DS114/13, 18 August 2000 125
Federal Republic of Germany and Others v Commission of the European Communities, C-281, 283, 284, 285 and 287/85, EU:C:1987:351 11

Dutch Cases

District Court of the Hague, *Novartis AG v Teva BV et al*, Decision of 30 March 2016, C/09/500844 / KG ZA 15-1829 229
Pharmaq AS v Intervet International BV, 9 April 2015, E-16/14. .... 120, 122
Rechtbank 's-Gravenhage, 18 August 2010, *Synthon BV et al against College ter Beoordeling van Geneesmiddelen (CBG)*, LJN: BN 7663 70

EU Cases

Abraxis Bioscience LLC v Comptroller General of Patents, C-443/17, EU:C:2019:238 .... 104–05, 227, 238, 254, 256–57
Actavis Group PTC EHF and Actavis UK Ltd v Boehringer Ingelheim Pharma GmbH & Co KG, C-577/13, EU:C:2015:165 94
Actavis Group PTC EHF and Actavis UK Ltd v Sanofi, C-443/12, EU:C:2013:833 .... 95, 131
Adriaan de Peijper, Managing Director of Centrafarm BV, C-104-75, EU:C:1976:67 4
AHP Manufacturing BV v Bureau voor de Industriële Eigendom, C-482/07, EU:C:2009:501 .... 93, 128
Arne Forsgren v Österreichisches Patentamt, C-631/13, EU:C:2015:13 .... 89, 107, 112, 132

xviii *Table of Cases*

Arnold André GmbH & Co KG v Landrat des Kreises Herford,
C-434/02, EU:C:2004:800 16–17
AstraZeneca A/S v Lægemiddelstyrelsen, C-223/01, EU:C:2003:546 76
AstraZeneca AB and AstraZeneca plc v European Commission,
T-321/05, EU:T:2010:266 71
Bayer CropScience AG v Deutsches Patent- und Markenamt,
C-11/13, EU:C:2014:2010 .... 89, 91, 113
Bernhard Schloh v Auto contrôle technique SPRL, C-50/85, EU:C:1986:244 13
Biogen Inc v Smithkline Beecham Biologicals,
C-181/95, EU:C:1997:32 .... 93, 128–30
Carlo Tedeschi v Denkavit Commerciale srl, C-5/77, EU:C:1977:144 14
Criminal proceedings against Tullio Ratti, C-148/78, EU:C:1979:110 14
*CSL Behring GmbH v European Commission and European Medicines
Agency (EMA)*, T-264/07, EU:T:2010:371 172
*Daiichi Sankyo Company v Comptroller General of Patents, Designs
and Trade Marks*, C-6/11, EU:C:2011:781 111
Eli Lilly and Company Ltd v Human Genome Sciences Inc, C-493/12,
EU:C:2013:835 .... 96, 98
Eli Lilly and Company v Genentech Inc, C-239/19,
EU:C:2019:687 .... 131, 232, 238
European Medicines Agency v Shire Pharmaceuticals Ireland Ltd,
C-359/18 P, EU:C:2019:639 .... 180, 182, 256
Farmitalia Carlo Erba Srl, C-392/97, EU:C:1999:416 .... 108, 110, 121–22
*Federal Republic of Germany v European Parliament and Council
of the European Union*, C-376/98, EU:C:2000:544 16–17
Generics, C-427/09, EU:C:2011:520 103
Georgetown University v Octrooicentrum Nederland,
C-484/12, EU:C:2013:828 .... 92, 94
*Glaxosmithkline Biologicals SA and Glaxosmithkline Biologicals, Niederlassung
der Smithkline Beecham Pharma GmbH & Co KG v Comptroller General
of Patents, Designs and Trade Marks*, C-210/13, EU:C:2013:762 .... 89, 104
Hässle AB v Ratiopharm GmbH, C-127/00, EU:C:2003:661 117–18
*Hauptzollamt Neubrandenburg v Leszek Labis and Sagpol SC Transport
Miedzynarodowy i Spedycja*, C-310/98 and C-406/98, EU:C:2000:154 235
Kingdom of Spain v Council of the European Union,
C-350/92, EU:C:1995:237 14
Laboratoires CTRS v European Commission, T-452/14, EU:T:2015:373 179
Massachusetts Institute of Technology, C-431/04, EU:C:2006:291 .... 88, 101
Medac Gesellschaft für klinische Spezialpräparate v Commission,
T-549/19, EU:T:2020:444 .... 180, 257
Medeva BV v Comptroller General of Patents, Designs and Trademarks,
C-322/10, EU:C:2011:773 .... 92, 94, 96, 98, 102, 110–12, 132, 228

Merck Sharp & Dohme Corp v Deutsches Patent- und Markenamt,
  C-125/10, EU:C:2011:812..85, 146, 228
Merck Sharp & Dohme Corporation v Comptroller-General of Patents,
  Designs and Trade Marks, C-567/16, EU:C:2017:948..107
MSD Animal Health Innovation GmbH and Internet International BV
  v European Medicines Agency, C-178/18, EU:C:2020:24......................................62
Neurim Pharmaceuticals (1991) Ltd v Comptroller-General of Patents,
  C-130/11, EU:C:2012:489..85, 91, 101–06, 110, 135, 254
Novartis AG v Actavis Deutschland GmbH & Co KG and Actavis Ltd,
  C-574/11, EU:C:2012:68...120
Novartis AG v Actavis UK Ltd, C-442/11, EU:C:2012:66 120
Novartis AG v Patent- och registreringsverket, C-354/19, EU:C:2020:81 106
Novartis AG, University College London and Institute of Microbiology and
  Epidemiology v Comptroller-General of Patents, Designs and Trade
  Marks for the United Kingdom and Ministre de l'Économie v Millennium
  Pharmaceuticals Inc, C-207 and 252/03, EU:C:2005:245 .... 90, 118
Now Pharm AG v European Commission,
  T-74/08, EU:T:2010:376 .... 158–59, 168–70
Nycomed Danmark ApS v European Medicines Agency (EMA),
  T-52/09, EU:T:2011:738 144–45
Olainfarm AS v Latvijas Republikas Veselības ministrija and
  Zāļu valsts aģentūra, C-104/13, EU:C:2014:2316.. 80, 82
Yissum Research and Development Company of the Hebrew
  University of Jerusalem v Comptroller-General of Patents,
  C-202/05, EU:C:2007:214... 89, 101
Astrazeneca AB v Comptroller General of Patents,
  C-617/12, EU:C:2014:28... 90, 118
Pfizer Ireland Pharmaceuticals, Operations Support Group v
  Orifarm GmbH, C-681/16, EU:C:2018:484..123
Pfizer v Commission and EMA, T-48/14, EU:T:2014:1091.......................................148
Philip Morris Brands SARL and Others v Secretary of State for Health,
  C-547/14, EU:C:2016:325...16
Presidenza del Consiglio dei Ministri and Others v Rina Services SpA
  and Others, C-593/13, EU:C:2015:399 123
Proceedings brought by Boston Scientific Ltd, C-527/17,
  EU:C:2018:867 115–16
PTC Therapeutics International Ltd v European Medicines Agency,
  C-157/18, EU:C:2020:23...62
Republic of Poland v European Parliament and Council of the
  European Union, C-358/14, EU:C:2016:323 16
Royalty Pharma Collection Trust v Deutsches Patent- und Markenamt,
  C-650/17, EU:C:2020:327...99

Santen SAS v Directeur général de l'Institut national de la propriété industrielle, C-673/18, EU:C:2020:34 .... 105–06, 256–57
Seattle Genetics Inc v Österreichisches Patentamt, C-471/14, EU:C:2015:659 87
Shire Pharmaceutical Contracts Ltd v European Commission, T-583/13, EU:T:2018:165 179
Shire Pharmaceuticals Ireland Ltd v European Medicines Agency, T-80/16, EU:T:2018:165 182
Snellers Auto's BV v Algemeen Directeur van de Dienst Wegverkeer, C-314/98, EU:C:2000:557 13
Synthon BV, C-195/09, EU:C:2011:518 103
Teva Pharma and Teva Pharmaceuticals Europe v EMA, T-547/12, EU:T:2014:1099 73
Teva Pharma BV and Teva Pharmaceuticals Europe BV v European Medicines Agency (EMA), C-138/15, EU:C:2016:136 .... 179, 182, 229
Teva Pharma BV and Teva Pharmaceuticals Europe BV v European Medicines Agency (EMA), T-140/12, EU:T:2015:41 177–78
Teva UK Ltd and Others v Gilead Sciences Inc, C-121/17, EU:C:2018:585 .... 98, 100
The Queen on the application of Novartis Pharmaceuticals UK Ltd v The Licensing Authority, C-106/01, EU:C:2004:245 .... 69, 72
The Queen v Secretary of State for Health, ex parte British American Tobacco (Investments) Ltd and Imperial Tobacco Ltd, C-491/01, EU:C:2002:741 .... 17, 254
The Queen v The Licensing Authority established by the Medicines Act 1968 (acting by The Medicines Control Agency), ex parte Generics (UK) Ltd, The Wellcome Foundation Ltd and Glaxo Operations UK Ltd and Others, C-368/96, EU:C:1998:583 69
The Queen, on the application of Approved Prescription Services Ltd v Licensing Authority, C-36/03, EU:C:2004:781 69
The Queen, on the application of Generics (UK) Ltd v Licensing Authority, C-527/07, EU:C:2009:379 .... 70, 82
The Queen, on the application of Synthon BV v Licensing Authority of the Department of Health, C-452/06, EU:C:2008:565 .... 60, 82
The Queen, on the application of: Swedish Match AB and Swedish Match UK Ltd v Secretary of State for Health, C-210/03, EU:C:2004:802 17
Una Coonan v Insurance Officer, C-110/79, EU:C:1980:112 13
University of Queensland and CSL Ltd v Comptroller General of Patents, Designs and Trade Marks, C-630/10, EU:C:2011:780 111
Yeda Research and Development Company Ltd and Aventis Holdings Inc v Comptroller General of Patents, Designs and Trade Marks, C-518/10, EU:C:2011:779 ....110–11, 121

German Cases

BPatG, Abamectin, 15 W (pat) 71/97 (2000) GRUR 398.......................................107
Cologne Administrative Court of 25 July 2008, Case 7 L 988/08 80
District Court of Düsseldorf, 15 November 2012, 4b O 123/12 (2012)
    open Jur 2013, 3044 92
District Court of Düsseldorf, Decision of 10 November 2011 (2012)
    BeckRS21620 130

Italian Cases

Tribunal of Milan, Decision of 23 February 2016, *Teva Italia*
    SRL et al v Novartis AG et al, Case 52274-1/2015...229

Swedish Cases

Sandoz AS v Searle, PMÖ 12172-18 92

UK Cases

E l du Pont Nemours & Co v United Kingdom Intellectual Property Office
    [2009] EWCA Civ 966 147–48
Eli Lilly and Co v Genentech Inc [2019] EWHC 388 (Pat) 232
Eli Lilly and Co v Human Genome Sciences Inc [2014] EWHC 2404............ 97, 111
Glaxosmithkline Biologicals SA v Comptroller-General of Patents,
    Designs and Trade Marks [2013] EWHC 619 (Pat)..132
MedImmune v Novartis [2012] EWHC 181 (Pat)..108
Pharmacia Italia SpA, formerly Pharmacia & Upjohn SpA, C-31/03,
    EU:C:2004:641. 101
Takeda Chemical Industries Ltd's SPC Applications (No.3) [2004] RPC 1,
    [2003] EWHC 649 (Pat) 109
Teva UK Ltd and Others v Merck Sharp & Dohme Corporation
    [2017] EWHC 539 (Pat) 98

UKIPO Cases

UK IPO, BL O/096/09, *E I du Pont de Nemours*, 9 April 2009 147
UK IPO, BL O/108/08, *Merck & Co Inc*, 14 April 2008..147
UK IPO, BL O/141/14, *Cerus Corporation*, 31 March 2014....................................114

UK IPO, BL O/328/14, *Leibniz-Institut für Neue Materialien Gemeinnützige GmbH*, 29 July 2014 114
UK IPO, BL O/466/15, *Angiotech Pharmaceuticals Inc and University of British Columbia*, 6 October 2015 115

US Cases

Fisons plc v Quigg, 876 F.2d 99, 101 (Fed. Cir. 1989) 235

TABLE OF LEGISLATION

Canadian Legislation

House of Commons of Canada, Bill C-30 (First Reading)
   31 October 2016 126

EU Legislation

Charter of Fundamental Rights of the European Union
   [2000] OJ C 364/1 221
Commission Decision of 30 November 2009 establishing a European Union
   Committee of Experts on Rare Diseases [2009] OJ L 315/18..........................212
Commission Directive 2003/94/EC of 8 October 2003 laying down
   the principles and guidelines of good manufacturing practice in respect of
   medicinal products for human use and investigational medicinal products
   for human use (Text with EEA relevance) [2003] OJ L 262/22..........................58
Commission Directive 2005/28/EC of 8 April 2005 laying down principles
   and detailed guidelines for good clinical practice as regards investigational
   medicinal products for human use, as well as the requirements for
   authorisation of the manufacturing or importation of such products
   (Text with EEA relevance) [2005] OJ L 91/13 184
Commission Directive 2009/120/EC of 14 September 2009 amending
   Directive 2001/83/EC of the European Parliament and of the Council
   on the Community code relating to medicinal products for human use as
   regards advanced therapy medicinal products (Text with EEA relevance)
   [2009] OJ L 242/3 183
Commission Directive 2015/565/EU of 8 April 2015 amending Directive
   2006/86/EC as regards certain technical requirements for the coding
   of human tissues and cells Text with EEA relevance [2015] OJ L 93/43.........190
Commission Directive 2015/566/EU of 8 April 2015 implementing Directive
   2004/23/EC as regards the procedures for verifying the equivalent
   standards of quality and safety of imported tissues and cells Text with
   EEA relevance [2015] OJ L 93/56...190
Article 7 190
Recital 2 190
Commission Regulation 488/2012/EU of 8 June 2012 amending

xxiv *Table of Legislation*

Regulation 658/2007/EC concerning financial penalties for infringement
of certain obligations in connection with marketing authorisations
granted under Regulation 726/2004/EC of the European Parliament
and of the Council [2012] OJ L 150/68 152
Commission Regulation 847/2000/EC of 27 April 2000 laying down the
provisions for implementation of the criteria for designation of a medicinal
product as an orphan medicinal product and definitions of the concepts
'similar medicinal product' and 'clinical superiority' [2000] OJ L 103/5 166
Article 2(1) 163
Article 3(3)(b) 174
Consolidated Version of the Treaty on the Functioning of
the European Union [2020] OJ C 202/1 .... 16, 18
Council Directive 65/65/EEC of 26 January 1965 on the approximation
of provisions laid down by Law, Regulation or Administrative
Action relating to proprietary medicinal products OJ 22/369 .... 2, 54, 67
Chapter 1 3
Chapter 2 3
Council Directive 75/318/EEC of 20 May 1975 on the approximation
of the laws of Member States relating to analytical, pharmaco-toxicological
and clinical standards and protocols in respect of the testing of
proprietary medicinal products [1975] OJ L 147/1 3
Council Directive 83/570/EEC of 26 October 1983 amending
Directives 65/65/EEC, 75/318/EEC and 75/319/EEC on
the approximation of provisions laid down by Law, Regulation or
Administrative Action relating to proprietary medicinal
products [1983] OJ L 332/1 4
Council Directive 87/21/EEC of 22 December 1986 amending
Directive 65/65/EEC on the approximation of provisions laid
down by law, regulation or administrative action relating to
proprietary medicinal products [1987] OJ L 15/36 67
Council Directive 87/22/EEC of 22 December 1986 on the approximation of
national measures relating to the placing on the market of high-technology
medicinal products, particularly those derived from biotechnology
[1986] OJ L 15/38 5
Council Directive 89/105/EEC of 21 December 1988 relating to
the transparency of measures regulating the prices of medicinal
products for human use and their inclusion in the scope of national
health insurance systems [1988] OJ L 40/8 .... 5, 201, 252
Council Directive 93/39/EEC of 14 June 1993 amending
Directives 65/65/EEC, 75/318/EEC and 75/319/EEC in respect
of medicinal products [1993] OJ L 214/22 6
Council Directive 93/42/EEC of 14 June 1993 concerning medical
devices [1993] OJ L 169/1 189

Table of Legislation xxv

Council Regulation 1768/92/EEC of 18 June 1992 concerning the
creation of a supplementary protection certificate for medicinal
products [1992] OJ L 182/1 .... 5, 83, 202
Article 36(1) 119
Council Regulation 2309/93/EEC of 22 July 1993 laying down Community
procedures for the authorisation and supervision of medicinal products
for human and veterinary use and establishing a European Agency
for the Evaluation of Medicinal Products [1993] OJ L 214/1 .... 5, 6, 37
Council Regulation 297/95/EC of 10 February 1995 on fees payable to the
European Agency for the Evaluation of Medicinal Products
[1995] OJ L 35/1 43
Directive 2001/20/EC of the European Parliament and of the Council of
4 April 2001 on the approximation of the laws, regulations and
administrative provisions of the Member States relating to the
implementation of good clinical practice in the conduct of clinical trials on
medicinal products for human use [2001] OJ L 121/34 .... 64, 137, 184, 217–18
Article 4 142
Directive 2001/83/EC of the European Parliament and of the Council of
6 November 2001 on the Community code relating to medicinal
products for human use [2001] OJ L 311/67 .... 31, 50, 54–55,
68, 157, 183, 189, 196
Article 10 70
Article 10(2)(a) 70
Article 18 60
Article 24(2) 62
Article 24(5) 61
Article 28(4) 107
Article 3 .... 64, 191
Article 6 .... 133, 139
Article 6(1) 72
Article 8 139
Section 2.1, Part IV, Annex 1 .... 183, 185–86, 192
Section 2.2, Part IV, Annex 1 186
Title IV 58
Directive 2002/98/EC of the European Parliament and of the Council of
27 January 2003 setting standards of quality and safety for the collection,
testing, processing, storage and distribution of human blood and blood
components and amending Directive 2001/83/EC [2003] OJ L 33/30 .... 67, 194
Directive 2004/109/EC of the European Parliament and of the Council
of 15 December 2004 on the harmonisation of transparency
requirements in relation to information about issuers whose
securities are admitted to trading on a regulated market and
amending Directive 2001/34/EC [2004] OJ L 390/38 6–7

xxvi *Table of Legislation*

Directive 2004/23/EC of the European Parliament and of the Council
of 31 March 2004 on setting standards of quality and safety for
the donation, procurement, testing, processing, preservation,
storage and distribution of human tissues and cells
[2004] OJ L 102/48 .... 189, 193–94, 221, 249
Article 6(1) 190
Directive 2004/24/EC of the European Parliament and of the Council
of 31 March 2004 amending, as regards traditional herbal medicinal
products, Directive 2001/83/EC on the Community code relating to
medicinal products for human use [2004] OJ L 136/85 .... 50, 67
Directive 2004/27/EC of the European Parliament and of the Council of
31 March 2004 amending Directive 2001/83/EC on the Community code
relating to medicinal products for human use (Text with EEA relevance)
[2004] OJ L 136/34 31
Article 10(1)3rd 76
Directive 2006/17/EC of 8 February 2006 implementing
Directive 2004/23/EC of the European Parliament and of the Council
as regards certain technical requirements for the donation, procurement
and testing of human tissues and cells (Text with EEA relevance)
[2006] OJ L 38/40 249
Directive 2006/86/EC of 24 October 2006 implementing
Directive 2004/23/EC of the European Parliament and of the Council as
regards traceability requirements, notification of serious adverse reactions
and events and certain technical requirements for the coding, processing,
preservation, storage and distribution of human tissues and cells
(Text with EEA relevance) [2006] OJ L 294/32 249
Directive 2010/84/EU of the European Parliament and of the Council of
15 December 2010 amending, as regards pharmacovigilance, Directive
2001/83/EC on the Community code relating to medicinal products for
human use Text with EEA relevance [2010] OJ L 348/74 7
Directive 2011/24/EU of the European Parliament and of the Council of
9 March 2011 on the application of patients' rights in cross-border
healthcare [2011] OJ L 88/45 .... 13, 213
Directive 95/46/EC of the European Parliament and of the Council of
24 October 1995 on the protection of individuals with regard to the
processing of personal data and on the free movement of such
data [1995] OJ L 281/31 194
Directive 98/43/EC of the European Parliament and of the Council of
6 July 1998 on the approximation of the laws, regulations and
administrative provisions of the Member States relating to the
advertising and sponsorship of tobacco products [1998] OJ L 213/9 16
Directive 98/44/EC of the European Parliament and of the Council of
6 July 1998 on the legal protection of biotechnological inventions
[1998] OJ L 213/13 .... 31, 198, 230, 250

European Patent Convention [2000] OJ EPO 2001/ 55 ....98, 196, 204
Protocol to the Convention on the elaboration of a European
    Pharmacopoeia [1994] OJ L 158/22 64
Regulation 1049/2001/EC of the European Parliament and of the
    Council of 30 May 2001 regarding public access to European Parliament,
    Council and Commission documents [2001] OJ L 145/43 63
Regulation 1257/2012/EU of the European Parliament and of the Council
    of 17 December 2012 implementing enhanced cooperation in the area
    of the creation of unitary patent protection [2012] OJ L 361/1 134
Regulation 1394/2007/EC of the European Parliament and of the Council
    of 13 November 2007 on advanced therapy medicinal products
    and amending Directive 2001/83/EC and Regulation
    (EC) No 726/2004 (Text with EEA relevance) OJ L 324/121 ....8, 50, 183–84
Article 28(2) 191
Articles 20–23 185
Regulation 141/2000/EC of the European Parliament and of
    the Council of 16 December 1999 on orphan medicinal
    products [1999] OJ L 18/1..7–8, 155
Article 1 214
Article 2 162
Article 3 181
Article 4 159
Article 8 65
Article 9 176
Preamble 8 149
Recital 2 8
Recital 8 ....8, 53
Recitals 67 and 68..181
Regulation 1610/96/EC of the European Parliament and of the Council
    of 23 July 1996 concerning the creation of a supplementary protection
    certificate for plant protection products [1996] OJ L 198/30 84–85
Regulation 1901/2006/EC of the European Parliament and of the Council
    of 12 December 2006 on medicinal products for paediatric use
    and amending Regulation (EEC) No 1768/92, Directive 2001/20/EC,
    Directive 2001/83/EC and Regulation (EC) No 726/2004
    (Text with EEA relevance) [2006] OJ L 378/1 ....7–8, 49, 83–84, 126, 137
Article 1(b) 88
Article 11 141
Article 20 141
Article 22 142
Article 25(7) 153
Article 28(1) 153
Article 31 150
Article 35 151

xxviii Table of Legislation

Article 36 173
Article 40 153
Article 7 139
Article 8 139
Preamble 6 138
Recital 19 .... 150, 231
Recital 2 8
Recital 4 8
Regulation 1902/2006/EC of the European Parliament and of
    the Council of 20 December 2006 amending Regulation 1901/2006
    on medicinal products for pediatric use (Text with EEA relevance)
    [2006] OJ L 378/20 218
Regulation 2017/745/EU of the European Parliament and of the Council of
    5 April 2017 on medical devices, amending Directive 2001/83/EC,
    Regulation (EC) No 178/2002 and Regulation (EC) No 1223/2009
    and repealing Council Directives 90/385/EEC and 93/42/EEC
    (Text with EEA relevance) [2017] OJ L 117/1 .... 54, 114
Regulation 2017/746/EU of the European Parliament and of the Council
    of 5 April 2017 on in vitro diagnostic medical devices and repealing
    Directive 98/79/EC and Commission Decision 2010/227/EU
    (Text with EEA relevance) [2017] OJ L 117/176 114
Regulation 2019/933/EU of the European Parliament and of the Council of
    20 May 2019 amending Regulation (EC) No 469/2009 concerning the
    supplementary protection certificate for medicinal products
    (Text with EEA relevance) [2019] OJ L 153/1 .... 124, 237
Regulation 282/2014/EU of the European Parliament and of the Council
    of 11 March 2014 on the establishment of a third Programme for the
    Union's action in the field of health (2014–2020) and repealing Decision
    No 1350/2007/EC Text with EEA relevance [2014] OJ L 86/1 20
Regulation 469/2009/EC of the European Parliament and of the Council of
    6 May 2009 concerning the supplementary protection certificate for
    medicinal products (Codified version) (Text with EEA relevance)
    [2009] OJ L 152/1 .... 8, 83, 196
Regulation 469/2009/EC, Recital 9 127
Regulation 536/2014/EU of the European Parliament and of the Council of
    16 April 2014 on clinical trials on medicinal products for human use,
    and repealing Directive 2001/20/EC Text with EEA relevance
    [2014] OJ L 158/1 ....68, 142
Regulation 726/2004/EC of the European Parliament and of the Council of
    31 March 2004 laying down Community procedures for the authorisation
    and supervision of medicinal products for human and veterinary
    use and establishing a European Medicines Agency
    [2004] OJ L 136/1 ....68, 78, 183, 189

Regulation 726/2004/EC, Article 13(1) 59
Regulation 726/2004/EC, Article 14(2) 62
Regulation 726/2004/EC, Article 14(4) 61
Regulation 726/2004/EC, Article 15(5) 61
Regulation 726/2004/EC, Article 32 58
Regulation 726/2004/EC, Article 6(3) 59
Regulation 726/2004/EC, Articles 5–15 150

Swiss Legislation

Federal Act on Medicinal Products and Medical Devices (Therapeutic
    Products Act, TPA) of 15 December 2000 (Status as of 1 January 2020)
    The Federal Assembly of the Swiss Confederation 228

US Legislation

Drug Price Competition and Patent Term Restoration Act of
    1984 (PL 98-417) 65
Orphan Drug Act, Public Law 97-414, 9th Congress,
    96 State 2049 [1983] 156
Pediatric Research Equity Act, 117 Stat 1936
    Public Law 108–155 – Dec 3, 2003 139

1

Regulating the EU Pharmaceutical Sector

A Multilayered Challenge

1. The Pharmaceutical Sector: A Need for Regulation

Regulating pharmaceutical products became an urgent necessity in the aftermath of the thalidomide crisis. Thalidomide was a pharmaceutical, initially put on the market in West Germany in 1957 and prescribed as a sleeping aid for pregnant women suffering from morning sickness. It was praised at the time as an outstanding pharmaceutical breakthrough. That was, of course, before the births of tens of thousands of babies with congenital anomalies, as well as the numerous cases of pregnant women who became ill with peripheral neuritis (a severe degenerative disease), which were traced back to side effects of thalidomide leading to its removal from the market in 1961. This tragedy in the history of pharmaceutical research also triggered an urgent interest in the control and regulation of commercialisation of pharmaceutical products.[1]

While the thalidomide tragedy was a wake-up call, that does not mean there was no public awareness of the potential dangers of pharmaceutical products prior to that. However, with exceptions only in the Nordic countries and the United States, the review and registration process of pharmaceuticals was limited to administrative control before the 1960s. The main objective of the first pharmaceutical regulation was to ensure that pharmaceutical products were not advertised in ways that would make patients believe they worked better than they actually did. In the beginning of the 1960s, all major jurisdictions reviewed their pharmaceutical regulation legislation. As thalidomide had been denied marketing authorisation

---

[1] For a review of the emergence and evolution of what is now called health law, see Tamara K Hervey and Jean V McHale, *Law in Context: Health Law and the European Union* (Cambridge University Press 2004). See also Gordon Bache, Mark L Flear and Tamara K Hervey, 'The Defining Features of the European Union's Approach to Regulating New Health Technologies', in Mark L Flear, Anne-Maree Farrell, Tamara K Hervey and Thérèse Murphy (eds), *European Law and New Health Technologies* (Oxford University Press 2013). For the regulatory effects of the thalidomide crisis, see Michael A Gallo 'History and Scope of Toxicology' in Curtic D Klaassen (ed), *Casarett and Doull's Toxicology: The Basic Science of Poisons* (8th edn, McGraw-Hill Education 2013).

in the United States prior to the crisis, the US system was considered a successful model to look at when considering different alternatives.[2]

The US regulatory system required pharmaceutical companies to submit detailed and reliable information in the packaging of pharmaceutical products, being particularly transparent with regard to potential adverse effects, in order for doctors and health professionals to make informed decisions when choosing between treatments and substances. It also included a federal regulatory office for pharmaceuticals, the Food and Drug Administration (FDA). As early as 1958, the US Congress granted the FDA a mandate to give pharmaceutical manufacturers licences, on the condition that they met certain safety and efficiency criteria. Several European countries followed the example set by the United States, slowly introducing new criteria in order for marketing authorisation to be granted, and also establishing independent bodies that would receive applications and review the efficacy and safety of pharmaceutical products. In the early 1970s, the system was further strengthened by requiring the submission of clinical trial evidence.

In Europe it soon became clear that there was a need to proceed to a form of supra-national regulation of the pharmaceutical industry, in addition to the initial national initiatives and reactions to the thalidomide crisis. Common health threats, as in the thalidomide case, had to be dealt with, and the most effective way to do so was to work proactively. Interestingly, several aspects of this first period of European pharmaceutical product regulation are important to this day. In 1963, the European Commission invited representatives of the public health sector, such as industry representatives, pharmacists and doctors, as well as consumer groups, to discuss potential directions that the European public health harmonisation should and could take.

Already in the first round of discussions, the parties participating in the negotiations had a major controversy, namely whether or not 'therapeutic potency' should be included as a requirement for marketing authorisation.[3] Two years later, the six Member States of what was then the European Economic Community (EEC) agreed on the necessity and importance of common controls and standards. The EC thus proceeded to adopt a legislative act in 1965: Directive 65/65/EEC on common authorisation requirements for new drugs.[4] This first piece of EU legislation introduced important terminology and definitions that are of central importance to this day.

---

[2] For a thorough review of the thalidomide crisis and how it has influenced the evolution of regulatory rights and the market-authorisation procedure, see Govin Permanand, *EU Pharmaceutical Regulation: The Politics of Policy-Making* (European Policy Research Unit Series, Manchester University Press 2006) 1–19.

[3] Doctors, pharmacists and consumer groups considered this necessary, while industry representatives did not – see the Commission's Press Release CEC IP 1963.

[4] Council Directive 65/65/EEC of 26 January 1965 on the approximation of provisions laid down by Law, Regulation or Administrative Action relating to proprietary medicinal products [1965] OJ 22 L369/73.

An important definition was that of a medicinal product: 'any substance or combinations of substances presented for treating or preventing disease in human beings or animals or any substance or combination of substances which may be administered to human beings or animals with a view to making a medical diagnosis or to restoring, correcting or modifying physiological functions in human beings or in animals'.[5] The Directive included a definition for proprietary pharmaceuticals as 'any ready prepared medicinal product placed on the market under a special name and in a special pack'.[6] The Directive also included a set of requirements for medicinal products to be placed on the market.[7] In order to receive market approval, a pharmaceutical manufacturer had to provide evidence of the product's efficacy, safety and therapeutic benefit. Lastly, another very important contribution of the Directive was to clarify that medicinal products may not be placed on the market of a Member State without the prior agreement and authorisation of the national authority of that specific Member State.[8] Guidelines related to time requirements and decision-making processes were also developed.[9]

During the early 1970s, when tariffs were gradually eliminated and the objective was to create an open internal market, yet another Directive was introduced, in order to facilitate the commercialisation of medicinal products. Directive 75/318/EEC introduced the process of mutual recognition and the procedures of the Committee for Proprietary Medicinal Products (CPMP).[10] Prior to this, applications for manufacturing authorisations had to be submitted to each Member State separately. By means of this Directive, a product granted marketing authorisation in one Member State could receive authorisations in five further Member States without any separate administrative procedure being necessary. The fact that this mutual recognition procedure was possible also necessitated the harmonisation of quality and safety requirements. The role of the CPMP was extended to include arbitration in cases where one Member State refused to grant an automatic manufacturing authorisation (confirming the validity of a marketing authorisation granted in another jurisdiction to also cover the jurisdiction of another Member State). Although this role was worded in an ambitious way, the mandate of the CPMP was in fact of a purely advisory character, which also meant that its proposals could be (and were in fact rather often) ignored. Member States did raise objections based on safety and health concerns and the facilitation of trade of pharmaceutical products was not always without friction.

---

[5] Article 1, Chapter 1, Directive 65/65/EEC.
[6] Ibid.
[7] See Chapter 2, Directive 65/65/EEC.
[8] Article 3, Chapter 2, Directive 65/65/EEC.
[9] For a compilation of Guidelines in the field of regulatory rights, see EudraBook V1 – May 2015/ EudraBook V20/ January 2017.
[10] Council Directive 75/318/EEC of 20 May 1975 on the approximation of the laws of Member States relating to analytical, pharmaco-toxicological and clinical standards and protocols in respect of the testing of proprietary medicinal products [1975] OJ L 147/1.

In the 83/570/EEC Directive, the minimum number of countries in which an applicant could receive an automatic authorisation was changed from five to two.[11] Manufacturers did not have to apply for authorisation in more than two countries, unless they wanted to. Although this system was more effective than the previous one, it led to a number of practical considerations and faced resistance from some Member States. By 1994, at least one objection per medicinal product was submitted by Member States. Although Community legislation was motivated by public health concerns, it has always been obvious that the creation of an internal market for pharmaceutical products was a central objective. It was also equally obvious that this objective was very difficult to achieve.

Already in the original 1985 White Paper on the Internal Market (CEC 1985), the goal was expressed clearly: national regimes should be brought together under a supra-national framework.[12] However, what this framework would look like and which steps had to be taken in this direction remained unclear. Thus, EU pharmaceutical competences developed gradually on an ad hoc basis. Member States' public health systems have also developed independently and in parallel with one another, in a strange form of isolation that has been strengthened by increasing financial constraints and public health budget considerations.

At the same time, as the interest in regulating the intra-community medicines market increased, a new business model emerged on the pharmaceutical market, namely that of parallel trade. Taking advantage of the differences in the pricing policies between countries, pharmaceutical product traders bought medicines in low-income Member States and sold them on more expensive markets. This new business model was – for obvious reasons – supported by patient organisations while – for equally obvious reasons – it met the resistance of pharmaceutical companies, which found their international business (and pricing) model challenged. The pharmaceutical industry went so far as to test its legality before the European Court of Justice in the 1976 *Peijper* case.[13] Unfortunately for them, the Court ruled that marketing authorisation rules could not be regarded as obstacles to intra-community movement until full market harmonisation of pharmaceuticals was achieved.

The Single European Market Programme adopted in 1986 provided that free movement of goods, services and capital would be possible by 1992.[14] In the same year, Paolo Checchini, a retired Commission official, received the mandate to lead

---

[11] Council Directive 83/570/EEC of 26 October 1983 amending Directives 65/65/EEC, 75/318/EEC and 75/319/EEC on the approximation of provisions laid down by Law, Regulation or Administrative Action relating to proprietary medicinal products [1983] OJ L 332/1.

[12] Completing the Internal Market: White Paper from the Commission to the European Council (Milan, 28–29 June 1985), COM [85] 310, Vol 1985/0130.

[13] Judgment of the Court of 20 May 1976, *Adriaan de Peijper, Managing Director of Centrafarm BV* (C-104-75), EU:C:1976:67.

[14] Jacques-Bernard Sauner-Leroy, 'The impact of the implementation of the Single Market Programme on productive efficiency and on mark-ups in the European Union manufacturing industry' [2003] European Economy-Economic Papers 2008–2015, 192, Directorate General Economic and Financial Affairs (DG ECFIN), European Commission.

an investigation on the costs of a 'non-European' pharmaceuticals market. The conclusions of his report, published in 1988, were that although pharmaceutical markets would always be closely linked to public health, they were included under the SEM umbrella.[15]

The 87/22/EEC Directive introduced yet another marketing authorisation procedure (this time, a centralised one), that would only be applicable to biotechnological and other high-tech pharmaceutical products.[16] In this new procedure, the manufacturers were to submit applications to the CPMP and one Member State (the primary intended market). When the CPMP and the national authority of that Member State finalised their respective evaluations, the communication between the applicant and other Member States would be facilitated.

In 1992, another interesting piece of Community legislation was enacted, namely Regulation (EEC) 1768/92, which created the Supplementary Protection Certificate (SPC), providing patentholders with a compensation for the patent term effectively lost due to the lengthy marketing authorisation procedure.[17]

Another area that was and remains controversial was that of the pricing and reimbursement of pharmaceuticals. The 89/105/EEC Directive (the Transparency Directive) introduced requirements concerning the transparency of Member States in relation to the pricing of pharmaceuticals.[18] A proposal for a second or amended Transparency Directive was abandoned already in 1992. In a 1996 Communication on the development of an official EU 'Industrial policy', the Commission concluded that barriers remained to the pharmaceuticals market harmonisation and that the requirements set for the single market were not fulfilled. The most important obstacle in the process was identified to be the lack of a strong public health agency with the mandate to make binding decisions.[19]

However, it took several years to proceed to the establishment of an independent agency with the mandate to regulate the process of marketing authorisation of pharmaceutical products. The European Medicines Agency (EMA) was founded in January 1995[20] and was granted the responsibility of actually enforcing the

---

[15] Paolo Cecchini, 'The Cost of Non-Agencies with Relevance to the Internal Market' (EU Parliament, 2016) www.europarl.europa.eu/RegData/etudes/STUD/2016/572702/IPOL_STU(2016)572702_EN.pdf [Accessed 22 January 2021].

[16] Council Directive 87/22/EEC of 22 December 1986 on the approximation of national measures relating to the placing on the market of high-technology medicinal products, particularly those derived from biotechnology [1986] OJ L 15/38.

[17] Council Regulation 1768/92/EEC of 18 June 1992 concerning the creation of a supplementary protection certificate for medicinal products [1992] OJ L 182/1.

[18] Council Directive 89/105/EEC of 21 December 1988 relating to the transparency of measures regulating the prices of medicinal products for human use and their inclusion in the scope of national health insurance systems [1988] OJ L 40/8.

[19] Commission of the European Communities, *An industrial competitiveness policy for the European chemical industry: an example. Communication from the Commission to the Council, the European Parliament and the Economic and Social Committee*, COM [96] 187 final, Brussels, 30.04.1996.

[20] Council Regulation 2309/93/EEC of 22 July 1993 laying down Community procedures for the authorisation and supervision of medicinal products for human and veterinary use and establishing a European Agency for the Evaluation of Medicinal Products [1993] OJ L 214/1.

regulatory framework, including all Directives and Regulations, going back to the first, 1965 Directive. By means of the Directive 93/39/EEC, the previous multi-state marketing authorisation procedure was replaced by a binding decentralised process.[21] While the granting of marketing authorisations is only part of the mandate of the EMA, the agency is not comparable to its US counterpart, the FDA. Formally, at least, healthcare policy is outside the mandate of the EMA.

A general conclusion on the gradual regulation of the pharmaceutical market over the past 50 years is that most of the legislation has been enacted under the Single Market Programme. This is, of course, largely due to the Commission's (and the European Union's) lack of competence (or at least very restricted competence) in the public health area. Nevertheless, the EU has managed to introduce at least two pieces of legislation with a public health legal basis, namely the Transparency Directive[22] and the EMA Regulation.[23] The fact that EU competences are far from clear in the pharmaceutical industry might also be one of the reasons why EU legislation is, in this respect, rather fragmented. Legislation is introduced when necessary or when the necessary stakeholder pressure is evident. Unfortunately, this has the side effect of a lack of a general overarching plan and a limited possibility to work with legislative architecture.

The regulation of the pharmaceutical market in the EU has mainly been the result of 'product regulation'. Diverging national standards concerning product safety would constitute an impediment to the internal market and thus also to the goals of the SEM. Most old pharmaceutical regulations are thus the result of some form of spill-over from the Single Market Programme.[24]

As a result, the EU pharmaceutical regulation adopted a negative integration approach early on and has been dependent on the support of the industry. Strategically, providing the preconditions for a single market in the field of pharmaceutical products has been a better way to convince Member States of the extended competence of the Commission. The strategic choice of a legal basis also constitutes a weakness of the legislative acts adopted, as the support of the industry also enables it to influence the objectives and contents of these acts.[25]

The gradually evolving and increasingly detailed legal framework under which pharmaceuticals are sold, as well as the new forms of therapies that are being

---

[21] Council Directive 93/39/EEC of 14 June 1993 amending Directives 65/65/EEC, 75/318/EEC and 75/319/EEC in respect of medicinal products [1993] OJ L 214/22.

[22] Directive 2004/109/EC of the European Parliament and of the Council of 15 December 2004 on the harmonisation of transparency requirements in relation to information about issuers whose securities are admitted to trading on a regulated market and amending Directive 2001/34/EC [2004] OJ L 390/38.

[23] Council Regulation 2309/93/EEC of 22 July 1993 laying down Community procedures for the authorisation and supervision of medicinal products for human and veterinary use and establishing a European Agency for the Evaluation of Medicinal Products [1993] OJ L 214/1.

[24] One could exclude from this the Transparency Directive and the establishment of the EMA, which were adopted with a healthcare and social dimension and can therefore be considered to be a form of process regulation.

[25] See *Permanand* (n 2) 48–68.

developed, have contributed to the gradual establishment of a new legal area: health law. Mapping regulations and legislation that constitute health law results in a long list of different regulative areas and Directives, which interact with and influence each other. These include the protection of intellectual property, the regulation of research processes, data protection, marketing and product safety legislation, funding, monitoring and surveillance, as well as pricing, reimbursement and coverage in healthcare systems. Naturally, the degree of regulation at an EU level varies considerably depending on which category of regulation we are looking at. Pricing and reimbursement is a matter of national competence and EU regulation in the field is limited to the disclosure of information on national pricing arrangements for pharmaceuticals.[26]

According to Bache, Flear and Hervey, health law evolves under the framework of three different areas, namely the markets (the objective of the internal market being of central importance, but other market structures are also of relevance), risk, and rights and ethics, which seem mainly to have the role of legitimising regulation.[27]

Enhancing the (internal) market has been of central importance for the evolution of health law, both when it comes to legitimising EU competence and with regard to the objectives of legislation. The objective in this respect has been to create a favourable regulatory environment for the European pharmaceutical industry. That being said, the regulatory system could not develop without a strong anchoring in a theory of risk control.[28] Both the Paediatric Regulation and the Orphan Drugs Regulation share their origin in an ethical discussion (the need to provide medicines to patients with orphan diseases and the need to provide medicines developed for children), in order to justify the creation of rights and thus also justify the regulatory market interference.[29] There is a certain conviction that the pharmaceutical companies will not, on the basis of the market as such, proceed with research into orphan drugs or paediatric studies, making governmental intervention necessary in order to achieve the existing societal and public health objectives.

---

[26] Directive 2004/109/EC of the European Parliament and of the Council of 15 December 2004 on the harmonisation of transparency requirements in relation to information about issuers whose securities are admitted to trading on a regulated market and amending Directive 2001/34/EC [2004] OJ L 390/38.

[27] Gordon Bache, Mark L Flear and Tamara K Hervey, 'The Defining Features of the European Union's Approach to Regulating New Health Technologies', in Mark L Flear, Anne-Maree Farrell, Tamara K Hervey and Thérèse Murphy (eds), *European Law and New Health Technologies* (Oxford University Press 2013).

[28] Directive 2010/84/EU of the European Parliament and of the Council of 15 December 2010 amending, as regards pharmacovigilance, Directive 2001/83/EC on the Community code relating to medicinal products for human use (Text with EEA relevance) [2010] OJ L 348/74, Recital 4.

[29] Regulation 1901/2006/EC of the European Parliament and of the Council of 12 December 2006 on medicinal products for paediatric use and amending Regulation (EEC) No 1768/92, Directive 2001/20/EC, Directive 2001/83/EC and Regulation (EC) No 726/2004 (Text with EEA relevance) [2006] OJ L 378/1. See also Regulation 141/2000/EC of the European Parliament and of the Council of 16 December 1999 on orphan medicinal products [1999] OJ L 18/1.

In the Paediatric Regulation, the starting point is the fact that 'market forces alone have proven insufficient to stimulate adequate research into, and the development and authorisation of, medicinal products for the Paediatric population'.[30] The Regulation thus seeks to provide objectives in order to promote 'the development of safe medicinal products for children'.[31] In the same way, the Orphan Drugs Regulation provides incentives by granting a 10-year market exclusivity and other benefits in terms of incentive schemes at a national level. This market exclusivity constitutes 'the strongest incentive for industry to invest in the development and marketing of orphan medicinal products'.[32] Data reveals that although the Orphan Drugs Regulation is the result of an ethical discourse, it is by no means a charitable affair, and conducting business in that specific segment of the pharmaceuticals market has proved to be rather lucrative.[33] Naturally, the ethical discourse does not stand alone, as a strong internal market imperative is expressed in the texts of the regulations, providing that European pharmaceutical industries shall enjoy the same regulatory system (and benefits) as their counterparts in the United States and Japan.[34] The creation of equal opportunities for pharmaceutical industries in Europe has been connected to the possibility of equal access to medicines for patients in Europe as those in the United States and Japan.[35]

2. The Structure of the Pharmaceutical Industry in Europe

The Commission's Final Report of the Pharmaceutical Sector Inquiry, though published in 2007 and thus based on more than 10-year-old data, still provides a very good overview of the pharmaceutical industry in Europe.[36] The conclusions drawn by the report are confirmed when compared with data available today and

---

[30] Regulation 1901/2006/EC, Recital 2.
[31] Regulation 1901/2006/EC, Recital 4.
[32] Regulation 141/2000/EC, Recital 8.
[33] Lucio Luzzatto, Hanna I Hyry, Arrigo Schieppati, et al, 'Outrageous Prices of Orphan Drugs: A Call for Collaboration' 392 [2018], *Lancet*, 10149, 791–94.
[34] Regulation 141/2000/EC, Recitals 2 and 8.
[35] Thus promoting a non-discrimination discourse, see Regulation 469/2009/EC of the European Parliament and of the Council of 6 May 2009 concerning the supplementary protection certificate for medicinal products (Codified version) (Text with EEA relevance) [2009] OJ L 152/1; Regulation 141/2000/EC of the European Parliament and of the Council of 16 December 1999 on orphan medicinal products [1999] OJ L 18/1; Regulation 1901/2006/EC of the European Parliament and of the Council of 12 December 2006 on medicinal products for paediatric use and amending Regulation 1768/92/EEC, Directive 2001/20/EC, Directive 2001/83/EC and Regulation 726/2004/EC (Text with EEA relevance) [2006] OJ L 378/1; Regulation 1394/2007/EC of the European Parliament and of the Council of 13 November 2007 on advanced therapy medicinal products and amending Directive 2001/83/EC and Regulation 726/2004/EC (Text with EEA relevance) [2007] OJ L 324/121.
[36] European Commission, '*Final Report of the Pharmaceutical Sector Inquiry*', 8 July 2009; see also Nicoleta Tuominen, 'An IP perspective on defensive patenting strategies of the EU pharmaceutical industry' (2012) 34 *European Intellectual Property Review*, 8, 541–51.

thus their relevance is, to this date, incontestable.[37] One of the interesting points made in the report is the structure of the generics industry and the variations in its importance and size in different Member States. For example, Croatia's generics industry has a 74 per cent market share, while Spain's has a mere 7.2 per cent.[38] At the same time, data seems to confirm that any delay in the entry of generics on the market has a considerable effect on the price of pharmaceuticals. Prices of generics are on average 25 per cent lower than those of originals.[39]

According to the Commission's conclusions, the costly R&D necessary for product development in the pharmaceutical industry is financed by up to 90 per cent by the industry itself. It is difficult for new commercial entities to enter the market, and thus, when a company disappears, it is seldom or only slowly replaced. The financial risk taken by pharmaceutical companies when developing a new product is, of course, non-negligible. The average cost for the development of a new pharmaceutical is 2.6 billion dollars, with an average R&D time of 10 years, while the chances that this is in fact leading to a marketable product are comparatively low.[40] Substances often prove to have very low or no therapeutic effects at all or, in other cases, their therapeutic effect is counterbalanced by their toxicity and a lack of patient safety. Product development in the pharmaceutical industry indicates that for approximately 5,000 molecules tested, only 250 will enter into preclinical testing, and 10 will reach the stage of clinical development. A project is very successful if one of these substances becomes subject to a marketing authorisation. Another aspect of decisive importance is the fact that the customers of the pharmaceutical industry are primarily national public health systems that naturally have considerable power and may influence both the profitability of the industry and the final commercialisation of specific pharmaceutical products. Pricing decisions constitute limitations to a fully competitive market in pharmaceuticals.[41]

The market for new health technologies and pharmaceuticals is thus not a traditional consumer-dependent market. The main target group of the products and services encompasses national health systems. As a result, traditional patterns of consumer behaviour are not applicable and more complicated political priorities play a central role.[42]

---

[37] The data that the report builds upon is confirmed by data released since. See, for instance, EFPIA (2019) The Pharmaceutical Industry in Figures, Key Data 2019.
[38] IFPMA, Regional Breakdown and Differentiation Between Originators and Generics, The Economic Footprint of the Pharmaceutical Industry [2015].
[39] Communication from the Commission, Executive Summary of Pharmaceutical Sector Inquiry Report, 3 Available at https://ec.europa.eu/competition/sectors/pharmaceuticals/inquiry/communication_en.pdf [Accessed 10 June 2020].
[40] Joseph A DiMasi, Jennifer Kim, Kenneth A Getz, 'The Impact of Collaborative and Risk-Sharing Innovation Approaches on Clinical and Regulatory Cycle Times' (2014) 48 *Therapeutic Innovation and Regulatory Science* (SAGE Journals), 4, 482–87.
[41] For a highly interesting review of the particularities of the pharmaceutical industry, see Margaret Kyle, 'Economic Analysis of Supplementary Protection Certificates in Europe', January 30, 2017 https://ec.europa.eu/info/publications/economic-analysis-supplementary-protection-certificates-europe_en [Accessed 22 January 2021].
[42] On the ways that the special character of the health technology market also influences the evolution of regulations in this specific market, see Mark L Flear, Anne-Maree Farrell, Tamara K Hervey

The pharmaceutical industry has traditionally adopted three major business models. The first and most central one is that of a big multinational company spending substantial sums of money in R&D and investing in the development and patent protection of new original pharmaceuticals. The second business model is that of smaller companies focusing mainly on biotechnological inventions and/or large molecules with medicinal properties. The products of these biotech companies are very often commercialised by third parties, including companies using business model one. The third category is that of generics, companies that invest little in the development of new pharmaceuticals and much in producing existing products at lower cost.

What makes this presentation interesting is the fact that the lines between these three different business models are becoming increasingly blurred. Pharmaceutical companies develop more and more generics and engage in research into big molecules and biologicals,[43] while the top R&D firms are also the top sellers of branded products in Europe. The top sellers of branded products include five US companies and one from Japan, while the top sellers of unbranded products include three Indian companies.

Another important factor to consider concerning product development and thus also clinical trials and marketing authorisation procedures is the nature of the diseases that are the focus of pharmaceutical product research. Diseases that develop slowly will also have a longer product development time, and thus assessing their effectiveness takes longer. Quickly developing diseases, on the other hand, take less time to assess and developing pharmaceutical treatment is subject to a shorter period of clinical trials. It has thus gradually become a more time-demanding process to prove product efficacy and safety, and clinical trials are lengthier than in the past. On the other hand, electronic simulation of disease development could facilitate drug testing in the future and have an impact on the length of clinical trials. That in turn would, of course, have an impact on how expensive and time-consuming marketing authorisation (MA) procedures will be as well as on the duration of the SPCs granted.

3. EU Competence in the Field of Public Health

3.1. EU Public Health Competence in Theory

The allocation of responsibility and power to regulate in the field of public health has been a controversial issue – and remains so to this day – as has already been

---

and Thérèse Murphy, 'Conclusion: A European Law of New Health Technologies?', in Mark L Flear, Anne-Maree Farrell, Tamara K Hervey and Thérèse Murphy (eds), *European Law and New Health Technologies* (Oxford University Press 2013).
[43] See Kyle, n 41, 7–11.

alluded to in this book.[44] In fact, the allocation of competence within the EU system of governance is a matter of concern, generally, and this concern was expressed in the Draft Treaty Establishing a Constitution for Europe (DCT).[45] In general, the legislative institutions of the EU have limited competence, and may act only on condition that they are granted such power through the EC Treaty and the Treaty of the European Union.[46] When the legal basis of the interventions of EU institutions is absent or institutions exceed the limits established, legislative acts may – under the scrutiny of the CJEU – be set aside as unlawful. Having said that, defining the limits of EU competence precisely is no simple matter. In fact, the EU might be able to resort to 'implied competence', where the EU, in order to achieve a Treaty objective, can proceed with certain measures despite lacking the formal competence to do so.[47]

The EC Treaty provided an explicit legal basis concerning the competence of the EU in public health matters, namely Article 152 (now Article 168). However, this is not the only provision employed when legislating in matters that have a direct or indirect impact on public health. Policy fields in which the EU is expected to legislate, such as the internal market, agricultural law and environmental law, are areas that may be related to public health regulation. As a result, a number of legal measures with implications for health have been adopted with legal basis in provisions such as Article 37 (ex 43) EC on the common agricultural policy, Article 71 (ex 75) EC on the common transport policy, Article 137 (ex 118a) EC on social policy, Article 153 (ex 129a) EC on consumer protection, Article 175 (ex 130s) EC on environmental policy, and Article 181 EC (ex 130y) on development cooperation. However, in order for these provisions to be viable legal bases, the legislative acts in question must have as their main goal one of the aforementioned policies,

---

[44] Until February 2010, the Directorate General – Enterprise and Industry (DG Enterprise) was responsible for the oversight of the pharmaceutical industry. The 2010 reorganisation led to a shift of the responsibility for pharmaceuticals to Directorate General – Health and Consumers (SANCO). SANCO was further divided into two entities in February 2012: 'Medicinal products – authorisations, EMA' and 'Medicinal products – quality, safety and efficacy'. The split was motivated by the workload of the European Commission related to the implementation of the Pharmacovigilance Legislation. DG Health and Consumers naturally has an important public health mandate. The DG Health and Consumers comprises six units: General Affairs, Consumers Affairs, Public Health, Health Systems and Products, Safety of the Food Chain, Food and Veterinary Office, Veterinary and International Affairs. The role of the Public Health unit has been reduced since the introduction of the Pharmacovigilance Risk Assessment Committee and the transfer of pharmacovigilance issues to this organ. The Biotechnology unit is part of the Safety of the Food Chain unit. It has been moved from DG Enterprise and Industry, which means that the focus will move from the promotion of competitiveness in biotechnology and pharmaceutical industries to health, safety and ethics issues.

[45] Laeken Declaration on the Future of the European Union, adopted by the Heads of State and Government at the Laeken Summit, 14–15 December 2001, Bulletin of the European Union, 2001, No 12. Luxembourg: Office for Official Publications of the European Communities. 'Presidency Conclusions of the Laeken European Council (14 and 15 December 2001)', 19–23.

[46] See Trevor Hartley, *The foundations of European Community law: An Introduction to the Constitutional and Administrative Law of the European Community* (Clarendon Press 1994) 105–118.

[47] See Judgment of the Court of 9 July 1987, Federal Republic of Germany and others v Commission of the European Communities, C-281, 283, 284, 285 and 287/85, EU:C:1987:351.

with the public health dimension being of secondary importance. In cases where a legislative act has straightforward public health issues as its main goal, Article 168 (ex 152) is the only appropriate legal basis.

Healthcare was not mentioned in the original EEC/EC Treaty, with one notable exception, namely that of legal exceptions to the fundamental freedoms based on public health concerns in Article 46 (now Article 52 TFEU). However, Article 2 EEC provided that one of the objectives of the Community was the 'raising of the standard of living' of EU citizens, and this provision has been interpreted as a possible alternative legal basis for measures related to public health protection.

In the Maastricht Treaty, Article 152 (now Article 168) was introduced, referring to public health protection in the same way as consumer and environmental protection. Public health was added to the list of activities covered by the Treaty in Article 3(1)(p) EC, and this was further linked to the core objective of raising the standard and quality of life as set out in Article 2 EC.[48]

In the Lisbon Treaty,[49] the 'protection and improvement of public health' of Article 6(a) of the TFEU was added as a legal basis. This means the EU shall have competence to carry out certain actions in support, coordination, or supplementation of these objectives. Article 2(5) TFEU clarifies that these actions may not be considered a harmonisation of national law.

Article 6(a) is also reflected in Article 168(1) TFEU providing that 'A high level of human health protection shall be ensured in the definition and implementation of all Union policies and activities'. This introduces the obligation on the EU legislative process to take into consideration the impact that any proposed legislation (even if it is not in principle directly related to public health) has on public health and make it part of its general evaluation process. This process of public health impact assessment is called 'mainstreaming'.[50]

Furthermore, Article 114(3) TFEU (previously Article 95 EC) states that the Commission 'will take as a base a high level of protection' with regard to legislative proposals that concern public health.[51]

Article 168 stipulates the importance of the cooperation between Member States and third countries as well as with competent international organisations as regards the improvement and promotion of health and prevention of ill health, and measures related to high standards of quality and safety. The role of the Commission is subsidiary, encouraging and promoting coordination between the

---

[48] For an elaborate discussion on EU competence in Health, see Tamara K Hervey, 'Community Competence in the Field of Health' in Tamara K Hervey and Jean V McHale (eds), *Law in Context: Health Law and the European Union* (Cambridge University Press 2004).

[49] Elias Mossialos and Martin McKee, 'Is a European Healthcare Policy Emerging?' [2001] BMJ (Clinical research ed), Vol 323(7307), 248, where it is suggested that the rising number of CJEU cases evidences the emergence of a new EU health framework.

[50] Gillian MacNaughton and Lisa Forman, 'The Value of Mainstreaming Human Rights into Health Impact Assessment' [2014] 11 *International Journal of Environmental Research and Public Health*, 10, 10076–90.

[51] This is rather contradictory given that the EU has very limited competence as regards legislation related to public health issues.

Member States. However, the same provision states that EU competence is limited to three areas: measures setting high standards of quality and safety of organs and substances of human origin, blood, and blood derivate (though these measures may not prevent Member States from introducing stricter rules), measures in the veterinary and phytosanitary fields which have as their direct objective the protection of public health, and measures setting high standards of quality and safety for medicinal products and devices for medical use.

Although the aforementioned provisions seem to considerably limit EU competence, the EU has moved to legislate in other areas as well, for instance in the case of the Patients' Rights Directives, which clearly do not fall under any of these three areas of competence.[52]

What becomes obvious is that there is limited room for harmonisation in this field. What has been considered of central importance (also in the case law of the CJEU) is safeguarding the powers of Member States to organise their respective social security systems.[53] The Member States are thus able to set the framework of their national social security systems and the criteria according to which benefits will be made available and to whom. Although there is a clear national competence in this field, Member States are also under obligation to comply with EU law and the tension between, for example, the free movement provisions and the public health competence of Member States is increasing.[54]

The internal market has a dominant place in the EU legal order, and thus constitutes the legal basis for a number of legislative acts in various areas of law. As a result, the legal basis provisions in the Treaty concerning the establishment and functioning of the common (Article 94 EC, ex 100a EEC) and the internal market (Article 95 EC, ex 100a EEC) are equally important as Article 152 when assessing EU competence in public health. The free movement of goods might in fact include risks to public health, since dangerous or potentially disease-carrying goods might be spread on the internal market. Article 30 (ex 36) provides that the Treaty 'shall not preclude prohibitions or restrictions on imports … justified on grounds … of the protection of health and life of humans …' The same provision states that such measures shall not 'constitute a means of arbitrary discrimination or a disguised restriction on trade between Member States'. The CJEU had the opportunity to provide guidelines as to how this provision should be applied in the cases of *Schloh* and *Snellers*, providing that the health and life of humans foremost among the property or interests to be protected by Article 30 of the Treaty.[55]

---

[52] Directive 2011/24/EU of the European Parliament and of the Council of 9 March 2011 on the application of patients' rights in cross-border healthcare [2011] OJ L 88/45.

[53] Judgment of the Court (Third Chamber) of 24 April 1980, *Una Coonan v Insurance Officer*, C-110/79 EU:C:1980:112, para 12.

[54] See European Commission, 'Guide to the Case Law of the European Court of Justice, on Articles 56 et seq. TFEU: Freedom to Provide Services', Available at http://ec.europa.eu/DocsRoom/documents/16743/attachments/1/translations [Accessed on 11 June 2020].

[55] Judgment of the Court (Third Chamber) of 12 June 1986, *Bernhard Schloh v Auto contrôle technique SPRL*, C-50/85, EU:C:1986:244; Judgment of the Court (Sixth Chamber) of 12 October 2000, *Snellers Auto's BV v Algemeen Directeur van de Dienst Wegverkeer*, C-314/98, EU:C:2000:557.

In fact, Member States have a significant level of discretion in how they draft and implement their public health policies. The last sentence of Article 30 provides for clear application of the principle of proportionality. Member States must be able to show that there is a risk to public health and that the goal is only to address this risk, and not to provide an obstacle to the internal market trade between Member States. On the other hand, the flexibilities of Article 30 cease to exist when EU-level measures are introduced in order to harmonise public health protection.[56] It seems that Article 30 has been used to provide the Member States with a possibility of derogation in circumstances justified by public health interests, rather than a general national public health competence.

The important interrelation between the internal market and public health was brought to light in 1992 at the time of the promulgation of the programme for the completion of the internal market. The new Article 100a (now 95 EC) provided that the Council should adopt harmonisation measures which had as an objective the establishment and functioning of the internal market, while Article 95(3) provided that in doing this, measures should provide a high level of protection with regard to health, safety, the environment and consumers.

The Court adopted a broad interpretation of Article 95 in the Supplementary Protection Certificate Case, a Regulation based on Article 100a (now 95) EC. Spain challenged the use of the specific article as a legal basis for this regulation and claimed that the provision which should have been used instead was 100 or 235 EC.[57] According to the Court, the goal with the Regulation was to prevent national legislation providing diverging remedies to patentholders and thereby creating obstacles and distorting competition. National measures could obstruct the free movement of pharmaceuticals and work to the detriment of the internal market in the specific industry.

3.2. EU Public Health Competence in Practice

In the field of healthcare, the European Commission is represented by the Directorate General for Health and Food Safety (DG Sante) and the Consumers, Health and Food Executive Agency (Chafea). On the other hand, pharmaceuticals are treated as an industrial good and as such are the responsibility of the Directorate General for Enterprise. Last, but not least, we have the role of the EMA and, of course, the Member States. Responsibility is fragmented, to say the least.

As a result of the subsidiarity principle, action at the EU level should only be taken in policy domains where there is a clear need to proceed at a more

---

[56] See Judgment of the Court of 5 October 1977, *Carlo Tedeschi v Denkavit Commerciale srl*, C-5/77, EU:C:1977:144; Judgment of the Court of 5 April 1979, *Criminal proceedings against Tullio Ratti*, C-148/78, EU:C:1979:110.

[57] Judgment of the Court of 13 July 1995, *Kingdom of Spain v Council of the European Union*, C-350/92, EU:C:1995:237.

centralised level. Concurrently, the proportionality principle dictates that EU action should not go beyond what is necessary in order to achieve the objectives of the EU Treaties.[58] Healthcare is the policy domain in which the subsidiarity principle has prevailed the most. Today, the EU has 28 member states, all with unique and rather complicated public health schemes, making a centralised approach a rather complicated endeavour. There has thus been a common understanding that healthcare is a matter of national competence where the EU has no formal legal mandate to develop its own centralised 'hard healthcare laws'. That being said, the EU has adopted a more indirect method of participating and coordinating, that of soft law and the open method of coordination, meaning that it strives to improve healthcare in Member States by promoting cooperation, financing certain public health projects, etc.[59]

Article 5(2) of the TEU provides for the principle of conferral according to which the EU may act only within the limits of the competences conferred upon it by the Member States. In other words, what is not explicitly conferred remains the competence of Member States. The basis for the competence of the EU in public health issues is found in Article 168 TFEU, where it is provided that all EU action directed at improving public health shall complement national policies. Thus, public health measures adopted at an EU level are only to be seen as complementary. In Article 168(5), a further delimitation of competence is provided, namely:

> The European Parliament and the Council, acting in accordance with the ordinary legislative procedure and after consulting the Economic and Social Committee and the Committee of the Regions, may also adopt incentive measures designed to protect and improve human health and in particular to combat the major cross-border health scourges, measures concerning monitoring, early warning of and combating serious cross-border threats to health, and measures which have as their direct objective the protection of public health regarding tobacco and the abuse of alcohol, excluding any harmonisation of the laws and regulations of the Member States.

A basis for EU competence in the field of public health is also provided in Article 114(3) TFEU, including an obligation for EU institutions to ensure a high level of health and consumer protection in their harmonising measures adopted under that Article.

Taking into consideration all the aforementioned provisions, it becomes clear that EU public health measures raise or might raise issues of competence. While EU public health measures should, according to Article 168(5), be merely complementary in nature – something that leaves fundamental decisions to Member States – the EU also has the responsibility under Article 114(3) of guaranteeing health and consumer protection. In an attempt to bring further clarity to this

---

[58] Martin McKee, Tamara Hervey and Anna Gilmore, 'Public Health Policies' in Elias Mossialos et al (eds), *Health Systems Governance in Europe: The Role of EU Law and Policy* (Cambridge University Press 2010) 265. See also Tamara Hervey, 'Up in Smoke? Community (Anti) Tobacco Law and Policy' (2001), 26 *European Law Review*, 2, 101–25, 104.

[59] See, for instance, Horizon 2020 and Health 2020.

question, the CJEU has, in the case of *Tobacco Advertising I*, provided that the EU may adopt measures on the basis of other Treaty provisions, if these provisions could also have an impact on the protection of public health.[60] The Court also stated that if the conditions for relying on Article 114 of the TFEU are fulfilled, EU legislation may not be prevented from relying on that Article as a legal basis solely on the grounds that public health concerns form a decisive factor therein.

An interesting and important question to address is what constitutes the basis of EU competence for the Regulations and Directives addressed in this book. In this respect, the question arises as to whether Article 114(1) is being abused in order to extend the powers of the EU in public health, causing them to develop into something that they were not originally supposed to.[61] Article 114(1) states that 'save where otherwise provided in the Treaties, the following provisions shall apply for the achievement of the objectives set out in Article 26'.[62] The provision is drafted in such a way as to constitute a general legal basis for cases where the EU would have to legislate for the purposes of the internal market, but where there is no other specific legal basis upon which such legislation could be based. This could, of course, also be used when there are provisions limiting EU competence, such as in the case of public health. At the same time, Article 114(1) may not be considered the legal basis for a general competence of the EU. The boundaries between the competence of the EU and its Member States are blurred and it seems that Article 114 can be used to harmonise any issue, even a purely public health one, with the justification that this contributes to the functioning of the internal market. The CJEU has provided some criteria under which the EU may refer to Article 114.[63] However, it has been noted that the EU has not always confined itself to these criteria, but has legislated in areas where harmonisation of national

---

[60] Judgment of the Court of 5 October 2000, *Federal Republic of Germany v European Parliament and Council of the European Union*, C-376/98, EU:C:2000:544. In this case, Germany brought a successful claim of invalidity against the Tobacco Advertising Directive (Directive 98/43/EC of the European Parliament and of the Council of 6 July 1998 on the approximation of the laws, regulations and administrative provisions of the Member States relating to the advertising and sponsorship of tobacco products [1998] OJ L 213/9 on the basis that this had been enacted outside the competence of the EU, since the conditions for making use of Article 114 TFEU were not fulfilled. In the specific case, the Commission argued that this legislation was important in order to avoid that Member States legislated in differing ways, as this would affect the internal market negatively. The Directive was considered not to have enough connection to the internal market, proving that the legislator had in fact acted outside its scope of competence. This was also the first time an EU legislative act was proclaimed invalid by the Court due to lack of competence.

[61] Scott Crosby, 'The New Tobacco Control Directive: An Illiberal and Illegal Disdain for the Law' [2002] 27 *European Law Review*, 2, 177–93, 184. See also, Derrick Wyatt, 'Community Competence to Regulate the Internal Market' [2007] *Oxford Legal Studies Research Paper*, No 9/2007 46.

[62] Article 26 in the Treaty on the Functioning of the European Union (TFEU).

[63] Judgment of the Court (Grand Chamber) of 14 December 2004, *Arnold André GmbH & Co. KG v Landrat des Kreises Herford*, C-434/02, EU:C:2004:800, para 30. See also the more recent Judgment of the Court (Second Chamber) of 4 May 2016 *Republic of Poland v European Parliament and Council of the European Union*, C-358/14, EU:C:2016:323, para 38, and Judgment of the Court (Second Chamber) of 4 May 2016, *Philip Morris Brands SARL and Others v Secretary of State for Health*, C-547/14, EU:C:2016:325, para 64.

rules would in fact facilitate trade or remove uncertainty from the system. It has been suggested that Article 114 has been used as an instrument for general EU governance.[64]

The limits for use of the said Article were set by the CJEU in the *Tobacco Advertising I* case. The uncertainty in the division of competences between the EU and the Member States concerning public health gives the CJEU the role of ex ante 'controller'. While it is reassuring to have CJEU case law as guidance and at the same time as a control mechanism concerning the limits of EU competence, this entails the risk of providing the Commission with a form of legislative drafting guide. This means that CJEU case law could work as a starting point for the EU legislator when drafting new legislative acts, opting for a choice of terms that complies with the Court's case law, making it hard for the CJEU to later on set aside the legislative act in question, for obvious reasons.[65] In fact, following the annulment of the *Tobacco Advertising I* Directive, the Commission proceeded to draft a new legislative act whose validity was attacked in the same way. However, the outcome was different. *Tobacco Advertising II* was re-worked, taking into consideration the CJEU ruling in the *Tobacco Advertising I* case. The new proposal for a Directive fulfilled the criteria of Article 114 TFEU, since the legislator used the previous CJEU ruling as a starting point for the legislative architecture and content.[66]

With regard to the limits of Article 114 TFEU, the opinion by AG Geelhoed is of interest, stating clearly that when a potential barrier to the internal market arises, the EU must be in a position to act, even in cases where the specific barrier is not the principal reason for action.[67]

The CJEU ruled in the cases *André* and *Swedish Match* that the existence of obstacles to the free movement of certain products – created by national laws of Member States – will in principle authorise the EU legislator to adopt measures on the basis of Article 114 TFEU.[68] At the same time, when regulating in these cases, the EU legislator must comply with fundamental legislative principles, such

---

[64] In this regard, the CJEU has stated that judicial measures that have their legal basis in Article 114 TFEU would be rendered nugatory if a mere finding of disparities between national rules were sufficient to justify the choice of Article 114 TFEU as a legal basis. See Judgment of the Court of 5 October 2000, *Federal Republic of Germany v European Parliament and Council of the European Union*, C-376/98, EU:C:2000:544, para 84.

[65] That being said, there are some cases where legislative acts under Article 114 TFEU have been successfully challenged, see *Tobacco Advertising I*.

[66] See also Mattias Kumm, 'Constitutionalising Subsidiarity in Integrated Markets: The Case of Tobacco Regulation in the European Union' [2006] 12 *European Law Journal*, 4, 503–33, 520.

[67] Judgment of the Court of 10 December 2002, *The Queen v Secretary of State for Health, ex parte British American Tobacco (Investments) Ltd and Imperial Tobacco Ltd*, C-491/01, EU:C:2002:741. See also Geraint Howells, *The Tobacco Challenge: Legal Policy and Consumer Protection* (Ashgate Publishing 2011), 227.

[68] See Judgment of the Court (Grand Chamber) of 14 December 2004, *Arnold André GmbH & Co KG v Landrat des Kreises Herford*, C-434/02, EU:C:2004:800; Judgment of the Court (Grand Chamber) of 14 December 2004, *The Queen, on the application of: Swedish Match AB and Swedish Match UK Ltd v Secretary of State for Health*, C-210/03, EU:C:2004:802.

as the principle of proportionality. In the case of the Regulations and Directives in focus in this book, it can be concluded that Article 114 TFEU works as their legal basis, as differences in the national regulation on marketing authorisation of pharmaceutical products and thus also of the Supplementary Protection Certificates would become obstacles on the internal market.[69]

The fact that Member States want to retain control over their national public health policies and pharmaceutical pricing has prevented the EU from proceeding further with the harmonisation process and with the creation of a true internal market for pharmaceuticals.

New to the provision of Article 168 TFEU is the expectation that the EU will encourage cooperation between Member States in order to improve health services in cross-border areas. In fact, the Commission is able to take initiatives in order to organise and coordinate the exchange of expertise between Member States and prepare the infrastructure for monitoring and evaluating cooperation initiatives. This new provision gives a broader mandate to the Commission, as well as a possibility to act proactively. Both the Parliament and the Council are able to adopt incentive measures designed to combat serious cross-border threats to health and measures regarding tobacco and the use of alcohol.[70] In general, it seems that there is a hierarchy in the generality of Treaty provisions that might constitute a legal basis for EU competence in the field of public health, with Article 308 being considered the most general basis, while Article 95 is more specific, albeit not as specific as other provisions. In order for the legitimacy of a legal act not to be questioned, the Commission needs to find and employ the most specific legal basis for the issue being regulated. When there is no specific legal provision, Article 95 might be an option. However, it cannot be claimed that the complex questions in relation to EU competence in the field of pharmaceuticals are settled. In particular, the application and interpretation of Article 308 remains obscure and complicated. The application of Article 95 is also not completely clear. The cases *Tobacco Advertising I* and *Tobacco Advertising II* lead to the conclusion that in order for Article 95 to be applicable, the objective of the legislative act must be to provide improved conditions for the establishment and functioning of the internal market and not merely to deal with an abstract risk of competition distortion.[71] This also means that in order to review the legitimacy of competence, one has to investigate whether the preamble of a legislative act is reflected in its provisions.[72]

---

[69] According to Article 26 in the Treaty on the Functioning of the European Union (TFEU), the internal market comprises 'an area without internal frontiers in which the free movement of goods, persons, services and capital is ensured in accordance with the provision of the Treaties'.

[70] See also Brigit Toebes and Janne Rothmar Herrmann, 'The European Union and Health and Human Rights' (2011), *European Human Rights Law Review*, No 4, 419–36.

[71] Stephen Weatherill, 'The Limits of Legislative Harmonization Ten Years after Tobacco Advertising: How the Court's Case Law has become a "Drafting Guide"' [2011] 12 *German Law Journal*, 03, 827–64.

[72] Han-Wei Liu, 'Harmonizing the Internal Market, or Public Health? Revisiting Case C-491/01 (*British American Tobacco*) and Case C-380/03 (*Tobacco Advertising II*)' [2009] 15 *Columbia Journal European Law Online*, 41.

3.3. The Public Health Programmes

Although the limits of EU competence in the field of public health have been and are contentious, what has been clear is that Article 168(7) TFEU gives a stable legal basis for the Council and the European Parliament to adopt incentive programmes funded by the EU and managed by the Commission itself or by EU agencies. These programmes are interesting, because most of the regulatory rights have been introduced after an initial EU engagement under the framework of a public health programme.[73]

What is interesting with these public health programmes is the way they are systematically used in order to open the door to a more extensive EU competence, albeit indirectly. By showing the level of activity of the EU in terms of research programmes and public health programmes, and connecting the outcomes of these and the lessons learned to a proposed legislative act, it seems possible to give the legislative act a solid foundation, gradually creating acceptance for EU competence in certain areas of public health.

An interesting example in this respect is that of rare diseases. The Commission, in its communication concerning a programme of Community action on rare diseases within the framework for action in the field of public health, decided to give rare diseases priority within the public health framework. The European Parliament and the Council have through Decision No 1295/1999/EC of 29 April 1999 adopted a programme of Community action on rare diseases within the framework for action in the field of public health (1999–2003) (2), including actions to provide information, to deal with clusters of rare diseases in a population, and to support relevant patient organisations. The Orphan Drugs Regulation, which was proposed later, implemented one of the priorities laid down in this programme of action, while the general framework of the regulation was built upon previous experiences.

3.3.1. The First Public Health Programme

The first public health programme (2003–08) addressed three objectives: improving health information and knowledge, responding rapidly to health threats, and addressing health determinants. Under the framework of this programme, the Commission proposed to stipulate EU-level action in comparing and assessing healthcare systems.

---

[73] Orphan drugs, paediatric medicine and advanced therapy medicinal products have all been promoted in EU public health programmes.

3.3.2. The EU Health Strategy

The EU Health Strategy 'Together for Health' from 2007 encompassed an initial plan of action for the period 2008–13, which was later extended and is still valid today. The 'Together for Health' strategy highlighted the importance of dealing with certain public health issues at an EU level. The public health issues identified included pandemics and bioterrorism on the one hand, and issues pertaining to the movement of goods and services, and other measures for guaranteeing health and quality standards across Europe, on the other. In this regard, this EU Health Strategy is a complement to national health policies, in accordance with Article 168 TFEU. This policy faces three challenges: the ageing population of the EU, the emerging threats to health (climate change, pandemics and bioterrorism), and new technologies (AI and other new technologies with the potential of revolutionising healthcare systems).[74]

This health strategy is built upon certain principles. Principle one concerns the shared health values of the EU: universality (no-one should be barred from access to healthcare), access to good-quality care, equity (equal access according to need, regardless of ethnicity, gender, etc.), solidarity (financial arrangements within the national health system to ensure accessibility of healthcare for all), citizens' empowerment (citizens should be informed and able to participate in public health decision making), reduction of health inequalities (targeted health promotion and best-practice exchange), and scientific evidence (health policy must be based on the best scientific evidence).

Principle two concludes that health is in fact the greatest wealth (healthcare is not to be considered merely as a cost, but also as a form of investment for the future), while principle three contends that health issues are of relevance in all policies, since many policy domains have a direct or indirect impact on health issues (making it important to establish cooperation and synergies between sectors and actors). In the fourth principle, the focus lies on global health and the impact that a unified EU public health front might have in addressing global health concerns.

3.3.3. The Third Health Programme (2014–20)

The third health programme is based on Regulation EU 282/2014.[75] With a total budget of €449.4 million and 23 priority areas, it is the most comprehensive initiative in the field and serves four specific objectives: to promote health, prevent

---

[74] See also European Commission, *'Together for Health: A Strategic Approach for the EU 2008–2013'* (White Paper) IP/07/1571, Brussels, 23 October 2007. See also European Commission, 'Investing in Health' (Commission Staff Working Document) SWD [2013] 43 Final.

[75] Regulation 282/2014/EU of the European Parliament and of the Council of 11 March 2014 on the establishment of a third Programme for the Union's action in the field of health (2014–2020) and repealing Decision No 1350/2007/EC (Text with EEA relevance) [2014] OJ L 86/1.

disease and foster healthy lifestyles through 'health in all policies', to protect EU citizens from serious cross-border health threats, to contribute to innovative, efficient and sustainable health systems, and lastly to facilitate access to high quality and safe healthcare for EU citizens.[76]

The objectives of the third Public Health Programme are to promote health, prevent diseases and foster supportive environments for healthy lifestyles. The Union is to address shortages of resources – both human and financial – and facilitate voluntary uptake of innovations in public health. Furthermore, the programme will enhance access to cross-border expertise in public health matters and promotes high specialisation, even with regards to rare medical conditions. Quality healthcare and patient safety are priorities to be guaranteed through the application of research results.[77]

3.3.4. Health 2020

Health 2020 is the World Health Organization's health policy framework for the European region and is the result of a two-year consultation; its final version was adopted by the 53 countries of the European Region already in September 2012. The programme takes into consideration contemporary developments in public health issues and economic, social and demographic factors that may be of relevance. A central aspect of the Health 2020 programme is eliminating inequalities within the EU concerning public health by providing a common framework for the exchange of knowledge and expertise and looking into social determinants of health, the objective being to create a strong public health sector in all Member States. Within Health 2020, access to public health is seen as a democracy issue.[78]

These health programmes provide the necessary background, data, and even legitimacy for the Commission to proceed with proposing legislation in this specific field. The programmes are also indirectly used in order to change perceptions and increase the public acceptability of expanding EU competences in the field of public health. It is undeniable that they have had an impact on how the mandate of the Commission (and of the EU legislator) is perceived and may also gradually impact on how protective Member States are of their exclusive national competence.

---

[76] European Commission, *Impact assessment accompanying the document 'Proposal for a Regulation of the European Parliament and of the Council establishing a Health for Growth Programme, the third programme of EU action in the field of health for the period 2014-2020'* (Commission Staff Working Paper) SEC [2011] 1322; See also citizens' responses considering the third health programme: https://ec.europa.eu/health/sites/health/files/programme/docs/summary-prog_en.pdf [Accessed on 11 June 2020].

[77] For the EU policy approach in the field of public health, see European Commission, *'Investing in health: Social investment package'* (Commission Staff Working Document) SWD [2013] 43 final.

[78] Health 2020. A European policy framework and strategy for the 21st century [2013], World Health Organization.

4. Effective Legislation and Regulatory Rights

Developing techniques for legislative evaluation is an important aspect to consider in modern legislation, at both the national and the EU level. Although there seems to be a consensus on the need for evaluation of legislative acts, there also seems to be a broad spectrum of views as to how this should be done and the models or techniques that should be employed. Moreover, there are different objectives that could be used to consider whether or not a certain piece of legislation is successful, namely legality, legitimacy, effectiveness, or legal certainty and proportionality. While the principles (and objectives) of legitimacy and effectiveness have often been separated, they are closely related.[79] Above all, they are two major legislative values that need to be considered when designing and implementing regulation. A non-legitimate piece of legislation will probably be lacking in effectiveness, as it will most likely not be enforced.[80]

Effective legislation is characterised by high certainty and predictability and lower transaction costs, providing for a better business environment. At the same time, such legislation is expected to have direct effects on the work of public institutions, as they are able to achieve better results with fewer resources. Another important parameter to consider is the fact that the effectiveness of a single rule has an impact on the legal system as a whole, not only in its current state but also potentially on its future application.[81] Considering the level of effectiveness of legislation usually becomes a question of considering its ineffectiveness, as it is rare that legal rules work as expected. There is indubitably a gap between the will of the legislator and that of the individuals, companies and markets – or even of the authorities – that are to apply the legislation in question. Side effects arising because of the specific legal rule's interaction with other legal rules, with the market, or with other exogenous parameters – whether said effects are known or unknown at the time of the drafting of the legislation – will have an impact on its results. The effectiveness of the rule might also depend on the administrative authority that is to apply and interpret the legislative act and works as a middleman between individuals or companies and the legal provision.[82] The regulations that are the focus of this book are all dependent on the effectiveness of administration and of general administrative rules. The functioning of the EMA is of key

---

[79] On the principle of legitimacy, see Martijn van der Brink, 'Justice, Legitimacy and the Authority of Legislation within the European Union' [2019] 82 *Modern Law Review*, 2, 293–318.

[80] There have been attempts to link effectiveness to legitimacy, for instance in the case of the Blood Directive and the Organ Donation Directive, see Anne-Maree Farrell, 'Risk, Legitimacy and EU Regulation of Health Technologies' in Mark L Flear, Anne-Maree Farrell, Tamara K Hervey and Thérèse Murphy (eds), *European Law and New Health Technologies* (Oxford University Press 2013) 203–21.

[81] See Maria de Benedetto, 'Effective Law from a Regulatory and Administrative Law Perspective' [2018] 9 *European Journal of Risk Regulation*, 3, 391–415.

[82] Concerning the contribution of administrative authorities concerning the effectiveness of legislation, see de Benedetto, n 81.

importance for the effectiveness of the system as a whole. Of course, the way that national patent and MA authorities are to apply certain aspects of the regulations also has an important share in the responsibility, and thus any malfunctioning of national patent offices (or marketing authorisation authorities) could be a source of weakness for the system and the objectives of the regulations.

In this book, the choice has been made to study four EU Regulations – the SPC Regulation, the Orphan Drugs Regulation, the Paediatric Regulation and the Advanced Therapy Medicinal Products (ATMP) Regulation – through the lens of effectiveness.

Needless to say, defining what is meant by effectiveness is not the easiest of tasks. Effectiveness could be a measurement standard encompassing anything from the general impact of the legislation on the legal system as a whole to the societal changes it brings or simply how the political objectives incentivising this specific piece of legislation are accommodated. Thus, the concept of effectiveness has been and remains blurred, both because of the lack of a unified definition and because of the different perspectives and views as to where and how effectiveness of a legal rule should be measured and evaluated.[83] One of the important (and contradictory) concepts to consider when defining effectiveness is that of 'results'. According to Zamboni, one could make a distinction between internal effectiveness, focusing on the impact that the new legislation has on the legal system, and external effectiveness, related to policy outcomes of the legislation measured in terms of economic, social and political outputs.[84]

There are other legislative objectives which, while not being the same as effectiveness, at least sound similar: efficacy (looking into the role of the law from a broader societal perspective) and efficiency (looking into the law from a pure cost/benefit approach). In recent works in the field of legislative studies, and in particular in the work of Mousmouti,[85] effectiveness has gained considerable attention. This may be because the aforementioned competing concepts are either too broad or too narrow, or because – as Mousmouti puts it – effectiveness manages to capture the role of a specific piece of legislation as part of a broader system, or simply because it provides the methodological framework necessary to look into the mechanics of legislation. What makes this perspective an interesting methodological basis is the fact that it actually follows and to some extent governs the reasoning of the legislator under the framework of his/her mandate and legislative powers. This methodology permits guiding of the ongoing process

---

[83] See Mauro Zamboni, 'Legislative Policy and Effectiveness: A (Small) Contribution from Legal Theory' [2018] 9 *European Journal of Risk Regulation*, 3, 416–30.
[84] Ibid 423.
[85] Maria Mousmouti, 'Operationalising Quality of Legislation Through the Effectiveness Test' [2012] 6 *Legisprudence*, 2, 192–105; Maria Mousmouti, 'Effectiveness as an Aspect of Quality of EU Legislation: Is It Feasible?' [2014] 2 *The Theory and Practice of Legislation*, 3, 309–27; Maria Mousmouti and Gianluca Crispi '"Good" Legislation as a Means of Ensuring Voice, Accountability, and the Delivery of Results in Urban Development' [2015] *The World Bank Legal Review*, Vol 6, 257–69.

of introducing a new piece of legislation, while it may at the same time constitute an evaluation tool for existing legislation. Applying the effectiveness test does not in any way guarantee the elaboration of the perfect piece of legislation. The system in itself provides considerable flexibility, taking into consideration that legislation is in fact influenced by parameters that may not be envisaged at the time of the drafting. Effectiveness is not a goal per se, but is defined and determined by a number of factors that it is expected to serve as a link for, such as political ideals, the specific situation at hand, and the results that it produces.[86] Thus, instead of having an objective that is external to the legislation as a starting point, you evaluate legislation on the basis of its objective, its content and its interaction with other components of the legal framework.

The effectiveness test provides a handy structure for how to proceed when looking into different parameters that may influence the effectiveness of legislative acts. The different aspects of the test include the objectives of the legislation, the content, the context and the results. These four aspects have been chosen with the ambition of covering all important angles of modern law making. The objective covers the intention of the legislator with introducing the specific piece of legislation and what the legislation is to achieve, while the content looks into how the legislation will achieve the desired results. Context relates to how the provisions will be integrated into the broader legal system and the results focus on what has actually been achieved.

What is important and intriguing with this evaluation model is the fact that although it has its origins and theoretical basis in academic research in the field of legislative studies it also depends on feedback and its own practical application when put to the test in the process of evaluating concrete legislative acts. Thus, this model is not meant to remain merely a theoretical exercise; its limits and potential should be tested based on specific legislative acts, and it is through such practical application that it receives feedback, a starting point for further adjustments, fine-tuning and further development.

The analytical framework presented by Mousmouti in her book 'Designing Effective Legislation' is certainly an interesting and tempting tool to use when considering the regulations that together constitute the basis for regulatory rights in the pharmaceutical industry.[87] However, one needs to keep in mind the fact that the subject matter of this book is EU legislation and the issue to consider is whether this test works as well for EU legislative works or whether it is better suited for national legislation.

Another question that may arise is whether an analytical kit like the one proposed under the effectiveness test is necessary, taking into consideration the fact that the EU has already put in place a number of internal legislative guidelines and legislative evaluation mechanisms.

---

[86] Zamboni (n 83) 429.
[87] Maria Mousmouti, *Designing Effective Legislation* (Edward Elgar Publishing, 2019).

It would be strange if the EU had not responded to what seems to constitute a central issue in the discussions concerning legislative drafting in terms of rationalisation and evaluation of legislation.[88] During recent decades, there have been a number of legislative evaluation models that were expected to streamline legislative drafting, both the process as such and its effects.[89] In the EU, the interest in streamlining legislative process was expressed in the Better Regulation Guidelines. The Better Regulation Guidelines include two parts, where one is guidance on what is considered to be the 'essential' aspects of better regulation, such as being proactive and providing for forward planning, political validation, stakeholder consultation, quality control, implementation support and monitoring. The Regulation includes a toolbox with practical, hands-on advice to drafters. However, this legislative toolbox is to be used 'selectively and with common sense', with the warning that it could not be considered a panacea in legislative drafting.[90]

Two main initiatives have been noted in this respect, namely the impact assessment and the public consultation.[91] The impact assessment concerns the decision-making process as such and the way this is to be structured, while the public consultation has as its main objective to provide for collection of information and ensure the broader participation of interested bodies or individuals in the EU legislative process.[92]

A practical and hands-on perspective has been adopted in a number of national jurisdictions that have elaborated templates either for legislation in general or for specific aspects of legislative drafting.[93] Other related initiatives are for instance the Joint Practical Guide for the Drafting of Community Legislation in the European

---

[88] European Commission, *Communication from the Commission to the European Parliament and the Council: Proposal for an Interinstitutional Agreement on Better Regulation* COM [2015] 216 final; European Commission, *Communication from the Commission to the European Parliament, the Council, the European Economic and Social Committee and the Committee of the Regions: Completing the Better Regulation Agenda: Better solutions for better results* COM [2017] 651 final; European Commission, 'Communication from the Commission to the European Parliament, the Council, the European Economic and Social Committee and the Committee of the Regions: The principles of subsidiarity and proportionality: Strengthening their role in the EU's policymaking' COM [2018] 703; European Commission, *Report from the Commission: Annual Report 2017 on the Application of the Principles of Subsidiarity and Proportionality* COM [2018] 490 final; European Commission, *Communication from the Commission to the European Parliament, the European Council and the Council, Better Regulation: Delivering better results for a stronger Union* COM [2016] 615 final.

[89] Mousmouti (n 85), 109. See also European Commission, *Communication from the Commission to the European Parliament, the Council, the European Economic and Social Committee and the Committee of the Regions: Better regulation for better results – An EU agenda* COM [2015] 215 final.

[90] European Commission, *Commission Staff Working Document: Better Regulation Guidelines* SWD [2017] 350.

[91] Impact assessments and public consultations are two major components of the Better Regulation Guidelines; however, they are not the only ones. Parts of the Guidelines concern monitoring and transposition.

[92] Impact assessments are reviewed by the Regulatory Scrutiny Board, on the basis of which it also provides recommendations and opinions.

[93] See, for example, the public consultation concerning the SPC system 12 October 2017 to 4 January 2018.

Union or the Guide de Légistique de France.[94] These initiatives have the objective of providing standardised practices concerning structure, use of language, accessibility and cross-referencing. Obviously, these legislative tools are in some cases too broad to be of any tangible assistance, while in others they are too limited and too specific to be applied in all legislative areas. Such legislative drafting toolkit guidelines are ambitious projects, but they very rarely cover all the needs of legislative drafting and also run the risk of quickly becoming outdated.

Taking into consideration how intensive legislative drafting has become in the past few decades, drafters are faced with considerable challenges and very little hands-on guidance, apart from the framework provided by the national constitution or, in some cases, parliamentary regulations. The OECD has been one of the first international actors to work with issues of legislative drafting and legislative quality. As early as 1995, it introduced guidelines and recommendations referring to principles that were to be considered when introducing new legislation, such as the principles of efficiency, clarity, effectiveness, simplicity, precision, consistency, etc.[95] The OECD has developed hands-on tools to assist drafters in their practical work, such as the OECD checklist with 10 questions that provide guidance in the legislative process. The questions concern important aspects of the choices the drafter or legislator has to make related to appropriateness, the relation between cost and benefit, accessibility, comprehensibility, etc.

4.1. The Impact Assessment

The impact assessment is an interesting legislative drafting tool that seems to be in line with the spirit of the effectiveness test.[96] Taking into consideration the fact that the legislative acts here constitute EU legislation and that the impact assessment is granted a particular status in the EU, it is important to reflect on its application and how this relates to the effectiveness test used in this book.[97]

Among the strengths of the impact assessment are the clarity of its structure and content. At the EU level, the impact assessment is codified by means of seven questions:[98]

- What is the problem and why is it a problem (to legislate for)?
- Why should the EU act?

[94] European Commission, *Joint practical guide of the European Parliament, the Council and the Commission for persons involved in the drafting of European Union legislation* (EU publication, Luxembourg: Publications Office of the European Union 2015); *Guide de Légistique de France* (3rd edn, La Documentation Française, Paris 2017).
[95] These recommendations were updated in 2005 and 2012.
[96] For a thorough review of the role of impact assessments in the EU legislation, see Anne C M Meuwese, *Impact Assessment in EU Lawmaking* (Wolters Kluwer 2008).
[97] Impact assessments are publicly available in the homepage of the Commission, see https://ec.europa.eu/transparency/regdoc/?fuseaction=ia [Accessed on 11 June 2020].
[98] Similar questions have been developed in national jurisdictions for the purposes of impact assessment.

- What should be achieved?
- What are the various options to achieve the objectives?
- What are their economic, social and environmental impacts and who will be affected?
- How do the different options compare (effectiveness, efficiency and coherence)?
- How will monitoring and subsequent retrospective evaluation be organised?

At the EU level, the impact assessment has been used as a toolkit to justify (or not) the necessity of regulation of the issue at hand. Usually, the discussion remains at a rather superficial level, simply providing a chosen policy option, but very rarely (if ever) analyzing any further considerations. Mousmouti offers examples of such considerations, illustrating that the results of the impact assessment in fact constitute the policy basis upon which law-making is supposed to be performed. This means that a number of crucial decisions will be made by the legislator to choose a concrete direction, structure and content for the regulation. Another critique of how the impact assessment is used in practice is that its central focus is very often cost versus benefit and how these may be quantified under the framework of the regulation at hand. The often rather exaggerated attempt to quantify incentives and effects of a regulation may constitute an internal weakness, since important aspects like moral values and other forms of policy interests that are not quantifiable are thus not included in the evaluation process.

That being said, impact assessments have been revised to also include objectives other than purely economic ones, such as concerns related to fundamental rights and gender issues. It remains to be seen how these principles will influence the process of the impact assessment and the final policy decisions reached. This is particularly so as it is unclear where these principles are placed in the hierarchy of objectives. For instance, what would be the final choice in cases where the most cost-effective decision is the one that most endangers the environment? Which principle would prevail? An overview of EU impact assessments does not provide a clear answer to this question.[99] Although they are suboptimal, impact assessments contribute considerably to the law-making process since they bring into the discussion important perspectives and data, for instance regarding the need to legislate and the identification of legislative provisions that do not work in practice. Furthermore, they highlight considerations related to compliance and implementation at an early stage. Mousmouti claims that impact assessments are not law-making tools – they are policy tools that inform the lawmaker about the general directions that the legislation needs to take, but never go so far as to provide practical guidance, and thus remain of limited use to legislative drafters.[100]

---

[99] As has been stated previously, impact assessments have in fact been used in different ways and thus it is difficult to proceed to an absolute generalisation. However, it can be stated that the majority of impact assessments function in this way.
[100] Mousmouti (n 85), 116.

In this book, impact assessments have provided an important insight to the background and objectives of the regulations and revealed frictions and challenges in both their introduction and their application. Considering the very limited preliminary works of EU legislative acts, these impact assessments constitute a unique source of information on the legislative history and political (and other) expectations in relation to the legislative acts. They constitute important sources that may be used in the application of the effectiveness test, providing information on the objectives, contents, and context of the regulations, and in some cases also on their effects. Equally important is what they choose to omit. Although impact assessments play an important role as a source, they do not replace the importance or role of the effectiveness test.

4.2. The Public Consultation

The public consultation has been broadly employed during the past decade as a tool for openness, transparency and participation of citizens in governance and regulation. It provides a flexible tool for testing how legislation has been communicated to the public, how it works in practice, and what the stakeholders on a specific market (as well as citizens) perceive as the strengths and weakness of its provisions.[101] What the consultation can contribute with depends on the questions that are posed and how open these questions are. Guidelines related to consultations very often concern technical issues, such as when the consultation should be published, how long it should be open, and how to proceed in order to succeed in reaching the target group. A general critique has been that consultations are rather static and that they only prioritise making the process more participatory by engaging stakeholders, rather than truly being interested in posing the right questions and receiving useful reactions and content to the answers given.[102]

Both impact assessments and public consultations could become important and valuable law-making tools, but their roles currently seem limited to being policy tools with rather restricted functions. While policy needs support and guidance at a broader level, law-making needs a much more hands-on approach, where a specific piece of legislation is to create specific measures serving a specific objective that could directly or indirectly, separately or in combination with other legislative acts, contribute to achieving a certain policy goal.[103]

---

[101] Public consultations are grouped based on the nature of the consultation: if it concerns new legislation, initial ideas, or simplification of existing legislation. The different categories are available on the Commission webpage, where all public consultations are also published: https://ec.europa.eu/info/law/better-regulation/have-your-say [Accessed 11 June 2020].

[102] See also Erik Lundberg and Erik Hysing, 'The Value of Participation: Exploring the Role of Public Consultations from the Vantage Point of Interest Groups' [2015] 39 *Scandinavian Political Studies*, 1, 1–21.

[103] See OECD, 'Improving Policy Instruments through Impact Assessment' [2001] SIGMA Papers, No 31, OECD Publishing, Paris.

Both impact assessments and public consultations are based on a set of different objectives such as efficacy, efficiency, rationality, legitimacy and transparency. However, these objectives are not in any way prioritised or placed in an internal structure. Furthermore, the longer the list of objectives to be taken into consideration, the more difficult it becomes to provide valuable feedback without also having access to a transparent internal hierarchy. Thus, applying the effectiveness test to both the design and the evaluation of EU legislation is not redundant. There are considerable differences in the approach between the effectiveness test and the Better Regulation or public consultation measures already applied by the Commission.[104]

One of the most important aspects that has led to the choice of this methodological perspective is the fact that it is not a mere theoretical model: its value lies in its application to specific pieces of legislation bringing long-awaited clarity to the different perspectives of legislation and how these work in practice. Although the effectiveness test may be used proactively, as guidance during the law-making process, its role in this book will be that of an evaluation toolkit. Furthermore, the effectiveness test leads the reader to concrete explanations as to potential legislative failures and may provide a reliable diagnosis for proceeding with future amendments and adjustments that could remedy the pathologies of the past.[105]

The advantage of the effectiveness tool is the fact that it is focused on the legislation's internal objectives and does not orient it towards a specific political perspective or goal. While it does not guarantee perfection in legislative drafting, it provides the legislator with a full picture, which is necessary in order to make choices based on reality, as opposed to intuition.[106]

4.3. Regulatory Rights and why the Effectiveness Test is Not Straightforward

While achieving effectiveness when introducing a legal rule is a central objective, measuring this effectiveness is not a frictionless enterprise. When looking at the field of regulatory rights, it becomes obvious that applying the test requires

---

[104] These are, in fact, two different philosophies or two different systems. The effectiveness test adopts a much more holistic view, where all different aspects of the Regulation are considered from an objective and regulation-internal point of view. On the other hand, a public consultation documents the reactions of stakeholders and other interested parties.
[105] See also Helen Xanthaki, 'An enlightened Approach to Legislative Scrutiny: Focusing on Effectiveness' [2019] 9 *European Journal of Risk Regulation*, 3, 431–44.
[106] Maria Mousmouti, 'Making Legislative Effectiveness an Operational Concept: Unfolding the Effectiveness Test as a Conceptual Tool for Lawmaking' [2018] 9 *European Journal of Risk Regulation*, 3, 445–64.

a number of adjustments.[107] The concept of 'compliance'[108] may not be central in the specific regulations that are analysed in this book; it has a clearer role in cases where the legislation is directed at individuals. However, cognitive rules also influence the way companies behave on the market and which strategic choices they make.[109] It is obvious in the case of the regulations analysed in this book that there is a basic assumption that exclusive rights and thus market monopolies serve societal needs, leading to more research and broader (and better) accessibility to medicinal products. In the case of regulatory rights, it is almost impossible to simplify the discussion on effectiveness. All these regulations create incentives for research and commercialisation; thus, compliance and enforcement are not central elements to consider. Still, proceeding to a numerical calculation of effectiveness by counting SPCs, orphan drug designations, or ATMP products on the market would be a direct, but overly simplistic way of measuring effectiveness.

Another source of complication is the fact that the legislative acts (the regulations in focus in this book) cannot be seen as isolated pieces of legislation. They interact directly and indirectly, they include cross-references to each other's provisions and they operate on the same market. This also means that the effectiveness (or ineffectiveness) of one has a direct impact on the effectiveness of the others. The fact that they work in a synergetic way means that the effectiveness must be tested not only regulation by regulation, but also of the regulations as a group, with particular focus on their interactions with one another and their interaction with the traditional intellectual property rights (IPR) system.

The special character of the specific market is also of relevance. It is characterised by considerable investment requirements and long research and development cycles, creating market entry thresholds. It is also a market with very few actors, divided into two major categories: the innovators (pharmaceutical companies that work with research and development in new fields of diseases or new substances) and the generics (companies that have as their business model to produce and sell pharmaceuticals that were originally developed by the innovators and which were previously protected by some form of exclusive right that has now expired). As has been previously mentioned, the line between these two categories is increasingly blurred, bringing some uncertainty to the basic assumptions of the system.

---

[107] See, for instance, Florentin Blanc, F, 'Tools for Effective Regulation: Is "More" Always "Better"?' [2018] 9 *European Journal of Risk Regulation*, 3, 455–82, describing that it is not only the regulation itself that is decisive for the effectiveness of the legal rules it introduces. Other important parameters need to be considered as well, such as the behavioural perspectives, ie, how the target group of the regulation perceives and accepts the legal rule and what forms of control are necessary in order to guarantee compliance. Thus, considering the effectiveness of a legal rule only on the basis of the legal rule as such gives a limited perspective. Concerning the behavioural impact on the effectiveness of rules, see Nicoletta Rangone, 'Making Law Effective: Behavioral Insights into Compliance' [2018] 9 *European Journal of Risk Regulation*, 3, 483–501. One of the interesting points made in Rangone's article is that compliance increases when giving a legal rule a fairness perspective.

[108] Ibid.

[109] Consider, for instance, the practice of shaming lists and the impact this has on shaping the behaviour of companies.

Another perspective of relevance when analyzing the effectiveness of regulatory rights is their legislative character. EU legislation in the field of regulatory rights has been fragmented, being found in several EU regulations.[110] At the same time, these regulations interact and to a certain extent depend on the provisions of a Directive (the Marketing Authorisation Directive),[111] which means that part of the system is dependent on national implementation. To make matters even more complicated, these regulations interact with the patent system and their application may be combined therewith (at least for reasons of business strategy). Patent law is extremely important on the pharmaceutical market, but is not harmonised at the EU level.[112] The context in which regulatory rights are to operate thus becomes of decisive importance. The fact that these different pieces of legislation interact in this direct way poses a challenge for legislative architecture. One needs to ensure that the objectives of these regulations are mutually supportive and that the effects of one are not to the detriment of the others. Naturally, this perspective and inherent interaction is an important aspect to be taken into consideration when reviewing the objectives, content and results of the respective legislative acts. If one does not take this intrinsic interrelation into consideration, testing of effectiveness will be piecemeal and incorrect.

Another issue that complicates matters when it comes to the application of the effectiveness test, and at the same time provides possibilities to further develop this evaluation model, is the fact that all regulations analysed and discussed in this book are the result of legal transplantation.[113] EU legislators have had as their inspiration, if not their model, previous similar legislation in the United States. This brings yet another perspective into the fine-tuning of the effectiveness test. The process of law making, when this is the result of legal transplantation, is not as transparent, since it becomes the result of transferring legislation from one jurisdiction to the other, making objectives and content more difficult to document, assess and evaluate.

---

[110] The regulations analysed in this book are merely one part of the regulations of relevance in the field of regulatory rights. As has been stated previously, one also needs to consider Directives in order to get a complete overview. The fact that regulatory rights are fragmented at different levels of EU legislation also makes national legislation very important, and thus the evaluation of any single piece of legislation becomes complicated.

[111] Directive 2001/83/EC of the European Parliament and of the Council of 6 November 2001 on the Community code relating to medicinal products for human use [2001] OJ L 311/67; Directive 2004/27/EC of the European Parliament and of the Council of 31 March 2004 amending Directive 2001/83/EC on the Community code relating to medicinal products for human use (Text with EEA relevance) [2004] OJ L 136/34.

[112] Directive 98/44/EC of the European Parliament and of the Council of 6 July 1998 on the legal protection of biotechnological inventions [1998] OJ L 213/13.

[113] On legal transplants, see Alan Watson, 'Legal Transplants and European Private Law' [2000] Electronic Journal of Comparative Law, Vol 4.4; Jonathan Miller, 'A Typology of Legal Transplants: Using Sociology, Legal History and Argentine Examples to Explain the Transplant Process' [2013] 51 The American Journal of Comparative Law 4, 839–85; Another interesting article concerning legal transplants in corporate law, is Holger Spamann, 'Contemporary Legal Transplants: Legal Families and the Diffusion of (Corporate) Law' [2009] Harvard Law School, Discussion Paper No 28.

Putting regulatory rights (ie legal transplants) under the effectiveness lens creates a challenge in connecting the original expectations on the legislation, the needs and objectives the first legislative act was introduced to fulfil, etc. In fact, in order to obtain a clear picture of the objectives, one would likely need to go back to the objectives of the original legislation (in the jurisdiction in which the legislation originated), with all the difficulties this entails in terms of both accessibility and understanding. Such a process would presuppose an insight into both the legal framework and societal, economic and other market needs that dictated the introduction of that specific legislation in the country of origin at the specific point in time of its introduction. The difficulties of tracing the objectives of the legal transplant is a demanding task, since the black letter objectives are not always identical to the real ones. For a legislator, deciding to transfer legislation from another jurisdiction has the benefit of previous experience regarding how the legislation works in practice and how effective it is in achieving its objectives. Very little is written concerning the effectiveness of transplanted legislation and most of the contributions focus on the borrowing of legal definitions from other jurisdictions or implementing international standards into national legislation.[114]

According to Xanthaki, in current legislative practice when legislators are faced with the challenge of drafting new legislation, they tend to turn to countries whose legal system, language and legal tradition are similar to their own.[115] The EU turning to the United States cannot be explained by a similarity of legal tradition and legal system. However, there are a number of common denominators in the political structure of the United States and the EU (federal states and Member States), the challenge of shared competences (federal vs. state), and, above all, the importance of two major objectives: boosting the pharmaceutical industry and safeguarding patient safety. The United States was first in dealing with the specific issues in terms of market failures and identified public health needs that also constitute the objectives of the regulations on which this book focuses. The structure and needs of the pharmaceutical industry in the United States and the EU are comparable, and the objectives of patient security and patient safety are identical. Several years of experience in applying and interpreting this legislation in the United States provide an invaluable insight into how these regulations could function in practice and how they interact with the legal system as such and with other pharmaceutical regulations. Furthermore, the adoption of the regulations in focus in this book are to a certain extent the result of lobbying by European companies and patient organisations to introduce in the EU systems comparable to those of the United States. It was thus only natural that the EU legislator looked to the US paradigm when drafting its legislative acts. The question is, of course, whether that was an appropriate move and whether transplanting a system from

---

[114] See Coen J P Van Lawer and Helen Xanthaki, 'Legal Transplants and Comparative Concepts: Eclecticism Defeated?' [2013] 34 *Statute Law Review*, 2, 128–37.

[115] Helen Xanthaki, 'Legal Transplants in Legislation: Defusing the Trap' [2008] 57 *The International and Comparative Law Quarterly*, 3, 659–73.

the United States to the EU in the specific case would be successful. According to Xanthaki, what is important when selecting a system for comparative examination is not necessarily the similarity of the two systems, but rather the functionality. In other words, the question the legislator should pose is 'What is the social need that the draft law addresses?' Naturally, the social need is not always straightforward, nor is it always disclosed in the legislative act itself. Preparatory works are often very laconic and when the social need is expressed, one needs to review that this is in conformity with the rest of the provisions of the legislative act (consider the case where one social need is identified in the text, while in fact another more important need exists in the background and is expressed in the provisions of the legislative act).[116]

One of the challenges of legislative drafting that needs to be taken into consideration when exploring the effectiveness of the system as a whole is the way it interacts with traditional intellectual property rights, and in particular patent law. In this respect, it is also worth considering the fact that although regulatory rights are not expressly intellectual property rights, they either build upon a *sui generis* exclusive right, like in the case of orphan drugs, or directly interact and very often also extend the exclusive rights granted by means of patent law, such as the Supplementary Protection Certificates or the Paediatric extension.

Legislative drafters have developed skills in drafting new legislative provisions, but often lack the skills and knowledge necessary to evaluate the effects that legislation has in terms of economic impact, societal changes, etc. This would not be a problem if their drafting of legal rules was scrutinised and reviewed in terms of effectiveness by a third party. Unfortunately, they seem to hold a rather monopolistic position in conducting the evaluation of legislation and reviewing the legislation's effectiveness. If you lack knowledge of the legal system as a whole, as well as the market, technical and societal conditions under which the legislation is to operate, it is very difficult, if not impossible, to proceed to an effectiveness review.[117] According to Zamboni, in order to create a certain outcome (ie an effect on society), legislation must first produce an output (ie an effect on the law). Non-legal experts, when drafting legislation, very often lack the skills and the legal experience to see a specific provision as part of a broader legal system, a piece in a bigger puzzle of legal provisions and regulations. Such experts also have to overcome the difficulty of not being aware of how the drafted provisions will be interpreted and applied by courts and administrative authorities. The way that the legal rule will actually work in practice (the output) is less foreseeable. Zamboni recommends that politicians be more involved in the process of legislative drafting and in the process of evaluation of effectiveness. The question is, of course, if this is possible in case of legislation like that considered in this book, requiring a very

---

[116] See also Geoffrey Bowmann, 'Legislation and Explanation' [2000] Loophole, available at www.calc.ngo/sites/default/files/loophole/jun-2000.pdf [Accessed on 11 June 2020].
[117] See Zamboni (n 83) for an elaborate analysis of the problematic aspects of legislative drafting when performed by non-legal experts.

specialised knowledge of the IP system, the pharmaceutical market and the technology underlying the products and services. Furthermore, it presupposes that the legislator adopts a holistic perspective, where one legislative act is drafted with the objectives, content and context of the other regulations kept in mind.[118]

5. The Structure of the Book

This book is structured into eight chapters. Chapter one introduces the subject and provides a factual and a methodological introduction. Chapters two and three concern central factors of the pharmaceutical market that influence the existence, application, and interpretation of regulatory rights, namely the EMA, committees, the MA procedure and the data exclusivity. Chapters four to seven discuss and analyse the contents of the regulations in focus in the book, while chapter eight provides an overall evaluation of these regulations and the system they belong to as a whole through the lens of the effectiveness test.

Chapter one of the book presents the pharmaceutical market, its special characteristics and the historical background to the modern regulatory rights system. It discusses issues that have come to influence the evolution of EU legislation in the field, with special focus on the limited EU competence in the field of public health. Finally, this chapter presents the methodological framework of the book, namely the effectiveness test, both as previously elaborated and with the fine-tuning necessary for its application in this specific case.

In **chapter two**, the EMA, its background, status, role and committees are presented and critically discussed. The same chapter includes a review of the marketing authorisation procedure, its different application routes, and the practicalities that influence the system as a whole.

Chapter three focuses on data protection, discussing the system as a whole, its different parameters, and the difficulties in application and interpretation. The role of chapters two and three is to provide the reader with a background and overall framework to increase clarity concerning the environment in which regulatory rights are expected to operate and which constitute necessary justifications for the evolution of the system as such. Chapters two and three describe the platforms upon which SPCs, orphan drugs, paediatric medicine and ATMPs are expected to 'meet' and interact.

In **chapter four**, the Supplementary Protection Regulation is discussed and analysed, looking into its background, but focusing mainly on its major provisions and how these have been interpreted in EU and national case law. It provides a detailed analysis of case law from the CJEU and a reflection as to how these cases influence the SPC system as such and other regulatory rights.

---

[118] Ibid.

The Structure of the Book

Chapter five concerns the Paediatric Regulation. Through analysis and interpretation of its core provisions and how these interact with other regulatory rights, this chapter provides valuable insight into the role of this Regulation and the ways it interacts with other regulations.

Chapter six focuses on the Orphan Drugs Regulation and claims that it actually introduces a new *sui generis* IP right. After discussing the major provisions of the regulation and how these have been interpreted by the EU and national case law, this chapter moves on to an analysis of the interrelation between orphan drugs and the Paediatric Regulation and the patent system, and considers the problem areas of these interfaces, some of which have been overlooked by the legislator.

With **Chapter seven**, this book looks into yet another regulatory right, namely that of ATMPs. Although ATMPs seem to be the outsiders of the system, where the points of interaction with the other regulations remain limited, they are interesting for several reasons. ATMPs represent a field of pharmaceutical research that is considered to be the future, namely that of personalised medicine. Furthermore, the special nature of these pharmaceutical products tests the applicability of other regulatory rights such as the Orphan Drugs Regulation, as well as creating frictions in for instance how the SPC system is to be applied and how MA procedures will be followed.

Lastly, **Chapter eight** is where chapters one to seven come together to be analysed under the lens of the effectiveness test. The SPCs, orphan drugs, paediatric medicine and ATMPs are critically discussed from an effectiveness perspective. This chapter gives an analysis of each regulation with regard to its objectives, content, context and results. In this chapter, an overall evaluation of the system in which these different regulations operate is presented.

2

Setting the Stage for Regulatory Rights

The Regulatory Agencies and the Marketing Authorisation Procedure

The European pharmaceutical regulatory rights landscape undoubtedly creates a multilayered challenge. Key factors in the system as a whole are the authorities that implement and apply the regulatory rights system. It is difficult – if not impossible – to discuss European regulatory rights and analyse their effectiveness without discussing the role of regulatory agencies vested with the tasks of implementing and interpreting the legal framework and making binding decisions related thereto. Furthermore, the MA procedure is a real *sine qua non* in the discussion on regulatory rights and a necessary ingredient. It is both a justification of why regulatory rights are structured in the way they are and one of the major reasons for their existence.[1]

The roles of the agencies and committees in the system are of central importance. In particular, the role and mandate of the EMA has been and is crucial, both because it is the EU agency with the primary responsibility for the European regulatory system and because it is an agency that has often been scrutinised, due to its special character and frequently contested mandate.[2]

---

[1] Thomas Christiansen, 'Reconstructing European Space: From Territorial Politics to Multilevel Governance', in Knud Erik Jørgensen (ed), *Reflective Approaches to European Governance* (Palgrave Macmillan 1997); Rita Banzi, Vittorio Bertele, Jacques Demotes-Mainard et al, 'Fostering EMA's transparency policy' [2014] 25 *European Journal of Internal Medicine*, 8, 681–84; see also Richard F Kingham, Peter W L Bogaert, Pamela S Eddy, 'The New European Medicines Agency' [1994] 49 *Food and Drug Law Journal*, 2, 301–22.

[2] Kıvanç Yüksel and Işık Tuğlular, 'Critical Review of European Medicines Agency (EMA) Assessment Report and Related Literature on Domperidone' [2019] 41 *International Journal of Clinical Pharmacy* 387–90.

1. Regulatory Authorities

1.1. The European Medicines Agency

1.1.1. Background

The EMA was established in 1995 under the name 'the European Agency for the Evaluation of Medicinal Products'.[3] Considering the headlines it made when introduced, such as 'A Drug Tsar is Born'[4] and 'A Real European Milestone',[5] the expectations regarding both the role and the impact of the agency on the European pharmaceutical industry were very high.[6] In 2005, the agency was re-introduced under a new name, that of 'the European Medicines Agency', while keeping the same acronym. Its status is a special one, when compared with other EU agencies: limited to providing recommendations and guidelines, since the specialised opinions of the EMA constitute the basis for the binding decisions of the Commission. This gives the EMA a quasi-regulatory role. What makes this extended mandate even more interesting is the fact that it operates in the pharmaceutical industry, where the EU competence is limited and often questioned.

The need to introduce an agency with this important mandate became urgent during the 1980s, when considerable concern was expressed regarding the way in which Community pharmaceutical authorisation regime functioned. At the time, it was uncontested that in order for the European pharmaceutical industry to be facilitated, a more efficient and reliable system was required. It is interesting that the official justification of the Commission for the introduction of the new agency was not based on internal market concerns, but rather on public health protection considerations. In fact, this is the predominant content in the press release at the inauguration of the agency, providing that 'the creation of the European Medicines Evaluation Agency is firstly a benefit for the European patient'.[7]

EMA, just as any other EU agency, operates under what could be considered a certain paradox, namely the fact that while uniformity in the politics and operation

---

[3] The EMA was established by means of Council Regulation 2309/93/EEC of 22 July 1993 laying down Community procedures for the authorisation and supervision of medicinal products for human and veterinary use and establishing a European Agency for the Evaluation of Medicinal Products [1993] OJ L 214/1.

[4] A Annon, 'A Drug Tsar is Born', *The Economist*, May 7, 1994, 74.

[5] Albedo, 'At Last, A Real European Milestone' [1995] *Pharmaceutical Technology Europe* 8–11.

[6] See also, P Etienne Barral, *Ten Years of Results in Pharmaceutical Research Throughout the World (1975–1984)* (Prospective et Sante Publique 1985); Hans Berlin and Bengt Jönsson, 'International Dissemination of New Drugs: A Comparative Study of Six Countries' [1986] 7 *Managerial and Decision Economics*, 4, 235–42.

[7] European Commission, *Inauguration of the European Agency for the Evaluation of Medicinal Products* (Press Release) 26 January 1995 https://ec.europa.eu/commission/presscorner/detail/en/IP_95_64 [Accessed on 12 June 2020].

of the agency is needed, centralisation of powers and politics is not a preferred steering model.[8] EU agencies have been given the flexibility to use different structures, financing sources and staff. While all other EU agencies are expected to regulate by independently gathering and sharing information, the EMA bases its decisions and opinions for the authorisation of pharmaceutical products on information it receives from pharmaceutical companies.

The fact that a single – effective and speedy – process would replace national marketing authorisation procedures was welcomed by the industry. The industry was growing in size and marketing authorisation applications were piling up, creating considerable delays in the process of putting products on the market. The technology behind pharmaceutical products had become increasingly complicated. This meant that the national authorisation agencies faced challenges in dealing with their workload, keeping up with technological developments, and finding the internal competence to handle high-tech applications. Furthermore, the mutual recognition procedure was deemed to be too slow and inefficient.

A report from 1988 on the work of the CPMP speeded up negotiations for the establishment of the EMA. This report was the result of a consultation with 'interested parties', which were asked what the optimal form for a system for the free movement of medicines would be. The 'interested parties' included both the industry and consumer organisations. However, taking into consideration the fact that the report was issued by the DG Industrial Affairs, without prior consultation with the DG Social Affairs, it is obvious that the central role of the agency is related to enhancement of the industry rather than the rights of patients or public health concerns.[9]

The report also reveals the Commission's objectives, stating that the number of applications in the multi-state route was too low compared with the hundreds of applications submitted at a national level each year. Furthermore, every pharmaceutical product that was to be put through the mutual recognition procedure had been the subject of reasoned objections and thus referred back to the CPMP, in spite of the fact that Member States were expected to take into serious consideration previous authorisations granted by other Member States.[10] According to the same report, this fragmented approach towards marketing authorisations for pharmaceuticals led to national barriers and thus a malfunctioning of the internal market in the pharmaceuticals industry. The Commission thus considered a unified system as an important ingredient for the promotion of a single market. In fact, one of the major conclusions of the Commission was that many national

---

[8] Renaud Dehousse, 'Regulation by Networks in the European Community: The Role of European Agencies' [1997] 4 *Journal of European Public Policy*, 2, 246–61.
[9] Ibid.
[10] European Commission, 'Report from the Commission to the Council on the Activities of the Committee for Proprietary Medicinal Products' COM [88] 143 final, Brussels, 22 March 1988.

regulatory standards were barriers to trade in disguise and that their primary purpose was to protect domestic procedures from international competition.[11]

Reading the 1996 compilation document of the Commission, it is clear that the establishment of the agency and the expectations upon it were not in any way the result of consensus. Even the industry representative, EFPIA, was against a 'fully centralized system with decisions being made by a European body' and suggested that not only would the workload of such an agency be too heavy, but also that the agency would be a political construct of a type that would be easy to influence.[12] Establishing a European FDA was not an attractive option, as this was considered to be an agency that operated under strong political control. Because of all these serious concerns, the EFPIA suggested that the industry be consulted and engaged in the drafting procedure. In order to safeguard the interests of the industry, the EFPIA asserted that pharmaceutical companies should be given the possibility to choose between mutual recognition and the centralised procedure, where the former would continue to constitute the central route in the system. At the same time, Member States would be under the obligation to recognise each other's marketing authorisation decisions, and the role of the CPMP would be reinforced, so that under the new system it would be able to make binding decisions in matters such as appeals. The EFPIA also proposed that the applicant (the pharmaceutical company) would be able to choose the rapporteur in the applications.[13] The chairperson of the CPMP at the time was of the opinion that the improvement of the mutual recognition system presupposed a reinforced legal position of the CPMP, which would only be possible when the Council of Ministers decided to grant it the mandate to produce operational and mandatory opinions.[14]

John Griffith, who was the director of the Association of British Pharmaceutical Industry at the time, claimed that the Commission's early vision of the agency was a 'recipe for disaster'.[15] Griffin's expression of concerns regarding the new system did not stop there. In a public letter to the *British Medical Journal* he posed the question 'Is patient safety being put at risk in the decision making process offered by the Commission?'[16] In the same letter, he expressed concerns regarding the system's credibility, since the experts in the CPMP were not always medically or scientifically trained. He also stated that the Committee should be composed of specialists in order for the decisions to be legitimate and correct.

---

[11] Ibid. See also David Vogel, 'The Globalization of Pharmaceutical Regulation' [1998] 11 *Governance: An International Journal of Policy and Administration*, 1, 1–22, 16.
[12] EFPIA was very active in the negotiations preceding the establishment of the EMA. See EFPIA, *Completing the Internal Market for Pharmaceuticals* (Brussels 1998); EFPIA, *EFPIA Comments on the New Proposals Contained in Preliminary Draft Rev. 5* [1992a]; EFPIA, *Memorandum on an Industrial Policy for the European Pharmaceutical Industry* (EFPIA III3485/92) [1992b].
[13] EFPIA, *Delivering High Quality Health Care in the European Union – Policy Concerns for the Pharmaceuticals Industry* (Brussels 1996).
[14] Duilio Poggiolini, chairperson of the CPMP.
[15] Marketletter, 'EC Drugs Move: Recipe for Disaster' [1989] 2 July 6.
[16] T D Griffin, 'Policies on Drugs in the New Europe' [1990] *British Medical Journal* 1536.

Concerning the positions of the Member States on the composition and mandate of EMA, these have been far from uniform. Although Member States highlighted the common interest in preserving national sovereignty and the status of the national marketing authorisation agencies, they expressed differing views as to the necessity and role of a centralised agency and a centralised procedure. Some countries, including Luxembourg and Ireland, presented the merits of such a procedure, while France preferred a reinforced mutual recognition procedure with a binding character. This is an interesting position, since a reinforced mutual recognition procedure presupposes a weakened national sovereignty, as marketing authorisation of expensive pharmaceuticals would have an impact on public health national budgets.[17]

Consumer organisations did not provide an equally coordinated view. The European Consumers Organisation (BEUC) reflected on the example of Halcion (a drug for sleeping disorders), which was withdrawn in the United Kingdom in 1993 for safety concerns, but continued to be marketed in other Member States.[18] The hope of the consumer organisations was that a centralised procedure would mean that safety and quality standards would be harmonised upwards. The BEUC was not favourably disposed to the industry enjoying too much flexibility in the system, or the right to choose between different systems and different MA routes. It expressed the view that the contrast of a centralised, highly scientific (and thus also more rigid) procedure and the procedure of a less experienced and less technical national agency – combined with the possibility for applicants to choose between the two – could result in a less safe and less efficient system.

At the same time, the Consumer's Consultative Committee (CCC) provided that it is important to give the marketing authorisation system the possibility to review the efficacy of new pharmaceuticals as compared with those already on the market, taking into consideration 'specific therapeutic advantages'.[19] This was in line with the EU Parliament, which promoted the view that the 'particular social significance' of certain pharmaceuticals should be used as a criterion in the marketing authorisation procedure.[20]

The Commission concluded in its preparatory works that a major transfer of executive competence was necessary in order to complete the objective of a truly single market. The 'Proposal for a Regulation laying down Community Procedures for the Authorization and Supervision of Medicinal Products for Human and Veterinary Use and Establishing a European Agency for the Evaluation

---

[17] See also Patricia M Danzon, Y Richard Wang, and Liang Wang, 'The Impact of Price Regulation on the Launch Delay of New Drugs – Evidence from Twenty-Five Major Markets in the 1990s' [2005] 14 *Health Economics*, 269–92.

[18] Consumer's Consultative Commission, 'Resolution of the Consumers' Consultative Commission Concerning the European Agency for the Evaluation of Medicinal Products', Brussels, 12 November 1991.

[19] Ibid.

[20] William Currie, 'European Registration: Today, Tomorrow, and Beyond' [1990] 30 *Journal of Clinical Pharmacology*, 5, 366–89.

of Medicinal Products' was submitted in November 1990.[21] The proposal was presented to the Council as part of a package of four future system instruments concerning a broader framework for the movement of medicines in the internal market.[22] Given the divergences between stakeholders, it was no surprise that the final agreement on a text did not come until July 1993 and only after several adjustments and amendments were made. The EMA was not in operation until two years later.

1.1.2. The Legal Basis for the Establishment of the EMA

The aim of the establishment of the EMA was, among other things, to introduce and impose an MA timeline of a maximum of 300 days from application to authorisation.[23] Two alternative marketing authorisation procedures would be available, while national authorities' objections to marketing authorisations granted under the decentralised procedure would only be possible under the precondition that they concerned 'objectively defined reasons of public order or public policy'. The CPMP would arbitrate in cases where a bilateral agreement was not possible.[24]

However, given the lack of clarity when it comes to EU competence in public health issues, one of the major concerns was what would be the legal basis of the regulatory framework of the new agency. According to the Commission, the legal basis for the establishment of the EMA was to be found in Article 100(a) EC. The German government rejected this approach, claiming that the subsidiarity principle precluded the EU from making decisions in public health matters; the only thing the German government would support was a limited (in status, resources and mandate) secretariat.[25] The approach of other governments was much less complicated; Ireland and Luxembourg accepted the proposal as it was presented, as well as its proposed legal basis. Denmark, Italy, Spain and the Netherlands were in favour of an administrative agency, while they expressed the view that the new system must guarantee that the technical competence of the national agencies was preserved. France, on the other hand, had a clear preference for the system as it

---

[21] Commission of the European Communities, *Proposal for a Regulation of the European Parliament and of the Council Laying Down Community Procedures for the Authorisation and Supervision of Medicinal Products for Human and Veterinary Use and Establishing a European Agency for the Evaluation of Medicinal Products* COM [2001] 404 final.

[22] Commission of the European Communities, *Future System for the Free Movement of Medicinal Products in the European Community* COM [90] 283 final http://aei.pitt.edu/10894/1/10894.pdf [Accessed on 12 June 2020].

[23] See, in this respect, Frederick M Abbott and Graham Dukes, *Global Pharmaceutical Policy* (Edward Elgar 2009).

[24] Govin Permanand, *EU Pharmaceutical Regulation: The Politics of Policy-Making* (European Policy Research Unit Series, Manchester University Press 2006) 47–69.

[25] According to DGIII, Robert Hankin, this was because of the federalist view of the German government which also meant that it was permitted for the EU to make decisions at the level of principles, but not concerning specific individual pharmaceutical products.

42 *Setting the Stage for Regulatory Rights*

was at the time, proposing only small adaptations to the way the mutual recognition procedure worked in practice.[26]

The UK government was positive, in principle, but rejected Article 100(a) EC as an appropriate legal basis, and instead promoted Article 235 EC. At the same time, the UK expressed the view that further consultation was necessary in order to ensure that the new system, whichever it would be, would satisfy the strict objectives of safety and quality of medicinal products. Article 235 EC was considered to constitute a much more appropriate alternative by the Belgian, Italian and Spanish governments as well, and even the German government gradually conceded. The French approach encompassed a combination of both: Article 100(a) EC, for the establishment of the agency, and Article 235 EC, for the establishment of the centralised procedure. Thus, although both the Parliament and the Economic and Social Committee had previously accepted the use of Article 100(a), a change of legal basis was decided during the Internal Market Council meeting. Proceeding with such an alternative legal basis seemed a rather risky project, as this required a consultation procedure in the Parliament as well as the unanimity of the Council. On the other hand, the Parliament would, under Article 235, be granted a single reading. Since it had already sent a number of proposed amendments to the Commission that the Commission had not seemed satisfied with, this seemed a rather attractive option.[27] In the discussions of the Parliament, particular critique was directed at the fact that the proposal seemed to pay limited attention to public health objectives. The Parliament suggested, for instance, that specific medicinal product categories (such as biotechnological products) should be added to the list of products that would fall under the sole competence of the EMA. This would also ensure that pharmaceutical products that had to reach the market quickly, for public health reasons, would be provided with alternative market authorisation routes.

A few weeks after the publication of the 1991 ESC report,[28] the Commission presented a new proposal, this time under Article 235 EC. The new proposal was welcomed by the majority of Member States, with the notable exception of Denmark, which considered the new proposed system to be much stricter than most national marketing authorisation regimes. While the Danish opposition was hardly an issue when the details of the new system were presented, another

---

[26] Permanand (n 24) 19–47.

[27] European Parliament, Minutes of Proceedings of the Sitting of Wednesday 12 June 1991: *Proposal for a Council Regulation Laying Down Community Procedures for the Authorisation and Supervision of Medicinal Products for Human Veterinary Use and Establishing a European Agency for the Evaluation of Medicinal Products*. The Parliament has traditionally constituted the forum, where open discussions took place and where societal concerns received more attention.

[28] Economic and Social Committee, *Opinion on the Proposal for a Council Regulation (EEC) Laying Down Community Procedures for the Authorisation and Supervision of Medicinal Products for Human Veterinary Use and Establishing a European Agency for the Evaluation of Medicinal Products*, Official Journal of the European Communities, 91/C 269/84.

problem arose: the seat of the new agency. Several Member States wanted the EMA to be situated in their territory, namely the Netherlands, Denmark, Ireland, Spain and the United Kingdom. In the end, on 29 October 1993, the heads of state and governments proclaimed London as the seat of the EMA.[29]

Having the EMA situated in London would give a considerable advantage to the UK pharmaceutical industry, which would have simple and direct access to the agency and thus easy access to the internal market. Another issue related to the functioning of the agency that raised concern was its financing. The question was whether the new agency would be financed through fees or whether its expenses would be covered by a Community subsidy. The disagreements concerning the financing of the agency contributed to further delays in its establishment, as budget issues had to be reviewed by the Parliament. In the end, the financing of the EMA was a mixed construct that was revised in 1998.[30] The revision led to primary financing through fees.

In the final draft, the Commission was interested in presenting the new agency as serving the first objective, namely patients' interests. In the press releases that followed, no reference was made to the need for an internal market in the pharmaceutical industry; what was underlined was the satisfaction of consumer interests, taking into consideration the fact that the new system entailed the introduction of more severe and stringent product testing. In fact, in information leaflets concerning the functioning of the EMA, it was claimed that the agency was introduced in order to meet the concerns of patients and as a response to demands from patient organisations. This is, of course, not the case, since the changes proposed by the Parliament and the requirements of consumer organisations – which addressed purely public health concerns – were all rejected. Transparency is the only aspect of the new system that can be traced back to the demands of the organisations.[31] Access to the decisions of the EMA and to the details of the products granted marketing authorisation by means of the centralised procedure has been a requirement of both the consumer organisations and the Parliament. In order to comply with the requirements on transparency, the EMA presents detailed information regarding its work on its website, including applicable legislation, summaries from meetings, assessments of operations, and pharmacovigilance alerts for products already on the market. The EMA also publishes two sets of documents. These are Summaries of Product Characteristics, with detailed information on new medicines in order to provide patients and medical doctors with necessary documentation

---

[29] Commission of the European Communities, *Commission Communication to the Council and the Parliament on the Outlines of an Industrial Policy for the Pharmaceutical Sector in the European Community* COM [93] 718, Brussels.

[30] See Council Regulation 297/95/EC of 10 February 1995 on fees payable to the European Agency for the Evaluation of Medicinal Products [1995] OJ L 35/1.

[31] See also European Medicines Agency, 'ICH Topic M 4 Common Technical Document for the Registration of Pharmaceuticals for Human Use – Organisation CTD, ICH Topic M 4 Common Technical Document for the Registration of Pharmaceuticals for Human Use – Organisation CTD', February 2004 (CPMP/ICH/2887/99).

concerning their effectiveness, and European Public Assessment Reports (EPARs). An EPAR provides for the detailed assessments of all new applications in centralised procedures. While the aforementioned publications had as a goal to contribute to making the EMA a modern, accessible and transparent agency, their nature and value in practice is questionable. One of the most serious critiques concerning the accessibility and transparency of the EMA comes from the International Society of Drug Bulletins, which has openly stated that the information on the EMA website is obsolete and of no value. The use of language in EPARs, in particular, decreases its accessibility, as it is impossible for a non-expert to comprehend their contents. There are also documents that are not made publicly available, such as the opinions leading to negative MA decisions. This is in contrast with the FDA, where 90 per cent of the documents produced by the agency are published.[32] Despite the critique, the accessibility of documents concerning the marketing authorisation of pharmaceuticals is much higher after the establishment of the EMA than with the previous decentralised and nation-oriented system.[33] Recently, considerable work has been done to increase accessibility by publishing documents related to clinical trials used in the MA applications.

On the other hand, the fact that the agency is primarily financed through application fees is referred to as a point of weakness in the legitimacy of its decisions, since this gives the agency a character of customer politics. Concerns have been raised that the industry exercises influence and power over the work of the agency. The special relationship between the EMA and the industry was illustrated in an interview with the head of EFPIA, Brian Ager, who stated that the EMA and the industry do not have the relationship of a regulator and a regulated party, but that of a partnership.[34] In the same interview, Ager concluded that the cooperative system of the EMA was not seen in the United States, where the FDA functions much more as a 'policing agency'.[35]

However, it seems that presenting the final regulatory framework of the EMA as a result of consumer demands was a way for the Commission to deal with potential critique of the complete lack of consumer representation in the final work of drafting procedures. Still, it is obvious that the Commission's primary concerns were the internal market and the development of the European pharmaceutical industry.

---

[32] NCC [1993], Balancing Acts – Conflict of Interest in the Regulation of Medicine. London: National Consumer Office.

[33] European Medicines Agency, *European Medicines Agency Policy on Publication of Clinical Data for Medicinal Products for Human Use*, 21 March 2019, EMA/144064/2019. In this regard, see also European Medicines Agency, *Questions and Answers on the European Medicines Agency Policy on Publication of Clinical Data for Medicinal Products for Human Use*, 21 March 2019 EMA/357536/2014, Rev 2.

[34] W Ross, 'It's no FDA – Maybe it Even Works a Little Better, an Interview with Brian P Ager, Director General of the European Federation of Pharmaceutical Industries and Associations' [2000] 35 *Medical Marketing and Media*, 8, 61–67.

[35] Henry I Miller, 'Sick Process' [1999] *Hoover Digest*, No 1.

Interestingly, the UK pharmaceutical industry organisation (the ABPI) already in 1988 published a policy paper in which it presented the ideal competencies of a new agency, stating that biotechnological products should fall under the exclusive competence of the new agency, while pharmaceutical companies would, for other products, have the possibility to choose between the new agency and the already-established marketing authorisation procedures. This proposal is very close to what became the final EMA scheme.[36]

1.1.3. The Mandate and Role of the EMA

The EMA has a central role in the referral procedures relating to medicinal products that are approved or under consideration by Member States for non-centralised authorisation.[37] However, its main task is to conduct scientific assessments of medicinal products and to coordinate the scientific evaluation of their safety, efficacy and quality.[38]

The EMA is also responsible for the monitoring of the safety of medicines through its pharmacovigilance network. Information reported on adverse drug reactions is stored in a central database, in order for the EMA to keep track of safety trends. If the documentation reveals that the balance of benefits to risks has changed, the EMA may act and can go as far as to suspend a marketing authorisation previously granted. One of the EMA's mandates is to stimulate innovation and research in the pharmaceutical sector. To achieve that, it has created a multinational pool of expert scientists from over 40 national competent authorities. It also represents the EU in the work of international organisations and initiatives like the European Pharmacopeia and the World Health Organization.

Seven scientific committees operate under the umbrella of the EMA. The committees that conduct its main scientific work are: the CHMP, the Committee for Medicinal Products for Veterinary Use (CVMP), the Committee for Products (COMP), the Committee on Herbal Medicinal Products (HMPC), the Paediatric Committee (PDCO), the Committee for Advanced Therapies (CAT), and the Pharmacovigilance Risk Assessment Committee (PRAC). In 2005, a new group was introduced, called the SME office: a specific unit within the EMA with the mandate to support small- and medium-sized enterprises. The support includes

---

[36] Permanand (n 24) 69–72.
[37] The EMA internal organisation includes an executive director who is under the supervision of an internal management board. The executive director has a secretariat with over 600 staff members. The management board is the supervisory body of the EMA, responsible for budgetary and planning matters. The management board includes two representatives from the European Commission, two representatives from the European Parliament, one representative from each Member State (heads of the national competent authorities) and the 'civil society' representatives: two representatives from the patient organisations and one representative from each of the doctor and vet organisations.
[38] For an overview of the EMA mandate, see www.ema.europa.eu/en/human-regulatory/research-development/innovation-medicines [Accessed on 12 June 2020].

reduction of fees for scientific advice and inspections, fee deferrals, or exemptions for marketing authorisation applications.

Of course, one can question whether the EMA lives up to its 'public health mandate' and whether its operation benefits the European patient.

According to a report of the DG Enterprise,[39] the fact that the EMA is able to proceed to efficient processing of marketing authorisation applications can mean that the public gains access to innovative medicines quickly. One can see a difference between the public health mandate of the EMA according to the Regulation 2309/93 and how this is communicated in the aforementioned report. In the original Regulation, the EMA was to protect public health 'by mobilizing the best scientific resources within the European Union', while at the same time it would promote public health 'through the effective regulation of pharmaceuticals within the single European market'. These objectives seem to have been abandoned, at least as far as can be gleaned from the reports concerning the evaluation of the EMA's work.[40]

One of the consumer organisations' ambitions with the new agency was to harmonise the standards of national agencies by making them more stringent and following technological developments more closely. However, what seems to have been the actual impact of the work of EMA is that applications are examined within the predetermined timeframe. The concern is that instead of the focus being on the safety and efficacy of pharmaceutical products, it is on processing applications in a timely manner. Certain national agencies have provided concrete examples of pharmaceutical products, granted marketing authorisation through the EMA, that would have been denied authorisation if subject to a national procedure, due to issues pertaining to lack of safety.[41] Furthermore, one can question whether more time-efficient application procedures contribute to public health objectives, since it is not certain that the products that receive marketing authorisation are those that are most needed from a public health perspective.

The EMA has no mandate to consider the issue of 'need' in relation to pharmaceutical products. It has been suggested as necessary to grant EMA the right to acquire the rights to drugs that are no longer manufactured by the product owner, or for which there is a lack of commercial interest, if they still have value in clinical use.[42] The fact that there is no (or very little) consumer participation in the work of the EMA also leads to limited references to the 'need' for pharmaceuticals.

---

[39] Commission of the European Communities, *Pharmaceuticals in the European Union, Commission of the European Communities, Enterprise Directorate-General*, Brussels, 2000.

[40] See, for instance, European Association of Euro-Pharmaceutical Companies, *Response to Consultation Paper by European Association of Euro-Pharmaceutical Companies (EAEPC)*, Brussels, 2001.

[41] John Abraham and Graham Lewis, 'Secrecy and Transparency of Medicines Licensing in the EU' [1998] *The Lancet*, 352 (9126) 480–82.

[42] Silvio Garattini and Vittorio Bertele, 'The Role of the EMEA in Regulating Pharmaceutical Products' in Elias Mosialos, M Monique Mrazek and Tom Walley (eds), *Regulating Pharmaceuticals in Europe: Striving for Efficiency, Equity and Quality* (European Observatory on Health Systems and Policies Series Maidenhead, Open University Press 2004) 441. In this respect, it has been claimed that

Contrary to the FDA, the EMA has rather limited competence concerning post-authorisation control of medicinal products. Although pharmacovigilance is part of such follow-up, the way in which this is performed and the consequences it might have are much weaker than those provided for under the FDA system.[43] The FDA reviews whether any medical errors have been committed due to a lack of information or faulty promotional labelling, as well as reporting on pharmaceutical product shortages and their causes. Furthermore, the US agency is able to proceed to a detailed review of 'therapeutic inequivalence', ie, the question of whether the therapeutic character of a certain product is outweighed by its toxicity or other side effects. The FDA has the possibility to sanction violations of post-authorisation rules. In comparison with the FDA, the EMA seems to have a much weaker mandate, something that in its turn seems to mean that the EMA has much more limited possibilities to fulfil public health objectives than its US counterpart.

Access to pharmaceuticals is, of course, not only dependent on the marketing authorisation as such, but also on decisions regarding pricing and reimbursement schemes. These fall outside the scope of the mandate of the EMA and are purely a matter for Member States.

1.1.4. Committees under the EMA

1.1.4.1. The Committee for Medicinal Products for Human Use

The CHMP is responsible for preparing the EMA's opinions on all matters concerning medicinal products for human use, in accordance with Regulation (EC) No 726/2004. This committee is also responsible for providing assistance to companies researching and developing new medicines and preparing scientific and regulatory guidelines for the industry. Post-authorisation and maintenance activities, including the assessment of modifications and extensions, are also the responsibility of the CHMP. Furthermore, disagreements that may arise in the decentralised procedures with regard to whether a medicinal product has potential risks to public health are arbitrated by the CHMP.[44]

The assessments made by the CHMP are based purely on scientific criteria and tests as to whether the pharmaceutical product fulfils the criteria for quality and safety. The CHMP publishes a European Public Assessment Report presenting the scientific criteria according to which the Commission should approve or reject the marketing authorisation application. If the application is approved, the CHMP will also draft the Summary of Product Characteristics and the labelling

---

the EMA could in fact acquire the ownership of these products and then license them to pharmaceutical companies that would be interested in proceeding with their manufacturing.

[43] Dan Kidd, 'The International Conference on Harmonization of Pharmaceutical Regulations, the European Medicines Evaluation Agency, and the FDA: Who's Zooming Who?' [1996] 4 *Indiana Journal of Global Legal Studies*, 1, 183–206.

[44] On the role and responsibilities of the CHMP, see https://web.archive.org/web/20070610065228/www.emea.europa.eu/htms/general/contacts/CHMP/CHMP.html [Accessed on 12 June 2020].

and packaging requirements. The EPARs are published on the EMA website and constitute public information. In order to increase transparency, the CHMP also publishes patient-friendly summaries of the EPARs, as one way of responding to previously expressed critique on the agency's lack of transparency.

Each Member State is to appoint one member of the CHMP, with five additional members chosen on the basis of scientific competence.

1.1.4.2. The Committee for Medicinal Products for Veterinary Use

The CVMP prepares EMA opinions for veterinary products in accordance with Regulation (EC) No 726/2004.[45] It has the same role as the CHMP, but for veterinary products. Apart from reviewing the safety and quality of veterinary products, the CVMP also decides on the permissible maximum residue limits (MRLs) of veterinary products in food produced from animals for human consumption. The CVMP decides on these limits before marketing authorisation is granted. This is a committee that works in close cooperation with both national veterinary agencies and veterinary product companies. One of the tasks of the CVMP – the preparation of guidelines – is in fact performed in cooperation with companies researching and developing new veterinary products, as well as in cooperation with international organisations. The procedure concerning the appointment of the CVMP members is similar to that of the CHMP, with one member per Member State plus five co-appointed members chosen based on their expertise.

1.1.4.3. The Committee for Orphan Medicinal Products

The Committee for Orphan Medicinal Products (COMP) is the authority responsible for examining orphan drug designation applications, and thus works with medicinal products for the diagnosis, prevention or treatment of orphan diseases (life-threatening or serious conditions that affect no more than five in 10,000 persons). The Council Regulation (EC) No 141/2000 of 16 December 1999 provides all relevant provisions for the examination procedure.[46]

Furthermore, the COMP advises the European Commission on the establishment and development of a policy on orphan medicinal products in the EU and assists the Commission in drafting guidelines in the field and in keeping in touch with and coordinating the international cooperation in the field of orphan drug protection and research. COMP members are designated by Member States, in consultation with the EMA Management Board. The criteria for the choice of the

---

[45] See European Medicines Agency, *Committee for Medicinal Products for Veterinary Use: Rules of Procedure*, 23 April 2020 EMA/CVMP/422/04 Rev. 2 EMA/MB/47098/2007. See also European Medicines Agency, *Committee for Medicinal Products for Veterinary Use (CVMP) Work Plan 2020*, 5 December 2019 EMA/CVMP/505315/2019.

[46] See European Medicines Agency, *Committee for Orphan Medicinal Products (COMP): Work Plan 2020 Adopted by the Committee on 22 January 2020*, 22 January 2020 EMA/COMP/478696/2019 Inspections, Human Medicines Pharmacovigilance and Committees Division.

members are based on their expertise in science and medicine, as well as in the valuation of medicinal products.[47]

The COMP also includes three representatives from patient organisations.

1.1.4.4. The Paediatric Committee

The Paediatric Committee (PDCO) was established by means of Regulation (EC) No 1901/2006.[48]

The role of the PDCO is to assess the content of paediatric investigation plans (PIPs) and to adopt opinions concerning their application.[49] However, the PDCO not only reviews and assesses the PIPs, but also their contents, and adopts opinions on the quality, safety or efficacy of any medicine that will be used on the paediatric population. The role of the PDCO is extended to providing assistance to national authorities with regard to the contents and format of data necessary to assess the safety and efficacy of medicines. It also advises and supports the EMA in the creation of a European network of persons and bodies with specific expertise of relevance for the paediatric population and provides advice on any matter relating to paediatric medicines to both the European Commission and the EMA executive director. Apart from its regulatory roles, the PDCO stores information regarding the needs in paediatric research and the arrangements necessary for conducting paediatric research.

Nevertheless, the PDCO does not grant marketing authorisation; only the CHMP has authority over the marketing authorisation procedure. The PDCO will, upon request from the CHMP, provide an opinion on the quality, safety and efficacy of a medicinal product for use in the paediatric population. The PDCO is composed of five CHMP members appointed by the CHMP itself, one member for every Member State,[50] three members representing health professionals, and three members representing patient organisations.

Both the mandate and the legal basis of the PDCO have been subject to the scrutiny of the CJEU.[51] In its judgment of 14 December 2011, the court held that the PDCO was correct in not taking into consideration the indication proposed by the applicant (who had applied for a waiver). The PDCO's sole obligation is to base its opinion on the scientific and objective evidence.

---

[47] The status of CHMP opinions has been clarified in the ruling of the CJEU in Judgment of the General Court (Second Chamber) of 5 December 2018, *Bristol-Myers Squibb Pharma EEIG v European Commission and European Medicines Agency*, T-329/16, EU:T:2018:878.

[48] Regulation 1901/2006/EC of the European Parliament and of the Council of 12 December 2006 on medicinal products for paediatric use and amending Regulation 1768/92/EEC, Directive 2001/20/EC, Directive 2001/83/EC and Regulation 726/2004/EC (Text with EEA relevance) [2006] OJ L 378/1.

[49] Another of the roles of the PDCO is to make assessments on full or partial waivers and deferrals. See European Medicines Agency, *Rules of Procedure of the Paediatric Committee (PDCO)*, 25 March 2020 EMA/348440/2008 Rev.2 Paediatric Committee (PDCO).

[50] Except for those Member States that are already represented in the PDCO through the CHMP.

[51] See European Medicines Agency, *Committee for Advanced Therapies (CAT) Rules of Procedure*, 19 March 2020 EMA/CAT/454446/2008 rev. 3, Committee for Advanced Therapies.

1.1.4.5. The Committee for Advanced Therapies

The Committee for Advanced Therapies (CAT) is the EMA committee responsible for assessing the quality, safety and efficacy of advanced therapy medicinal products (ATMPs) and following scientific developments in the field. The committee has a multidisciplinary character, gathering some of the best available experts in Europe. The committee was established by means of Regulation (EC) No 1394/2007 on ATMPs.[52]

The central role of the CAT is to prepare draft opinions on ATMP applications submitted to the EMA before the CHMP adopts a final opinion on the granting, variation, suspension, or revocation of a marketing authorisation for the medicine concerned. However, at the request of the EMA executive director or of the European Commission, an opinion may also be produced on any scientific matter relating to ATMPs.[53]

The CAT consists of five members from the CHMP, one member from each Member State not represented through the CHMP, two members appointed by the European Commission representing the health profession, and two members representing patient organisations.[54]

1.1.4.6. The Committee on Herbal Medicinal Products (HMPC)

This Committee was established by means of Regulation (EC) No 726/2004 and Directive 2004/24/EC, introducing a simplified registration procedure for traditional herbal medicinal products in the EU Member States.[55]

The HMPC is also involved in the standardisation and harmonisation of procedures and provisions concerning herbal medicinal products in EU Member States. Furthermore, it provides its scientific opinion to the EU Member States and the European institutions concerning issues related to herbal medicinal products. Its role also extends to drafting a list of herbal substances, preparations and combinations, and establishing EU herbal monographs.

The Committee consists of one member appointed by each of the EU Member States, as well as one member appointed by Iceland and one appointed by Norway.[56]

---

[52] Regulation 1394/2007/EC of the European Parliament and of the Council of 13 November 2007 on advanced therapy medicinal products and amending Directive 2001/83/EC and Regulation 726/2004/EC (Text with EEA relevance) [2007] OJ L 324/121.

[53] See European Medicines Agency, *Committee for Advanced Therapies (CAT) Rules of Procedure*, 19 March 2020 EMA/CAT/454446/2008 Rev. 3.

[54] For more information on the work of CAT, see www.ema.europa.eu/en/committees/committee-advanced-therapies-cat [Accessed on 12 June 2020].

[55] Regulation (EC) No 726/2004 of the European Parliament and of the Council of 31 March 2004 laying down Community procedures for the authorisation and supervision of medicinal products for human and veterinary use and establishing a European Medicines Agency; Directive 2004/24/EC of the European Parliament and of the Council of 31 March 2004 amending, as regards traditional herbal medicinal products, Directive 2001/83/EC on the Community code relating to medicinal products for human use.

[56] Further members can be appointed on the basis of expertise.

1.1.4.7. The Pharmacovigilance Risk Assessment Committee

The Pharmacovigilance Risk Assessment Committee (PRAC) is the EMA committee responsible for assessing and monitoring the safety of human medicines. The mandate of PRAC includes the detection, assessment, minimisation and communication of the risks related to each medicine, with account taken of the therapeutic effect of the medicine. The PRAC prepares recommendations on any matters relating to pharmacovigilance activity.

PRAC recommendations are considered by the CHMP when it adopts opinions concerning centrally authorised medicines and referral procedures. The members of the PRAC are nominated by the EU Member States in consultation with the EMA Management Board, on the basis of scientific criteria. The Commission appoints two representatives for health professionals and two representatives from patient organisations.[57]

1.1.5. *Other Working Groups of Interest for the EMA*

1.1.5.1. The Heads of Medicines Agencies

The Heads of Medicines Agencies (HMA) is a committee that includes the Heads of Agencies for Human Medicines and the Heads of Agencies for Veterinary Medicines from each Member State. Their appointments depend on the domestic procedures of each of the Member States. They meet often, to exchange information, discuss strategic issues and share best practices within the EU.[58] They provide support to the network of European medicines agencies through the provision of professional and scientific resources. Although the Heads of Medicines Agencies is not established by means of a Regulation or Directive, it still plays a central role in producing a balanced view on the operation of the European procedures and their resource implications for the Member States agencies. It has a very important role, since it collects information from the Member States' competent authorities and communicates it to the EMA and to the Commission. It may also provide solutions to practical problems faced by the national competent authorities.[59]

1.1.5.2. The National Competent Authorities of European Member States

The role of the national competent authorities is central, since it is these authorities that are responsible for the assessment of marketing authorisations. Inspections concerning Good Clinical Practices (GCP), Good Manufacturing Practices

---

[57] European Medicines Agency, *Pharmacovigilance Risk Assessment Committee Rules of Procedure*, 14 April 2020 EMA/PRAC/567515/2012 Rev.2.
[58] Usually meeting four times a year.
[59] For more information on the role of the Heads of Medicines Agencies, see www.hma.eu/ [Accessed on 12 June 2020].

(GMP), and pharmacovigilance inspections are performed by the employees of the national authorities.[60]

1.1.5.3. The Coordination Group for Mutual Recognition and Decentralised Procedures: Human (CMDh)

The CMDh replaced the informal Mutual Recognition Facilitation Group in 2005. It examines issues that relate to marketing authorisations of human medicines in two or more EU Member States. In case of disagreement between Member States during the assessment of data based on the grounds of potential serious risk to public health, the CMDh considers the issue and tries to assist in reaching an agreement within 60 days. If this is not successful, the issue is subjected to the arbitration of the CHMP.

Furthermore, the CMDh is responsible for matters relating to the safety of non-centrally authorised medicines marketed in the EU. The CMDh adopts a position on safety-related EU referral procedures, taking into account the recommendations of the PRAC, and creates a list of medicines for which harmonised product information should be collected. The CMDh consists of representatives from each Member State, plus one representative each from of Norway, Iceland and Liechtenstein.

1.1.5.4. The European Directorate for the Quality of Medicines

The European Directorate for the Quality of Medicines (EDQM) was established in 1996 under the Council of Europe. The EDQM is responsible for the Technical Secretariat of the European Pharmacopoeia Commission, set up in 1964 by means of the European Pharmacopoeia Convention. The EDQM is responsible for organising activities related to the procedure for assessment and approval of certificates of suitability. It is also responsible for the surveillance of medicinal products distributed in Europe, and for this reason coordinates a European network of official medicine control laboratories and sets standards used in quality control testing.

1.1.5.5. The International Conference on Harmonisation of Technical Requirements for Registration of Pharmaceuticals for Human Use (ICH)

The International Conference is a meeting place for the regulatory authorities of Europe, Japan and the United States, and the experts of these regions, where they can discuss scientific and regulatory concerns.

---

[60] Procedural differences in the work of national authorities create further friction in the application of regulatory rights, since even the provisions of the SPC Regulation are dependent on their application and interpretation by national authorities. A coordination group thus plays an important role in working towards a less fragmented application of the regulation.

Already in the early 1980s, there were major initiatives towards some form of international harmonisation, alongside the EU working towards a single market for pharmaceuticals. In 1989, the WHO Conference of Drug Regulatory Authorities (ICDRA) laid out specific plans as to how this cooperation and harmonisation should work. The next step was taken in April 1990, when representatives of regulatory agencies of Europe, Japan and the United States met in Brussels. This is also where and when the ICH was established.[61]

The purpose of the ICH is to make recommendations on ways to achieve greater harmonisation in the interpretation and application of technical guidelines and requirements for product registration, in order to reduce the need to duplicate testing carried out during the research development of new medicines. International harmonisation is important since it removes obstacles to international development and availability of the new medicines, while also safeguarding safety and efficacy.

2. The Marketing Authorisation Procedure

The central component of the regulatory legal framework for the pharmaceutical industry is the marketing authorisation procedure.

A pharmaceutical product, whether patented or not, may not be placed on the market without first obtaining marketing authorisation. The granting of an SPC is dependent on the marketing authorisation procedure and its timing in relation to the patent granted. The paediatric extension made possible by the Paediatric Regulation depends on procedures pertaining to the marketing authorisation regulatory framework. The Orphan Drugs Regulation grants market exclusivity, which is also dependent on the marketing authorisation of the orphan drug.[62]

The marketing authorisation, its legal framework and practicalities are thus undoubtedly of vital importance for the operation, granting and interpretation of all regulatory rights.

Under the framework of the MA procedure, the product owner has to provide data supporting the safety, quality and efficacy of the pharmaceutical in question, for a specific dosage, under specific conditions, and for a specific patient group.[63] During this process, the economic perspective is not taken into consideration; the issue of reimbursement to the product owner is a matter for the national health authorities to consider.

---

[61] This is a conference which convenes often – at least twice a year.
[62] Article 8, Regulation 141/2000/EC.
[63] This imposes certain requirements on the applicant, which must be taken into account in their application.

2.1. The Legal Framework

Directive 65/65/EEC[64] of 1965 was the first attempt to provide harmonisation in the field of regulatory rights. A fragmented national legislation-based regulatory framework would make product development and commercialisation of pharmaceuticals even more cumbersome and costly.[65]

Directive 2001/83/EC[66] codified the previous Directives from the 1960s onwards, as well as national legislation and case law. This Directive has been subject to a number of subsequent amendments in order to accommodate changes in the industry and the subsequent introduction of relevant regulations, such as the Advanced Therapies Regulation.[67]

The Directive provides that a pharmaceutical may not be put on the market unless marketing authorisation has been granted – either by the national competent authority, for the product to be commercialised in the specific jurisdiction, or by the European Commission, when a marketing authorisation is to cover the whole EU. The regulation complements the provisions of the Directive regarding the functioning of the European Medicines Agency (EMA) and the 'centralised procedure' for the granting of marketing authorisation.

However, the marketing authorisation system is even more fragmented, since issues pertaining to the marketing authorisation of orphan drugs or paediatric pharmaceuticals are regulated separately. Furthermore, the applicant needs to take into consideration a number of soft law legal sources, such as the 'Notice to Applicants' guidelines, and other implementing legislation and guidelines published on the European Commission's website.

The already fragmented and arguably over-regulated area of medicinal products is supplemented by a long list of guidelines. While guidelines usually include further explanations and clarifications whose objective is to facilitate the application of a legal rule, in this case the guidelines constitute a central component of the legal framework as such. The most important guidelines are found in the document Notice to Applicants (NTA). The NTA is published by the European Commission under Eudralex and is the result of co-operation between the EMA, the Commission and the national MA authorities. Its first publication was is 1986, but it has been subject to several revisions. The first volume of the NTA includes

---

[64] Council Directive 65/65/EEC of 26 January 1965 on the approximation of provisions laid down by Law, Regulation or Administrative Action relating to proprietary medicinal products [1965] OJ 22/369.

[65] See Preamble of Council Directive 65/65/EEC: 'Whereas trade in proprietary medicinal products within the Community is hindered by disparities between certain national provisions, in particular between provisions relating to medicinal products (excluding substances or combinations of substances which are foods, animal feeding-stuffs or toilet preparations); and whereas such disparities directly affect the establishment and functioning of the common market'.

[66] Directive 2001/83/EC of the European Parliament and of the Council of 6 November 2001 on the Community code relating to medicinal products for human use [2001] OJ L 311/67.

[67] See also Regulation 2017/745/EU of the European Parliament and of the Council of 5 April 2017 on medical devices, amending Directive 2001/83/EC, Regulation 178/2002/EC and Regulation 1223/2009/EC and repealing Council Directives 90/385/EEC and 93/42/EEC [2017] OJ L 117/1.

a consolidated version of Directive 2001/83/EC and a list of relevant national legislation and links thereto.

2.2. The Application Dossier

Article 8(3) of Directive 2001/83/EC provides the requirements applicable to the marketing authorisation application and in particular the documentation to be submitted along with it.[68] According to Article 8(3), the application shall include a list of mandatory information such as the name of the applicant, the name of manufacturer, the name of the medicinal product and its active ingredient(s), a description of the manufacturing method, therapeutic indications and contraindications, dose and pharmaceutical form, methods of administration, reasons for any safety and precautionary measures, a description of control methods, results of pharmaceutical toxicological and clinical trial results, and a Summary of Product Characteristics (SmPC). Annex 1 of the same Directive describes further requirements on how these documents are to be presented, while detailed guidance is provided in the Notice to Applicants, Volume 2B, Common Technical Document (CTD).

The CTD is a uniform set of specifications that has been adopted by the EU, the United States and Japan, and comprises five parts: administrative and prescription information, the overview and summary of modules 3–5, the quality of the product (pharmaceutical documentation), its safety (toxicology), and its efficacy (clinical trials).

The marketing authorisation application must include a detailed description of the manufacturing process, the equipment used, the ingredients, the timing and conditions, and the quality controls to be performed on the end product. In addition to the main requirements specified in Article 8(3), there are provisions in the Directive (Articles 10, 10a, 10b and 10c) that include exceptions for applications that do not require a full dossier.[69]

The MA application must provide information on the quality not only of the active substance(s), but also of all the other constituents of the medicinal product (excipients). The same applies to data supporting the efficacy and safety of all constituents, as well as of the end product as a whole.

New active ingredients fall under a different set of rules, and thus the definition of what constitutes a 'new' active ingredient is very important.[70] A new active ingredient is a chemical, biological or radiopharmaceutical substance not

---

[68] Directive 2001/83/EC of the European Parliament and of the Council of 6 November 2001 on the Community code relating to medicinal products for human use [2001] OJ L 311/67.
[69] Among the exceptions listed, we find orphan drugs and medicinal products whose active substances have had a well-known and consistent medicinal use in the Community for at least 10 years.
[70] Naturally, defining the active ingredient in the application is one of the most important steps in the process, and also the grounds upon which a certain exception can prove to be applicable.

previously authorised as a medicinal product in the EU. An isomer (derivative, salt) of a chemical substance previously authorised in the EU, but differing significantly from the previously authorised substance in relation to safety and efficacy issues, a biological substance that has been previously authorised in the EU, but differing in molecular structure, nature of source material, or manufacturing process, or a radiopharmaceutical substance that is a radionuclide not previously authorised as a medicinal product in the EU, or where the coupling mechanism linking the molecule and the radionuclide has not previously been authorised in the EU, are examples of what would be considered 'new ingredients'.

In order to simplify the process of information provision, the applicant may apply for and receive certificates of suitability (CEPs). Such certificates are granted by the European Directorate for the Quality of Medicines (EDQM) and serve as confirmation that the active substance has been produced in accordance with the requirements of the European Pharmacopoeia. Making use of a CEP simplifies the marketing authorisation procedure and enables submission of a more condensed version of the marketing authorisation dossier.[71]

The information included in the application must encompass proposed packaging details, such as the expected shelf-life of the pharmaceutical product.[72] The applicant needs to provide information on the outer packaging of the product, in accordance with Article 54, the immediate packaging of the medicinal product, in accordance with Article 55, and the information on the packaging leaflet as provided for in Article 59 of the Directive 2001/83/EC. The package leaflet must have been approved in consultation with the target patient groups, to ensure that it is clear and easy to understand.[73]

The application shall also include a SmPC containing a description of the medicinal product's properties and the conditions of use. The SmPC includes information that will later be available to health professionals and visible on the packaging. Although the SmPC does not include detailed information regarding the medical conditions that will be treated, a short reference to these and to the patient groups targeted should be included.[74]

---

[71] The role of a certificate of suitability (CEP) is to certify the compliance of a material with the requirements laid down in the relevant monograph of the European Pharmacopoeia. Active pharmaceutical ingredients for which a certificate of suitability has been granted are suitable for use in medicinal products.

[72] For some products, such as eye gels, the in-use shelf-life (after the packaging has been opened) also has to be included.

[73] See Articles 59 and 61(1) of the Directive. This is referred to as 'user testing' or 'readability testing'.

[74] A document describing the properties and the officially approved conditions of use of a medicine. Summaries of Product Characteristics provide basic information to healthcare professionals on how to use the medicine safely and effectively. The EMA has developed guidelines concerning the content and clarity of SmPCs. See, for instance, European Medicines Agency, *EMA action plan related to the European Commission's recommendations on product information*, 14 November 2017 EMA/680018/2017. The development of adequate and clear information on a product is also one of the pillars of the Commission report: European Commission, *Report from the Commission to the European Parliament and the Council in Accordance with Article 59(4) of Directive 2001/83/EC of the European Parliament and of the Council of 6 November 2001 on the Community Code Relating to Medicinal Products for Human Use*, COM [2017] 135 final.

The applications shall also include reference to potential environmental risks. Any specific precautions and safety measures to be taken into consideration in the use, storage and disposal of the pharmaceutical must be specified in the application.[75]

2.3. Alternative Marketing Authorisation Procedures

While there are four different alternative ways of proceeding with a marketing authorisation application, the requirements and the procedures to be followed do not differ dramatically. All four alternatives require that the applicant submits comprehensive data concerning the safety and quality of the pharmaceutical product in question. The application for an innovative product shall include results of pre-clinical and clinical trials,[76] a proposed summary of product characteristics, and other information of relevance. For generic products, the list of required documents can be shorter, if the so-called abridged procedure of marketing authorisation is used.

The first step in proceeding with a MA procedure is to choose the appropriate or best route from a strategic point of view. In some cases, one of the routes is mandatory, so no choice can be made.

The four alternative routes are:

- The centralised procedure (CP), wherein the European Commission can grant a marketing authorisation valid in the entire EU. This alternative is mandatory for some pharmaceuticals (such as orphan drugs).
- The mutual recognition procedure (MRP). This procedure requires the applicant to select the Member States in which it wants protection. One of the states is designated as a Reference Member State (RMS), while the others are Concerned Member States (CMS). The RMS will prepare a report for the CMS that the CMS must recognise.
- The decentralised procedure, where approval is granted by a Member State. This is procedurally close to the MRP.
- The national procedure, wherein national authorisations are granted by national authorities.[77]

In cases where a choice can be made, a number of strategic criteria are to be taken into consideration. The CP is a good alternative for big pharmaceutical companies that opt for an EU-wide commercialisation of pharmaceutical products, while SMEs usually prefer the national procedure, in particular when they want to

---

[75] In this respect, the applicant will take into consideration the CHMP note for Guidance on Environmental Risk. Brussels, 22.3.2017 COM [2017] 135. See also European Commission, *A Guideline on Summary of Product Characteristics*, (SmPC) September 2009.

[76] In a Common Technical Document (CTDoc).

[77] European Commission, Volume 2A, *Procedures for Marketing Authorisation Chapter 2 Mutual Recognition February 2007* Brussels, ENTR/F2/ SM.

58 Setting the Stage for Regulatory Rights

commercialise the product only in their own jurisdiction. It is important to note that the holder of the marketing authorisation can be either a natural or a legal person.

In order to obtain a marketing authorisation, the manufacturer of the product must be the holder of a manufacturing authorisation. As such, the manufacturer guarantees the consistent quality of the products by following Good Manufacturing Practices (GMPs) and by using starting materials that have been produced under the GMP requirements.[78] GMPs for pharmaceuticals intended for human use are specified in Directive 2003/94/EC.[79]

In cases where the holder of the marketing authorisation is not the same as the manufacturer, the two parties are required to sign an agreement stipulating that the manufacturer will follow GMP requirements as well as any other local requirements, and respects the manufacturing conditions as specified in the marketing authorisation dossier.

The manufacturer has to have a GMP certificate issued by a competent authority and, in order to receive this, has to undergo extensive reviews and periodic inspections. GMP certificates are site-specific and can be limited to specific manufacturing activities. Where the application concerns manufacturing capacities outside the EU, a qualified person needs to ensure that each imported batch has undergone the testing specified in Paragraph 1(b) of Article 51 (Directive 2003/83/EC). Furthermore, an official document that certifies that the specific manufacturer has a manufacturing authorisation in its home country is required. Medicinal products produced inside the EU must have a certification from a qualified person that each batch has been tested and follows the requirements of the Directive and the specifications of the marketing authorisation.[80]

2.3.1. The Centralised Procedure

The centralised procedure allows the applicant to commercialise its product in the entire EU, with the same SmPC (translated into the official languages of the Member States), using the same brand name.[81] This means that it is important to find a name that works on the entire internal market. In exceptional cases, the Commission may allow a different name to be used in a specific Member State where the name does not work for reasons related to trademark law. The centralised procedure has the downside of considerable fees.

---

[78] See Title IV of Directive 2001/83/EC.
[79] Commission Directive 2003/94/EC of 8 October 2003 laying down the principles and guidelines of good manufacturing practice in respect of medicinal products for human use and investigational medicinal products for human use (Text with EEA relevance) [2003] OJ L 262/22.
[80] European Medicines Agency, *Pharmacovigilance Risk Assessment Committee, Rules of Procedure*, 14 April 2020, EMA/PRAC/567515/2012 Rev. 2.
[81] Article 32 of Regulation 726/2004/EC of the European Parliament and of the Council of 31 March 2004 laying down Community procedures for the authorisation and supervision of medicinal products for human and veterinary use and establishing a European Medicines Agency [2004] OJ L 136/1.

The centralised procedure is mandatory for the following categories of pharmaceutical products: medicinal products produced by means of recombinant DNA technology, hybridoma and monoclonal antibody methods, and controlled expression of genes coding for biologically active proteins in prokaryotes or eukaryotes, medicinal products for veterinary use used mainly as performance enhancers, medicinal products designated as orphan drugs, and medicinal products for human use including a new active substance for which the therapeutic indication includes HIV/AIDS, cancer, neurodegenerative diseases, diabetes, auto-immune diseases, or viral diseases.

Applications in the CP are handled by the EMA. It is the EMA's scientific committee (the CHMP) that performs a scientific evaluation and submits its results to the EMA. The EMA prepares the report proposing the granting (or not) of marketing authorisation and submits it to the Commission, which makes the final decision.[82]

The CHMP is granted a maximum of 210 days to reach a decision.[83] Both the CHMP and the applicant can request an oral hearing in order for the contents of the application to be explained in greater detail.

Should an applicant decide to withdraw its application before a decision is made by the Commission, they must explain the reasons for this to the EMA. The EMA will then proceed to publication after deleting any information that might be considered commercially sensitive.

Marketing authorisations granted through the CP will be published in the Official Journal of the EU. This publication is to contain all the vital information regarding the marketing authorisation and the pharmaceutical product in question.[84]

Once granted, the marketing authorisation is valid in the entire EU and provides the same rights and obligations as a marketing authorisation under a Directive 2001/83/EC procedure. Following authorisation, the product may be placed on the market, subject to local requirements concerning reimbursement and pricing. The holder of a marketing authorisation is not under any obligation to immediately market the product; however, it is important to consider the 'sunset clause', according to which a marketing authorisation may be repealed if the product is not marketed within a standard five-year period. Thus, the MA holder must inform the EMA of the marketing of the product in any EU country, as well as if marketing ceases, permanently or temporarily.[85]

There are some special categories of marketing authorisations, such as compassionate use and conditional authorisation. A 'compassionate use' opinion

---

[82] Article 13(1) of the Regulation 726/2004/EC.
[83] The maximum period of 210 days may be interrupted when the CHMP poses questions to the applicant or requires further information. See Article 6(3) Regulation 726/2004/EC.
[84] Such as the date of authorisation, the registration number, the pharmaceutical form of the medicinal product, etc, see European Medicines Agency, *Human Medicines Evaluation Division European Medicines Agency pre-authorisation procedural advice for users of the centralised procedure*, 14 May 2020 EMA/821278/2015.
[85] See Sally Shorthose, *Guide to EU Pharmaceutical Regulatory Law* (7th edn, Wolters Kluwer 2017).

is submitted by the CHMP and concerns medicinal products that would not otherwise be eligible under the centralised procedure. This applies to medicinal products currently lacking marketing authorisation, that are made available for the treatment of patients suffering from chronically or seriously debilitating diseases or whose disease is considered to be life-threatening and who cannot be treated successfully with any authorised product. In order to be subject to 'compassionate use', the pharmaceutical has to be undergoing either a marketing authorisation application procedure or clinical trials.

Furthermore, it is possible to apply for a conditional authorisation, which is valid for one year and renewable. Conditional authorisation can be granted subject to certain conditions, such as requiring the applicant to introduce specific safety procedures or to notify competent authorities of any incident relating to use of the medicinal product.

Products that hold major public interest may be subject to an accelerated assessment procedure. This involves providing evidence that the product promotes public health through therapeutic innovation.

2.3.2. *The Mutual Recognition Procedure (MRP)*

The CMS are bound by the marketing authorisation granted by the RMS, within 90 days from the date of the receipt of the application and the assessment report. There is one possibility for a CMS to deny authorisation: if it considers there to be serious threat to public health.[86] The public health objection is considered on a strictly case-by-case basis and covers situations where there is no scientific justification to support the claims of efficacy, where there is not enough evidence to show that all potential safety issues have been appropriately and adequately addressed, where production and quality control mechanisms may be inadequate, where the potential risks of the product outweigh its intended benefits, or where the product information is misleading. Although a disagreement between Member States may lead to delays in the procedure, the MRS route is still fairly efficient. The applicant has the possibility to appeal a negative decision from a CMS within a 90-day period.

It is important to note that the applicant has the possibility to use post-RMS application data to respond to the public health concerns of a CMS.

Although the MRP route facilitates marketing authorisation for applicants interested in several Member State markets, it does not ensure simultaneous launch of the product on these markets. This causes costs for the applicant since it will not be able to use a coordinated marketing campaign, as in the centralised and decentralised procedures.[87]

---

[86] See Article 18 Directive 2001/83/EC.
[87] Judgment of the Court (First Chamber) of 16 October 2008, *The Queen, on the Application of Synthon BV v Licensing Authority of the Department of Health*, C-452/06, EU:C:2008:565.

2.3.3. The Decentralised Procedure (DCP)

The decentralised procedure has the positive effect of allowing the applicant to proceed to a simultaneous launch of the same product in multiple EU countries. This is positive for the product owner, as it reduces launch costs, and facilitates use of a centralised marketing campaign contributing to a stronger brand. On the other hand, in the DCP, the RMS is under the obligation to deal with all CMS objections at the same time, something that may delay the entire procedure.[88]

2.3.4. The National Procedure

A marketing authorisation granted under a purely national procedure will be valid only in the specific member state. This makes it attractive to applicants wishing to commercialise the product only on one specific national market. Furthermore, it is possible for an applicant to combine this with a subsequent MRP, in order to receive marketing authorisation in other EU countries.

2.3.5. The Name of the Product

One of the prerequisites for the commercialisation of a pharmaceutical product is being awarded an appropriate name. The name of the active substance will be the international non-proprietary name (INN) designated by the World Health Organization. Thus, if the active substance does not have a name, the product owner should apply for one from the WHO. The applicant should provide three alternatives to be considered by the consultation committee. The chosen name will be published by the WHO. The name of the active substance may be either an invented name or the name of a chemical substance.[89]

2.3.6. Validity, Renewal and Termination

A marketing authorisation ceases to be valid if the medicinal product is not placed on the Community market within three years after marketing authorisation was granted or if a product previously placed on the market is not present on the market for three consecutive years.[90] Placing the product on the market means making the product available in at least one Member State and for at least one of the packaging options. Furthermore, the product is considered to be on the market as soon as it is in the distribution chain (ie leaves the control of the holder of the

---

[88] Further delays are possible in case a referral to the CMD is made (and in case the arbitration of the CHMP is required). There may also be delays at the national level (when granting the marketing authorisations in each RMS and CMS).

[89] WHO, Guidance on the use of International Nonproprietary Names (INNs), 12 July 2017.

[90] Articles 14(4) and 15(5) of the Regulation 726/2004/EC and Articles 24(5) Directive 2001/83/EC. This is called the 'sunset clause'.

marketing authorisation). In cases of special public health issues, the Commission may grant exemptions to the three-year rule.[91]

A marketing authorisation is valid for a period of five years from the date of approval, and is renewable if the competent authority after review concludes that the benefits outweigh the risks.[92] After this renewal, the marketing authorisation will be valid for an unlimited period of time.

2.3.7. Transparency of the MA Procedure

In two recent rulings of the CJEU in the *PTC Therapeutics International v EMA* case (C-175/18 P)[93] and the *MSD Animal Health Innovation and Intervet International v EMA* case (C-178/18 P),[94] the CJEU was for the first time called to consider the right of access to EU documents that were submitted in an MA application. In both cases, the European Medicines Agency (EMA) approved a third party's request for access to documents, including toxicological reports and clinical studies. Only a very limited portion of the documents was classified as confidential. The request was approved after MA had been granted and while the products were on the market (ie not while the application was under review).

Both the EMA and the General Court had previously considered that the documents were not confidential, apart from certain sections already removed, and that they could therefore be made available to third parties. The appellants had failed to establish that each of the elements of the report constituted commercially confidential information. The Court of Justice clarified that in order for the documents to be considered confidential, the risk of a protected interest being undermined had to be reasonably foreseeable and not purely hypothetical.

The General Court and the Court of Justice stated that, according to the EMA's own policy, the EMA did not disclose commercially confidential information, such as detailed information on the quality and manufacturing of medicinal products. Therefore, even if another undertaking were to use the data contained in the report at issue, that undertaking would have to carry out its own relevant studies and trials and thus successfully develop its own medicinal product. Furthermore, the appellants were granted a 10-year market exclusivity during which no other party could apply for an MA in the EU. Contrary to the General Court, the Court of Justice clarified that there did not have to be any evaluation of 'seriousness' as to the potential commercial harm inflicted or the exceptions provided for in Article 4 of Regulation No 1049/2000, and that the General Court committed an error of

---

[91] This may also occur in exceptional circumstances (which are outside the control of the applicant and justified).
[92] See Article 14(2) Regulation 726/2004/EC; Article 24(2) Directive 2001/83/EC.
[93] Judgment of the Court (Fourth Chamber) of 22 January 2020, *PTC Therapeutics International Ltd v European Medicines Agency*, C-157/18, EU:C:2020:23.
[94] Judgment of the Court (Fourth Chamber) of 22 January 2020, *MSD Animal Health Innovation GmbH and Internet International BV v European Medicines Agency*, C-178/18, EU:C:2020:24.

law in that respect. However, this requirement was not decisive for the ruling of the General Court and thus not of such importance as to lead to annulment of the decision.[95]

The appellants claimed that documents submitted to an EU institution, agency, body, or office fall under a presumption of confidentiality. With regard to this claimed general presumption of confidentiality, the Court ruled that although an institution, agency, or office would be able to apply general assumptions to determine whether disclosure of documents would undermine the interests protected by one or more of the exceptions of Article 4 of the Regulation No 1049/2000, this was not required.[96] The general presumption of confidentiality is not a strict obligation.

Lastly, with regard to the appellants' criticism that the disclosure of the reports during the data exclusivity period could in fact seriously undermine the decision-making process, the Court of Justice concluded that the decision-making process of relevance was that of the MA for the medicinal products in question, which was already closed at the time when the documents were made available.

These two cases are important for two reasons: they clarify an important principle in EU law – that of transparency – and also clarify the status of documents submitted in MA proceedings and thus provide an interpretation of Article 4 of Regulation No 1049/2000.[97] In its ruling, the Court of Justice elaborated on the importance of transparency of EU documents and stated that such transparency constitutes the grounds for the legitimacy of the EU agencies, such as the EMA.

3. Concluding Remarks

Understanding the technicalities of the MA and how these are at times challenged by regulatory rights is crucial. It is this procedure that gives rise to the existence of such rights, for instance in the field of SPC or within the framework of the paediatric extension. The rather complicated system guarantees the safety and efficiency of pharmaceuticals in Europe, while also being the *sine qua non* for them being placed on the market. Thus, it functions as an unchanging foundation, background and – in some cases – challenge in the evolution of regulatory rights and the strategic choices made by the pharmaceutical industry.

The EMA and the Committees under its umbrella have the important task of applying and interpreting the regulatory framework and are thus crucial factors to take into consideration when evaluating the regulatory rights as such, and the regulatory system as a whole.

---

[95] Regulation 1049/2001/EC of the European Parliament and of the Council of 30 May 2001 regarding public access to European Parliament, Council and Commission documents [2001] OJ L 145/43.
[96] Ibid.
[97] Ibid.

Although medical law in Europe is clear, no medicinal product may be put on the market without an MA. This straightforward rule does not necessarily apply to products that are exceptionally prepared in a pharmacy. This exception is regulated in Article 3 of Directive 2001/83/EC as formula magistralis ('prepared in a pharmacy in accordance with a medical prescription for an individual patient') and formula officinalis ('prepared in a pharmacy in accordance with the prescriptions of a pharmacopoeia and 'intended to be supplied directly to the patients served by the pharmacy in question). This practice goes under the general name replacement compounding, and whether it is a legal practice or not will be a matter for national legislation to regulate.[98]

However, it seems that the exception of Article 3 Directive 2001/83/EC[99] has a very limited scope of application, and this limited scope has been considered necessary in order to preserve the general trust of pharmaceutical companies in the system as a whole. National initiatives have stretched the limits of this exception. In particular, in the Netherlands, the Amsterdam Medical Centre hospital, in cooperation with the main national insurance companies, proceeded to 'replacement compounding' products on the national market on such a large scale that the entire national population of an orphan disease was covered by this alternative pharmaceutical.[100] Naturally, this affected the sales of the authorised orphan drug.[101] Other national initiatives seem to be moving in the same direction because of health budget constraints, which risks the creation of a crack in the system as a whole.

A similar exception, the use of which is also growing, is hospital exemption in the ATMP regulation. In the same way as with compounding, the hospital exemption allows hospitals to provide ATMPs that have not undergone MA, thus circumventing the regulatory rights system.

Both compounding and the hospital exemption illustrate the importance that the MA system has on the regulatory rights system. The structure of the system and the way the MA system interacts with it, circumventing the requirement for an MA, means in the end circumventing the rights of the product holder. Thus, while MA seems to constitute a burden for the product holder, it definitely constitutes a means of fending off generic manufacturers. At the same time, regulatory rights are dependent on the MA system in one way or another, either basing the right on the existence of a previous MA such as in the SPC and paediatric extension, or identifying the exclusive right granted with the MA as in the case of orphan drugs and ATMPs. Either way, the MA legal framework constitutes a cornerstone of all regulatory rights, and its possibilities and limitations thus have an impact on the system as a whole.

---

[98] National legislation is limited by means of the Convention on the Elaboration of a European Pharmacopeia L158, 25 June 1994 19.

[99] Article 3 of Directive 2001/83/EC.

[100] Cerebrotendinous xanthomatosis (CTX).

[101] This practice has been confirmed in decisions of the Dutch Health and Youth Care Inspectorate (ICJ), as well as the Minister for Medical Care.

3

Data Exclusivity

1. The Legal Framework

'All industries are different, but some are more different than others. The pharmaceutical industry fits the latter category.'[1]

There could not be a more illustrative quotation regarding the complexities and special characteristics of the pharmaceutical industry. There is no doubt that this industry is subject to constraints and challenges that are rather unique. These challenges and constraints, which are related to both product development and product marketing, influence the way the IP system is applied and used, while they also constitute the motor behind strategic decisions that pharmaceutical companies resort to and are often criticised for. There are two factors of central importance in this respect. First, we have the fact that product development is very lengthy and expensive: typical product development takes 10–15 years and costs over 2 billion euros. Furthermore, pharmaceutical products may not be placed on the market without first (successfully) undergoing a strictly regulated marketing authorisation procedure.[2]

Another important perspective to consider is the fact that pharmaceuticals are divided into two major categories: traditional chemical pharmaceutical products and biological pharmaceuticals. The differences between these two segments of the industry are non-negligible and influence the way the market is regulated.

Looking back at the pharmaceutical product development and the requirements on pre-clinical and clinical trials during the past 20 years, it is obvious that the time required to place a pharmaceutical on the market has become much longer, while the efforts necessary have also increased. In the 1960s, it took approximately 7.9 years from the day when the active ingredient was identified to the day that the pharmaceutical product containing the active ingredient was placed on the market. Already in the 1990s, this time had increased to 12.8 years.[3]

---

[1] Frederic M Scherer, *Industry Structure, Strategy, and Public Policy* (Prentice Hall 1996) 336.

[2] Data exclusivity was first introduced in the United States in 1984 with the Drug Price Competition and Patent Term Restoration Act of 1984 (PL 98-417), also known as the Hatch-Waxman Amendments. The Act provided several types of additional exclusivities to innovators as trade-offs for provisions to make market entry of generics easier and quicker.

[3] Joseph A DiMasi, Henry G Grabowski and Ronald W Hansen, 'Innovation in the Pharmaceutical Industry: New Estimates of R&D Costs' [2016] 47 *Journal of Health Economics*, 20–33.

Clinical trials are performed in a stringent regulatory environment requiring an increased number of patients in the test groups, and the application of the efficiency and safety requirements is much stricter nowadays. Furthermore, there is a large degree of economic and scientific uncertainty. In fact, behind each drug placed on the market, there are often between 5,000 and 10,000 substances that have been subject to pre-clinical and clinical trials.[4]

The total costs for R&D of new pharmaceuticals were approximately 1.3 billion euro in 2003,[5] increasing to 2.6 billion in 2019 according to some studies. Thus, it seems that the costs of product development doubled within 16 years.[6]

The need to provide for some form of protection for data submitted in an MA application is based on two major aspects. One is the fact that this data is very costly and time-consuming to generate. At the same time, the requirement of submitting clinical data does not apply to all medicinal products, at least not to the same extent. In fact, generic medicines may use the clinical data produced by the originators (the original product developers), thus giving manufacturers of generics a faster and cheaper route onto the market. Although this direct access of generics is in accordance with modern public health policies – encouraging the entrance of generic alternatives and thus the possibility to replace expensive originals with cheaper generic versions – it creates a crucial market failure. The expensive and time-consuming process of collecting clinical data is not protected in any way; competitors in the generics field are actually permitted to use it. In order to avoid this and remunerate the originator for its contributions, a data exclusivity system was introduced. The data exclusivity provides protection against competition from generics for a period of 8 + 2 + 1 years. During the first eight years of protection, no generics company may make use of the clinical data submitted by the originator. During the following two years, no generics company is able to submit an application for MA. If the originator provides a new therapeutic indication with significant benefits, an additional year is added to the duration of market exclusivity.

Data protection was recognised as a priority at the international level, in the TRIPS Agreement.[7] Article 39(3) TRIPS states that

> Members, when requiring, as a condition of approving the marketing of pharmaceutical or of agricultural chemical products which utilize new chemical entities, the submission of undisclosed data or other data, the origination of which involves a considerable effort,

---

[4] See Michael Dickson and Jean Paul Gagnon, 'Key Factors in the Rising Cost of New Drug Discovery and Development' [2004] 3 *Nature Reviews Drug Discovery*, 5, 417–29, 418.

[5] Joseph A DiMasi, Ronald W Hansen and Henry G Grabowski, 'The Price of Innovation: New Estimates of Drug Development Costs' [2003] 22 *Journal of Health Economics*, 151–85.

[6] It has been estimated that the costs of collection of clinical data in order to receive a marketing authorisation range between US$1.5 billion to, in some cases, more than US$1.8 billion. See Jorge Mestre-Ferrandiz, Jon Sussex and Adrian Towse, 'The R&D cost of a new medicine' (Office of Health Economics 2012).

[7] The TRIPS Agreement is Annex 1C of the Marrakesh Agreement Establishing the World Trade Organization (WTO), signed in Marrakesh, Morocco, on 15 April 1994.

shall protect such data against unfair commercial use. In addition, Members shall protect such data against disclosure, except where necessary to protect the public, or unless steps are taken to ensure that the data are protected against unfair commercial use.

In the EU, the data protection has its origins in Directive 65/65/EEC,[8] introducing detailed data submission requirements to be satisfied by MA applicants. EU legislation protecting such scientific data was introduced for the first time in Directive 87/21/EC.[9]

2. Clinical Data

Clinical data is the data (information on the efficiency and safety of a medicinal product) generated during pre-clinical and clinical trials and subsequently submitted in the application dossier in the MA procedure.[10]

Chemical pharmaceuticals consist of active substances and auxiliaries. Active substances are the ingredients that have a specific pharmacologic effect, while auxiliaries are necessary to compose a suitable dosage form and administer the active substance to the human body. The pharmacological properties of an active substance and the targets in the human body are nowadays often identified through computerised processes.[11]

The identification of an active substance and its target(s) leads to the next step: experimentation regarding the substance's effects by means of screening methods, firstly on cell cultures and then through animal testing. In the majority of the cases, the screening yields at least two candidates for further clinical studies.[12]

Clinical trials are traditionally divided into three phases. Phase I includes the first testing of the active substance on humans. During this phase, 10 to 30

---

[8] Council Directive 65/65/EEC of 26 January 1965 on the approximation of provisions laid down by Law, Regulation or Administrative Action relating to proprietary medicinal products [1965] OJ L 22/369–73.

[9] Council Directive 87/21/EEC of 22 December 1986 amending Directive 65/65/EEC on the approximation of provisions laid down by law, regulation or administrative action relating to proprietary medicinal products [1987] OJ L 15/36.

[10] The procedure and rules that must be followed in order for such data to be collected are found in the Directive 2001/20/EC of the European Parliament and of the Council of 4 April 2001 on the approximation of the laws, regulations and administrative provisions of the Member States relating to the implementation of good clinical practice in the conduct of clinical trials on medicinal products for human use [2001] OJ L 121/34.

[11] An important part of the clinical trials concerns the pharmacovigilance test. In this respect, the pharmacovigilance guidelines are of importance, www.ema.europa.eu/en/human-regulatory/post-authorisation/pharmacovigilance/good-pharmacovigilance-practices.

[12] Directive 2001/83/EC as amended by Directive 2002/98/EC of the European Parliament and of the Council of 27 January 2003 setting standards of quality and safety for the collection, testing, processing, storage and distribution of human blood and blood components and amending Directive 2001/83/EC [2003] OJ L 33/30. See also Directive 2004/24/EC of the European Parliament and of the Council of 31 March 2004 amending, as regards traditional herbal medicinal products, Directive 2001/83/EC on the Community code relating to medicinal products for human use [2004] OJ L 136/85.

68 Data Exclusivity

volunteers are tested for a period of one to seven days in order to review the significance of pharmacological results from clinical studies for human applications, on the one hand, and the safety of the substance, on the other. Phase II examines the substance's effect as regards the specific medical indication, with several hundreds of volunteers and 8 to 12 weeks of testing. Phase II serves to determine the efficacy, compatibility and risk profile of the active substance. Phase II leads to a final hypothesis that is further tested in Phase III, namely that substance X in dosage Y will have a positive therapeutic effect for indication A.[13]

Phase III proceeds with an even broader group of test persons (usually over 1,000 patients) and takes several years to conclude. The objective of Phase III is to confirm the hypothesis from Phase II. Phase III, documentation thereof, expert opinions and the results from the clinical trials, constitute parts of the basis for an application for marketing authorisation.[14]

After Phase III and application for marketing authorisation, clinical trials may continue. The term Phase IV is used to describe clinical studies related to clinical compatibility (side effects) and comparative studies. In some cases, these studies lead to the discovery of further medical indications. When this is used as the basis for an application to extend the term of the MA, the MA authority will require supplementary data covering these new indications.

3. The Marketing Authorisation Procedure and Directive 2001/83 – Original Pharmaceuticals

In the EU, placing a pharmaceutical product on the market presupposes either marketing authorisation granted by a national competent authority (under the implementing national legislation of Directive 2001/83)[15] or marketing authorisation granted by the Community competent authority under Regulation 726/2004.[16]

---

[13] European Medicines Agency, 'ICH Topic E8 General Considerations for Clinical Trials, note for guidance on general considerations for clinical trials' CPMP/ICH/291/95, www.ema.europa.eu/en/documents/scientific-guideline/ich-e-8-general-considerations-clinical-trials-step-5_en.pdf.

[14] On 6 April 2014, the European Commission adopted the new Regulation 536/2014/EU of the European Parliament and of the Council of 16 April 2014 on clinical trials on medicinal products for human use, and repealing Directive 2001/20/EC Text with EEA relevance [2014] OJ L 158/1, repealing Directive 2001/20/EC. See also European Medicines Agency, 'Working Group on Clinical Trials conducted outside of the EU/EEA Reflection paper on ethical and GCP aspects of clinical trials of medicinal products for human use conducted outside of the EU/EEA and submitted in marketing authorisation applications to the EU Regulatory Authorities' 16 April 2012 EMA/121340/2011.

[15] Directive 2001/83/EC of the European Parliament and of the Council of 6 November 2001 on the Community code relating to medicinal products for human use [2001] OJ L 311/67.

[16] Consolidated text: Regulation 726/2004/EC of the European Parliament and of the Council of 31 March 2004 laying down Community procedures for the authorisation and supervision of medicinal products for human and veterinary use and establishing a European Medicines Agency [2004] OJ L 136/1.

When the pharmaceutical product in question is a high-tech medicinal product, there is a compulsory centralised procedure under Regulation 726/2004. In cases where the market authorisation application is approved, it leads to the granting of an EU-wide marketing authorisation.[17] This unified procedure gives the holder of the marketing authorisaton the possibility to place the product on the market in all EU Member States at the same time (a one stop-shop).[18]

With regard to pharmaceuticals that are not classified as high-tech medicinal products, the choice of application procedure will depend upon the intended market. Where the holder of the marketing authorisation opts for an EU-wide market authorisation, the mutual recognition procedure will be prioritised (in accordance with Directive 2001/83). Using this procedure means that the first marketing authorisation at a Member State level can be used as a reference recognised by all subsequent Member States in which the MA holder seeks to extend their protection.

Lastly, national marketing authorisation is an alternative for pharmaceuticals marketed in one Member State only. In order to avoid discrepancies in the interpretation of Directive 2001/83, it is not possible to hand in national applications for the same pharmaceutical product in several different Member States.[19]

4. Marketing Authorisation for Generic Products

4.1. What Constitutes a Generic Product?

The definition of the term 'generic product' is a codification of the CJEU case law in *Generics*,[20] *Novartis*,[21] and *Approved Prescription Services*.[22] The definition, now codified under Article 10(2)(b), provides that a generic is a 'medicinal product which has the same qualitative and quantitative composition in active substances and the same pharmaceutical form as the reference medicinal product, and whose bioequivalence with the reference medicinal product has been demonstrated by appropriate bioavailability studies'.

---

[17] See ch 2 of this book.

[18] See also European Commission, *An Evaluation of the European Medicines Agency*, January 2010.

[19] This serves to prevent the same application from being treated in different ways in different Member States.

[20] Judgment of the Court (Fifth Chamber) of 3 December 1998, *The Queen v The Licensing Authority Established by the Medicines Act 1968 (Acting by The Medicines Control Agency), ex parte Generics (UK) Ltd, The Wellcome Foundation Ltd and Glaxo Operations UK Ltd and Others*, C-368/96), EU:C:1998:583, para 36.

[21] Judgment of the Court (Sixth Chamber) of 29 April 2004, *The Queen on the Application of Novartis Pharmaceuticals UK Ltd v The Licensing Authority*, C-106/01, EU:C:2004:245, para 66.

[22] Judgment of the Court (Second Chamber) of 9 December 2004, *The Queen, on the Application of Approved Prescription Services Ltd v Licensing Authority*, C-36/03, EU:C:2004:781, para 30.

Another very important definition is that of a 'reference product'. A 'reference' product is an authorised medicinal product whose scientific data is referred to by a third party in support of its own MA application.[23] Only medicinal products that have a full set of scientific data as evidence for their safety, quality and efficacy may constitute reference products. Although a generics company may refer to a dossier based on well-established use, fixed combinations, or informed consent, it is not possible to have another generic medicinal product as a reference product.[24]

Determining which products may be used as 'reference products' also entails checking how (ie through which procedure) MA was granted and thus which criteria the dossier was based on. In order for the generics company to be able to use an abridged application and thus submit a 'reference' dossier, the original MA must have been subject to the requirements of EU medicinal law.

One important question has been the status of dossiers related to medicinal products authorised in Member States prior to their accession. Two important rulings of the CJEU have contributed to answering this question, namely *Generics UK*[25] and *Synthon*.[26] Both of these rulings concern medicinal products granted marketing authorisation pre-EU accession, where the dossiers in question were never 'upgraded' in accordance with EU law requirements. Marketing authorisations granted by EU Member States at a time when the EU standards did not apply cannot trigger a global MA and consequently no data exclusivity.

4.2. Data Exclusivity and Generics

Generics manufacturers commercialise copies of products that have previously been subject to MA procedures. Consequently, the safety and efficiency of these pharmaceuticals have previously been tested and confirmed. In fact, a generics manufacturer is not required to produce pre-clinical and clinical data, if it is possible to 'demonstrate that the medicinal product is a generic of a reference medicinal product which is or has been authorised under Article 6 for not less than eight years in a Member State or in the Community'.[27]

The question is whether the generics manufacturer is able to use the clinical data submitted in the first MA application. According to Article 10c of the Directive, the generics manufacturer can use the original application as a reference, on condition

---

[23] Article 10(2)(a) of the Medicinal Code (Directive 2001/83/EC).
[24] European Commission, *Notice to Applicants: Volume 2A Procedures for marketing authorisation Chapter 1 Marketing Authorisation* [2013] at para 5.3.1.1.
[25] Judgment of the Court (First Chamber) of 18 June 2009, *The Queen, on the Application of Generics (UK) Ltd v Licensing Authority*, C-527/07, EU:C:2009:379. This case is often referred to as Galanthamine, Nivalin's active ingredient.
[26] *Rechtbank 's-Gravenhage*, 18 August 2010, *Synthon BV et al against College ter Beoordeling van Geneesmiddelen* (CBG), LJN: BN 7663.
[27] Article 10, Directive 2001/83/EC.

that the generics manufacturer has the approval of the initial authorisation holder. Thus, the generics manufacturer must, in its own marketing authorisation application, provide reference to the original application procedure and evidence of therapeutic identity between the generic drug and the original product.[28] If the application is based on bibliographic data, the safety and efficiency of the drug must be shown by means of detailed scientific data. Article 10a requires that the 'active substances of the medicinal product have been in well-established medicinal use with the Community for at least 10 years, with recognised efficacy and an acceptable level of safety'.

A generics manufacturer may also proceed to an application for MA with reference to the dossier submitted by the original MA holder by making use of Article 10(1) of the same Directive. However, this application may not be submitted before the term of data exclusivity has expired. For the purposes of its MA, the generics manufacturer will have to prove that the new pharmaceutical really is a generic version of the original medicinal product. The term generic is defined as a medicinal product which has the same qualitative and quantitative composition in active substances and the same pharmaceutical form as the reference medicinal product, and whose bioequivalence with the reference medicinal product has been demonstrated through appropriate bioavailability studies.[29] Proving bioavailability and bioequivalence entails certain costs for the generics manufacturer, but these are only a fraction of the costs for new pre-clinical and clinical trials.

According to Article 10(1)(1) of the Directive, it is not necessary that the marketing authorisation for the reference pharmaceutical to be valid; it is enough that the reference pharmaceutical is or has been subject to a previous MA.[30]

It is important to remember that data exclusivity applies whether or not the pharmaceutical product is patented. There are different forms of data exclusivity, depending on the grounds upon which MA was granted and the status of the pharmaceutical it covers.

Although the system allows for a generics manufacturer to use the clinical trials of the bioequivalent original product in order to provide evidence of the safety and efficiency of its own product, the original manufacturer enjoys a form of protection for the investment made in the data submitted in the MA application. Data exclusivity enters into force as soon as the pharmaceutical is granted

---

[28] The combination of the two is indirect proof of the safety and efficiency of the generic pharmaceutical. Therapeutic identity is at hand if two tested drugs show identical bioavailability (their effects related to efficacy and safety are the same).
[29] Bioequivalence is defined as the therapeutic identity of two substances.
[30] This prevents the holder of the reference pharmaceutical from withdrawing its marketing authorisation and in that way hindering the generics manufacturer from using the dossier of pre-clinical and clinical trials for its own marketing authorisation application. This practice has also been characterised by the EU Court of Justice as abuse of a dominant position (Article 102 TFEU), see Judgment of the General Court (Sixth Chamber, extended composition) of 1 July 2010, *AstraZeneca AB and AstraZeneca plc v European Commission*, T-321/05, EU:T:2010:266.

marketing authorisation.[31] If the pharmaceutical product is removed from the market or the marketing authorisation is withdrawn, the term of the data exclusivity is not impacted.[32]

Market exclusivity is a positive side effect of the marketing authorisation procedure; no further requirements need to be fulfilled in order for it to apply. According to Article 6(1), protection is automatic as soon as a pharmaceutical receives marketing authorisation. However, data exclusivity is not granted for pharmaceuticals with active ingredients that are already authorised (or where the active substance is identical to or a modification of a previously authorised drug).

In this respect, the global marketing authorisation concept applies, meaning that only one period of data protection applies for all medicinal products in the same family authorised through separate procedures, including cases where these are authorised in different Member States and under different names.[33] The global MA concept was introduced in the CJEU ruling of *Novartis* and is now codified in Article 6(1) of the Medicinal Code.[34]

In fact, Article 6(1)(2) specifies that a global marketing authorisation covers any additional strengths, pharmaceutical forms, administration routes, presentations and variations. Any such authorisation shall be considered as belonging to the same global marketing authorisation. This means that the data exclusivity under Article 10(1) is provided only once per MA.

Data exclusivity has a minimum length of eight years. As mentioned in this chapter, the generics manufacturer does not need to provide pre-clinical and clinical data if its product can be proven to be a generic of pharmaceutical that has previously been authorised under Article 6 in a Member State or in the Community, for not less than eight years. Thus, the eight-year term of protection applies regardless of whether the MA granted was provided under a national, a centralised, or a decentralised procedure.

The global MA concept covers all line extensions of medicinal products. These can enjoy the remaining period of data and marketing protection afforded to the

---

[31] Article 6(1) of the Directive 2001/83/EC.
[32] This means that a generics applicant cannot use such data in its own application, even in cases where the original MA is no longer in force.
[33] As long as the active ingredient is the same.
[34] Judgment of the Court (Sixth Chamber) of 29 April 2004, *The Queen, on the Application of Novartis Pharmaceuticals UK Ltd v The Licensing Authority Established by the Medicines Act 1968 (Acting by the Medicines Control Agency)*, C-106/01, EU:C:2004:245. It is interesting in this respect to look into the AG's Opinion dated 23 January 2003, providing that if the application pertains to a new product C and is made under point 8(a)(iii) of the third paragraph of Article 4, making reference to a product A which was authorised more than six to ten years previously, a competent authority is entitled, when verifying that the documents and particulars submitted in support of the application comply with Article 4, to cross-refer to data submitted in support of product B which was authorised within the previous six to ten years, without consent of the person responsible for the marketing of product B, provided that products A and B are essentially similar or differ only in respect of their pharmaceutical form, dose, or therapeutic use.

initial medicinal product, and will not be subject to separate data exclusivity.[35] One important parameter to consider is what is meant by the 'same MA holder'. The question is whether the 'same MA holder' presupposes the same legal person. The interpretation provided by the NTA rather generously states that the 'same MA holder' includes cases where:

(i) the MA holder/applicant belongs to the same company group or is controlled by the same natural or legal person, or where
(ii) the MA holder/applicant has concluded explicit or implicit agreements concerning the marketing of the same medicinal product. This includes joint marketing and licensing agreements.

Still, there are products that fall outside the scope of the global MA.

One major category of such products is fixed combination products (ie products containing two or more active substances included in authorised medicinal products that are not used in combination for therapeutic purposes).[36] Fixed combination products are considered to be distinct products in the global MA concept. This means that the new clinical trials required in the new MA procedure for the combination product will generate a new data and marketing protection term.[37] A global MA does not apply to independently developed medicinal products, provided the company is not encompassed in the meaning of the 'same MA holder'. When the applicant is unrelated to the original MA holder, it must submit a full regulatory dossier based on its own tests and trials. The transfer of an MA from one MA holder to another does not restart, prolong or alter the existing period of data protection.

Furthermore, it is important to note that the global MA only applies if it relates to the same active substance. Therefore, if the medicinal product assessed contains a modification of an existing substance belonging to the same MA holder, it should be determined by the Committee for Medicinal Products for Human Use (CHMP) during the MA process whether the modified active substance qualifies as a new active substance or if it is included in the authorisation of the previously reviewed

---

[35] This concept is further elaborated upon and interpreted in European Commission, *Notice to Applicants: Volume 2A Procedures for marketing authorisation Chapter 1 Marketing Authorisation* [2013], at paras 2.3 and 2.8.

[36] See Article 10b of the Medicinal Code. Here, the interpretation of Article 10b by Teva for the MA of the generic Kivexa can be mentioned. The issue in the specific case was whether a previous triple-fixed combination precluded data and marketing protection for the first fixed combination of two of the active substances, abacavir/lamivudine. According to Teva, Kivexa was a fixed-dose combination combining two active substances which had been supplied and used within the EU as components of a number of different medicinal products for some years; thus, Kivexa could not qualify as a fixed-combination product. The case was withdrawn, so we have no ruling on this very interesting case (*Teva Pharma and Teva Pharmaceuticals Europe v EMA*, T-547/12, EU:T:2014:1099). Order of the General Court of 5 December 2014 to remove the case from the register.

[37] It is important to note that this does not apply to products that have merely been 'bundled' together with no clear therapeutic effect for this specific combination.

74 Data Exclusivity

medicinal product. The CHMP will only assess the data submitted by the applicant and will not actively search for additional data in the public domain.[38] Annex I of the NTA 2013 provides a definition of the term 'new active substance', that may be helpful in assessing whether modifications have led to a modified substance (still falling under the previously granted MA), or to a new one. It is up to the applicant to provide necessary evidence to prove that there is a new substance designation. In order to structure the evidence, one could analogously apply the criteria stipulated in Article 8.22 and 8.23. Further guidance can be found in Article 10(2)(b), which describes the requirements for when two substances could be considered two separate active substances, and which also states that 'salts, esters, ethers, isomers, mixtures of isomers complexes or derivatives of an active substance shall be considered to be the same active substance unless they differ significantly in properties with regard to safety and/or efficacy'.

Furthermore, Part II, Annex I of the Medicinal Code states that 'where the active substance of an essentially similar medicinal product contains the same therapeutic moiety as the original authorised product associated with a different salt/ester complex/derivative evidence that there is no change in the pharmacokinetics of the moiety, pharmacodynamics and/or in toxicity which could change the safety/efficacy profile shall be demonstrated'.[39] Thus, when a substance had received authorisation, any new active substance status will apply, provided that the chemical substance has significantly different properties regarding safety and efficacy.

Two CJEU cases, *Aubagio*[40] and *Tecfidera*,[41] involving the reversal of the CHMP Opinions, provide some clarification in the field. These cases illustrate the difficulties the pharmaceutical industry may be faced with when a new active substance designation is not recognised. In fact, the definition of the term 'active substance' is considered to be of such commercial importance for originator companies seeking to gain new data and marketing protection periods that further case law in the field is to be expected.

The concept of the global MA and its scope is an important and as yet unresolved issue. An interesting and important aspect of this concerns the potential extension of the global MA concept to hybrid abridged applications submitted by third-party applicants (ie applicants not related to the MA holder of the reference product).[42]

---

[38] EMA: New Active Substance categorisation and Orphan Similarity – SME workshop: Focus on quality for medicines containing medical entities, www.ema.europa.eu/en/events/sme-workshop-micro-small-medium-sized-enterprises-focus-quality-medicines-containing-chemical [Accessed on 20 January 2021].

[39] See Article 3, Part II, Annex 1 Medicinal Code.

[40] European Medicines Agency, *Summary of Opinion (initial authorisation): Aubagio* 27 June 2013 EMA/379992/2013 Committee for Medicinal Products for Human Use (CHMP).

[41] European Medicines Agency, *Summary of Opinion (initial authorisation) Tecfidera Dimethyl fumarate* 27 November 2013 EMA/167897/2013/Rev 2 Committee for Medicinal Products for Human Use (CHMP).

[42] See Article 10(3) of the Medicinal Code.

Marketing Authorisation for Generic Products 75

Article 10(3) allows a partial derogation of the legal requirement to submit results from appropriate pre-clinical or clinical trials in cases where the medicinal product does not fall within the definition of a generic medicinal product, where bioequivalence cannot be demonstrated through bioavailability studies, or in case of changes in the active substance, therapeutic indications, strength, pharmaceutical form, or route of administration.

The question that arises is whether the hybrid abridged data generated by an unrelated company falls under the global MA concept, which would mean that it is excluded from data and marketing protection.

In the earlier version of the NTA (2005), an illustration of the difference between generic dossiers and original pharmaceutical dossiers was provided. This clarified that an MA application for a generic does not contain all the relevant information on the safety and efficiency of the medicinal product, and thus cannot constitute a reference dossier.[43] This has introduced the principle of 'no generic of a generic'. In other words, a medicinal product authorised under the Article 10(1) or Article 10(3) of the Medicinal Code may not serve as reference medicinal product for the purposes of a generic application, as the dossier is not complete.[44] One might say that information provided under the dossier of a generic enjoys indefinite protection, since no other party may use this information for its own application. However, this is contrary to the principle providing that the global MA concept applies to any product authorised under Article 10(3), whether such product is developed by the holder of the original MA or by a separate entity. This would also mean that a product authorised under Article 10(3) would not benefit from any form of protection.[45]

After the eight-year period, reference to the original pre-clinical and clinical data is possible. However, marketing authorisation may not be granted for an additional two-year period (Article 10(1)(2) of Directive 2001/83 and Article 14(11) of Regulation 726/2004).

This additional two-year period during which no marketing authorisation may be granted is not data exclusivity per se, but indirectly extends the exclusivity period. In practice, the generics manufacturer proceeds to apply for a marketing authorisation. The application procedure takes some months to complete, although very rarely two years. If the marketing authorisation authority is ready to reach a decision and the two years have not yet elapsed, the procedure will be temporarily suspended.

---

[43] European Commission, *Notice to Applicants: Volume 2A Procedures for marketing authorisation Chapter 1 Marketing Authorisation*, November 2005.
[44] This was further developed in NTA 2013.
[45] See the Guidance of the Coordination Group for Mutual Recognition and Decentralised Procedures (CMD(h), Doc Ref: CMEDh/272/2012, Rev0 October 2012, www.hma.eu/216.html?&L=0 [Accessed on 20 January 2021]; see also Maria I Manley and G Strachan, 'Regulatory Data Protection', in Maria I Manley and Marina Vickers (eds), *Navigating European Pharmaceutical Law* (Oxford University Press 2015) 255–76.

76   Data Exclusivity

In fact, the eight- plus two-year term of protection was the result of a compromise. The Commission had initially proposed 10-year data exclusivity. The protection would then be 10.5 or 11.5 years, as a generic's market entrance would be even further delayed, given that the process for submitting the application could not, according to the initial proposal of the Commission, begin before the ten years had elapsed.

Another interesting question to investigate is what happens when the originator (the holder of the original MA) decides to withdraw the MA. Would the dossier of the withdrawn marketing authorisation be valid as a 'reference' dossier? This question was clarified in the CJEU *AstraZeneca* case.[46] AstraZeneca had withdrawn the MA for the reference product, but had maintained the MA for a line extension product. The questions on which the CJEU was called to reply in this case were: (1) Does the withdrawal of the MA mean that the generics manufacturer is precluded from using it as a reference dossier? (2) Does the MA need to be in force (i) at the time when an application for a generic is submitted, or (ii) at the time when an application for a generic is approved?

The CJEU concluded that in order for a generic to make use of the abridged procedure, it was necessary that the original MA was in force, in the Member State concerned, at the time of submission of the MA application. This ruling creates considerable flexibility for the pharmaceutical industry, which could be used to obstruct or stall entrance of generics. In order to avoid potential abuse, the legislator enacted a new provision,[47] introducing the European reference product concept. This stipulated that as long as the reference product had at some stage been authorised in an EU Member State, such Member State could be called upon to provide the 'full composition of the reference product and if necessary other relevant documentation'.[48]

4.3. The Nature of the Protection Granted

National regulatory authorities and the EMA cannot, during the term of data exclusivity, grant a generics applicant access to the pre-clinical and clinical data (previously submitted by the original MA holder) necessary to proceed to a marketing authorisation. This means that the generics manufacturer will not be able to base its claims of the safety and efficiency of its product on the data submitted by the original product manufacturer.[49] This does not mean that the generics manufacturer needs to have detailed knowledge of the data previously submitted and proceed to any testing; a mere reference will suffice.

---

[46] Judgment of the Court (Sixth Chamber) of 16 October 2003, *AstraZeneca A/S v Lægemiddelstyrelsen*, C-223/01 EU:C:2003:546.
[47] Introduced as Article 10(1) 3rd para of the Medicinal Code Directive 2004/27/EC.
[48] Article 10(1) 3rd para of the Medicinal Code.
[49] Meir Pugatch, 'Measuring the Strength of National Pharmaceutical Intellectual Property Regimes: Creating a New Pharmaceutical IP Index' (2006) 9 *Journal of World Intellectual Property*, 4, 373–91.

The exclusive right granted to the product owner by means of the data exclusivity is enforceable against the marketing authorisation authority. No reference to this data is allowed before the eight-year period has elapsed. However, data exclusivity does not mean that a generics manufacturer may not proceed with its own clinical and pre-clinical trials and produce its own data to be submitted under a marketing authorisation application before the eight-year period has elapsed.

This limitation in the protection granted is the main difference between data exclusivity and patent rights. Nevertheless, it should be noted that the cost and time required to collect the necessary clinical data means that data exclusivity is a valuable right.

4.4. Improvements to Already Existing Pharmaceuticals

Improvements to an already existing pharmaceutical include new therapeutic indications, substitution of its active ingredient (by making use of derivatives, salts, enantiomers), introducing new dosage forms, or routes of administration. In all these cases, an MA for such improvements will not require the submission of a full set of pre-clinical and clinical data; the safety and efficiency of the improvement can partly be proven by reference to the clinical data provided for the first product. Article 10(3) provides that the product manufacturer is required to submit only such data concerning the safety and efficiency of the pharmaceutical that are necessary to bridge the differences between the two versions of the medicinal product (the original and the improved version). The possibility of enjoying a somewhat simplified marketing authorisation procedure leads to the question of whether or not this would give rise to a new period of data exclusivity.[50]

4.4.1. New Therapeutic Indications with Significant Clinical Benefits

One of the major changes provided by means of the 2004–05 revision of the MA legal framework was to accommodate the protection for pharmaceuticals that constitute improvements to already authorised products.[51] The current version of 10(1)(4) of the Medicinal Code stipulates that the two-year market exclusivity period (which follows the eight-year data exclusivity) will be extended by one year, leading to a de facto market exclusivity totalling 11 years if the marketing authorisation holder is able to obtain a marketing authorisation for one or more new therapeutic indications, with a considerable clinical benefit according to the

---

[50] The answer to this question depends on what kind of changes have occurred and how important these improvements have been for the functioning of the pharmaceutical.
[51] See Article 10(1)(4) of the Medicinal Code.

scientific evaluation performed before authorisation. Such a one-year extension can be granted only once.[52]

Thus, the question arises of what the product owner has to show in order to prove a clinical benefit. How this concept should be interpreted remains unclear. However, one way of defining this concept is found in Regulation 726/2004 and Article 3(2)(1)(b), providing that a pharmaceutical will be subject to the centralised procedure if the applicant shows that the product constitutes a significant therapeutic, scientific, or technical innovation.[53] Taking into consideration that these concepts have been applied since 1995, there could be guidance available for the interpretation of 'significant clinical benefit'.

4.4.2. Separate Data Exclusivity for Significant Pre-clinical or Clinical Studies for New Therapeutic Indications

According to Article 10(5), 'where an application is made for a new indication for a well-established substance, a non-cumulative period of one year of data exclusivity shall be granted provided that significant pre-clinical or clinical studies were carried out in relation to the new indication'.

However, there is not sufficient guidance as to what constitutes a 'well-established substance'. In the German implementing legislation (Section 24(6) of the German Act on Medicinal Products), the term has been interpreted as requiring a minimum of 10 years of medicinal use. Furthermore, the Directive does not provide any interpretation guidance for the term 'significant studies' either, and it is thus uncertain how much time and how many studies are needed in order to meet the requirement.

It is important to note that this one-year extension covers pre-clinical and clinical data concerning the new therapeutic indication only, and thus data and pre-clinical data related to the first marketing authorisation application do not receive additional protection.

4.4.3. Data Exclusivity for Derivatives, New Dosages and Other Variations of the Original Pharmaceutical

According to Article 6(1)(2), marketing authorisations of 'any additional strengths, pharmaceutical forms, administration routes, presentation as well as any variations and extensions shall be considered as belonging to the same global marketing

---

[52] Since it is the same medicinal product, it cannot receive a longer term of protection than 8 + 2 + 1 years.
[53] Regulation 726/2004/EC of the European Parliament and of the Council of 31 March 2004 laying down Community procedures for the authorisation and supervision of medicinal products for human and veterinary use and establishing a European Medicines Agency (Text with EEA relevance) [2004] OJ L 136/ 1.

authorisation in particular for the purposes of Article 10(1)'. This means that after the expiration of the data exclusivity for the first-generation drug, reference can be made to test data for both the 'old' and the 'new' generation drug.

It is important to note that this does not apply for combination drugs. Article 10b requires complete pre-clinical and clinical trials for such pharmaceuticals. These are thus considered to be new products, which also means that a new market exclusivity or 8 + 2 years will be granted.

4.4.4. Extension of Data Exclusivity for Rx-to-OTC Switches

Article 74a provides that a marketing authorisation holder enjoys one additional year of data exclusivity in case a 'change of classification of a medicinal product has been authorised on the basis of significant pre-clinical and clinical trials'.[54]

The most important change of classification is that of pharmaceuticals previously sold under prescription (Rx) that are, subject to certain requirements, subsequently sold over-the-counter (OTC).[55] Since OTC pharmaceuticals are sold without the supervision of a medical practitioner, the requirements on safety and efficacy are particularly strict. In order to proceed to a change of status, the exclusion of risks listed in Article 71(1) has to be proven for the pharmaceutical. The risk of abuse by patients has to be limited and treatment without professional medical supervision must not constitute a health hazard. In order to receive the additional one year of protection, the applicant has to show that significant pre-clinical or clinical tests were performed that were directly relevant for the change of classification (such as new galenic formulations, modified doses of the drug's active ingredient, or new therapy plans).

This one year of market exclusivity covers only the new test data and does not constitute an extension of the original marketing authorisation as such (*cf* Article 10(1)(4)).

According to the 2013 NTA, a marketing authorisation application for a generic may refer to the dossier of a medicinal product authorised under Article 10(a) of the Medicinal Code. This means that a product authorised under Article 10(a) can act as a reference pharmaceutical, and that this dossier can stand on its own (both efficacy evidence and safety evidence are contained in the dossier). One question that is not answered in the NTA is whether a product authorised based on Well Established Use (WEU) would enjoy data and marketing protection. This is interesting, as WEU applications do not provide new clinical data, but are based solely on bibliographic references.

---

[54] Article 74a of the Medicinal Code.
[55] See European Commission, *A Guideline on Changing the Classification for the Supply of a Medicinal Product for Human Use* (Revision January 2006), Part 3 Data Exclusivity for data submitted to 'switch' the legal status of a medicinal product from prescription to non-prescription (change in classification).

80 Data Exclusivity

The following questions were posed by a Latvian court to the CJEU in the *Olainfarm* case:[56]

(a) Can a WEU medicinal product be used as a reference medicinal product for the purposes of an application related to a generic?
(b) Does an MA for a WEU medicinal product afford the MA holder a right to challenge the lawfulness of the authorisation of a generic which has been granted by reference to that medicinal product?

According to the Advocate General, the answers to both questions should be affirmative.[57] This would mean that the MA holder of a reference medicinal product has the right to challenge an MA application related to a generic which refers to the regulatory dossier of its product, if authorisation was granted during the period of regulatory data protection covering the reference medicinal product. At the same time, the AG stated that a generics manufacturer may submit an independent application under Article 10(a) for a WEU product. The Court concurred and answered both questions in the affirmative but chose to remain silent as regards the question if a WEU medicinal product may benefit from independent data and marketing protection.

5. The Weaknesses of the System

According to Article 10(a) of the Medicinal Code, an applicant may submit an MA application with reference made to well-established medicinal use within the Community, during at least ten years, with recognised efficacy and an acceptable level of safety.[58] In the majority of such cases, results of pre-clinical and clinical trials are published in scientific journals. Generics companies have attempted to use scientific literature and references in order to circumvent data and marketing protection.[59]

In a case known as *Plavix*, the generics manufacturer (Yes Pharmaceutical) was able to obtain an MA from the German regulatory authority (BfArM) on the basis of a bibliographic application, before the expiry of the Plavix data protection.[60] In its application, Yes Pharmaceutical referred to a variety of documents, including 10 years of WEU of the active substance, starting from the date of

---

[56] Judgment of the Court (Fifth Chamber) of 23 October 2014, *Olainfarm AS v Latvijas Republikas Veselības ministrija and Zāļu valsts aģentūra*, C-104/13, EU:C:2014:2316.
[57] Opinion of Advocate General Wall C104-13, ECLI:EU:C:2014:342.
[58] See also Annex 1 of the Medicinal Code.
[59] EU law places originators of medicinal products under the obligation to publish the results of pre-clinical and clinical trials within one year from the end of these trials. See para 4.2 of the 'Commission Guideline – Guidance on posting and publication of result-related information on clinical trials in relation to the implementation of Article 57(2) of Regulation 726/2004/EC' (2012/C/302/03).
[60] Decision of the Cologne Administrative Court of 25 July 2008, Case No 7 L 988/08.

publication of a pivotal clinical trial (the CAPRIE study), data obtained from the FDA in the United States, and the EPAR report.[61] In reality, all these documents encompassed data submitted for the MA of Plavix, which were thus covered by data exclusivity.

The Commission was very critical of the German authority's approach and stated that allowing this would mean that generics manufacturers were not only able to circumvent data and marketing protection exclusivity, but were also rewarded when they did so.

6. Data Exclusivity for Paediatric Medicines that are Not Patent-Protected

The 'Paediatric Use Marketing Authorisation' (PUMA) was introduced by means of Regulation 1901/2006. This is a new category of marketing authorisation that covers only medicinal products for paediatric use.

In order to be granted a PUMA, a pharmaceutical must be provided in doses that are adapted to the needs of the paediatric population or as special dosage form of a pharmaceutical used in adults. A PUMA holder is granted an (8 + 2)-year market exclusivity (Article 38 of Regulation 1901/2006) and the protection covers only the paediatric application of the pharmaceutical. The requirements for the granting of protection follow the same rules as for other marketing authorisations, as stipulated in Articles 10(1) and 14(11) of Regulation 726/2004.

7. Concluding Remarks

The objective of the data exclusivity is not to incentivise innovation as such, but to provide some protection of the commercial value of the often very costly pre-clinical and clinical trials. Thus, the ultimate objective is to guarantee safety and efficacy. No qualitative requirements are imposed – the product does not need to be better than those already on the market). However, the system includes some incentives for better versions of existing pharmaceuticals, as an extra year of protection is granted for pharmaceuticals with proven significant benefits.

The exclusive rights are not exercised by the MA holder as such, but by the public authority; thus, complaints on how these rights are applied can only be directed at the national MA authority.[62]

---

[61] The EPAR report is the scientific report of the EMA regarding the clinical data and other data submitted by the originator company when applying for MA.

[62] It is the agency that is not allowed to grant MA to a third party on the basis of the dossier of another MA covered by data exclusivity.

It is important to note that not all Member States provide the procedural options necessary in order to litigate on the basis of a regulatory right. In the *Olainfarm* case,[63] the CJEU clarified that not providing the means to defend a regulatory right constitutes an EU law violation. In particular in jurisdictions where originators previously enjoyed very few or no possibilities to challenge a marketing authorisation for a generic granted as a result of infringement of data and marketing protection, the *Olainfarm* case constituted a very important development.

One of the issues that remains open is what the obligation of the CMS is in relation to the examination already concluded by the RMS in respect of the data protection potentially violated by a generics company. One plausible interpretation is that the CMS is under a legal obligation to conduct an independent assessment of each application related to a generic, in order to guarantee the most solid regulatory data protection possible.[64] This would also include an obligation to check that the reference pharmaceutical has been granted a marketing authorisation in accordance with EU law.[65]

Data exclusivity undoubtedly provides a form of protection for medicinal products. Medicinal products that constitute sub-patentable inventions may resort to data protection as a means of keeping a dominant position on the market and delaying the entrance of generics. Even pharmaceutical products that enjoy patent protection may find data exclusivity to provide a very effective form of protection. Generic versions of a pharmaceutical that do not use the patented technology and thus do not constitute an infringement could be covered by data exclusivity on the basis of bioequivalence.

Data exclusivity is an important, if unorthodox, form of exclusivity, with definite value for the pharmaceutical industry. Its interrelation with the regulatory rights discussed in this book is obvious. The Paediatric Regulation has challenged its scope with the PUMA procedure, while it shares objectives and background with the SPC Regulation, in wanting to compensate for the time and money invested in the MA procedure.[66] The Orphan Drugs Regulation proposes a kind of exclusivity shaped on the basis of data protection, while the interactions with the provisions of the ATMP Regulation are not yet exhaustively explored.

Thus, data exclusivity is a unique mixture of a background to the regulatory rights discussed in this book, an important component thereof, and a parallel right thereto. Regardless, it is an exclusive right that cannot be overlooked when discussing the effectiveness of the system as a whole.

---

[63] Judgment of the Court (Fifth Chamber) of 23 October 2014, *Olainfarm AS v Latvijas Republikas Veselības ministrija and Zāļu valsts aģentūra*, C-104/13, EU:C:2014:2316.

[64] In fact, an opposite interpretation would constitute an erroneous interpretation of the *Synthon* case (*Synthon BV*, C-452/06, EU:C:2008:565) which concerns only the scientific data and assessment made by the CMS.

[65] See, for instance, the Judgment of the Court (First Chamber) of 18 June 2009, *The Queen, on the Application of Generics (UK) Ltd v Licensing Authority*, C-527/07, EU:C:2009:379.

[66] The SPC has a slightly different focus, compensating for the patent protection term lost because of MA proceedings.

4

The Supplementary Protection Certificate

1. Background to the Legal Framework

R&D costs in the pharmaceutical industry are high and the time it takes to put a new medicinal product on the market is non-negligible. Although the patent system provides for an exclusive right that compensates adequately for the time and effort necessary to create a new product in most industries, the 20 years provided by the system are deemed not to be enough in the pharmaceutical sector. In fact, during the past three decades, the development of regulatory legal framework has created an additional hurdle for the innovators of the pharmaceutical industry and a cost that is difficult to compensate for through the exclusivity offered during the patent term. This is often further strengthened, as the patent application is handed in as early as possible in the R&D process in order to avoid concerns related to novelty and inventive steps. At the same time, the marketing authorisation procedure has become stricter and much more demanding, which means that the product owner has to spend a number of years (and resources) on the pre-clinical and clinical trials necessary for a complete marketing authorisation dossier.

In order to compensate for the effective term of patent protection that is lost during the marketing authorisation procedure, jurisdictions introduced different patent extension mechanisms. The Supplementary Protection Certificate (SPC), introduced in EU law in 1992, by means of the 1769/1992 EU Regulation, has been considered an important tool for bringing a desirable harmonisation to the system of patent extension for pharmaceutical products. The system was created in order to compensate for the time lost due to lengthy market authorisation procedures.[1] The SPC Regulation was amended a number of times before being replaced by a new codified version, Regulation (EC) No 469/2009.[2]

---

[1] Council Regulation 1768/92/EEC of 18 June 1992 concerning the creation of a supplementary protection certificate for medicinal products [1992] OJ L 182/1, as amended Regulation 1901/2006/EC of the European Parliament and of the Council of 12 December 2006 on medicinal products for paediatric use and amending Regulation 1768/92/EEC, Directive 2001/20/EC, Directive 2001/83/EC and Regulation 726/2004/EC (Text with EEA relevance) [2006] OJ L 378/1.

[2] See Regulation 469/2009/EC of the European Parliament and of the Council of 6 May 2009 concerning the supplementary protection certificate for medicinal products (Codified version) (Text with EEA relevance) [2009] OJ L 152/1;

84 *The Supplementary Protection Certificate*

An SPC grants a *sui generis* right that has a double basis, partly in the patent system, partly in the regulatory system. Although the SPC system is regulated by an EU Regulation it does not provide for any centralised grant procedure and the only way to acquire an SPC is by applying on a country-by-country basis.

The duration of an SPC is equal to the period elapsed between patent filing and granting of the first MA in the EEA,[3] less five years, and subject to a maximum duration of five years. The Paediatric Regulation provides for a six-month extension to the SPC term for certain products on which trials are completed in accordance with an approved Paediatric Investigation Plan, and regardless of whether the results are positive or negative.[4]

Obtaining up to five years of protection extension made this new legal institution a very attractive resort for pharmaceutical companies, whose patented drugs faced competition from generic alternatives directly upon patent protection expiry. By 2011, 14,620 SPC applications had been handed in, in EU countries, with the majority of applicants in France, Italy, the United Kingdom, Germany, Belgium, the Netherlands, Sweden, Austria and Switzerland. Taking the structure of the pharmaceutical industry into consideration, it is not surprising that the group of applicants is dominated by a few well-known pharmaceutical companies.[5]

Despite the fact that it introduced a completely new system, the SPC Regulation had what one could call a harmonious first period of application. The Regulation included a number of rather vague and poorly defined terms and concepts, but there were very few cases from the national courts or the CJEU relating to the scope and definition of the Regulation's central terms and provisions. While the Regulation had an uneventful childhood, it has experienced a very turbulent adolescence in recent years. New cases are constantly being added to the case law related to the SPC Regulation, while the system does not seem to be getting any clearer.

Major questions related to the application of the Regulation and the scope of the protection granted have been the favourite subject of both national and CJEU decisions. They could be summarised in the following three questions, directly related to the patent rights on which they are based: (a) What is a product in the meaning of the Regulation? (b) What is meant by 'protected by a basic patent'? (c) What happens when a single basic patent protects more than one 'product', or where one 'product' is covered by multiple basic patents? Other questions have

---

See also Regulation 1610/96/EC of the European Parliament and of the Council of 23 July 1996 concerning the creation of a supplementary protection certificate for plant protection products [1996] OJ L 198/30.

[3] The European Economic Area, comprising the 27 Member States of the EU plus Iceland, Lichtenstein and Norway.

[4] Regulation 1901/2006/EC, amending Regulation 1768/92, Directive 2001/20/EC, and Regulation 726/2004.

[5] Among applicants we find Novartis, GlaxoSmithKline, Bayer, Aventis, Janssen, BMS, and AstraZeneca. See A Pastor, SPC News 26, May 2011, 1 (applications from January 1991 to December 2011 published until the end of April 2012).

concerned the marketing authorisation, with a primary focus on what constitutes a 'valid authorisation' and what constitutes the 'first authorisation'.

In order to see all the important perspectives, challenges and potential of the SPC Regulation, it should not be read in isolation. To make a correct interpretation of the provisions of the Regulation, one needs to read it in conjunction with other legislative acts, such as the Plant Protection Regulation, whose provisions apply mutatis mutandis to the SPC Regulation.[6] This is not apparent to the reader of the SPC Regulation, and no attempt to incorporate these provisions has been made, not even during the 2009 revision process. Naturally, one should also take into account the provisions of the Paediatric Regulation, since it provides for a six-month extension of the SPC when certain requirements are fulfilled. The maximum duration of an SPC is five years and six months, which is not easy to see when reading the SPC Regulation in isolation. Issues such as the negative SPC term stipulated in recent case law[7] reveal the difficulties with the determination of the SPC term of protection and interplay with the Paediatric Regulation. Furthermore, one needs to read the SPC Regulation in light of the EEA Agreement, which while not incorporated in the text of the Regulation is still of relevance for its interpretation. Interpreting the SPC Regulation has been a difficult endeavour and the CJEU has expressed the view that the text of the Regulation needs to be subject to a teleological interpretation.[8] The objective of the Regulation is to 'ensure sufficient protection to encourage pharmaceutical research'. Further assistance to the interpretation of the Regulation may be found in the Commission's original proposal for the SPC Regulation (SPC Explanatory Memorandum), emphasising that 'all pharmaceutical research provided that it leads to a new invention that can be patented … must be encouraged … and must be able to be given an SPC'.

Current developments related to the entry into force of the Unitary Patent Package (UPP), will naturally have an impact on the SPC system. SPCs are national rights, connected to national basic patents that provide valuable protection for pharmaceutical products when the patent right has expired. It is thus of major importance to clarify how these will be used and enforced under the framework of the Unitary Patent Package.[9] It remains unclear whether SPCs will also take the form of unitary rights or whether the existing system of national SPCs will

[6] Regulation 1610/96/EC of the European Parliament and of the Council of 23 July 1996 concerning the creation of a supplementary protection certificate for plant protection products [1996] OJ L 198/30. See in particular recitals 10–14.

[7] See Judgment of the Court (Second Chamber) of 8 December 2011, *Merck Sharp & Dohme Corp v Deutsches Patent- und Markenamt*, C-125/10, EU:C:2011:812.

[8] See, for instance, judgment of the Court (Fourth Chamber) of 19 July 2012, *Neurim Pharmaceuticals (1991) Ltd v Comptroller-General of Patents*, C-130/11, EU:C:2012:489.

[9] One of the important questions that has been raised in the text of the Regulation with regard to SPCs is the right to 'opt out'. According to Rule 5.2 of the Rules of Procedure, an 'opt-out' automatically extends to an SPC that is issued for a product protected by the 'opted out' patent. Furthermore, Rule 5.1 provides that a standard European patent that has expired can be 'opted out', with any SPC granted based on that patent automatically being 'opted out' as a result. However, if an assignment has been made, so that the owner of the SPC is different from the proprietor of the patent on which it is based, the SPC owner must lodge the 'opt-out' application together with the patent proprietor for the 'opt-out' to be effective.

be adapted to cover unitary patents as an alternative to basic patents. Choosing to preserve the national character of SPCs, could deprive the unitary patent of some of its major advantages.[10] The way SPCs on unitary patents will work raises other very important issues, such as the question of marketing authorisations and whether these should be centralised, decentralised, or simply national. The importance of SPCs for the pharmaceutical industry in Europe, combined with the obscurities that its application already entails, creates a pressing need for further clarifications in the field.[11]

Apart from these new challenges brought by means of the UPP, the SPC legal framework is under considerable pressure, which of course becomes obvious when looking into the number and the complexity of recent CJEU rulings, relating to its application and interpretation. Case law reveals that more than 20 years after its entry into force, there is still significant uncertainty as to the meaning and scope of the Regulation's central terms and provisions. While parts of this cumbersome interpretation process have their source in the problematic original drafting of the text of the Regulation, other parts are a side effect of technological advances in the field of pharmaceutical innovation. This calls into question if this Regulation is adequate to protect modern pharmaceuticals and to support the modern pharmaceutical industry.

2. The Legal Framework

2.1. Requirements for Protection

The application for SPC protection is filed with the patent office of the Member State which granted the basic patent. In order to be processed, the application has to be filed either within six months of the decision in a Member State to place the product on the market as a medicinal product, or – where the authorisation effective in a Member State is granted before the basic patent is granted in such Member State – within six months from the date of approval of the patent.

In the *Abbott Laboratories* case, concerning the deadline for an application filed at the UK Intellectual Property Office, the UKIPO held that the six-month deadline started on the date of the authorisation and not the date on which the marketing authorisation was published.[12] On the other hand, the sixth-month period in respect of marketing authorisations granted under the centralised procedure

---

[10] While unitary patents provide for a unitary exclusive right, the national SPCs would contribute to the continued tradition of national rights and would work in the opposite direction to the general goal of the Unitary Patent Package.

[11] Margareta Ydreskog, 'Opting Out of the Unified Patent Court and 'Opting In'. Reflections from a Patent Attorney Perspective' [2014] *Nordiskt Immateriellt Rättsskydd* 104–06. See also, from Swedish case law, PBR 11-087 (Sevelamerkarbonat), stating that an SPC for a product does not preclude SPC for a derivative.

[12] *Abbott Laboratories' SPC Application*, Patent Office (Mr R J Walker): July 25, 2002 [2004] RPC 20.

may start with the date when the applicant was notified of the approval, at least in some European countries. The CJEU has furthermore ruled on the meaning of the date of first authorisation in Article 13(1) SPC Regulation. Authorisation to proceed with clinical trials is not a marketing authorisation.[13]

Article 3 of the SPC Regulation poses a limitation: the product shall not be subject to another SPC. However, this limitation has a very narrow scope, covering only the SPCs granted in the specific Member State. The application must include information on the marketing authorisation and on the basic patent such as: the registration number of the basic patent, the title of the invention, the number and date of the marketing authorisation, and a copy of the authorisation under which the product is identified. If the market authorisation provided is not the first authorisation for placing the product on the market, the applicant is required to submit information regarding the identity of the product which was the subject of the first authorisation in the Community, the legal provision under which that authorisation took place, and a copy of the notice of the authorisation published in the appropriate official publication.[14]

Where the applicant is not the holder of the first marketing authorisation, there is no obligation to submit a copy of the marketing authorisation. The national authority granting the SPC can contact the national authority that granted the first marketing authorisation and request a copy. The SPC application is published and the applicant is informed about potential weaknesses of the application or requirements of completion and given the possibility to complete the application or make amendments. If these amendments and new documents are not submitted in time, the application will be rejected.

The term 'medicinal product' is defined in Article 1(a) of the SPC Regulation as 'any substance or combination of substances presented for treating or preventing disease in human beings or animals and any substance or combination of substances which may be administered to human beings or animals with a view to making a medical diagnosis or to restoring, correcting or modifying physiological functions in humans or in animals'. This definition differs from the one provided under Article 1(2) of the Directive 2001/83/EC (The Medicinal Code). In the latter provision, it is stated that a medicinal product is one that exerts 'a pharmacological, immunological or metabolic action'. The impact of the difference in the two definitions was analysed in a decision of the UK Intellectual Property Office in the *Cerus* case, concerning the application for an SPC covering a medical device.[15] The UKIPO concluded that the difference in wording was not material, since a medicinal product is eligible for an SPC only if it has been granted an MA under

---

[13] Judgment of the Court (Eighth Chamber) of 6 October 2015, *Seattle Genetics Inc v Österreichisches Patentamt*, C-471/14, EU:C:2015:659.

[14] Frantzeska Papadopoulou, 'Supplementary Protection Certificates: Still a Grey Area?' [2016] 11 *Journal of Intellectual Property Law and Practice*, 5, 372–81.

[15] Intellectual Property Office, 'Applicant: Cerus Corporation Issue: Whether applications SPC/GB/07/043 and SPC/GB/07/044 meet the requirements of Article 2 and Article 3(b) of the Regulation', BL O/14/14.

the Medicinal Code. Thus, in practice, the meaning and interpretation of the two definitions coincide.

It is important to note that the SPC protects a product and not an invention.[16] The choice of the term 'product', which has been criticised as rather unfortunate, since it is not equivalent to either 'invention' or 'medicinal product', was based on the fact that it was considered to be the closest 'terminological' bridge between the patent system and the MA legal framework.[17] A definition of the term 'product' is provided in Article 1(b) of the SPC Regulation, stating that it is 'the active ingredient or combination of active ingredients of a medicinal product' and should not be confused with the product specified in the marketing authorisation. In fact, the SPC covers only the active ingredient or the combination of active ingredients covered by the marketing authorisation, not ingredients (or all active ingredients) covered by the basic patent.[18] An SPC is granted for one product, although minor improvements to an existing product (eg providing a use as an ester or salt) will be covered by the first SPC. The lack of European harmonisation of substantive patent law makes national legislation important for the operation of the SPC and thus contributes to its fragmented application. Therefore, uniform interpretation of the text of the Regulation has proven to be a challenge, and the CJEU has a crucial role in SPC-related referral questions. No definition of the term 'active substance' is provided under the Regulation, but the CJEU is clear on the fact that this concept needs to be interpreted restrictively.

Since the SPC protection is based on the term 'product', its definition is naturally of central importance. It is unsurprising that its interpretation has given rise to extensive case law. Not only the granting of the SPC depends on the definition of this term, but also its validity. In the case *Massachusetts Institute of Technology* (*MIT*), the CJEU clarified that the term 'product' for the purposes of the SPC Regulation was to be interpreted to cover only 'active substances' and 'active ingredients'.[19] The terms 'active substance' and 'active ingredient' will only include substances that have an effect on the animal or human body. In this specific case, the applicant, MIT, attempted to argue that a new product was formed by means of the combination of active ingredients and an excipient (a substance that does not have its own medicinal effect). The Court was of the opposite opinion, even in cases where this excipient improves the toxicological profile of the product to such an extent that it could in fact be considered to bestow it with a new indication.

The narrow interpretation of the term 'product' in *MIT* was partly overturned in a later case, *Yissum*. In this case, the active ingredient had been the subject of a basic patent for one medical indication, while the substance itself was the subject of

---

[16] See Article 2 of the SPC Regulation.

[17] Article 1(b) of the Regulation 1901/2006/EC. See also Edward H Mazer, 'Supplementary Protection Certificates in the European Economic Community' [1993] 48 *Food & Drug Law Journal*, 4, 571–74.

[18] See also Article 4 of the SPC Regulation and the question of whether an SPC may be granted for further uses of a known pharmaceutical (for which an SPC had previously been granted).

[19] Judgment of the Court (Second Chamber) of 4 May 2006, *Massachusetts Institute of Technology*, C-431/04, EU:C:2006:291.

an earlier marketing authorisation for another medical indication. The CJEU held that where there is a new medical use of a known medicinal product, this new use will not fall under the definition of the product.[20] In *GlaxoSmithKline Biologicals SA* (*GSK*), the Court provided once more that the term 'product' was to be interpreted narrowly and stated that an 'active ingredient' could not be a substance that has no therapeutic effect on its own and that the combination of such a substance with an active ingredient was not to be considered to be a 'combination of active ingredients'.[21] In the case *Arne Forsgren v Österreichisches Patentamt*, the Austrian Court asked the CJEU whether a protein (covered by a basic patent) that is bound to other active ingredients in a medicinal product but retains its own activity is an active ingredient within the meaning of Article 1(b). The Court stated that the question as to whether or not a substance is an active ingredient will depend on whether it has its own pharmacological, immunological, or metabolic action, independently of any covalent binding with other active ingredients.[22] If this is the case, then the fact that it is covalently bound to another active ingredient will not prevent it from receiving SPC protection. On the other hand, the therapeutic effect of the covalently bound active substance must be covered by the marketing authorisation.[23] However, what is meant by 'covered' will be an issue for the courts to decide on a case-by-case basis.[24]

2.2. The SPC Application

Although the SPC Regulation is clear in that the SPC is granted to the patent holder, the question is who is able to apply. Here, the practices of Member States differ. In certain major jurisdictions (Germany, Denmark, France, etc), the application may not be filed by a licensee even if the patent holder has granted its express authorisation.[25] In some other countries, such as the United Kingdom, a licensee may submit an SPC application. However, if the SPC application is approved, the

---

[20] Order of the Court (Eighth Chamber) of 17 April 2007, *Yissum Research and Development Company of the Hebrew University of Jerusalem v Comptroller-General of Patents*, C-202/05, EU:C:2007:214.

[21] Order of the Court (Eighth Chamber) of 14 November 2013, *Glaxosmithkline Biologicals SA and Glaxosmithkline Biologicals, Niederlassung der Smithkline Beecham Pharma GmbH & Co. KG v Comptroller General of Patents, Designs and Trade Marks*, C-210/13, EU:C:2013:762.

[22] See also the decision related to the implementation of the Plant Protection Regulation namely the Judgment of the Court (Third Chamber) of 19 June 2014, *Bayer CropScience AG v Deutsches Patent- und Markenamt*, C-11/13, EU:C:2014:2010 where the meaning of 'active substance, covered by the MA' was clarified.

[23] Judgment of the Court (Eighth Chamber) of 15 January 2015, *Arne Forsgren v Österreichisches Patentamt*, C-631/13, EU:C:2015:13.

[24] This means that the definition of the term 'product' is even narrower than that of 'medicinal product'.

[25] See, for instance, Supplementary Protection Certificates in https://e-courses.epo.org/wbts_int/litigation/SPCs.pdf [Accessed on 1 June 2020].

90   *The Supplementary Protection Certificate*

SPC right will be owned by the patent holder. This rule is so rigid that in most jurisdictions, if there has been a transfer of patent ownership and this transfer is not registered in the national patent office, the SPC may only be applied for and granted to the registered patent holder. Some national patent offices allow the SPC to be applied for and granted to the assignee on condition that it can prove that a transfer of rights has taken place.

With regard to multiple proprietors of the same patent, most jurisdictions require that all patent holders submit jointly the SPC application or through a common representative.[26] On the other hand, certain national patent authorities do not require that the patent holder is also the holder of the MA. In fact, there is no provision in the SPC Regulation that requires that there is some link or identity between the patent holder and the holder of the MA.[27] Lastly, the requirement of submission of a copy of the MA may be remedied by means of the national patent authority contacting the MA authority or the online registers.[28]

There are also certain differences in how national patent authorities review the description of the product for which SPC is sought.

CJEU case law is clear on the fact that in order for a first market authorisation to be considered a basis for the granting of an SPC, it has to be granted in accordance with the EC Directive 2001/83. However, a certain complication can occur when the first authorisation takes place in a non-EU Member State and that MA is automatically recognised in an EEA state, for instance when a market authorisation granted in Switzerland is automatically recognised in Liechtenstein (EEA state). In the *Novartis* case, the CJEU provided that the Swiss MA was the first MA for the purposes of calculating the SPC duration.[29] However, due to continuing divergent national interpretations, the English Patents Court referred the *AstraZeneca* case to the CJEU.[30] The medicinal product in question (gefitinib) had been authorised in Switzerland under a fast-track procedure in March 2004, but the authorisation was subsequently suspended. A centralised MA was granted in June 2009 and the Swiss suspension was lifted on 8 December 2010. The CJEU confirmed that the pharmaceutical in question was eligible for SPC protection, but with regard to the duration of the SPC protection, the Court stated that it had to be calculated with reference to the Swiss MA, since this was the first MA.[31]

---

[26] In fact, in the Netherlands, the SPC application is always submitted by a common representative who does not have to show that it has been granted the mandate to act on behalf of all patent holders.

[27] In Germany and France, differing ownership between the holder of the patent and the holder of the MA may be relevant for the substantive examination of the SPC application.

[28] Greece, Lithuania and Portugal reject applications that do not have a copy of the MA.

[29] Judgment of the Court (Second Chamber) of 21 April 2005, *Novartis AG, University College London and Institute of Microbiology and Epidemiology v Comptroller-General of Patents, Designs and Trade Marks for the United Kingdom and Ministre de l'Économie v Millennium Pharmaceuticals Inc*, C-207/03 and C-252/03, EU:C:2005:245.

[30] Order of the Court (Eighth Chamber) of 17 January 2014, *AstraZeneca AB v Comptroller General of Patents*, C-617/12, EU:C:2014:28.

[31] For an elaboration of this see section 5 below.

In *Neurim*, the Court opened for more generous interpretation of what constitutes 'first authorisation'. As has been stated previously, Neurim's UK SPC application was rejected on the grounds that the 'product' that would be the subject of the SPC was the same as an earlier medicinal product which had been granted an MA in 2003. The Court stated that the previous MA did not preclude a second SPC on the new use of the same substance. In fact, the Court ruled that the 'first' MA to place the product on the market as a medicinal product was to be understood as the first MA to fall within the limits of protection of the basic patent relied upon for the SPC application (the first MA to infringe the basic patent). This is a very broad approach to Article 3(d), since it limits the definition of the term 'product' to cover only a particular new therapeutic application of the product which falls within the scope of the patent relied upon for the purposes of Article 3(a).[32]

However attractive this interpretation might have been for patentees, it seems hard to reconcile it with Article 3(c) and its interpretation in light of the Plant Protection Regulation (one SPC per patentee per product). Article 3(c) provides that in order to be granted an SPC, the product cannot be subject to an earlier certificate.[33] The same provision is found in Article 3 of the Regulation 1610/96 for Plant Protection products, but is also complemented by the provision in Article 3(2) stating the following: 'the holder of more than one patent for the same product shall not be granted more than one certificate for that product. However, where two or more applications concerning the same product and emanating from two or more holders of different patents are pending, one certificate for this product may be issued to each of these holders.'[34]

2.3. The Relation between the SPC Application and the MA

There is no doubt that there is a strong relation – if not dependence – between the subject of the SPC application and the subject of the MA. The question is what the level of dependence is, and whether and to what extent any mismatches between the subjects of SPC and the granted MA may influence the fate of the SPC application.

The initial interpretation of Article 3(b) was that in order for an SPC to be granted the product definition in the SPC application had to be identical to that

---

[32] This is also why the CJEU chose to re-evaluate the *Neurim* ruling in the subsequent *Abraxis* and *Santen* rulings.

[33] V-Cumaran Arunasalam and Filip De Corte, 'Supplementary Protection Certificates for Plant Protection Products: The Story of "The Ugly Duckling"' [2016] 11 *Journal of Intellectual Property Law & Practice*, 11 833–40; Euros Jones, 'On the Relevance of Supplementary Plant Protection Certificates on the Basis of Marketing Authorizations for Combination Products' [2011] *GRUR International* 1017.

[34] Judgment of the Court (Third Chamber) of 19 June 2014, *Bayer CropScience AG v Deutsches Patent- und Markenamt*, C-11/13, EU:C:2014:2010.

in the MA. This approach was abandoned in the CJEU rulings in the *Medeva*[35] and *Georgetown I* cases. In *Medeva*, the Court ruled that the MA requirement was satisfied when authorisation was granted for the product for which SPC was sought. In *Georgetown I*, an MA for substances A + B was considered to be a valid marketing authorisation for the SPC protection of product A. This is also the MA that will be the grounds for calculation of the duration of the certificate.[36] The application and interpretation of these cases in national law seems unproblematic. In the Swedish Court of Patent Appeals case,[37] the Court ruled that *Medeva* was not applicable when an earlier MA had been granted for A + B and a certificate has been requested for A only, on the basis of a more recent MA granted for the active ingredient A. According to the Swedish court, the combination of substances in the earlier MA was a different product in terms of Article 1(b) of the Regulation, and the later MA containing only A had a different composition and could not be considered to be the same product.[38]

Another important perspective of Article 3(b) is whether the MA must be in force on the date the SPC is requested. Member States have answered to this question in different ways, and one of the explanations for that is the fact that the translation of the text of the SPC Regulation into different languages opens for differing interpretations.[39] Naturally, this is an issue of limited practical importance, given the fact that it is the granting of the MA that forms the basis for the deadline that the applicants have to relate to in order to apply for SPC protection. Although it is theoretically possible that the MA will be revoked or invalidated during this time, this will not have occurred often in practice.

2.4. Procedural Rules: A Case for National Accommodation

Article 19(1) Regulation 469/2009 and Article 18(1) Regulation 1610/96 provide that national law applies to the procedural issues that are not regulated by the Regulation itself. Furthermore, national law is applied where issues of substantive law are left out of the Regulations. Due to the lack of implementing regulations and common guidelines, details on the examination procedures are addressed in the guidelines of national authorities.

In the field of SPC applications, EU Member States have chosen to proceed in different ways. Some have chosen to develop national guidelines, while others

---

[35] Judgment of the Court (Fourth Chamber) of 24 November 2011, *Medeva BV v Comptroller General of Patents, Designs and Trademarks*, C-322/10, EU:C:2011:773.
[36] See Article 13 of the SPC Regulation.
[37] *Sandoz AS v Searle* PMÖ 12172-18.
[38] The District Court of Düsseldorf limited the scope of *Medeva* providing that this applies to combinations, but not to monotherapy products. See District Court of Düsseldorf, Decision of 15 November 2012, 4b O 123/12 (2012) open Jur 2013, 3044.
[39] Spanish, Italian and French versions seem to require a valid MA, while the English version opens for a more flexible interpretation.

base the rules of examination of SPC applications on other internal procedural guidelines. Others do not hesitate to implement the national guidelines of other Member States when faced with new or particularly complicated issues.[40]

3. The Subject of Protection

3.1. Complex Pharmaceuticals

The technologies with which modern pharmaceuticals are developed today are quite different from those used at the time the text of the Regulation was drafted. Modern pharmaceuticals are in most the cases based on biological products, second medical indications of already known substances, or combination products. This creates certain challenges in the application of the SPC Regulation, in particular with regard to the definition of the subject of protection.

The provision determining the terms and conditions for the granting of an SPC is Article 3(c), which is also one of the most litigated provisions of the Regulation. According to Article 3(c), only one certificate may be granted for a basic patent; furthermore, this cannot have been subject to a previous certificate.[41] In the *Biogen* case, the CJEU provided that 'where a product is protected by a number of basic patents in force, which may belong to a number of patent holders, each of these patents may be designated as a basis for the grant of a certificate'.[42] This meant that the basic assumption of the system, that one patent may only lead to one SPC, was no longer true and the floor was open for more generous interpretations. In the same case, the Advocate General (AG) proposed a solution, namely to either allow the patent owner to acquire new certificates in respect of new products which rely on its invention and which are authorised to be marketed as medicinal products, or to extend the protection of an existing certificate to cover other new applications.[43] The AG stated that 'it is nowhere stated that a patent can be subject to only one certificate, or of a certificate only in respect on one medical product, as the same patent may be used for widely differing medicinal products'.[44] In 2011, yet another CJEU ruling came – much to the disappointment of those who hoped for a broad interpretation of Article 3(c) of the Regulation: 'where a patent protects a product, in accordance with Article 3(c) of the Regulation No 469/2009, only

---

[40] See European Commission, *Study on the Legal Aspects of Supplementary Protection Certificates in the EU*, Final Report [2018] Max Planck Institute for Innovation and Competition 484.
[41] Judgment of the Court (Sixth Chamber) of 23 January 1997, *Biogen Inc v Smithkline Beecham Biologicals*, C-181/95, EU:C:1997:32.
[42] Ibid, para 28.
[43] AG Fennelly's Opinion, C-181/95, EU:C:1996:370, para 53.
[44] See n 38 (*Biogen*, C-181/95, EU:C:1997:32); See also judgment of the Court (Third Chamber) of 3 September 2009, *AHP Manufacturing BV v Bureau voor de Industriële Agendum*, C-482/07, EU:C:2009:501.

one certificate may be granted for that basic patent'.[45] It was feared that this ruling would contribute to a return to the 'one patent, one SPC' rule.

Given the importance of bringing clarity to the meaning and scope of Article 3(c), it was obvious that the referral questions that could be brought to the CJEU on the specific matter were not exhausted. In 2013, two CJEU cases made noteworthy contributions to this end. In the first case, Sanofi obtained an SPC for Irbesartan and subsequently for the combination Irbesartan and Hydrochlorothiazide (the 'combination SPC') based on the same basic patent. Actavis challenged the validity of the Sanofi Combination SPC, arguing, inter alia, that the SPC had been granted based on the same patent as the Irbesartan SPC, which would by contrary to Article 3(c), as this has been interpreted in *Medeva*.[46] Actavis provided that if an SPC had already been granted for the active ingredient A, which is the core of the inventive advance of the patent, the grant of an SPC for the combination of A with another ingredient B, which is covered by the MA but not by the basic patent, is precluded. The second important case was *Georgetown II*, in which Georgetown applied for the granting of a series of SPCs concerning active ingredients that were either proteins of single HPV types or combinations of proteins from different HPV types. All SPC applications were supported by the same basic patent and two MAs for the virus-like particles of the recombinant L1.[47] The CJEU was thus to consider whether the existence of an SPC covering a combination product, based on an MA for this combination product, precluded the granting of SPCs directed at the individual active ingredients in the combination product. The Court clarified that it is possible to acquire an SPC on the specific active ingredients on condition that even these were individually also protected by the patent.

At the same time, these two cases stated that where a first SPC protects an active ingredient either isolated or in combination, it is not possible to obtain further SPCs for the same active ingredient in combination with another active ingredient, if the other active ingredient is not protected by the basic patent.[48]

On 12 March 2015, the CJEU ruling in *Actavis v Boehringer* partially confirmed previous case law, while at the same time raising a new interesting question.[49] Boehringer was granted an SPC for the single active ingredient, Telmisartan, which is used in the treatment of high blood pressure. On the basis of the same patent and for a subsequent market authorisation, Boehringer was granted a new SPC for the combination of Telmisartan and the diuretic hydrocholthiazide (HCTZ).

---

[45] Judgment of the Court (Fourth Chamber) of 24 November 2011, *Medeva BV v Comptroller General of Patents, Designs and Trademarks*, C-322/10, EU:C:2011:773.

[46] Ibid.

[47] Judgment of the Court (Third Chamber) of 12 December 2013, *Georgetown University v Octrooicentrum Nederland*, C-484/12, EU:C:2013:828.

[48] It is not possible even if this active ingredient has been referred to in general terms in the wording of the claims, if it is not explicitly covered by the patent claims.

[49] Judgment of the Court (Eighth Chamber) of 12 March 2015, *Actavis Group PTC EHF and Actavis UK Ltd v Boehringer Ingelheim Pharma GmbH & Co. KG*, C-577/13, EU:C:2015:165.

When obtaining the new SPC, Boehringer added a new claim to its initial patent, in which both active ingredients were mentioned. Actavis contested the validity of the 'combination SPC' to the UK High Court, and the case was referred to the CJEU, which had the task of clarifying the extent to which Article 3(c) of the SPC Regulation precluded the granting of multiple SPCs, when these were based on the same basic patent. Further, the Court was to determine whether it was allowable to amend the basic patent after granting, in order to comply with Article 3(a). The first question is almost identical to the question answered in the *Actavis* ruling. The second *Actavis v Boehringer* question was brought to CJEU for the first time. With regard to the first referral question, the Court ruled in conformity with the earlier *Actavis* ruling.[50] Boehringer's argument was that the facts in the specific case were not the same as in *Actavis*, since both substances A and B were specified in the wording of the claim, and thus should be considered to be independently protected as such by the basic patent. However, according to the CJEU, in order for an SPC to be granted for an active ingredient, that active ingredient must constitute the subject of the invention covered by the basic patent. However, the decision does not specify how the 'subject of the invention' is to be defined and how it relates to the 'core inventive advance' test from the earlier *Actavis* case. If the CJEU was referring to the same term as previously, the choice of a differing terminology was highly unfortunate. The Court chose not to explain what was meant when stating that although substance B and the combination fell under the scope of the claim of the basic patent, it did not constitute the subject of the patent. The Court chose not to answer the second question, relating to the amendment of post-grant patent claims, thus leaving space for further CJEU contributions.

These very important rulings of the CJEU have not exhausted the list of relevant questions relating to the interpretation of Article 3(c). A general conclusion that could be drawn is that where a basic patent covers an active ingredient alone or in combination, and a market authorisation covers the active ingredient, it also covers the use of the active ingredient in a fixed combination. However, the granting of a new SPC would require that the other active ingredient used in the new combination is also covered by the basic patent either for use as an isolated substance or in combination. In other words, where a basic patent protects more than one product, more than one SPC may be granted for that patent, at least under most circumstances. However, where a basic patent protects both a first active ingredient and a combination of that active ingredient with another substance, and an SPC has been granted for the first active ingredient on the basis of an MA covering one of the substances, an SPC for the combination product will not be granted under the same basic patent on the basis of a subsequent marketing authorisation.

Furthermore, the CJEU case law does not address another very important question, namely that of post-grant amendments. Taking into consideration how

---

[50] Judgment of the Court (Third Chamber), 12 December 2013, *Actavis Group PTC EHF and Actavis UK Ltd v Sanofi*, C-443/12, EU:C:2013:833.

often patent owners make such amendments, this uncertainty gives SPC applicants considerable leeway in their interpretation. Patent holders may also consider filing divisional applications in order to circumvent the limitations of Article 3.[51]

3.2. Is the Product Part of the Patent and how is the Scope of Article 3(a) of the Regulation Defined?

According to CJEU case law,[52] in order to determine whether a product is protected by a patent, the Court would have to examine whether a product is 'specified' in the wording of the patent claims. In both *Lilly*[53] and *Actavis*,[54] the CJEU attempted to apply this method and found it rather complicated. In *Actavis*, Sanofi was granted an SPC for a combination therapy comprising an antihypertensive agent (Irbesartan) together with HCTZ, a diuretic. The claims of the basic patent included Irbesartan in combination with a diuretic, but HCTZ was not named in the patent claims. The CJEU provided in its ruling that in order for an active ingredient to be regarded as protected by a 'basic patent in force', (i) it is not necessary for an active ingredient to be identified in the claims of a patent by a structural formula, and (ii) the use of a functional definition for an active ingredient will be sufficient provided that the claims 'relate implicitly but necessarily and specifically' to the active ingredient in question, when interpreted in accordance with Article 69 EPC.[55] In the specific case, Sanofi's second SPC was considered to be invalid, since the active ingredient (the diuretic) was not protected as such by the basic patent. Unfortunately, the CJEU did not consider it necessary to answer the first referral question, namely, what the criteria are for deciding whether 'the product is protected by a basic patent in force'.

The same question was posed in the *Eli Lilly* case, in which the CJEU specified that the active ingredient need not be identified by a structural formula in the claims of the patent. In order for an SPC to be granted in the case where the active ingredient is described by means of a functional formula, the claims have to be interpreted in the light of Article 69 of the EPC and in a way that means the active ingredient was mentioned 'implicitly but necessarily and specifically'.[56]

In this case, the holder of the basic patent was Human Genome Science (HGS). The patent covered a new protein and the antibodies which bound specifically to

---

[51] The patent holder has the possibility to divide any pending European patent applications, thus resulting in multiple patents. In this respect, a patent applicant could separate different versions of the invention and apply for a patent for a specific combination of active ingredients.

[52] Judgment of the Court (Fourth Chamber) of 24 November 2011, *Medeva BV v Comptroller General of Patents, Designs and Trademarks*, C-322/10, EU:C:2011:773.

[53] Judgment of the Court (Third Chamber) of 12 December 2013, *Eli Lilly and Company Ltd v Human Genome Sciences Inc*, C-493/12, EU:C:2013:835.

[54] Ibid.

[55] According to Article 69 EPC, the extent of protection conferred by a European patent shall be determined by the claims and the description and drawings should be used to interpret said claims.

[56] *Eli Lilly and Company*, C-493/12, EU:C:2013:835.

that protein. The active substance in the specific SPC application was developed after research by a third party, Eli Lilly. This new active substance, Tabalumab, was not expressly named in the claims and was not otherwise specified in the patent. However, if defined functionally, it was clear that Tabalumab would infringe the claims of HGS's patent which covered 'an isolated antibody or portion thereof that binds specifically'. The High Court of Justice referred an interesting question to the CJEU: 'in the case of a claim to an antibody or a class of antibodies, is it sufficient that the antibody or antibodies are defined in terms of their binding characteristics to a target protein, or is it necessary to provide a structural definition for the antibody or antibodies, and if so, how much?' The CJEU confirmed that an active ingredient is covered by the basic patent only when it is identified in the patent claims by means of a structural or functional definition. However, it is not necessary that the active ingredient is identified by means of a structural definition or formula. Where the active ingredient is covered by a functional definition or formula in the claims of a patent issued by the European Patents Office, an SPC may, in principle, be granted for that active ingredient, provided that the claims, interpreted in light of the description of the invention, permit the conclusion that they relate 'implicitly but necessarily and specifically' to the active ingredient. The final conclusion regarding this latter part must be reached by the national court. Thus, claims interpretation at the national level will also impact on whether or not an active ingredient can be protected by an SPC. Obviously, the flexibility provided by national interpretation will most probably lead to further divergences in national case law.

Shortly after the CJEU ruling, both Eli Lilly and HGS applied to the High Court for judgment in their favour, proof of the ambivalent meaning of the CJEU's answers to the referral questions, giving the national courts the possibility to interpret and apply the CJEU ruling with a certain degree of freedom.[57] Eli Lilly claimed that the use of the term 'identified' in the CJEU's decision meant that the patent had to contain a description or definition of the active ingredient. HGS, on the other hand, considered that the specific substance, Tumalubam, was 'implicitly but necessarily and specifically' described in claim 13 of the patent. The High Court ruled in favour of HGS and stated that Tumalubam fell under the scope of the patent.[58]

It seems that the clarification brought by the CJEU, though welcome, may prove to be of little help to national courts. Reference to Article 69 EPC, combined with the conclusion that claims should relate 'implicitly but necessarily and specifically' to the active ingredient in question, makes the determination of what falls inside the scope of the patent a rather complicated task. Taking into consideration the

---

[57] *Eli Lilly and Co v Human Genome Sciences Inc* [2014] EWHC 2404.
[58] The High Court made considerable comments on paragraph 43 of the CJEU ruling related to the issue of the research steps taken by the patentee to be granted marketing authorisations. According to the High Court, the CJEU exceeded the limits of its jurisdiction and took factual matters into consideration in its ruling.

fact that the EU is not party to the European Patent Convention,[59] the CJEU has been unable to provide for a specific interpretation of Article 69.

In *Teva*, the case concerned an SPC granted to Gilead for its antiretroviral medicinal product, marketed under the name TRUVADA.[60] The medicinal product included two active ingredients, tenofir disoproxil (TD) and emtricitabine, which had shown a combined effect for the specific treatment. The basic patent did not contain reference to specific substances but indicated in rather general terms a series of molecules which are helpful in the therapeutic treatment of a number of viral infections in humans and animals, in particular HIV. The claimants in the main proceedings claimed that the SPC in question did not fulfil the requirements of Article 3(a) of the Regulation, since the product was not 'specified in the wording of the claims'.[61] In cases where there is a function definition provided, the claim must relate implicitly, but necessarily and specifically, to that product, in accordance with the ruling in the *Eli Lilly* case.[62] The claimants submitted that emtricitabine was not specified in the wording of the claim upon which the SPC is based and no structural or function reference thereto was provided. Gilead claimed that the term used in claim 27 of its basic patent, 'other therapeutic ingredients', related implicitly, but necessarily, to emtricitabine.

The referring court, the High Court of Justice (England and Wales), considered the divergent decisions in a number of Member States and the many CJEU rulings on the question of application of Article 3(a) SPC, and decided to refer a very straightforward question to the CJEU, namely the following: What are the criteria for deciding whether 'the product' is protected by a basic patent in force in Article 3(a) of Regulation No 469/2009? The CJEU confirmed that given the lack of EU harmonised patent rules, the interpretation of the scope of a basic patent would proceed on the basis of non-EU rules.[63] The Court clarified the important role of the man skilled in the art, meaning that it is necessary to ascertain whether a person skilled in the art can understand, without a doubt, on the basis of their general knowledge and in light of the description and drawings of the invention in the basic patent, that the product to which the claims of the basic patent relate is a specification required for the solution of the technical problem disclosed by that patent. However, this assessment is to be made on the basis of what was the state of the art at the filing date or priority date, thus excluding later research results. Thus, the person skilled in the art must be able to identify that product specifically, in

---

[59] European Patent Convention [2000], OJ EPO 2001, Special edition No 4 55.
[60] *Teva UK Ltd and Others v Merck Sharp & Dohme Corporation* [2017] EWHC 539 (Pat); Judgment of the Court (Grand Chamber) of 25 July 2018, *Teva UK Ltd and Others v Gilead Sciences Inc*, C-121/17, EU:C:2018:585; see Nicola Dagg, Steve Baldwin and Dr Tony Rollins, 'From Takeda to Teva v Merck: Are we Treading the Right Path on Combination Product SPCs? (Part 2)' [2017] 39 *European Intellectual Property Review* 11, 697–704.
[61] See Judgment of the Court (Fourth Chamber) of 24 November 2011, *Medeva BV v Comptroller General of Patents, Designs and Trademarks*, C-322/10, EU:C:2011:773, para 28.
[62] *Eli Lilly and Company*, C-493/12, EU:C:2013:835.
[63] Ibid.

light of all the information disclosed by that patent, on the basis of the state of the art at the filing date or priority date of the patent concerned. Although the question of whether or not this was at hand in the specific case, was left to the national court, the CJEU stated that the patent did not contain any information as to the possibility that the invention covered by that patent could relate specifically to a combined effect of TD and emtricitabine for the purposes of HIV treatment.

Although it seemed that the answer of the CJEU was rather straightforward, the national courts were not satisfied by the level of clarity in the *Teva* ruling. This led to yet another case, the *Royalty Pharma Collection Trust*, concerning the meaning and application of Article 3(a).[64] In this case, Royalty Pharma was the proprietor of a patent (the basic patent) covering a method for lowering blood sugar levels in mammals through the administration of inhibitors of the enzyme dipeptidyl peptidase IV (DP IV). Sitagliptin is a DP IV inhibitor, but this product was developed by a licensee of the basic patent in question. Sitagliptin as such was patented and subsequently subject to an SPC.[65] The German Patent Office rejected the SPC application of Royalty Pharma for the 'basic patent', claiming that the medicinal product, the subject of the application, had not been disclosed in the patent application. This decision was appealed to the Bundespatentgericht. According to Royalty Pharma, the DP IV inhibitor fell within the 'core of the patented invention'. It asserted that the CJEU has not in its previous case law required that in order for a substance to be granted an SPC, it had to be indicated in an individualised form in the claims of the basic patent. The Bundespatentgericht decided to stay proceedings and referred three very specific questions to the CJEU, all related to the application and interpretation of Article 3(a) SPC. Despite the ruling in the *Teva* case (and despite the question posed by the CJEU as to whether there was a need for further clarification of Article 3(a)), the Bundespatentgericht maintained its request, stating that it is not yet clear whether the concept of 'core inventive advance' was of any relevance for the purposes of interpreting Article 3(a) of the Regulation. The questions posed were: (1) Is a product protected by a basic patent in force pursuant to Article 3(a) of Regulation [No 469/2009] only if it forms part of the subject of protection as defined in the claims and is thus provided to the expert as a specific embodiment? (2) Is it not therefore sufficient for the requirements of Article 3(a) of Regulation [No 469/2009] if the product in question satisfies the general functional definition of a class of active ingredients in the claims, even if it is not otherwise indicated in individualised form as a specific embodiment of the method protected by the basic patent? (3) Is a product not protected by a basic patent in force under Article 3(a) of Regulation [No 469/2009] if it is covered by the functional definition in the claims, but was developed only after the filing date of the basic patent, as a result of an independent inventive step?

---

[64] Judgment of the Court (Fourth Chamber) of 30 April 2020, *Royalty Pharma Collection Trust v Deutsches Patent- und Markenamt*, C-650/17, EU:C:2020:327.
[65] Ibid.

Interestingly enough, before even addressing the questions referred, the Court clarified that, in its previous *Teva* ruling, it relied on an interpretation of Article 3(a), where the term 'core inventive advance' was not relevant. With respect to questions (1) and (2), the Court underlined the consistency in the CJEU case law with regard to the important role of the patent claims, and the role of Article 69 and of its Protocol in determining the scope of the claims. In cases where the product is not expressly mentioned in the claims, assessment must be made of whether that product is necessarily and specifically covered by one of the claims. In this assessment, two criteria must be fulfilled cumulatively, namely that the product must, from the point of view of the person skilled in the art, and in light of the description and drawings of the basic patent, necessarily come under the invention covered by that patent, and the person skilled in the art must be able to identify that product specifically in light of all the information disclosed in that patent, on the basis of the state of the art at the filing date of the patent concerned.[66] The CJEU turned to the specific case at the Bundespatentgericht and stated that while the first condition seemed to be fulfilled, the second raised concerns. It is with regard to this second condition that the Court provided some further guidance, stating that even when the product that is the subject of the SPC is not in individualised form as a specific embodiment of the method of that patent, the granting of an SPC is not, in principle, excluded. It will be a matter of assessing whether a person skilled in the art is, at the filing date (or priority date), objectively able to infer the product directly and unequivocally from the specification of that patent and based on that person's general knowledge of the field. Finally, the Court answered the third question by simply confirming that a product is covered by a functional definition given in the claims of the patent, even if it was developed after the filing date of the application for the basic patent following an independent inventive step.

These rulings could entail that broad patents, drafted at an early stage of the research into a medicinal substance, will not be able to support SPCs that cover products including active ingredients that were found after subsequent research. This creates a clear incentive to file applications for additional patents where specific active ingredients have been identified.[67]

3.3. New Use, Old Substance: What Constitutes a New Active Ingredient in View of the SPC Regulation?

Article 3(d) has constituted an obstacle to applicants that wished to acquire SPC protection for active substances that have previously been covered by an MA for a medicinal or veterinary product. According to Article 3(d), the MA that forms the basis of an SPC has to be the first marketing authorisation for this substance.

---

[66] See *Teva UK Ltd and Others v Gilead Sciences Inc*, C-121/17, EU:C:2018:585, para 52.
[67] Furthermore, in the case of combination products, where not all ingredients are covered by the basic patent, it might be preferable to apply for a separate patent protection.

A number of CJEU cases have been concerned with the question of the definition of the term 'product' under the SPC Regulation framework. In *Pharmacia Italia*, the question was whether the market authorisation of an active ingredient for animals precluded the later granting of an SPC for the same active ingredient when used for humans.[68] *Yissum*[69] focused on the question of whether an earlier market authorisation of a medical use precluded an SPC for a subsequent second medical indication. Lastly, *MIT*[70] ruled on the question of which requirements a combination of active ingredients has to satisfy in order to fall under the scope of the Regulation. Both *MIT* and *Yissum* referred to Article 1(b) of the SPC Regulation and provided useful conclusions relating to the meaning of the term 'product'. The term 'active ingredient' is not defined in the text of the Regulation, and should, according to the CJEU, be given a narrow interpretation.[71] In pharmacology, the same term is defined as an ingredient that has a medicinal effect on its own. In other words, in order to have a combination of active ingredients, there has to be a combination of substances that each have a medicinal effect on their own. The CJEU held in *Yissum*, confirming MIT and *Pharmacia Italia*, that the term 'product' does not cover all the possible therapeutic uses of an active ingredient protected by the basic patent. In *MIT*, the CJEU clarified that the concept of 'a combination of active ingredients of a medicinal product' does not include a combination of two substances, only one of which has therapeutic effects of its own. According to the same case, the term 'active ingredient' does not cover carrier or auxiliary substances, even if these are essential in order to achieve the medical effect of an active ingredient.

In *Pharmacia Italia*, the second medical indication (and thus also the second MA) concerned an active ingredient that was used for the same indication, but for another species (the first was for veterinary use, the second for human medicinal use).[72] Another potential scenario could be a case where the second MA concerns the use of the same active ingredient for the same species (here humans) but for another indication; this situation was at hand in the *Yissum* ruling.[73] Finally, *Neurim* concerned an MA for a different species and a different indication.

Although all of these decisions concerned Article 1(a) and Article 1(b) of the Regulation, they have had a direct impact on the interpretation and application of Article 3(d).[74] Before the *Neurim* ruling, CJEU case law was clear: Article 3(d)

---

[68] Judgment of the Court (Fifth Chamber) of 19 October 2004, *Pharmacia Italia SpA, formerly Pharmacia & Upjohn SpA*, C-31/03, EU:C:2004:641.

[69] Order of the Court (Eighth Chamber) of 17 April 2007, *Yissum Research and Development Company of the Hebrew University of Jerusalem v Comptroller-General of Patents*, C-202/05, EU:C:2007:214.

[70] Judgment of the Court (Second Chamber) of 4 May 2006, *Massachusetts Institute of Technology*, C-431/04, EU:C:2006:291.

[71] See both the *Massachusetts Institute of Technology*, C-431/04, EU:C:2006:291 and *Yissum*, C-202/05, EU:C:2007:214 cases.

[72] *Pharmacia Italia*, C-31/03, EU:C:2004:641.

[73] *Yissum*, C-202/05, EU:C:2007:214.

[74] Central terms, such as marketing authorisation and active ingredient, are to be interpreted in the same way as in the Regulation.

focused on the active ingredients as such, not on their use. Thus, when an MA had previously been granted and was different from the MA invoked by the applicant in the SPC application, no SPC could be granted for this substance. This rather stable approach of the CJEU was overturned in *Neurim*.[75]

When Neurim applied for an SPC for its pharmaceutical, Circadin, the Intellectual Property Office (IPO) denied it on the basis that Circadin was the second medical indication patent of another pharmaceutical, Regulin, a medicinal product for animals, used to regulate the reproductive cycle of sheep. The question arose whether the MA for Regulin meant that Circadin was subject to an earlier MA, thereby preventing the granting of an SPC for Circadin's new use.[76] The English Patents Court applied CJEU case law[77] and concluded that an SPC could not be granted on the basis of the specific factual premises. The English Court of Appeal considered the results of such an outcome detrimental to second medical indication research and thus referred the matter to the CJEU for a preliminary ruling. The CJEU provided a very important clarification: a second medical indication product covered by a new patent on a specific use is entitled to obtain an SPC.[78]

The *Neurim* ruling did not come as a complete surprise. With the 2000 EPC Revision, a broader support for the protection of second medical use inventions was manifested. The goal and objectives of the Regulation were the decisive factors upon which the CJEU based its decision in favour of Neurim. The Court proceeded to a teleological interpretation of the text of the Regulation,[79] providing that it was important to ensure sufficient protection in order to encourage research in the pharmaceutical field. A patent protecting a new use of a known product may, in accordance with Article 2 SPC Regulation, enable the granting of an SPC. The CJEU assumed that there was a connection between the authorisation for placing on the market mentioned in Articles 3(b) and 3(d) SPC Regulation and the basic patent mentioned in Article 3(a) of the same Regulation. The Court held that the marketing authorisation of a medicinal product relating to the therapeutic use, as protected by the basic patent on which the application for a supplementary protection certificate was based, could be considered the first authorisation in the spirit of Article 3(d).[80] A patent for a new therapeutic use of a known active ingredient can

---

[75] Judgment of the Court (Fourth Chamber) of 19 July 2012, *Neurim Pharmaceuticals (1991) Ltd v Comptroller-General of Patents*, C-130/11, EU:C:2012:489.

[76] With reference to Articles 3(b) and 3 (d) of the SPC Regulation. See also Christopher Brückner, *Supplementary Protection Certificates with Paediatric Extension of Duration* (2nd edn, Heymanns 2015), Art 3, marginal note 569.

[77] For instance *Medeva* (Judgment of the Court (Fourth Chamber) of 24 November 2011, *Medeva BV v Comptroller General of Patents, Designs and Trademarks*, C-322/10, EU:C:2011:773).

[78] See also from the Swedish case law, *Patentbesvärsrättens dom*, Mål nr 10-027, on the SPC protection for a second medical indication.

[79] See the Opinion of AG Trstenjak, focusing on whether the patented invention as such actually deserves an extension of the term of protection.

[80] In the *Neurim Pharmaceuticals*, C-130/11, EU:C:2012:489, AG Trstenjak's Opinion provided that the MA should count under Article 3(d) only if the earlier MA allowed its holder to work within the scope of the patent.

enable the patent proprietor to obtain an SPC even if the relevant active ingredient has already been put on the market in the form of a medicinal product for animals or humans for a different therapeutic indication.[81] However, the protection of the certificate would not extend to the active ingredient as such, but would be limited to the second medical indication.[82] Naturally, one could already at this stage question the scope of the *Neurim* ruling, as it concerned a very special case, namely a new, second medical indication for a new species. It is thus not certain that the CJEU intended to overrule the established case law of *Pharmacia Italia* and *Yissum* or to introduce some kind of exception to the rule developed by means of these decisions. The ruling in *Neurim* was considered to be contrary to the objectives of the SPC regulation.[83] The CJEU (and the AG Opinion) have been accused of using the Explanatory Memorandum[84] for the interpretation of Article 3(d) in a selective way. By doing that, the AG and the CJEU based a non-negligible part of their reasoning on paragraph 12 of the Memorandum stating that 'all research ... must be granted adequate protection'. However, they omitted reference to paragraphs 11 and 29, which clarify that there is no room for exceptions from the requirements to suggest that any patented pharmaceutical inventions should or would have the possibility to enjoy SPC protection.[85] Paragraph 35 is even more concrete in this regard, stating that when several marketing authorisations have been granted for the first substance, only the first marketing authorisation in the specific Member State will be considered.

A challenge posed by the *Neurim* ruling concerns the internal hierarchy of the Regulation. While in case law related to the application of Article 1(b), the term 'product' is defined on the basis of the active substance in focus in the MA, case law related to Article 3(d) links the term 'product' to the subject of the basic patent. According to previous case law on the application of Article 1(b), SPCs are not to be granted for uses of a known active ingredient, whether for other species or for a second medical indication. In what was to be a criticised case, the Court found that a product first placed on the EU/EEA market as a medicinal product in another way than in accordance with the Medicinal Code was not within the scope of the SPC Regulation as provided in Article 2 and would thus not be granted an SPC.[86] This means that second medical indication products fall outside the scope of the SPC Regulation. Though the *Neurim* case did not actually provide a ruling on the internal hierarchy between the two provisions, Article 3(d) and Article 1(b)

---

[81] *Neurim Pharmaceuticals*, C-130/11, EU:C:2012:489, n1 para 25 et seq.
[82] See also Jürgen Schell, 'Neurim: A New Definition of "Product" in Supplementary Protection Certificates?' [2013] 8 *Journal of Intellectual Property Law & Practice*, 9, 723–28.
[83] See European Commission, *Study on the Legal Aspects of Supplementary Protection Certificates in the EU*, Final Report [2018] Max Planck Institute for Innovation and Competition 230–31.
[84] Commission of the European Communities, *Proposal for a Council Regulation (EEC) concerning the creation of a supplementary protection certificate for medicinal products*, COM [90] 101 final.
[85] Thus, the examination of an SPC application adopted a different character that deviated from the original purpose of the Regulation, namely, to compensate for the patent protection term lost due to the MA.
[86] See *Synthon BV*, C-195/09, EU:C:2011:518 and *Generics*, C-427/09, EU:C:2011:520.

of the Regulation, it is valuable to study the respective roles of the provisions in the Regulation, to gain a better understanding of the SPC system and the relevant case law. Article 1(b) covers the subject matter protected by means of the Regulation, while Article 3(d) relates to the extent to which the 'product' is protected by means of the basic patent being a condition for SPC protection. A strict interpretation of Article 1(b) would make it incompatible with the CJEU ruling in *Neurim*.[87]

Equally surprising is an interesting legal argument that could be raised in this regard, namely that the roles of the EPC 2000 revision and Article 54(5) of the EPC 2000 were not considered by either the AG or the CJEU. One important question to be addressed is whether the SPC serves to provide some form of remuneration or compensation for an advancement in the pharmaceutical research or if it is the cumbersome MA procedure that forms the basis for SPC protection. In the *Neurim* ruling, it seemed that the former objective was to be prioritised. But would a hybrid authorisation under Article 10 of the Directive 2001/83 for an active ingredient already authorised or a variation of an existing MA for a new indication be entitled to an SPC? How important the *Neurim* ruling would be for the application and interpretation of the SPC Regulation depends on how it would be applied. The flexibility in the scope of the *Neurim* ruling could have led to considerable divergence, and it did for a while in the approaches of national patent offices and national courts, if it were not for a new case from the CJEU treating the same issue of SPC eligibility for a second medical indication. In its post-*Neurim* rulings, the CJEU has confirmed that that specific case does not mean that the narrow interpretation of Article 1(b) is to be abandoned. More specifically, when having to decide upon the protection of adjuvants and safeners after resorting to Directive 2001/83 and Regulation 1107/2009, the CJEU concluded that these are not to be considered 'active ingredients', leaving them outside the scope of Article 1(b).[88]

The ruling in the *Abraxis* case[89] brought the question of SPCs for new medical indications under new light, and removed the concerns from those worrying that the SPC Regulation is taking a direction that deviates from the will of the legislator. In this case, the Court concluded that Article 3(d) in the Regulation (EC) No 469/2009 shall be read in conjunction with Article 1(b). Thus, it should be interpreted to mean that the marketing authorisation stipulated in Article 3(b) of the Regulation relied on in support of an application for an SPC concerning a new formulation of an already known ingredient cannot be regarded as being the

---

[87] See Commission of the European Communities, 'Proposal for a Council Regulation (EEC) concerning the creation of a supplementary protection certificate for medicinal products', COM [90] 101 final; see also Recitals 13 and 17 of the SPC Regulation.

[88] Order of the Court (Eighth Chamber) of 14 November 2013, *Glaxosmithkline Biologicals SA and Glaxosmithkline Biologicals, Niederlassung der Smithkline Beecham Pharma GmbH & Co. KG v Comptroller General of Patents, Designs and Trade Marks*, C-210/13, EU:C:2013:762.

[89] Judgment of the Court (Fourth Chamber) of 21 March 2019, *Abraxis Bioscience LLC v Comptroller General of Patents*, C-443/17, EU:C:2019:238.

first marketing authorisation for the product, if that active ingredient has already been the subject of a marketing authorisation as an active ingredient. In other words, where an active ingredient has been the subject of a previous marketing authorisation, a new marketing authorisation covering the same substance, even for another use, will not constitute a marketing authorisation under the meaning of Article 3(b); thus, the new medical indication cannot be granted an SPC. Although *Abraxis* seemed to be rather clear on the stance chosen by the CJEU with regards to second medical indication inventions and the possibility for them to receive SPC protection, yet a new case was referred to the CJEU, this time by the Paris Court of Appeal.[90]

In the *Santen* case, the final word (it seems) is said about the possibility to acquire an SPC for a second medical indication. By ruling as a Grand Chamber of 13 judges testifies to the significance of the issues at stake and the need for the CJEU to actually bring clarity on the future impact (if any) of the *Neurim* case. This was also the approach of the Advocate General who had provided that it was time for the Court to either reject the *Neurim* case or simply embrace it wholeheartedly.[91] The Court concluded that:

> Article 3(d) of [the SPC Regulation] must be interpreted as meaning that a marketing authorisation cannot be considered to be the first marketing authorisation, for the purpose of that provision, where it covers a new therapeutic application of an active ingredient, or of a combination of active ingredients, and that active ingredient or combination has already been the subject of a marketing authorisation for a different therapeutic application.

According to the Court, Article 1(b) defines the 'product' of an SPC independently from its use or its approved therapeutic application. Thus, when an active ingredient is used for a new therapeutic application, this does not make it a different 'product' if the same active ingredient has already been used for a different therapeutic application previously (and this has received a marketing authorisation). This part of the ruling is based on the same conclusion reached by the Court in *Yissum* (C-200/05).

Another important aspect that was addressed by the Court was that of the 'first marketing authorisation within the scope of the protection of the basic patent', that had been part of the reasoning of the ruling in *Neurim*. The Court clarifies that the wording of Article 3(d) does not in fact concern the scope of protection of the basic patent. Article 3(d) must instead be understood as relating to the first marketing authorisation for any medicinal product incorporating the active ingredient (or combination of active ingredients) under consideration, regardless of the therapeutic application for which it is approved. In this regard, the Court also

---

[90] Judgment of the Court (Grand Chamber), *Santen SAS v Directeur général de l'Institut national de la propriété industrielle*, C-673/18, EU:C:2020:531.
[91] Opinion of Advocate General Giovanni Pitruzzella, *Santen SAS v Directeur général de l'Institut national de la propriété industrielle*, C-673/18, EU:C:2020:34.

referred to the intentions of the legislator to provide for a clear, simple and predictable system for the grant of SPCs, and one where there will be as little room as possible for national interpretations and divergences.

In paragraph 53 of the *Santen* judgment the Court went as far as to actually state that its conclusion, namely that the scope of the basic patent is of no relevance for determining which is the first marketing authorisation within the meaning of Article 3(d), was in fact contrary to what the Court held in paragraph 27 of the judgment in *Neurim*. While this is the only part where the Court discusses the relation of the ruling to the *Neurim* case, it seems clear that *Neurim* is overturned.

This ruling also rendered obsolete the referral made by the Swedish Patent and Market Court of Appeal in the case *Novartis* (C-354/19).[92] This referral concerned the question of whether the grant of a second SPC for a different therapeutic application is precluded if the second SPC is filed by the same rights holder who has already been granted a first SPC for the same active ingredient. The referral was withdrawn on 7 September 2020.

This is a further indication of the fact that the question of SPC protection for second medical indications will most probably not concern the CJEU, at least for some time to come.

3.4. One Product, One SPC, One Patent?

Article 1(b) SPC states that a product is 'the active ingredient or combination of active ingredients of a medicinal product'. The CJEU has further clarified the meaning of this provision in a number of important cases.

There are certainly several situations that may create interpretational hurdles with regard to what seems to be a straightforward requirement: that the product that will be subject to the SPC has to be protected by a basic patent, which is in force, as well as by a valid marketing authorisation. The process of acquiring a patent in the pharmaceutical sector and the marketing authorisation procedure are far from straightforward. In theory (and unfortunately sometimes in practice), an applicant may submit an SPC application while the basic patent is still in force, but without having been granted a marketing authorisation, or an SPC application may be filed soon after a marketing authorisation is granted, but after the basic patent has expired. In the first case, the SPC application fails to fulfil the requirement of Article 3(b) according to which an MA is to be granted, while in the second, it is inconsistent with Article 3(a), since the product is not protected by a patent in force. The applicant is left with no means to deal with this situation. In the first case, it will not be possible to invoke the *restitutio in integrum* provided under domestic law. In the second case, the lack of an MA is not something that can be remedied under Article 10(3) of the SPC Regulation, since only formal

---

[92] Order of the Court of 25 September 2020, *Novartis AG v Patent- och registreringsverket*, C-354/19, EU:C:2020:819.

deficiencies may be rectified after submission according to this provision.[93] The scenario that has been put forward in the CJEU is that in the Referral C-567/16, concerning an applicant that argued that an End of Procedure Notice issued by a Reference Member State was equivalent to a granted MA under Article 3(b).[94,95] In the specific case, Merck Sharp & Dohme (MSD) began development of a fixed-dose combination of ezetimibe and atorvastatin in September 2006. Seven years later, in September 2013, MSD filed MAs for Atozet in a number of Member States, using the decentralised procedure (DCP). MSD designated Germany as the Reference Member State (RMS). As the RMS, the German regulatory authority (Bundesinstitut für Arzneimittel und Medizinprodukte) coordinated the approval process, preparing the draft documents and, most importantly, the draft summary of product characteristics (SmPc).

The German medicines authority did not accept that MSD had filed a valid application until 13 February 2014. On 12 September that year, one day before the patent expired, MSD applied for its UK SPC at the UK Intellectual Property Office (IPO). However, MSD did not have a UK MA. Instead, MSD submitted, with its SPC application, a copy of the end of procedure (EoP) notice from the German medicines authority, stating that the DCP had ended with approval. MSD explained that the effect of the EoP notice was that concerned Member States, including the United Kingdom, had agreed to grant an MA for Atozet. The UK IPO reached the conclusion that MSD's application did not comply with Article 3(b), because they did not have a valid UK MA at the time of filing their SPC application. The EoP notice did not satisfy that requirement. The IPO also objected to the application on Article 3(c) grounds. Three weeks later, on 10 October 2014, the UK MHRA granted the MA. MSD submitted a copy of the UK MA, together with the first EU MA (from France), and asserted that these documents would rectify any irregularities in the application. The UKIPO decided that the application did not fulfil Article 3(b) and the irregularities presented were not such that could be rectified under Article 10(3). The CJEU confirmed the decision of the UK IPO, providing that an end of procedure notice may not be considered equivalent to a granted MA for the purposes of Article 3(b) of the SPC Regulation.[96] Furthermore, this was not the type of irregularity that could be rectified under Article 10(3), since a

---

[93] In the United States, there is a possibility to request an interim extension if the patent is about to expire. In Germany, this question was posed and answered in 1999 in the *Abamectin* case (*BPatG, Abamectin*, 15 W (pat) 71/97 (2000) GRUR 398), where it was provided that denying such patents the possibility to receive SPC protection would be contrary to the objective of the Regulation. Although this was noted, the court concluded that this is not something that could be remedied by means of a court decision and that a revision of the Regulation in this respect was necessary.

[94] See Article 28(4) of Directive 2001/83/EC.

[95] Judgment of the Court (Seventh Chamber) of 7 December 2017, *Merck Sharp & Dohme Corporation v Comptroller-General of Patents, Designs and Trade Marks*, C-567/16, EU:C:2017:948.

[96] In this respect, see also judgment of the Court (Eighth Chamber) of 15 January 2015, *Arne Forsgren v Österreichisches Patentamt*, C-631/13, EU:C:2015:13, para 54 providing that a patented product may not give rise to the granting of a SPC unless it has been granted a marketing authorisation as a medicinal product.

prerequisite for invoking Article 10(2), according to the CJEU, is to have an MA on the specific medicinal product.

Another situation that may lead to doubts as regards the granting of an SPC, is that where the patent is granted after its expiration. In such case, the requirements set out in the SPC Regulation are not fulfilled and thus the product in question will not be granted protection. This situation occurs rarely and thus has rather limited practical value.[97] Should the number of such patents increase, it would be an issue to look into from a patent law perspective.

Already in 1997, in the *Farmitalia* decision,[98] the German Federal Court of Justice asked the CJEU whether it was necessary to take into consideration the wording of the patent claims or the scope of protection of the claims in order to proceed to the interpretation of Article 3(a) of the Regulation. The CJEU ruled that since there was a lack of substantive patent law harmonisation on the EU level, it would be a question of national law to decide whether a product was protected by a basic patent or not. National courts were thus faced with a difficult task: defining the scope of the patent. One might wonder why this is a difficult task, since this is what a national court is expected to do in infringement proceedings, for instance. The difficulty lies in the interpretation. Is 'covered by a basic patent' to be interpreted as a concept disconnected from the SPC (and thus an EU law concept), or does its interpretation follow that of traditional patent law (and thus become a national law concept)? If it is the former, the CJEU will be competent to develop the interpretation of the provision; if it is the latter, this will be a matter for national courts. The question posed in the *Farmitalia* referral was whether the product was to be considered to be covered by the basic product according to Article 3(a) when a protection certificate is sought for the free base of an active ingredient, including any of its salts, but the basic patent in its claims mentions only the free base of this substance and a single salt of this free base. Is it the wording of the claim that is decisive or is it a matter for interpretation? The Court responded that in order to be able to determine whether a substance is covered by the basic patent, reference must be made to rules which govern the patent, which are national patent rules. This ruling was not entirely uncomplicated, as the Court did not explain which patent rules were to be used and, more importantly, how a harmonised interpretation of the SPC Regulation would be possible when the most important aspect of the SPC system – what is actually protected – depends on the divergent national patent laws.[99]

---

[97] According to the European Commission, *Study on the Legal Aspects of Supplementary Protection Certificates in the EU*, Final Report [2018] Max Planck Institute for Innovation and Competition, since 1973, only 49 patent applications had been approved after the expiry date. According to the recommendations of the same report, if this were to occur more often it would be an issue for the patent system to remedy, as it would constitute a very unfortunate situation.

[98] Judgment of the Court (Fifth Chamber) of 16 September 1999, *Farmitalia Carlo Erba Srl*, C-392/97, EU:C:1999:416.

[99] The weaknesses of the CJEU ruling were identified by Lord Justice Arnold in *MedImmune v Novartis* [2012] EWHC 181 (Pat).

Gradually, two tests were applied: 'the infringement test', used to determine whether the product defined in the SPC application infringed the rights deriving from the basic patent, and the 'disclosure test', used to determine whether the product defined in the SPC application was disclosed in the wording of the claims of the basic patent.[100] Naturally, national courts applied different perspectives. In Germany, the courts adopted the perspective that deciding whether a substance was covered by the basic patent required the interpretation of whether the product fell under the scope of the claims of the patent. This meant that it could be covered by the basic patent only due to the application of doctrine of equivalence, even if a substance that has not been mentioned at all in the description of the invention.[101]

In the United Kingdom, on the other hand, the Court had the opportunity to consider a complicated scenario in the *Takeda* decision.[102] This case concerned two basic patents designated for six SPC applications. The two basic patents concerned a pyridine derivative and the use of this pyridine derivative for manufacturing a pharmaceutical product. No reference to a pyridine derivative combined with another pharmaceutical agent was included in the patent applications. The SPC application included a pyridine derivative combined with two antibiotics. The application was rejected on the basis of Article 3(a), since the SPC application was not covered by the basic patent. Under the framework of this specific ruling, the *Takeda* test was developed, which encompasses two steps: if the SPC is requested for a combination of two products and this combination falls under the scope of the patent only because one of the two active ingredients falls under the scope of the patent, the combination is not protected. In cases where the SPC is requested for the combination of two ingredients and the combination is claimed as such in the patent, the combination is protected by the patent. In cases where only one ingredient is sought, it seems that the *Takeda* test is the same as the traditional infringement test. With regard to situations where the application concerns a combination of ingredients, the *Takeda* decision has been referred to as the 'disclosure test', according to which the requirement is that the combination must have been specifically disclosed and claimed in the patent specification.[103]

---

[100] Ibid.

[101] According to the European Commission, 'Study on the Legal Aspects of Supplementary Protection Certificates in the EU', Final Report (2018) Max Planck Institute for Innovation and Competition, the German courts did not deal with the scenario where the patent claimed only one single compound and did not include any other patent claim for that compound in combination with another pharmaceutical agent.

[102] *Takeda Chemical Industries Ltd's SPC Applications (No 1)* (2004) RPC 1; *Takeda Chemical Industries Ltd's SPC Applications (No 3)* [2004] RPC 1, [2003] EWHC 649 (Pat).

[103] This interpretation is not supported by the European Commission, *Study on the Legal Aspects of Supplementary Protection Certificates in the EU*, Final Report [2018] Max Planck Institute for Innovation and Competition, which provides that this approach is not supported in any way in the *Takeda* ruling. The same report includes an interesting categorisation of potential claims that was not treated in the *Takeda* ruling but might be applicable in practice. See European Commission, *Study on the Legal Aspects of Supplementary Protection Certificates in the EU*, Final Report [2018] Max Planck Institute for Innovation and Competition 184–85.

110 *The Supplementary Protection Certificate*

The ruling in the *Farmitalia* case opened for considerable flexibility by letting national courts decide on how to interpret the coverage and scope of the basic patent in relation to the SPC Regulation. However, this flexibility did not prove to be satisfactory in practice. The Court of Appeal of England and Wales turned to the CJEU in the *Medeva* case, asking how Article 3(a) of the Regulation was to be interpreted given a lack of substantive patent law harmonisation.[104] The case concerned a vaccine, the result of pharmaceutical research that is often characterised by a focus on combination of ingredients. In the specific case, two interesting mismatches were noted: between the product obtained through the process claimed by the patent and the product definition in the SPC application and between the subject of the MA and the product definition in the SPC application. The patent claims concerned the combination of two ingredients, with no reference made to potential combinations with other ingredients.[105] The CJEU ruled that to be protected by a basic patent, the active ingredients have to be specified in the wording of the claims. In fact, *Medeva* was seen as abandoning the 'infringement test',[106] which had been applied by national courts previously and entailed that a product, as specified in the SPC application, was 'protected' if it were to infringe the claims of a patent. However, what the term 'specified' meant remained unclear, despite subsequent case law. Although it became obvious that the CJEU in its ruling rejected the infringement test,[107] there was no clear explanation as to why. In fact, some suggest that there is no discrepancy between *Farmitalia* and *Medeva*.[108] This interpretation is based on the fact that *Medeva* and *Farmitalia* related to different facts and even different legal issues. In *Farmitalia*, the question was whether the SPC could be granted in a way that covered all variants of the same free base, even when the patent only covered one salt and the MA was granted for a medicinal product covering one salt. *Medeva* involved a completely different situation where the MA covered a combination of substances that was not protected (at least not explicitly) by the basic patent.

A strict interpretation of the *Medeva* case would have as an effect that in order to be supported by a basic patent, the substance would have to be explicitly disclosed in the claims, which would significantly limit the applicant's possibilities of getting an SPC, in particular if the underlying patent claims were broadly worded. The CJEU has stated that the substance must be specified in the wording

---

[104] *Medeva* (Judgment of the Court (Fourth Chamber) of 24 November 2011, *Medeva BV v Comptroller General of Patents, Designs and Trademarks*, C-322/10, EU:C:2011:773). See also order of the Court (Fourth Chamber) of 25 November 2011, *Yeda Research and Development Company Ltd and Aventis Holdings Inc v Comptroller General of Patents, Designs and Trade Marks*, C-518/10, EU:C:2011:779.

[105] There was a reference to other ingredients in the disclosure in order to illustrate the differences between the specific invention and other inventions.

[106] These are two examples of such cases.

[107] AG Trstenjak's Opinion in *Neurim Pharmaceuticals* makes apparent that this is the case (C-130/11, EU:C:2012:268).

[108] European Commission, *Study on the Legal Aspects of Supplementary Protection Certificates in the EU*, Final Report [2018] Max Planck Institute for Innovation and Competition, 187.

of the claims, and what this means is yet another issue. The *Medeva* ruling was applied, though with some slight variation, in three parallel referrals in *Daiichi Sankyo Company, Yeda* and the *University of Queensland*.[109] More specifically, in the *University of Queensland* case, the CJEU stated that in order for an active ingredient to be supported by the basic patent it had to be 'identified' in the wording of the claims. It would be interesting to know if the change of terminology was simply a linguistic matter, or if it entailed a substantial change in the meaning of the requirement. The main question that arose in the aftermath of this case was whether a product or substance had to be explicitly identified by name or by means of a specific formula, or if it was sufficient for the product to be referred to generically or by function.

Eli Lilly initiated yet another phase in the CJEU's interpretation of Article 3(a). The patent claims covered a new polypeptide, Neutrokine, as well as antibodies that could specifically bind Neutrokine. In the patent specification, it was stated that such antibodies might be effective against autoimmune diseases. While the patent specification did not disclose the structure of any antibody mentioned, it mentioned standard procedures for their preparation. The question in the specific case was thus whether a product could be considered to be specified or identified in the wording of a claim even if the claim or patent specification did not mention such product by structure or otherwise.

The *Eli Lilly* ruling brings clarification as to how to interpret the *Medeva* requirement. In order to satisfy the requirement, it is not necessary for the patent claim to indicate the structure of the product. On the other hand, the claim when interpreted in light of Article 69 of the EPC, will have to relate implicitly but *necessarily and specifically* to the active ingredient in question. Needless to say, the case has not brought clear answers to the questions posed – resulting in further uncertainty. One interpretation of the *Eli Lilly* case could be that in order to be covered by an SPC, reference to the substance in the claims is enough. On the other hand, it could be interpreted as showing that for *Eli Lilly* it was enough that the substance was included in the description and that it was not necessary to include it in the claims.[110]

In the *Teva* case, Justice Arnold supported the 'core inventive' test, stating that in his view this requirement provided that the product must embody the core

---

[109] Order of the Court (Fourth Chamber) of 25 November 2011, *Yeda Research and Development Company Ltd and Aventis Holdings Inc v Comptroller General of Patents, Designs and Trade Marks*, C-518/10, EU:C:2011:779; Order of the Court (Fourth Chamber) of 25 November 2011, *University of Queensland and CSL Ltd v Comptroller General of Patents, Designs and Trade Marks*, C-630/10, EU:C:2011:780; Order of the Court (Fourth Chamber) of 25 November 2011, *Daiichi Sankyo Company v Comptroller General of Patents, Designs and Trade Marks*, C-6/11, EU:C:2011:781. In the *Daiichi* case, the Court ruled on the interpretation of Article 3(a) of the Regulation and stated that supplementary protection certificates may not be granted to active ingredients which are not identified in the wording of the claims of the basic patent.

[110] This second interpretation was also followed by the High Court in *Eli Lilly Company v Human Genome Sciences Ltd* [2014] EWHC 2404 (Pat).

inventive advance of the basic patent and thus replaced the previous requirement 'specified in the wording of the claim', as opposed to being an addition to it.[111]

The majority of cases with problematic aspects in regard to the application of Article 3(a) involve combination products. In the United States, it is not possible to acquire patent extension protection for combinations of active ingredients that have been authorised in the past.[112] Thus, a patent claiming a combination of A and B is only eligible for term extension if either A or B had not previously been marketed.[113] If the EU were to adopt a different approach than the jurisdiction from whence the SPC regulation was transplanted, there would need to be an explanation. Another important issue to consider is whether the protection of combination (of known substances) is compatible with the objectives of the Regulation: to support the research and development of new substances.

In one of the latest CJEU cases, new interesting contributions have been added to the attempted definition of the term 'product'. In *Forsgren*,[114] the CJEU was faced with the question of whether an SPC could, in principle, be granted for a first active ingredient, when that ingredient is present in an already authorised medicinal product, in a covalent bond with another active ingredient. Another important question in the same case was whether the MA had to be related to the therapeutic effect associated with the first active ingredient. The CJEU concluded that an SPC may be granted for a first active ingredient which is present in an authorised medicinal product in a covalent bond with another active ingredient. Nevertheless, it is necessary that the therapeutic effect of the first active ingredient in isolation falls within the therapeutic indications covered by the wording of the MA in order to comply with Article 3(b) of Regulation 469/2009. The Court also suggested that where a carrier protein in a medicinal product is chemically bonded to a polysaccharide antigen, that carrier protein (in isolation) may be categorised as an active ingredient for the purposes of Article 1(b) of the Regulation, if it can be shown that it produces a 'pharmacological, immunological, or metabolic action' of its own which is covered by the therapeutic indications of the MA.

The CJEU resorted to the text of the Directive 2001/83/EC as amended by Directive 2011/62/EU in order to proceed to the definition of the term 'active substance' (or else 'active ingredient'), indicating that in order for a substance to be an active ingredient it must at least produce a pharmacological, immunological or metabolic action of its own. This interpretation is in line with the ruling in

---

[111] Under the framework of the European Commission, *Study on the Legal Aspects of Supplementary Protection Certificates in the EU*, Final Report [2018] Max Planck Institute for Innovation and Competition, stakeholders were asked which was the best alternative interpretation of the Article. The stakeholders could choose between the *Medeva* requirement, the infringement test and the core inventive advantage step. The results showed that the infringement test was expected to bring more clarity than the *Medeva* requirement.

[112] 35 USC §156 (a)(5)(A) requires that the regulatory review period must be for the first commercial marketing or use of the product.

[113] See n 106, Annex II of the study.

[114] Judgment of the Court (Eighth Chamber) of 15 January 2015, *Arne Forsgren v Österreichisches Patentamt*, C-631/13, EU:C:2015:13.

Bayer,[115] where the Court required that a substance has a toxic, phytotoxic, or plant protection action of its own for it to be an active substance under the Plant Protection Product Regulation. On the other hand, *Forsgren* takes the interpretation a step further and requires that the therapeutic effect associated with a given substance falls within the therapeutic indications covered by the wording of the MA, if that substance is to be considered a 'product' that can be subject to an SPC. The way the MA system works today, MAs can be amended to refer to new therapeutic effects when appropriate clinical trials are available. However, it will be interesting to see how this will be combined with Article 3(b)[116] and Article 3(d) of the Regulation[117] and in particular what documentation will be required for these amendments to comply with the requirements of a 'marketing authorisation'.

The CJEU did not provide any concrete guidance on how to determine whether a substance can be classified as an active ingredient[118] and has chosen to leave it to the national courts to make their own interpretations. However, in *GlaxoSmithKline Biologicals* (*GSK*), it was confirmed that the way a substance is defined in the MA can influence whether it may be classified as an active ingredient or not. In fact, if the MA refers to the substance as an 'adjuvant' or an 'excipient', this would preclude the substance from being considered an 'active ingredient' for which an SPC may be granted. The CJEU distinguished between the *Forsgren* case and the *GSK* decision, taking into consideration the fact that the active ingredient in question in *Forsgren* was not an adjuvant based on the wording of the MA. It thus becomes obvious that the precise choice of terminology in the MA application can be of fundamental importance for the subsequent granting or not of an SPC.

In general, there is no requirement of absolute identity between an active ingredient protected by an SPC and the medicinal product described in an MA upon which the SPC is based. Furthermore, if all other conditions are fulfilled, an SPC is appropriate for an active compound bound to an active or inactive carrier, provided that the therapeutic effect of the active compound falls within the wording of the MA. Lastly, an SPC may be granted when it relates to a portion of a molecule that is considered a carrier for another active ingredient, provided that the carrier has its own therapeutic effect and falls within the wording of the MA.

3.5. The Excluded Subject Matter

The objectives presented and promoted for medicinal products justifying the granting of SPCs are equally viable and applicable to other industries that suffer

---

[115] Judgment of the Court (Third Chamber) of 19 June 2014, *Bayer CropScience AG v Deutsches Patent- und Markenamt*, C-11/13, EU:C:2014:2010.
[116] Requiring that an MA supports the SPC.
[117] Requiring that there is no earlier MA for the same product.
[118] In other words, whether or not the product has a pharmacological, immunological or metabolic action of its own.

114 *The Supplementary Protection Certificate*

from the same problems of regulatory control and loss of effective patent term. One important example of this is the medical devices and diagnostics industry. In fact, in 2017, two EU Regulations were introduced that changed the way in which products in this industry were placed on the market.[119] These new Regulations introduced more rigid control regimes for high-risk devices and increased the requirements on clinical evidence, by imposing the requirement of a Certificate of Conformity on such products.[120] Clinical evidence is produced in Member States and the Certificate of Conformity is issued by notified bodies.[121] Although the relevance of patents is as high as in the pharmaceutical industry and the regulatory controls seem to be as rigid, products are brought to the market more quickly and at a lower cost,[122] something that means that this specific industry may not be in as urgent a need of SPCs as the pharmaceutical sector.[123]

3.5.1. The Case of Medical Devices

The commercialisation of medical devices is regulated, though not under Directive 2001/83, the regulatory framework concerning medicinal products. Medical devices fall under Directives 93/42, 90/385 and 98/79 (and now under the transitional provisions of Regulations 2017/745 and 2017/746).

The question of the eligibility of these devices for SPC has been dependent on whether their particular regulatory regime might be considered to fulfil the requirements set out in Article 3(b) of the SPC Regulation. In the United Kingdom, three SPC applications were denied protection, namely *Leibniz Institut BL O/328/14* (Nanotherm, iron oxide particles for treating tumours),[124] *Cerus Corp BL 0/141/14* (Intercept Blood System, that inactivates pathogens in blood platelets or plasma before transfusion),[125] and *Angiotech Pharmaceuticals Inc BL 0/466/15* (Taxus, drug-eluting stent). All three devices had undergone lengthy regulatory procedures, as provided for under Directive 93/42, meaning that 8–12 years of effective patent protection were lost. Nevertheless, all three were

---

[119] Regulation 2017/745/EU of the European Parliament and of the Council of 5 April 2017 on medical devices, amending Directive 2001/83/EC, Regulation 178/2002/EC and Regulation 1223/2009/EC and repealing Council Directives 90/385/EEC and 93/42/EEC (Text with EEA relevance) [2017] OJ L 117/1 and Regulation 2017/746/EU of the European Parliament and of the Council of 5 April 2017 on in vitro diagnostic medical devices and repealing Directive 98/79/EC and Commission Decision 2010/227/EU (Text with EEA relevance) [2017] OJ L 117/176 entering into force in 2022.

[120] The Certificate of Conformity is a guarantee that the products fulfil technical regulatory and safety requirements.

[121] Notified bodies operate under the responsibility of the Member States.

[122] See n 106.

[123] In this respect, claims have been made that an equivalent to the SPC system must be introduced for food and seeds, taking into consideration the regulatory controls to which they are subjected. However, with regard to food, it seems that intellectual property rights do not play a central role in the way the industry operates today, except in the case of genetically modified organisms.

[124] UK IPO, BL O/328/14, *Leibniz-Institut für Neue Materialien Gemeinnützige GmbH*, Decision of 29 July 2014.

[125] UK IPO, BL O/141/14, *Cerus Corporation*, Decision of 31 March 2014.

denied SPC protection on the grounds of not fulfilling Article 3(b) requirements, as the regulatory procedure they had undergone was not that of Directive 2001/83 or Directive 2001/82.[126]

On the other hand, there are some cases where an SPC had been granted for a medical device, such as Genzyme's Synvise replacement joint fluid (a medical device authorised under Directive 93/42). A special category of products, that of mixed devices and substances, such as implants containing active ingredients or condoms coated with spermicides, may be regulated by means of either Directive 2001/83 as a medicinal product or Directive 93/42 as a medical device, depending on what the principal mode of action of the combination is. Guidance on the choice between the two regulatory systems, and how this is to be made, is to be found in the European Commission's guidance document MEDDEV 2.1/3 rev 3 concerning 'Borderline products drug-delivery products and medical devices incorporating as an integral part, an ancillary medicinal substance or an ancillary human blood derivative'. For example, the guidance states that 'wound dressings with antimicrobial agent' are to be regulated as medical products, while 'wound dressings' where the sole function is to administer an antimicrobial substance are to be regulated as medicinal devices. In order to answer the question as to what the 'principal' versus the 'ancillary' action of a product is, one needs to look into the principal intended action of a medical device as it can be deduced from the scientific data regarding the mechanism of action and the manufacturer's labelling.[127]

The status and classification of such borderline products will thus be dependent on what the principal use of a product is. In C-109/12 *Laboratoires Lyocentre*,[128] the CJEU concluded that the same product might in fact be considered a medical device in one Member State and a medicinal product in another.

The CJEU was given the opportunity to consider this rather complicated situation once more in the case C-527/17.[129] Boston Scientific applied for an SPC in Germany for a drug-eluting stent (TAXUS Express 2). The product was a mixed product (drug and device) that had been authorised as a medical device under Directive 93/42. The German Patent and Trademark Office decided that the SPC could not be granted on the grounds of lacking compliance with Article 2 of the SPC Regulation (and thus also with Article 3(b)). The applicant appealed to the German Federal Patents Court, claiming that the authorisation procedure for the drug-device combination under the Medical Device Directive 93/42 was equivalent to the authorisation procedure as stipulated under the Medicinal

---

[126] UK IPO, BL O/466/15, *Angiotech Pharmaceuticals Inc and University of British Columbia*, Decision of 6 October 2015, para 83.
[127] Medical Device Coordination Group, 'Guidance on the renewal of designation and monitoring of notified bodies under Directives 90/385/EEC and 93/42/EEC to be performed in accordance with Commission Implementing Regulation (EU) 2020/666 amending Commission Implementing Regulation (EU) 920/2013', MDCG 2020-11, May 2020.
[128] *Laboratoires Lyocentre v Lääkealan turvallisuus-ja kehittämiskeskus* and *Sosiaali-ja terveysalan lupa-ja valvontavirasto*, C109/17, ECLI:EU:C:2013:626.
[129] *Boston Scientific*, C-527/17, ECLI:EU:C:2018:867.

Products Directive 2001/83. In fact, the Medical Device Directive provides that where a device incorporates as an integral part, a substance, which if used separately may be considered to be a medical product as defined in Article 1 of the Directive 2001/83/EC and which can act upon the body with action ancillary to that of the device, the quality, safety and usefulness of the substance must be verified by analogy to the methods specified in Annex I to Directive 2001/83/EC.

As a consequence, the regulatory authority that is to decide upon the marketing authorisation of the device-drug product must follow a procedure equivalent to that of Directive 2001/83. This would mean that the procedure should be considered equivalent in view of the application of Article 2 (and thus also 3(b)) of the SPC Regulation. The Federal Patent Court was sympathetic to this interpretation, as it was in accordance with the spirit and objectives of the SPC Regulation: compensating pharmaceutical or medical device patent holders that had effectively lost part of their patent term. The fact that different Member States had interpreted this provision in different ways, led the Federal Patent Court to refer a question to the CJEU:

> Must Article 2 of Regulation [No 469/2009] be interpreted as meaning that, for the purposes of that regulation, an authorisation under Directive [93/42] for a combined medical device and medicinal product within the meaning of Article 1(4) of [that directive] is to be treated as a valid [MA] under Directive [2001/83], where, as part of the authorisation procedure laid down in Annex I, Section 7.4, first paragraph, to Directive [93/42], the quality, safety and usefulness of the medicinal product component has been verified by the medicinal products authority of a Member State in accordance with Directive [2001/83]?

The ruling of the CJEU was clear – and contrary to the preliminary interpretation made by the German Federal Patent Court, providing that Article 2 of the SPC Regulation may not be interpreted extensively and in any case not in a teleological manner. Thus, in order for a product to qualify for SPC protection it has to have been subject to the marketing authorisation procedure of Directive 2001/83.[130] The CJEU also clarified that a product may be classified as either a medical device or a medicinal product, not both. A substance having an ancillary function in a medical device will not be classified as a medicinal product, even if it would have been, had it been sold separately. The CJEU was also clear in its conclusion that the authorisation of a drug-device combination is not to be considered equivalent to an authorisation for a medicinal product under Directive 2001/83, since the medical substance component in a drug-device combination is not focused on the medicinal product as such, but on the intended purpose of the medical device and of the incorporation of the substance into the device.

The conclusion of the CJEU ruling is that an SPC shall not be available for a product that is authorised as a medical device under Directive 93/42, even if the product incorporates, as an integral part, a substance which – if used

---

[130] Judgment of the Court (Ninth Chamber) of 25 October 2018, *Proceedings Brought by Boston Scientific Ltd*, C-527/17, EU:C:2018:867.

separately – might have been considered a medicinal product, even if the quality and safety of the substance has been controlled by analogy to the method applied to medicinal products under Directive 2001/83. On the other hand, the ruling does not exclude drug-combination products that have been classified as medicinal products (where the primary use of the product is the application of the active substance). Thus, it seems that the category under which a combination product is classified will also determine whether or not it can receive an SPC.[131]

4. The Rights Granted

4.1. The Term of Protection

An SPC is granted for a product that enjoys both a valid basic patent protection and a marketing authorisation in the country where the SPC is sought. In order to calculate the term of the SPC, one needs to specify the date of approval of the basic patent and the date of the granting of the marketing authorisation. According to Article 13 of the SPC Regulation, the maximum term of an SPC is five years. This in its turn gives a maximum effective patent term of 15 years.

The duration of the SPC will depend on the time that has elapsed between the filing of the patent application and the date of the first MA in the EEA. The difficulties that may rise with the identification of the 'first MA' were considered in the *Hässle* case.[132] The applicant had referred to a German MA (compliant with Directive 65/65) granted in 1 January 1988. An MA was granted in France and Luxembourg before the date of the German MA (also compliant with Directive 65/65). The applicant argued that the MA granted in France and Luxembourg could not be relevant for the purposes of the SPC application since the medicinal product could not be marketed in the specific countries without first being compliant with national pricing legislation. The CJEU rejected Hässle's argument ruling that the 'first authorisation to place (the product) on the market' does not refer to anything other than an MA compliant with Directive 65/65. This meant that it was not relevant whether or not the product could de facto be placed on the market. The Court stated that this should be interpreted in the same way throughout the Regulation and referred to any MA in accordance with Directive 65/65 (or the subsequent Medicinal Code).[133]

---

[131] In the European Commission, *Study on the Legal Aspects of Supplementary Protection Certificates in the EU*, Final Report [2018] Max Planck Institute for Innovation and Competition, the question was raised as to what would happen if a drug-combination product contained a substance that was authorised for the first time under the framework of this combination.

[132] Judgment of the Court (Sixth Chamber) of 11 December 2003, *Hässle AB v Ratiopharm GmbH*, C-127/00, EU:C:2003:661.

[133] Although the case does not expressly refer to Article 13, it could be concluded that it applies in the same way as it would apply for Article 19.

118 *The Supplementary Protection Certificate*

Both the *Novartis* and *AstraZeneca* cases,[134] concern whether a Swiss MA that is automatically recognised in Liechtenstein would constitute a 'first MA' for the purposes of the SPC Regulation. The CJEU ruled that this is the case in *Novartis*, and confirmed its ruling in the *AstraZeneca* case. In *Hässle*, the court had already provided that 'first MA' should in fact be interpreted in the same way throughout the Regulation, but in *Novartis* and *AstraZeneca* the CJEU was willing to read in Article 13 the changes that must be read into Article 3(b) of the SPC Regulation as a consequence of the EEA Agreement.

Article 3(b) provides that a valid authorisation to place the product on the market as a medicinal product has been granted in accordance with Directive 2001/83/EC (for the purposes of this subparagraph and the Articles which refer to it). An authorisation to place the product on the market granted in accordance with the national legislation of an EFTA State shall be treated as an authorisation in accordance with Directive 65/65/EEC.

In fact, Article 3(b) states that a Swiss MA automatically recognised in Liechtenstein is to be considered to be compliant with the Medicinal Code. One might hesitate in endorsing this interpretation, since the amendment is explicitly delimited to 'this subparagraph and the Articles which refer to it'. Article 13 includes no reference to Article 3(b). Article 3(b) refers to the MA granted by the Member State where the SPC has been sought, while Article 13 concerns the first MA granted anywhere in the EEA. Consequently, Article 13 could not be read in any other way than including the first authorisation granted in accordance with the Medicinal Code.

One of the concerns of the CJEU in the *Novartis* case was the fact that unless a Swiss MA automatically recognised in Liechtenstein constitutes the first MA in the EEA for the purposes of Article 13 of the SPC Regulation, there was a risk that the 15-year period of SPC duration would be exceeded.[135] However, this risk does not seem to be as great as the CJEU envisioned it.

The *AstraZeneca* case concerned the duration of the patent for gefitinib, a pharmaceutical marketed under the name Iresse for the treatment of non-small-cell lung cancer. In July 2002, AstraZeneca applied for an MA in Switzerland under the fast-track procedure. The application was approved in March 2004 on condition that AstraZeneca submitted Phase III data. The MA was suspended three years later and reinstated in December 2010. AstraZeneca also applied to the EMA for

---

[134] Judgment of the Court (Second Chamber) of 21 April 2005, *Novartis AG, University College London and Institute of Microbiology and Epidemiology v Comptroller-General of Patents, Designs and Trade Marks for the United Kingdom, and Ministre de l'Économie v Millennium Pharmaceuticals Inc*, C-207/03 and C-252/03, EU:C:2005:245; Order of the Court (Eighth Chamber) of 17 January 2014, *AstraZeneca AB v Comptroller General of Patents*, C-617/12, EU:C:2014:28.

[135] However, this disregards the principle of double marketability. See the Advocate General's Opinion in joined cases (Opinion of AG Ruiz-Jarabo Colomer of 21 April 2005, *Novartis AG, University College London and Institute of Microbiology and Epidemiology v Comptroller-General of Patents, Designs and Trade Marks for the United Kingdom and Ministre de l'Économie v Millennium Pharmaceuticals Inc*, C-207/03 and C-252/03, EU:C:2004:491).

an MA in January 2003, and because of its failure to provide necessary data, the MA was granted only in 2009. This was the first MA granted for Iresse. If the Swiss application were to be seen as the first MA, the SPC would result in less than three years of protection, while having the EMA MA as a basis for the SPC application would lead to a maximum duration of protection. While certain national jurisdictions accepted the EMA MA as the first MA, the UK opted for the Swiss MA. AstraZeneca appealed and the English High Court made a reference to the CJEU. The court applied the *Novartis* ruling in the specific case and concluded that the Swiss MA should in fact constitute the 'first' MA, to ensure that AstraZeneca would not get more than a total of 15 years of protection.[136] The Court chose not to consider AstraZeneca's main argument, namely the fact that such an interpretation is contrary to the purpose of the SPC Regulation, which seeks to compensate for the time, effort and money required to acquire an MA in accordance with the Medicinal Code (or its predecessor).

Another interesting issue concerns SPCs with a nil or negative term of protection. When the marketing authorisation is granted at a date earlier than five years from the grant of the basic patent, the term of the SPC will be nil or even negative. For a number of years, applying for an SPC protection for such pharmaceuticals was therefore considered pointless. However, the entry into force of the Paediatric Regulation and the possibility to receive a six-month extension raised an interest in receiving even a negative term of SPC protection, as a few days of exclusivity can generate considerable revenue in the pharmaceutical sector. The paediatric extension and the conditions which the SPC-protected medicinal product must fulfil for it to be applicable are found in Article 36 of the Paediatric Regulation and Article 13(3) of the SPC Regulation.[137]

The extension of the duration of the SPC may be expected to be used more often taking into account the fact that it is now mandatory to agree upon and submit a PIP in order to receive a marketing authorisation for a medicinal product, regardless of whether it will be used for the paediatric population or not.[138]

4.2. The Nature of the Rights Granted and their Enforcement

A medicinal product that falls under the scope of Article 1(b) of the SPC Regulation is protected in the same way as the basic patent would. Article 5 of the SPC Regulation provides that the protection granted carries the same rights and the same limitations and obligations.

The SPC application does not require (or permit) an independent description of the product that will be protected. According to Article 4 of the Regulation, the

---

[136] As stated previously, this is rather misguided as the 15 years should be calculated on the basis of the first MA to be granted pursuant to the Medicinal Code.
[137] See Article 36(1) of Regulation 1768/92/EEC.
[138] Unless the competent authority has issued a general or specific waiver or a deferral.

product that is to be covered by the SPC will be defined by means of the MA, while its scope will be determined by means of a combination of the scope of the patent and that of the granted MA. However, it seems that the product description, which has previously been considered to have an informative role only, is becoming more and more central in the process of attempting to match the scope of the MA and that of the basic patent. A failure to do so could lead to the invalidity of the SPC.

Thus, the principles that govern the interpretation of whether an SPC has been infringed upon will be the same as those used for a patent. However, it is important to note that the scope of the exclusive right granted by means of an SPC will not be the same as that of the basic patent.[139] In the CJEU case of *Novartis AG v Actavis UK Ltd*,[140] the Court held that Articles 4 and 5 of the SPC Regulation must be interpreted as meaning where 'a product' consisting of an active ingredient was protected by a basic patent and the holder of that patent was able to rely on the protection conferred by that patent for that 'product' to oppose the marketing of a medicinal product containing that active ingredient in combination with one or more other active ingredients.

Thus, the SPC holder may enforce an SPC that covers active ingredient A against a third party that uses a 'product' comprising active ingredient A (eg a product combining A with B or A with B and C, etc), provided that this would infringe on the basic patent.

Another important question to discuss is which criteria are to be used to determine whether a product falls under the scope of the certificate. One criterion that has been promoted has been that of the legal basis of the MA granted for the alleged infringing product. Thus, if the alleged infringer has submitted an application as a generic version of the original product, one could conclude that there is infringement. In the case of E-16/14,[141] the Oslo District Court asked the EFTA Court to clarify the role of whether the MA for the alleged infringer was a dependent one or a standalone. The Court responded that what is important is that the alleged infringer sells an active substance that is referred to in the marketing authorisation and has the therapeutic effects for which the marketing authorisation was granted. The legal basis of the alleged infringer's MA was not important. Thus, according to the EFTA Court, the route that the alleged infringer had taken in order to place the product on the market was considered to be decisive.[142] The role that the legal basis of an MA might play is interesting. A viable conclusion would be that the fact

---

[139] The SPC covers a 'product', while the patent covers an 'invention'.

[140] Order of the Court (Eighth Chamber) of 9 February 2012, *Novartis AG v Actavis UK Ltd*, C-442/11, EU:C:2012:66; and Order of the Court (Eighth Chamber) of 9 February 2012, *Novartis AG v Actavis Deutschland GmbH & Co KG and Actavis Ltd*, C-574/11, EU:C:2012:68.

[141] Request for an Advisory Opinion from the EFTA Court by the Oslo District Court received on 23 July 2014 in the case *Pharmaq AS v Intervet International BV*.

[142] The Swiss Federal Patent Court in its ruling of 12 October 2017 reached a different conclusion, stating that the fact that the alleged infringer had applied and received an MA by determining that the alleged infringed product was a reference drug X, meant that the generic was infringing on the SPC of product X.

that the MA application of the second drug is presented as a 'generic version' of the original is a strong indication that the second drug is infringing. On the other hand, the fact that the second drug has proceeded with a separate MA application does not necessarily mean that no infringement has occurred.

According to Article 15 of the SPC Regulation, the grounds of invalidity of an SPC are the same as those for the basic patent, but also include the reasons for which an SPC should not have been granted in the first place:

(i) patent granted contrary to Article 3;
(ii) the basic patent has lapsed before its lawful term expires;
(iii) the basic patent has been revoked or limited to the extent that the product for which the SPC was granted would no longer be protected by the claims of the basic patent or, after the basic patent has expired, grounds for revocation exist which would have justified such revocation or limitation.

The list of grounds of invalidity in Article 15(1) of the SPC Regulation are non-exhaustive.

Article 4 of the SPC Regulation provides that 'within the limits of the protection conferred by the basic patent, the exclusive right conferred by a certificate shall extend only to the product covered by the authorisation to place the corresponding medicinal product on the market and for any use of the product as a medicinal product that has been authorised before the expiry of the certificate'.

While there seems to be a general preference for broad claims in applications, specific claim-drafting, in particular with regard to the specification of the active substance and its chemical substance, appears to be more favourable for the granting and enforcement of SPC protection.

In the *Farmitalia* case,[143] the CJEU provided that where an active ingredient in the form of a salt is referred to in the MA concerned and is protected by a basic patent in force, the SPC can cover the active ingredient as such and its various derived forms, such as salts and esters, as medicinal products as long as these are covered by the basic patent. The same case also confirms that the national interpretation of the scope of patent claims will in fact also influence the interpretation of the scope of the SPC protection. The Court stated that the scope of the SPC could not exceed the scope of the basic patent. In the *Yeda* case,[144] the Court of Hague and the Council of the State were concerned with the wording of a product description. In the specific case, the applicant applied for an SPC on the basis of an MA for Humira adalimumab. The applicant provided in its product description that the product was defined as 'human monoclonal antibodies against tumour necrosis factor alpha'. The Dutch patent office granted an SPC for the product adalimumab,

---

[143] Judgment of the Court (Fifth Chamber) of 16 September 1999, *Farmitalia Carlo Erba Srl*; C-392/97 ECLI:EU:C:1999:416.

[144] Order of the Court (Fourth Chamber) of 25 November 2011, *Yeda Research and Development Company Ltd and Aventis Holdings Inc v Comptroller General of Patents, Designs and Trade Marks*, C-518/10, EU:C:2011:779.

but refused to grant an SPC based on the product description provided by the applicant. Obviously, the applicant attempted to extend the scope of the SPC by using a 'generous' product description that also contained other elements, antibodies, not provided under the specification of the MA. However, these elements were covered by the basic patent. In support of this, the applicant referred to *Farmitalia*, which according to the applicant's interpretation allowed the SPC to cover even derivatives of the free bases covered by the MA. The Court of Hague upheld the decision of the Dutch patent office, stating that *Farmitalia* could not be used to allow the inclusion of antibodies under the scope of an SPC. The molecular structure of antibodies provides that they may not be considered to be implicitly included in an MA that makes no explicit reference to them. While salts and esters (as in the *Farmitalia* case) are considered to be the same active ingredient under Article 10(2)(b) Dir 2001/83, this is not the case with antibodies.[145]

Yet another interesting ruling attempted to clarify the scope of the SPC protection by considering whether it would be possible to invalidate a certificate that was broader than the scope of the MA.[146] In this case, which was referred to the EFTA Court, the Norwegian Court asked about the interpretation of the Articles 2, 3 and 4 of the Regulation, wanting to know whether such an SPC would be valid and – if so – whether the scope of the SPC would be limited to the scope of the granted MA. The EFTA Court replied that such an SPC would be held invalid.[147]

A paediatric extension would seem to have the same scope as the SPC, since it merely constitutes its direct extension. This has not yet been subject to the scrutiny of the CJEU. However, it is clear that the extension will not be limited to the paediatric indication (if any), since the Paediatric Regulation is clear in this respect: the extension is provided for fulfilling the PIP and not for finding a paediatric use of the pharmaceutical.

Article 5 of the Regulation provides that 'subject to the provisions of Article 4, the certificate shall grant the same rights conferred by the basic patent and shall be subject to the same limitations and the same obligations'. It is important to note that a pending SPC application does not confer on the applicant the same rights as a pending patent application. Very often, this is of limited practical importance since the SPC is granted before the patent lapses (the pharmaceutical in question is thus protected in any case). However, there are situations where the patent expires before an SPC is granted. In such cases, generics companies usually avoid entering the market to minimise costs and legal risks, which probably also explains why there are no cases concerning this situation.

Article 5 seems to be clear when it comes to defining the scope of rights granted by means of an SPC, which is the same as for the rights entailed by the patents. However, this clarity decreases when taking into consideration the fact that the

---

[145] Salts and esters of an active ingredient that has previously been subject to a marketing authorisation may make use of the abridged procedure in Article 10 of the Directive 2001/83.
[146] The case concerned the invalidity of SPC No 2011014 granted by the Norwegian Patent Office.
[147] *Pharmaq AS v Intervet International BV*, 9 April 2015, E-16/14.

SPC system is based on an EU Regulation while patent law is, to this day and with the exception of the Biotech Directive, an area of law that is not subject to EU harmonisation.[148]

The SPC system includes the so-called 'specific mechanism'. In general, goods placed on the market in a Member State may be imported to another Member State, regardless of any intellectual property rights that may be applicable.[149] The specific mechanism is an exception to this rule and is included in Annex IV of the Accession Treaty. The specific mechanism was introduced due to the fact that it was not possible, until the early 1990s, to obtain patent protection for pharmaceuticals in a number of countries, in particular in the former communist states.[150] Placing a product on these markets, before their EU accession, meant that the product could not be re-imported to the EU, since the rights to the product in question were not exhausted. Once they joined the EU, the principle of exhaustion applied to them as well. An intermediate solution was necessary, as the prices of pharmaceuticals in these countries were so low at the time of accession that applying the general principle of exhaustion would mean that parallel importers would be able to halve the prices. To avoid strategic measures of patent holders in terms of either refraining from placing their products on these markets, or considerably increasing the prices of these pharmaceuticals, which could have an impact on their accessibility, the specific mechanism was introduced. Under this mechanism, a party interested in importing pharmaceuticals from the Member States in question had to demonstrate to competent authorities in the import application that one month's prior notification has been given to the holder or beneficiary of protection. In the C-593/13 *Merck* case, the CJEU provided that the patent (or SPC) holder does not have to indicate its intentions to act within the one-month period stipulated in the procedure. On the other hand, the notification does not have to be given by the party intending to proceed with the import, but it should identify the party clearly.[151]

The specific mechanism is a means to provide compensation to the right holder for the unavailability of sufficient protection in the new EU Member States prior to their accession to the EU. However, the question is what kind of protection one would be expected to be granted. In the *Pfizer* case, no equivalent patent or SPC was available on the application date of the patent in the new EU Member States (31 August 1990) and equivalent SPC protection was available on the application date of the SPC in the new EU Member States (26 June 2003).[152] According to the Opinion of the Advocate General, the specific mechanism should not be limited to

---

[148] With the exception also of the Bolar exemption.
[149] See Article 34 TFEU.
[150] Such as Poland, Hungary, the Slovak Republic, Latvia, Estonia, Lithuania, the Czech Republic and Slovenia.
[151] Judgment of the Court (Grand Chamber) of 16 June 2015, *Presidenza del Consiglio dei Ministri and Others v Rina Services SpA and Others*, C-593/13, EU:C:2015:399.
[152] Judgment of the Court (Second Chamber) of 21 June 2018, *Pfizer Ireland Pharmaceuticals, Operations Support Group v Orifarm GmbH*, C-681/16, EU:C:2018:484.

situations where SPC protection was available on the relevant date, but also where it was practically possible for the SPC holder to obtain an SPC at that time.[153] Since it was not possible for the applicant to acquire a patent protection, the SPC protection would only be a theoretical possibility. In practice, the application would not fulfil one of the basic requirements: patent protection. The specific mechanism would be unavailable only if patent protection was an alternative, and the applicant chose not to use it. Finally, since the paediatric extension is not an independent right, but an extension of the SPC term, the Specific Mechanism is also relevant throughout the term of the paediatric extension.

4.3. The SPC Manufacturing Waiver

A proposal for a regulation amending SPC Regulation was published in May 2018. The objective was to introduce an exception, referred to as the 'manufacturing waiver'. The justification of this new regulation is to support the generics and biosimilars industry and thus contribute to it becoming competitive at an international level. This proposal was not uncontroversial.[154] In fact, the pharmaceutical industry in both Europe and the United States expressed their opposition to this exception, which would entail that manufacturing of pharmaceuticals protected by an SPC could start six months before the expiry of SPC protection.[155]

The Commission stated that the lack of such an exception has had two major effects on the European pharmaceutical market:[156]

(1) it had prevented manufacturers (or 'makers' in the final text of the Parliament and the Council) of generic and biosimilar medicaments established in the Union from manufacturing, even for the purpose of exporting to third-country markets in which such protection does not exist or has expired; and

(2) it had made it more difficult for those manufacturers (makers) to enter the Union market immediately after expiry of the SPC, given that they were not able to build up production capacity ('for export and for the purpose of entering the market of a Member State' as the Parliament and Council added to the text of the proposal) until the protection provided by the certificate had lapsed, unlike manufacturers located in third countries where protection did not exist or had expired.

---

[153] Opinion of the Advocate General Tanchev C-681/16, ECLI:EU:C:2018:69.

[154] Medicines for Europe published a document entitled 'Comparison of expiry dates of protection worldwide', where it compared the situation of the protection conferred to 109 products in the EU, the United States, Korea, China, India and Canada. In all cases, the protection conferred in Europe expired later than in Canada, India and China. It expired later in Europe than in the United States in 88 per cent of the cases (97 against 12) and later in Europe than in Korea in 94 per cent of the cases (103 against 6): www.spcwaiver.com/files/Comparison_expiry_dates.pdf [Accessed on 16 June 2020].

[155] See Regulation 2019/933/EU of the European Parliament and of the Council of 20 May 2019 amending Regulation 469/2009/EC concerning the supplementary protection certificate for medicinal products (Text with EEA relevance) [2019] OJ L 153/1–10.

[156] Ibid. Recital 4.

The Commission concluded that the lack of an exception had put European manufacturers of generics and biosimilars at a clear competitive disadvantage, and the EU had a responsibility to act, since the industry was under threat. Although the TRIPS Agreement is not applicable to SPCs, the new Regulation was drafted to comply with the requirements of Article 30 of the TRIPS Agreement.

This is not the first time the EU has attempted to clarify and regulate the question of the manufacturing of pharmaceuticals covered by an SPC and their stockpiling, in order to be able to enter the market directly after the expiry of the patent protection. Already in 2003, European Institutions presented a proposal according to which manufacturing of pharmaceutical products should be considered an infringement under certain conditions.[157] The Commission proposed to modify Directive 2001/83 and include a Bolar-type exception.[158] The European Parliament in its turn extended this exception to include not only a marketing authorisation procedure but also the possibility to export to third countries.[159] The Commission was opposed to this proposal and the export exception was not adopted.[160]

Only two years before the presentation of the latest proposal for the manufacturing waiver, a free trade agreement was signed that had a clear impact on the political support for the amendment of the SPC Regulation. The Comprehensive Economic and Trade Agreement (CETA) was signed on 30 October 2016 between the EU, its Member States and Canada.[161] According to Article 20 of the CETA,

---

[157] This was a few years after the Canada/EU case and the loss of the Commission in the case *Canada – Patent Protection of Pharmaceutical Products – Arbitration under Article 21.3(c) of the Understanding on Rules and Procedures Governing the Settlement of Disputes – Award of the Arbitrator*, WT/DS114/13, 18 August 2000.

[158] On 23 January 2019, the Committee on Legal Affairs voted to include a further subparagraph (ia) to Article 5(2)(a) to also exempt from the scope of protection of the SPC 'making a product, or a medicinal product containing that product, for the purpose of storing in the Member State of making, during the final 2 years of validity of the certificate referred to in paragraph 1, in order to place that product on the market of Member States as from day 1 after the expiry of the certificate in those Member States', and (iia) to 'any act or activity for the purpose of import of medicinal products, or parts thereof, into the Union merely for the purpose of repackaging and re-exporting'. The first limitation means introducing a day-one entry to the EU and the second makes clear that activities intended only for repackaging or re-exporting are not covered by the exclusive right of the SPC. Recitals 7 to 11 are modified in the sense of including an application of the exception not only to exports but also to 'entry into the EU market as from day 1 after the certificate has expired'. See also the proposal of modification to Recital 20. The text was widely endorsed in the three committees that gave their opinion and finally approved by 21 votes in favour and two against. The limitation of two years was introduced by the JURI Committee, not by the other two committees, INTA and ENVI (Committee on Legal Affairs, 'Compromise amendments on the draft report on supplementary protection certificate for medicinal products', 2018/0161(COD), Brussels, 23 January 2019, www.europarl.europa.eu/cmsdata/159901/juri-committee-voting-list-supplementary-protection-certificate.pdf [Accessed on 16 June 2020].

[159] The justification serves to support the export of generics.

[160] See also European Commission, *Guide to the Comprehensive Economic and Trade Agreement (CETA)* [2017]: https://trade.ec.europa.eu/doclib/docs/2017/september/tradoc_156062.pdf [Accessed on 17 June 2020].

[161] Article 22.27(6) of CETA establishes that it is 'without prejudice to a possible extension of the period of *sui generis* protection by a Party as an incentive or a reward for research in certain target populations, such as children'. In the case of the European SPCs, this additional extension is for

parties to the agreement are under an obligation to grant *sui generis* rights to pharmaceutical products. The EU had granted such *sui generis* right since 1992, under the name SPC. According to CETA, the term of protection of the *sui generis* right would be between two (minimum) and five (maximum) years. The signature of CETA led to an amendment to the Canadian Patent Act.[162] One of the most important changes was the introduction of Articles 104–22, regulating the new Certificate of Supplementary Protection (the CSP). The term of this new right would be maximum two years.[163] The regulation of the CSP included an exception for pharmaceuticals that were manufactured in order to be exported from Canada.

At the same time, the DG Internal Market, Industry, Entrepreneurship and SMEs (DG Growth) commissioned Charles Rivers Associates to conduct a study to evaluate the economic impact that exceptions to patent rights and SPC rights (such as the Bolar provision, exports during the term of protection, stockpiling) would have on the European pharmaceuticals industry. The report was published on 5 October 2017 and the conclusion was clear: the European pharmaceuticals industry would in fact benefit from such exceptions.[164] In the Commission's proposal, the title of Article 4 would be modified from 'Subject matter of protection' to 'Subject matter of protection and exceptions to rights conferred', so as to include the manufacturing waiver. However, the Parliament decided after a number of amendment proposals that the right place for the manufacturing waiver would be Article 5 'Effects of the certificate'. This approach would take into consideration the fact that the manufacturing waiver is an exception to the rights conferred by the certificate; as such, it should be placed in Article 5 of the Regulation (EC) No 469/2009. Article 5(2) presents the exception and includes the four conditions that need to be fulfilled in order for the exception to be applicable (such as labelling, communication, etc).[165]

---

six months according to Regulation 1901/2006/EC of the European Parliament and of the Council of 12 December 2006 on medicinal products for paediatric use and amending Regulation 1768/92/EEC, Directive 2001/20/EC, Directive 2001/83/EC and Regulation 726/2004/EC, published in [2006] OJ L 378/1.

[162] See House of Commons of Canada, Bill C-30, (First Reading) 31 October 2016.

[163] Ibid. Article 116(3).

[164] European Commission, *Assessing the economic impacts of changing exemption provisions during patent and SPC protection in Europe*, Charles River Associates, February 2016.

[165] In European Commission, *Communication to the European Parliament, the Council, the European Economic and Social Committee and the Committee of the Regions, Upgrading the Single Market: more opportunities for people and business*, COM [2015] 550 final, the Commission stated that '[t]o strengthen EU-based manufacturing and competitiveness in industry sectors whose products are subject to regulated market authorisations, the Commission will explore a recalibration of certain aspects of patent and SPC protection. An SPC manufacturing waiver could allow the European generic and biosimilar medicines industries to create thousands of high-tech jobs in the EU and many new companies'; Thyra De Jongh, Alfred Radauer, Sven Bostyn and Joost Poort, a team in the Technopolis Group, explained at p 86 of the report 'Effects of supplementary protection mechanisms for pharmaceutical products' (Final report, May 2018) that '[i]n 2015, the Commission issued a communication in which it expressed its intent to consider the introduction of a targeted SPC manufacturing waiver for export purposes. Rationale for this waiver is that, as long as SPC protection on the reference product is still in force in European markets, manufacturers of generics or biosimilars are not allowed to produce in

The acts covered by the exception are the making of a product for the purpose of export to third countries, storing it in the Member States where it is to be made in order to be placed on the market of the Member States after the expiry of the certificate, and any related act that is strictly necessary for its making in the Union.[166] The exception includes yet another category of acts, such as those that are 'strictly necessary for that making or for the actual export and the actual storing'. Such acts are referred to in the Recital of the Regulation and include: the processing, supplying, offering to supply, importing, using, synthesising an active ingredient, temporary storing, advertising and related acts performed by third parties that have a contractual relation with the SPC holder.[167]

The Regulation also includes a list of acts that are not covered by the exception and that would thus constitute SPC infringement. These include placing on the market of a Member State product that was initially intended for export, storing products that are intended to be placed on the market for other reasons than export, re-importation of products that were produced in order to be exported, and any act or activity that in fact does not fall under the scope of the exception. Most of the limitations were included in the first proposal of the Commission,[168] one of the most important perspectives being to safeguard that pharmaceutical products that were meant to be exported were re-imported to the EU as long as the SPC was valid.[169]

Providing for an exception that means that generic products can enter the market on the day after the SPC protection expires seems to be an important and natural measure in order to support the generics industry, but was not included in the initial proposal of the Commission. In fact, it was the amendment introduced by the European Parliament that provided for this exception. The initial proposal was that the manufacturing could be initiated two years before the expiry of the

---

EU Member States. This is said to put EU-based manufacturers at a disadvantage compared to non-EU-based operators. The waiver is primarily intended to promote Europe-based manufacturing, and thereby accelerate access to generic products for European consumers but is also hoped to have a knock-on effect on innovation by promoting increased investment in high skill jobs in Europe' www.ivir.nl/publicaties/download/effects-of-supplementary-protection-mechanisms-for-pharmaceutical-products.pdf [Accessed on 16 June 2020].

[166] The term 'making' has its origin in Article 29 of the Community Patent Convention as one of the acts falling under the scope of the exclusive right of the patent holder. The same term is found in Article 7 of the Proposal of 1 August 2000 for a Council Regulation on the Community patent and Article 25 of the Agreement on a Unified Patent Court.

[167] See Recital 9 of Regulation 469/2009/EC.

[168] All limitations except the storing limitation.

[169] In relation to the date on which the patent expires, the Committee on Legal Affairs voted on 23 January 2019 to modify paragraph 5 of Article 4 and Recitals 21 and 22 accordingly, in the sense that the exception contemplated in paragraph 2 'shall apply to certificates that are applied for on or after the entry into force of this Regulation. It shall also apply in the case only of certificates for which the basic patent expired on or after 1 January 2021': Committee on Legal Affairs, *Compromise amendments on the draft report on supplementary protection certificate for medicinal products*, 2018/0161(COD), Brussels, 23 January 2019, www.europarl.europa.eu/cmsdata/159901/juri-committee-voting-list-supplementary-protection-certificate.pdf [Accessed on 16 June 2020].

SPC; this was limited to six months by the Council.[170] In economic reports on the effects of SPC protection on the industry, six months has been referred to as the time period needed by generics manufacturers to enter the market. However, this specific period has been criticised as being too short, in particular for biosimilars, where there is a longer production time.[171]

Naturally, the manufacturing waiver is counterbalanced by a detailed system of requirements on the entity making use of the exception, concerning the labelling of the products to be exported and the obligation to inform clients (and also all contractual parties that are involved in the distribution of these pharmaceuticals) that the products in question have been produced under the scope of this specific exception. The same obligation is applicable to those that store and contribute to placing the products on the market the day after the SPC protection has expired. Furthermore, the regulation includes a number of measures that will guarantee the transparency of the system, placing an obligation on the party that makes use of the exception to provide state authorities with information as well as to be of assistance in this respect also to the SPC holder. Information that is communicated to the state authorities that could be of sensitive commercial nature may be considered confidential.[172]

5. The SPC Beneficiary

5.1. Several Patent Holders for the same Product?

According to *Biogen*, two different patents may be issued an SPC for the same product.[173] The regulation was drafted with the basic assumption that the patent and the MA were in fact in the same hands.

In *AHP Manufacturing v Bureau voor de Industrielle Eigendoom*,[174] the Dutch Industrial Property Office rejected an application for an SPC for a product on the basis of there being different patents with different patent holders. The CJEU ruled that the granting of an SPC for an identical product on the basis of another patent is possible. In this case, the CJEU stated that it is important that the interpretation

---

[170] The Permanent Representatives Committee approved the proposal of the Parliament after shortening it to six months.

[171] Miguel Vidal-Quadras, 'Analysis of EU Regulation 2019/933 on the SPC Manufacturing Waiver Exception' [2019] 50 *International Review of Intellectual Property and Competition Law*, 1, 971–1005.

[172] In the original proposal of the Commission, the manufacturing waiver would be applicable only to such SPCs as were granted on or after the date of the first day of the third month that followed the month in which the amending regulation would be published. This provision was amended after the reading of the Parliament and the Council placing the date of application on 2 July 2022.

[173] Judgment of the Court (Sixth Chamber) of 23 January 1997, *Biogen Inc v Smithkline Beecham Biologicals*, C-181/95, EU:C:1997:32, para 28.

[174] Judgment of the Court (Third Chamber) of 3 September 2009, *AHP Manufacturing BV v Bureau voor de Industriële Agendum*, C-482/07, EU:C:2009:501 para 40 and para 41.

of the regulation is not merely literal, but also teleological, where the general objectives of the regulation are to be given a dominating role.

A general conclusion could be that the prohibition in Article 3(c) only applies in situations where the same patent holder has already obtained an SPC for the same product.[175]

5.2. Making Use of a Third-party MA

The Opinion of the AG in the *Biogen* case[176] expressed the view that, when drafting the SPC Regulation, the legislator had a rather simplistic approach to the structure of the pharmaceutical industry where the patent and the MA are in the hands of the same commercial entity. This does not always seem to correspond to practices in the pharmaceutical industry. Several different cases are imaginable where the patent holder is not the holder of the MA. For instance, a company might have developed the invention and acquired the patent, while a licensee might have proceeded to clinical trials and received the MA. Another scenario is where a company has developed the invention and, knowing that another company is doing research in the same field, proceeds to a joint venture in order to further develop the product. When the entity holding the patent and the one holding the MA are related in some way, the situation does not seem to be problematic. However, in a situation where one entity develops a patented invention and another entity (without a clear commercial link) receives an MA for a product that partly covers the patented invention, this might become more controversial. In the *Biogen* case, an SPC was granted against the opposition of the MA holder.

In the *Eli Lilly* case, the CJEU ruled that when the patent holder has identified, at the time of the granting of the patent, the product that later becomes the subject matter of the MA and if the patent holder proceeds to investments concerning the product development, this means that the SPC must be granted, regardless of who the holder of the MA is. The question is how the examination of this criterion to be performed and what kind of evidence the national patent offices will have to provide. The application of this case law by national patent offices is divergent and problematic to say the least. In fact, the Greek patent office does not grant SPCs when the applications lack a copy of the MA for the product. That means that where the MA holder is opposed to the SPC application of the patent holder, it will be impossible for the patent holder to be granted the SPC, at least in principle. Of course, this becomes very important when it comes to infringement proceedings. Will the holder of the SPC in this situation be able to enforce the rights on the MA holder?

---

[175] See European Commission, *Study on the Legal Aspects of Supplementary Protection Certificates in the EU*, Final Report [2018] Max Planck Institute for Innovation and Competition 251.
[176] Judgment of the Court (Sixth Chamber) of 23 January 1997, *Biogen Inc v Smithkline Beecham Biologicals*, C-181/95, EU:C:1997:32, Opinion of AG Fennelly.

130 *The Supplementary Protection Certificate*

In this regard, there is a very interesting case from the Dusseldorf District Court[177] providing that the patent holder that receives an SPC may in fact enforce the rights of the SPC on the holder of the MA.[178]

The question of whether it will be possible to grant an SPC when the MA holder opposes such an application has raised an interesting discussion in literature. One of the most interesting proposals on how to address this rather complicated practical situation is that the third-party MA would trigger the deadline by which the SPC is to be filed (unless the patent is granted after the MA grant).[179] This remains a controversial issue to be further clarified by the CJEU.

Having different entities as holders of patent rights and marketing authorisation rights respectively, is not at all rare in practice. The patent holder may in fact be the licensor, and the licensee may be the party responsible for proceeding with the marketing authorisation in order to place the product on the market. In this case, one of the difficulties the patent holder might face in complying with Article 8(1) of the SPC Regulation is providing for a copy of the marketing authorisation. However, this is not a serious obstacle, as the competent national authority may request a copy from the MA authority. There could be other sources of complications, where the holder of the marketing authorisation is also the holder of another patent that it attempts to use as the basic patent for a separate SPC application. Complications could also arise from infringement proceedings between the holder of the basic patent and the holder of the marketing authorisation.

Complications between licensee and licensor with regard to an SPC application were dealt with in the *Biogen v SmithKline Beechams Biologicals SA* case.[180] In this case, SmithKline Beecham was the licensee of a marketing authorisation concerning two different patents owned by two different licensors, Biogen and Institute Pasteur. Since the interpretation of the SPC Regulation has led to the conclusion that it is only one medicinal product that will be granted SPC protection, there were concerns that the SPC application of one of the patent holders would preclude other parties from applying for an SPC. Biogen filed a complaint on the basis of the fact that SmithKline provided Institute Pasteur with a copy of the Belgian marketing authorisation, while refusing the same request from Biogen. In this case, the MA of Biogen was refused.

The CJEU concluded that where the patent holder and the marketing authorisation holder are two different commercial entities, the fact that the patent holder does not have a copy of the marketing authorisation shall not be grounds for the refusal of an SPC. Thus, there is no requirement that the patent holder and the

---

[177] Düsseldorf District Court, Decision of 10 November 2011 (2012) BeckRS21620.
[178] The reasoning of the Court is in fact based on *Biogen*, C-181/95, EU:C:1997:32.
[179] In the United States, it is only possible for the patentee that has proceeded to the marketing authorisation to acquire an SPC. Also, it is interesting to look into what the term 'connected' actually means. See European Commission, 'Study on the Legal Aspects of Supplementary Protection Certificates in the EU', Final Report (2018) Max Planck Institute for Innovation and Competition, 274.
[180] Judgment of the Court (Sixth Chamber) of 23 January 1997, *Biogen Inc v Smithkline Beecham Biologicals*, C-181/95, EU:C:1997:32.

marketing authorisation holder be the same, but the marketing authorisation holder cannot limit or restrict the patent holder.

The CJEU was recently called to consider a referral for a preliminary ruling concerning whether the SPC Regulation precluded the grant of an SPC to the holder of a basic patent in respect of a product which was the subject of a marketing authorisation held by a third party without that party's consent. The conflict in the national court concerned Genetech's EP No 1 641 822. Eli Lilly markets a formulation of an antibody called ixekizumab, under the name Taltz, as a treatment of severe plaque psoriasis and psoriatic arthritis. Genetec claimed that this substance fell under the scope of its patent. Genetech filed an application for an SPC on the basis of the basic patent and the MA for ixekizumab. In a parallel proceeding, the Court held the patent invalid. Eli Lilly argued in the main proceedings that the fact that the patent was invalid led to the conclusion that the SPC application could not be granted on two grounds, both because it did not comply with Article 3(a) of the Regulation, since there was no basic patent in force, and because of Articles 2 and 3(b), according to which it is not permitted to rely on the MA of a third party in an SPC application.[181]

The CJEU, taking into consideration the dispute in the main proceedings, stated that the question posed to the Court was hypothetical and irrelevant in the specific case. Thus, the CJEU, based on procedural hindrances,[182] chose not to answer the referred question, since it considered it to be unrelated to the case at hand. It is a pity that the Court chose to decline the possibility of bringing clarity to this question, since the rather complex business models in the pharmaceutical industry, where product development is not as straightforward as in the past, will also entail that depending on a third-party MA might become a frequent phenomenon.

6. Concluding Remarks

During the past few years, the CJEU has had several opportunities to clarify the terms of the Regulation and provide a stable and transparent SPC system. Taking into consideration the amount of case law and the choice of the questions referred to the CJEU in the past few years, it could be expected that the rules and provisions surrounding supplementary patent protection would stand on clear and solid ground, allowing for frictionless application of the system. This is unfortunately not the case.

The Court has, without a doubt, provided interesting rulings and contributed to answering some questions of practical importance for the application of the Regulation.[183] A question the Court has extensively dealt with is what constitutes a basic patent for the purposes of the Regulation. The CJEU clarified that

---

[181] *Eli Lilly and Company v Genentech Inc*, C-239/19, EU:C:2019:687.
[182] In particular, Article 53(2) of the Rules of Procedure of the Court of Justice of the European Union.
[183] *Actavis*, C-443/12, EU:C:2013:833.

an SPC was available only for products protected 'as such' by a basic patent, thus referring back to the definition of Article 1(c) of the Regulation, and the interpretation of the wording 'as such'. The CJEU held that, in order to protect the product 'as such', the 'active ingredient' had to constitute the subject matter of the invention covered by a basic patent.[184]

Furthermore, in *Forsgren*,[185] the Court stated that there was no requirement of absolute identity between an active ingredient protected by an SPC and the medicinal product as described in a marketing authorisation on which the SPC was based. If all other conditions are met, an SPC is clearly appropriate for an active compound bound to an active or inactive carrier, provided that the therapeutic effect of the active compound falls within the wording of the marketing authorisation. If all other conditions are met, an SPC is permitted where it relates to a portion of a molecule that is considered to be a carrier for another ingredient, provided that the carrier has its own therapeutic effect within the wording of the marketing authorisation.

Despite these interesting clarifications, the system still has a number of weaknesses. The CJEU does not seem to have satisfactorily answered the questions posed by national courts, making the application of the Regulation cumbersome and uncertain. Justice Arnold stated in 2014, that it was the third time in six months that he had had to refer questions to the CJEU and clarified that this is a result of the dysfunctional state of the SPC and its poor drafting, but also of the fact that CJEU case law is so problematic.[186]

There is a long list of practical questions related to the interpretation of specific provisions of the Regulation that have not yet been referred to the CJEU, or that the Court has chosen not to answer. On the list of specific questions of practical importance that remain unanswered we find the question of what happens if the patent holder wants to surrender a granted SPC in order to file an SPC application for another active ingredient. The CJEU did not provide a ruling on this question, though it had the opportunity in the *Forsgren* case.[187]

Furthermore, while the Court seems to be clear on the fact that a second SPC could be claimed for a combination product comprising ingredients that are not structurally stated in patent claims, it leaves room for interpretation concerning whether SPCs may be granted for combinations including entirely new and innovative ingredients. A further question of interest is how the duration of the SPC is to be calculated in such a case.[188]

---

[184] *Medeva*, C-322/10, EU:C:2011:773.
[185] *Arne Forsgren*, C-631/13, EU:C:2015:13.
[186] *Glaxosmithkline Biologicals SA v Comptroller-General of Patents, Designs and Trade Marks* [2013] EWHC 619 (Pat) para 86.
[187] However, the AG considered the surrender of a SPC to be governed by Article 14 of Regulation 469/2009 and thus that it did not apply retroactively.
[188] See, for instance, the rulings in *Medeva* (Judgment of the Court (Fourth Chamber) of 24 November 2011, *Medeva BV v Comptroller General of Patents, Designs and Trademarks*, C-322/10, EU:C:2011:773).

Naturally, one does not envy the task of the CJEU in interpreting the text of the Regulation. In addition to the rather poor formulation of the text, a major source of complication is the natural but rather problematic linkage between the SPC system, the patent system, and market authorisation system. This linkage has direct practical effects. In order to bring clarity to central provisions of the SPC Regulation, the CJEU has in several cases chosen to resort to the Market Authorisation Directive and the Market Authorisation Regulation,[189] which is natural, as the two systems intertwine. For instance, an adjuvant is not considered to be an active substance under the MA Directive, and thus not a protectable subject matter under the SPC Regulation.[190]

This linkage itself has led to further complications. The choice of the term 'product' in the text of the SPC Regulation, which has proven to be rather unfortunate in practice, was justified by its connection to MA law. Unfortunately, the choice of terminology is not always coordinated. The SPC Regulations uses the term 'active ingredient', while the MA Directive employs another term – 'active substance'. This raises the justified question of whether these two terms are synonyms or whether there are slight nuances to be considered when using one or the other. The term 'derivatives' is defined in the MA legislation, but not in the SPC Regulation, and the question is whether it would be possible to simply transfer the definition from the one system to the other. In the text of the MPA Directive, the term 'initial market authorisation' is used,[191] while this is not at all mentioned in the text of the SPC.

In addition to the terminological differences between the three systems, there are other more overarching issues that have an impact on the way the SPC system functions, such as their respective background and objectives. The MA system has as an objective to provide the market with safe pharmaceuticals, while the patent system serves to reward inventors with exclusive rights, with the SPC somewhere in the middle: rewarding patent holders that have lost patent protection time during the MA procedure. The objective of the SPC system is to provide a patent protection extension, and this explains the system's dependence on the claims and validity of the basic patent. Article 5 of the Regulation provides that the SPC confers the same rights and entails the same limitations and obligations as those that apply to the basic patent. However, that does not mean that it provides the same scope of protection. Defining the scope of protection is not a simple endeavour. An example of the difficulties in the interpretation of what is covered and what is not by means of the basic patent for the purposes of the SPC protection, could concern the interpretation of Markush claims. Will the patent claims cover every single combination falling under the span of a Markush claim? And will all

---

[189] Directive 2001/83 and Regulation 1107/2009.
[190] European Commission, *Study on the Legal Aspects of Supplementary Protection Certificates in the EU. Annex IV: Fact Finding Methodology*, Max Planck Institute for Innovation and Competition, Ref. Ares(2018)2748080 – 28/05/2018.
[191] See Article 6 of the Directive 2001/83/EC.

these different combinations be considered to have been 'implicitly but necessarily and specifically' described in the claims of the basic patent for the purposes of the SPC Regulation?

On the other hand, the fact that the SPC is to compensate the patent holder for the patent protection time lost during the MA procedure provides an explanation as to why the SPC only protects the part of the patented subject matter that has been subject to an MA. Recent CJEU case law reveals that formulations employed in the MA application are decisive for subsequent SPC applications.[192]

Obviously, the lack of national harmonisation of substantive patent law is behind a share of complications. The CJEU's reference to patent claims interpretation on the basis of Article 69 EPC is not helpful.[193] With the CJEU constantly throwing the ball back to national courts, it seems that harmonisation in the field of SPC protection is not a realistic expectation. In fact, it is rather interesting to note which national courts usually raise referral questions to the CJEU for the interpretation of the Regulation. The majority of referrals from national courts to the CJEU relating to SPCs, originate in Germany, the United Kingdom and the Netherlands. One cannot fail to wonder on the reasons for this. Are these jurisdictions those with most difficulties in applying the Regulation, or those which have acquired enough experience in the SPC Regulation to be able to realise the complications caused by an erroneous or at least inconsistent interpretation of its provisions?

This interrelation and interdependence between the three systems is proof of the interesting approach adopted in the United States. The US one-package system where the patent extension system, the market authorisation rules and the Bolar exemption are part of the same Act – the Hatch-Waxman Act – present the clear advantage that they belong to the same system, employing the same terminology and evolving in the same direction.[194] The Unitary Patent Package (UPP) could both provide a more holistic approach, closer to the US alternative, and contribute to substantive patent law harmonisation in the EU.[195] While the final product of the UPP negotiations did not bring the expected results, the Agreement on the Unified Court makes a direct reference to the SPC system and signals in this way the changes that will have to occur with the entry into force of the Regulation.[196]

---

[192] There are also procedural difficulties, since it is still possible to choose between a centralised and a decentralised procedure, which is also problematic when one is to determine the 'first marketing authorisation'.

[193] Article 69 has been interpreted differently in different EU Member States.

[194] Drug Price Competition and Patent Term Restoration (Hatch-Waxman) Act of 1984, Pub. L. No. 98-417, 98 Stat. 1585.

[195] Regulation 1257/2012/EU of the European Parliament and of the Council of 17 December 2012 implementing enhanced cooperation in the area of the creation of unitary patent protection [2012] OJ L 361/1.

[196] Georgia Gavriilidou, 'Pediatrics' in Maria Isabel Manley and Marina Vickers (eds), *Navigating European Pharmaceutical Law* (Oxford University Press 2015) 182 with further references.

Concluding Remarks 135

Apart from the terminological and procedural difficulties with implications for the application of the SPC Regulation, one should not fail to note the considerable changes that have occurred in the pharmaceutical industry and that have a clear impact on the patent and patent extension systems. The contemporary economic conditions for the development of new pharmaceuticals in the market vary substantially from the reality that pharmaceutical companies had to face at the time the SPC Regulation was negotiated. The generics industry, which in the past was in the periphery of the pharmaceutical industry, now holds an important position on the market. Attitudes towards generics have changed, with national public authorities awarding them the important task of providing the market with good-quality alternatives to original pharmaceuticals when patent protection expires.[197] This change of priorities is expressed in the way that the system has evolved in the United States, with Congress adopting the Biosimilars Act in relation to the regulatory approval of biopharmaceuticals, and thus carving out the scope of the Hatch-Waxman Act. While the Hatch Waxman Act was to a large extent patent-centric, the Biosimilars Act, has been characterised as almost patent-agnostic.[198] Thus, it seems that regulatory reforms are now, to a greater extent, based on patient needs and health economics, and less dependent on the strength of exclusive rights.[199]

The need to provide for a more flexible interpretation of the text of the SPC Regulation is also obvious in the CJEU rulings. In both the *Neurim* and the *Eli Lilly* case, the CJEU has opted (rather unsuccessfully) for a teleological analysis and interpretation of the text of the Regulation, thus having as a starting point the question of whether the patent holder is worthy of patent term extension as well as whether a specific interpretation is compliant with the overarching goals of the Regulation. A teleological interpretation of the text of the Regulation would of course be welcome, since it would create a vital flexibility in the system.

However, the question remains: is there any point in expecting further clarifications from the CJEU? Is the SPC Regulation a text upon which the vital supplementary protection system could be based? Or is it an outdated text, with no chance of being satisfactorily applied under the new challenges that the pharmaceutical sector currently faces. If this is the case, it might not too late for the Unitary Patent Package (UPP) to provide both the opportunity and a credible excuse for more radical changes in the SPC system. It seems that the industry

---

[197] Approximately 84 per cent of prescriptions in the United States are for generic drugs: IMS Institute for Healthcare Informatics, 'Declining Medicine Use and Costs: For Better or Worse? A Review of the Use of Medicines in the United States in 2012', May 2013 (citing IMS Health, National Prescription Audit (2012)).
[198] See Robert A Armitage, 'The Hatch-Waxman Act: A Path Forward for Making it More Modern' [2014] 40 *William Mitchell Law Review*, 4, 1200–58.
[199] See also Joanna T Brougher, 'The Biosimilars Act: Promoting or Discouraging the Development of Generic Biologics?' [2010] 7 *Biotechnology Healthcare*, Winter, 10, 22–23.

is confident that a unitary SPC is an indispensable asset to the UPP, and one to guarantee that the latter will prove important for the industry.[200] There are in fact interesting proposals as to how an administrative body granting unitary SPCs could be composed and financed, and the unitary patent court most certainly provides for a solid basis for an appeal system.[201] However, it would be a pity to limit the discussion to administrative issues, which though important will not solve the substantive difficulties in the application of the Regulation and will not clarify its ambiguous provisions.

---

[200] The industry here includes the European Crop Protection, the European Federation of Pharmaceutical Industries and Associations (EFPIA), and the Animal Health Industry (IFAH Europe).

[201] ECPA, EFPIA, and IFAH-EUROPE Joint Position Paper on a Proposal for a Unitary SPC, 1 July 2015, www.efpia.eu/media/15414/ecpa-efpia-and-ifah-europe-joint-position-paper-proposal-for-a-unitary-spc-july-2015.pdf [Accessed on 16 June 2020].

5
The Paediatric Extension

1. Background

Given how important it is for society to be able to provide medicines to children that are both safe and efficient, it is peculiar that the intense regulation of the pharmaceutical sector of the past 20 years did not, until recently, include the introduction of any specific measure for paediatric pharmaceuticals. Prior to the Paediatric Regulation, concerns on pharmaceuticals directed at the paediatric population were expressed in the International Conference on Harmonisation (ICH) guideline[1] and the Clinical Trials Directive.[2] However, these peripheral references did not have as an objective to change practices in the development of medicinal products and provide products that were particularly designed and/or tested for the paediatric population. That, in its turn, meant that the majority of pharmaceuticals used on children were developed and tested on adults, sometimes even for other medicinal conditions than the ones for which they were used in the paediatric population.[3]

In the EU, the discussions on the introduction of incentives regarding research on paediatric medicines started in 1997 under the auspices of the EMA.[4] It was not until 2006 that the EU adopted the EU Regulation on Paediatric Use (EC) No 1901/2006.[5] In order to incentivise research in this particular field, the Regulation provides for a set of obligations, incentives and rewards.[6]

One of the major findings, which also constituted a background for the Regulation, was the fact that 50–70 per cent of the pharmaceuticals prescribed

---

[1] European Medicines Agency, 'ICH E11(R1) guideline on clinical investigation of medicinal products in the paediatric population', 1 September 2017, EMA/CPMP/ICH/2711/1999.
[2] Directive 2001/20/EC of the European Parliament and of the Council of 4 April 2001 on the approximation of the laws, regulations and administrative provisions of the Member States relating to the implementation of good clinical practice in the conduct of clinical trials on medicinal products for human use [2001] OJ L 121/34.
[3] See Georgia Gavriilidou, 'Paediatrics', in Maria I Manley and Marina Vickers (eds), *Navigating European Pharmaceutical Law* (Oxford University Press 2015) 181–98.
[4] See ch 4, n 193.
[5] Which entered into force on 26 January 2007.
[6] Regulation 1901/2006/EC of the European Parliament and of the Council of 12 December 2006 on medicinal products for paediatric use and amending Regulation (EEC) No 1768/92, Directive 2001/20/EC, Directive 2001/83/EC and Regulation (EC) No 726/2004 (Text with EEA relevance) [2006] OJ L 378/1.

for the paediatric population have not been tested or licensed for paediatric use. Thus, the prescribing doctor must take responsibility for this off-label prescription and even decide (on the basic of vague criteria) on the adequate dosage. A common procedure is to adjust the dosage of an adult to the weight of the child. Naturally, this is not a safe way to proceed, since there are other factors than weight influencing the appropriate dosage, such as the age of the child. In general, children cannot be treated as small adults and in order to decide on correct dosage one needs to take their physiological characteristics into consideration.[7]

Before the Paediatric regulation was adopted, ethical concerns had been employed in order to justify the lack of testing on children. However, off-label paediatric prescription has worked as an unregulated form of testing and thus been both dangerous and unethical. More specifically, in the majority of the cases, children are either harmed by overdoses or not treated at all, because the dosage calculated is too small to have an effect.[8]

The reluctance of pharmaceutical companies to conduct clinical trials on children coincides with a lack of commercial incentives to develop pharmaceuticals for children, since the market is considered to be too limited. This lack of commercial incentives and the historic lack of clinical data on the paediatric population have led to an urgent need for a new regulatory framework.

2. The General Legal Framework

The Paediatric Regulation provides a set of rewards and incentives, as well as a series of obligations, in order to contribute to the development and accessibility of paediatric medicinal products. It has as an objective ensuring the achievement of these objectives without subjecting the paediatric population to unnecessary clinical trials, and without at the same time having the negative effect of delaying the marketing authorisation of adult pharmaceuticals.[9]

The major change in the obligations placed on the pharmaceutical product developers concerns the submission of a Paediatric Investigation Plan (PIP) at a relatively early stage of product development. In the PIP, the pharmaceutical

---

[7] See European Medicines Agency, *Concept Paper on the Development of a Quality Guideline on Pharmaceutical Development of Medicines for Paediatric Use* [2008] Doc. Ref. EMEA/138931/2008, 4–5.

[8] Albert Wertheimer, 'Off-label Prescribing of Drugs for Children' [2011] 6 *Current Drug Safety*, 1, 46–48; Committee on Paediatric Studies Conducted Under the Best Pharmaceuticals for Children Act (BPCA) and the Paediatric Research Equity Act (PREA), Board on Health Sciences Policy, Institute of Medicine, Marilyn J Field and Thomas F Boat (eds), 'Safe and Effective Medicines for Children: Paediatric Studies Conducted Under the Best Pharmaceuticals for Children Act and the Paediatric Research Equity Act' (National Academies Press 2012).

[9] Preamble 6 of Regulation 1901/2006/EC.

company must specify the paediatric studies that are to be completed before the application for a marketing authorisation is handed in. The PIP is submitted, at the latest, upon completion of the first phase of human pharmacokinetic studies.

This requirement applies irrespective of if the application concerns a second medical indication, new pharmaceutical forms, or new routes of administration of authorised medicinal products which are protected by an SPC or a patent qualifying for an SPC.[10] It is important to note that the scope of the Paediatric Regulation is broad, and equally applicable to all medicinal products, as well as to orphan drugs, something that differentiates the EU system from that in the US. The corresponding US legislation (the Pediatric Research Equity Act)[11] explicitly excludes orphan drugs from its scope.

Article 7 of the Paediatric Regulation will apply only if the applicant does not hold a marketing authorisation for that particular substance at the time the Paediatric Regulation came into force. However, if the applicant applies for an MA for a substance previously granted an MA but for another indication, form, or route of administration, the requirements of Article 7 will not be considered to be fulfilled.[12]

One of the aspects that requires interpretation and that concerns the scope of applicability of the regulation is Article 8 and what the wording 'patent which qualifies for the granting of a supplementary protection certificate' actually means. While the SPC Regulation stipulates the requirements to be fulfilled in order for a patent to receive SPC protection, the extensive and at times contradictory case law concerning the interpretation of key provisions of the SPC Regulation reveals considerable difficulties in this interpretation.[13]

Article 8 primarily requires a self-assessment of the applicant, who at the time of the PIP needs to determine whether or not the medicinal product developed can be granted a patent. The EMA and the national competent authorities do not have the mandate to review or change this assessment; thus, the applicant's own determination is binding throughout the regulatory procedure. This puts a considerable burden on the applicant, since failure to make a proper assessment will have an impact on the reward provided for under the Paediatric Regulation, while it can also lead to penalties for failing to provide accurate information to the regulatory authority.[14] In cases where the requirements of Article 8 are not met, the

---

[10] See Article 8 of Regulation 1901/2006/EC.
[11] Pediatric Research Equity Act, 117 STAT. 1936 PUBLIC LAW 108-55-3 December 2003.
[12] Article 7 of Regulation 1901/2006/EC makes a direct reference to Articles 6 and 8 of Directive 2001/83/EC of the European Parliament and of the Council of 6 November 2001 on the Community code relating to medicinal products for human use [2001] OJ L 311/67, and its applicable rules and requirements.
[13] See ch 4.
[14] Article 8 clarifies that: 'Article 7 of this Regulation shall apply to applications for authorisation of new indications, including paediatric indications, new pharmaceutical forms and new routes of administration'.

140 *The Paediatric Extension*

application for a new medicinal application or route of administration will not require the submission of a PIP or a decision of waiver or deferral. However, the applicant might still have the possibility to proceed to a paediatric use marketing authorisation (PUMA).

What remains unclear, however, is whether the applicant is able to proceed to a voluntary PIP if the requirements of Articles 7 and 8 of the Regulation are not fulfilled.[15]

3. A New Committee to Implement the Legal Framework: The Role of the Paediatric Committee (PDCO)

The PDCO consists of:[16]

- five members from the Committee for medicinal products for human use (CHMP);
- one member appointed by each Member State not represented through CHMP members (experts from national competent authorities);
- three members to represent patient organisations; and
- three members to represent health professionals.

The main task of the PDCO is to review and assess the contents of the PIP submitted for approval. It discusses the content and structure of the PIP with the applicant and issues an opinion. The PDCO may request the applicant to supplement the PIP with additional research and widen its study to include different subclasses of the paediatric population. In that case, the procedure will be paused until these modifications are made. The applicant has the right to request a clarification meeting with the Committee. It is also the PDCO that checks if the applicant has complied with the submitted PIP.

In order to facilitate for applicants, the PDCO has developed standard PIPs. It also has the product-specific task of granting waivers and deferral schemes. Furthermore, it is vested with the responsibility of supporting a European network for paediatric clinical trials, establishing an inventory of specific paediatric medicinal product needs, and providing advice regarding paediatric clinical trials.[17]

---

[15] Such an interpretation would be consistent with the objectives of the regulation, since the objective is to collect information about the paediatric applications of pharmaceuticals, irrespective of whether or not they will in the end be used for a paediatric population.

[16] See also ch 2.

[17] See also, in this respect, European Commission, *Communication from the Commission: Guideline on the format and content of applications for agreement or modification of a paediatric investigation plan and requests for waivers or deferrals and concerning the operation of the compliance check and on criteria for assessing significant studies* (Text with EEA relevance) [2008] OJ C-338/1.

Although the Committee has an extensive role in implementing the legal framework, it does not hold the primary role in the granting of MAs for medicinal products for paediatric use. This is done by the CHMP or a national competent authority. However, the PDCO can, upon the request of the CHMP, issue an opinion concerning the quality, safety and efficacy of a medicinal product for use in paediatric population.

The formally competent authority to reach a decision is the EMA, not the Commission – as is the case with MAs. The decision of the EMA is published publicly, but any information of potentially commercially sensitive nature is removed from the published documents.

4. The PIP

The PIP constitutes a description and documentation of the research and development programme for testing a specific pharmaceutical for paediatric use. It is a necessary step in the collection of data, and is thus a prerequisite for applying for a marketing authorisation (a general one) or a PUMA. The completion of the PIP will provide the data necessary to conclude which indications could be treated with the pharmaceutical and in what ways it could be used on the paediatric population. Naturally, the completion of the research could lead to the conclusion that the specific pharmaceutical cannot be used for the paediatric population at all. The outcome of the research does not have to be positive in order for the medicinal product to be granted an MA or to enjoy the rewards provided for under the Paediatric Regulation.

Article 7 of Regulation 1901/2006 provides that all applications for marketing authorisations for new medicines must include one of the following:

(a) the results of all studies performed and details of all information collected in compliance with an agreed paediatric investigation plan;
(b) a decision of the Agency granting a product-specific waiver;[18]
(c) a decision of the Agency granting a class-waiver pursuant to Article 11;[19] or
(d) a decision of the Agency granting a deferral.[20]

---

[18] For a review of decisions granting a product-specific waiver, see Heidrun Albrecht, 'Experiences with PIPs and their required revisions on the critical path of the development of medicines in indications for adult patients', Master of Drugs Regulatory Affairs, Bonn 2013: www.dgra.de/media/pdf/studium/masterthesis/master_albrecht_h.pdf [Accessed on 17 June 2020].

[19] According to Article 11 of the Regulation 1901/2006/EC, a waiver for a product or a whole class of products may be granted for three different reasons, '(a) that the specific medicinal product or class of medicinal products is likely to be ineffective or unsafe in part or all of the paediatric population; (b) that the disease or condition for which the specific medicinal product or class is intended occurs only in adult populations; (c) that the specific medicinal product does not represent a significant therapeutic benefit over existing treatments for paediatric patients'.

[20] Deferrals shall be granted according to Article 20 of the Regulation 1901/2006/EC if 'justified on scientific and technical grounds or on grounds related to public health. In any event, a deferral shall be

Article 7 also states that all documents submitted according to (a) shall cover all subsets of the paediatric population.

Thus, the major obligation placed on the pharmaceutical companies by means of the Regulation is the requirement to fulfil the research and development proposed in the PIP (and agreed with the EMA in advance). With the exception of deferrals and waivers, an MA application will be dependent on the submission of a completed PIP.

According to Article 8, the scope of Article 7 extends to applications for an MA for new therapeutic indications, pharmaceutical forms and routes of administration.[21]

The PIP must include an outline of each proposed trial and each part of the PIP must include:

(a) the processes in place to assess safety, quality and efficacy;
(b) the processes in place to facilitate the use of the medicinal product by making its use easier, safer and more effective; and
(c) a proposal for the age-appropriate formulation with respect to all of the different subsets of the paediatric population.

The PIP must specify which measures will be adopted in order for the pain, distress and fear of the children taking part in the trials to be minimised. Concerning trials conducted on a paediatric population, the EMA encourages clinical trial structures that enhance the selection of results while using a limited sample.[22]

Should the applicant disagree with the EMA's decision on the structure and content of the PIP, they may file an application for annulment before the General Court of the EU. In case the agreed PIP proves to be impossible or unrealistic, the applicant may initiate a modification procedure in accordance with Article 22 of the Paediatric Regulation.[23]

5. PIP Compliance Control

After completion of the PIP, a compliance control is conducted in order to monitor that all steps included in the PIP have been completed within the agreed timelines.

---

granted when it is appropriate to conduct studies in adults prior to initiating studies in the paediatric population or when studies in the paediatric population will take longer to conduct than studies in adults'.

[21] Article 8 applies where an authorised product is protected by an SPC or a patent that qualifies for an SPC; the studies must cover both new and existing formulations, indications etc.

[22] Paediatric clinical trials must be conducted in compliance with the requirements set out in Directive 2001/20/EC (Article 4), now replaced by Regulation 536/2014/EU, which entered into force in May 2016.

[23] The applicant may ask for both a modification of the PIP and a deferral or waiver while in the process of performing the PIP, if the request can be justified for reasons that were not foreseeable at the time the PIP was decided (Article 22 of the Regulation 1901/2006/EC).

Since the entry into force of the regulation, some provisions have proven to be more complicated to apply than others. One such provision is Article 16(1), stating that the PIP has to be submitted at the latest upon completion of the first phase of human pharmacokinetic studies for the new pharmaceutical indication in adults. Applicants usually consider this to be a very early stage in the product development and it has been noted that this deadline is very rarely respected.

The EMA has clarified that respecting timelines is a very important part of the application procedure, even if the timelines are not mandatory.[24] The EMA has also stated that if there is a need for a modification of the PIP, this is always possible under the PIP modification procedure.[25]

Other practical issues relate to the ethical concerns that may be raised by national or local ethical committees, in particular concerning authorisations for clinical trials performed on the paediatric population. An important complication occurs when national ethics committees challenge the structure and content of PIPs that were agreed upon by the PDCO. Differences in the approaches concerning PIPs between the FDA and PDCO have been a source of complication for applicants applying for MAs in several jurisdictions.[26]

Another situation that raises the concerns of applicants is when the PDCO makes requests to the applicant to study further or new paediatric indications, thus going beyond the indications on which the application giving rise to a PIP is based (an example is off-label use). Experience of the way PDCO works leads to the conclusion that it is keen on requesting clinical trials with a very broad scope. However, this could be very burdensome and rather discouraging for the applicant. It seems important to determine the scope of the PIP and how far the obligations of the MA applicant may stretch. This also raises the question of how to define the conditions that are subject to the PIP.

This very situation has been the subject of litigation. An MA applicant, Nycomed Denmark, brought an action against the EMA, claiming that the opinion of the PDCO to refuse the granting of a PDCO waiver under Article 11(1)(b) of Regulation (EC) No 1901/2006 for a medical imaging agent (perflubatane) for taking echocardiographs by ultrasound, sold under the brand Imagify, should be annulled. Supporting its application, Nycomed argued that the imaging agent was designed to diagnose coronary artery disease (CAD), a condition appearing only in the adult population. The PDCO rejected the waiver application and claimed in

---

[24] See European Medicines Agency, *How to better apply the Paediatric Regulation to boost development of medicines for children: Report on a multi-stakeholder workshop held at EMA on 20 March 2018*: www.ema.europa.eu/en/documents/report/how-better-apply-paediatric-legislation-boost-development-medicines-children-report-multi_en.pdf [Accessed on 17 June 2020].

[25] It is very often the case that the PIP is subject to four to five modifications from the adoption of the PIP to its final completion.

[26] See, for instance, Principles of Interactions between EMA and FDA Pediatric Therapeutics. June 2007: https://ec.europa.eu/health/sites/health/files/files/paediatrics/docs/peds_principles-of-interactions_en.pdf [Accessed on 17 June 2020]. See also European Medicines Agency, *Paediatric Gaucher disease: A strategic collaborative approach from EMA and FDA*, 6 July 2017, EMA/237265/2017.

144 *The Paediatric Extension*

support of this that the actual intended use of the product was not only CAD, but also improving the visibility of blood flow in heart muscle during ultrasound scans to detect myocardial perfusion defects. Such defects are a sign of multiple diseases, some of which occur in the paediatric population.[27]

Nycomed appealed and provided that the concept of 'disease or condition for which the medicinal product is intended' (Article 11(1)(b)) had been misinterpreted and that it was up to the applicant to define the scope of the indication for which the marketing authorisation of the medicinal product requested was intended. Nycomed argued further that the PDCO did not have the mandate to request a modification of the applicant's intended use or that PIP included uses that were possible but expected by the applicant.

The General Court upheld the EMA's decision and refused the waiver, finding that the indications referred to by the applicant merely constituted the starting point for the spectrum of possible applications and that the PDCO was able to take into account potential uses of the medicine in paediatric populations. In the specific case, the decision was based on the fact that the product was intend to help detect myocardial perfusion abnormalities, which are not characteristic only of adult conditions. The Court added that if the applicant could independently determine the scope and uses of the indications, the obligation of performing paediatric studies would be considerably limited, if not circumvented. Such a development would seriously endanger the objectives of the Regulation: to provide suitably adapted medicinal products for the paediatric population.[28]

Nycomed is an interesting case, since it provides a good illustration of the mandate and powers of the PDCO, which are very broad. It has been shown that the PDCO has considerable flexibility in assessing applications for PIP waivers and deferrals and thus plays a decisive role in the granting of paediatric extensions.

6. Exemptions and Waivers

According to Article 9 of the regulation, some product categories are exempted from the scope of Articles 7 and 8. These are generics, hybrid medicinal products, biosimilars, homeopathic and traditional medicinal products, and medicinal products containing one or more active substances of well-established medicinal use.

These products have to follow the traditional marketing authorisation procedure, but do not have to prove compliance with the requirements of Regulation (EC) No 1901/2006.

---

[27] Judgment of the General Court (Third Chamber) of 14 December 2011, *Nycomed Danmark ApS v European Medicines Agency (EMA)*, T-52/09, EU:T:2011:738.
[28] Should the determination of medicinal uses be left only to the applicant, that would create flexibility that could be manipulated and abused.

Article 11 of Regulation (EC) No 1901/2006 provides that the requirements set out in Article 7(1)(a) may be waived for some products and categories of products. A waiver may be granted for products:

(i) likely to be ineffective or unsafe in part or for all of the paediatric population;
(ii) intended for a disease or condition that occurs only in the adult population;
(iii) do not represent a significant therapeutic benefit over existing treatments for paediatric patients.

In fact, it is not only the applicant that may request a waiver. The PDCO may itself decide on a product-specific waiver when it considers the aforementioned requirements to be fulfilled. There are some notable difficulties in interpreting the second category of products, in particular, for example when a certain pharmaceutical is intended for an indication found only in the adult population, but could potentially be used in other indications in the paediatric population.[29]

According to Article 20 of the regulation, applicants may, when submitting a PIP, request a deferral of the initiation or completion of some or all the measures contained in the PIP in cases where:

(a) there is a justification on scientific or technical grounds;
(b) there is a justification on grounds related to public health;
(c) it is appropriate to conduct studies in adults prior to commencing studies on the paediatric population;
(d) studies in the paediatric population will take longer than in adults.

Article 21(1) of the Regulation clarifies that the granting of a referral must be accompanied by specific time limits for initiating or completing the measures concerned. These are to be determined on a case-to-case basis.[30]

7. The Incentives of the Regulation

Non-orphan medicinal products that fulfil the requirements of Article 36 of the Paediatric Regulation and for which applications have been submitted in accordance with Articles 7 and 8 will receive a six-month extension of the SPC term of protection. The extension will be granted to the holder of the patent or the SPC. This six-month extension is applicable even if the results of the PIP are not favourable (that is even if the PIP leads to the conclusion that the pharmaceutical in question may not be used for the paediatric population). The objective of the

---

[29] *Nycomed*, T-52/09, EU:T:2011:738.
[30] The possibility to ask for and be granted a referral is based on the wish to avoid the Regulation having the adverse effect of delaying the availability of a pharmaceutical for the adult population.

regulation is to incentivise research into pharmaceuticals for the paediatric population, not to reward results. This is also one of the main differences between the incentive scheme of the Paediatric Regulation and that of the patent system.

In order to obtain this six-month extension period, Article 36 states that:

(i) the marketing authorisation application shall include results of all paediatric studies, which must have been conducted in accordance with the agreed PIP;
(ii) the product is authorised in all Member States;
(iii) the product has not been designated as an orphan product;[31]
(iv) in the case of a new paediatric indication authorised under Article 8, the product must not have obtained the one-year extension of the period for marketing protection.

The calculation of the term of the SPC is based on Regulation (EC) No 469/2009. The SPC is calculated on the basis of the time that has elapsed between the filing of the patent and the date of the first marketing authorisation within the EU, less five years, and for a maximum period of five years. It is thus possible that the term of the SPC will be negative or nil. The question has been whether it is possible to grant an SPC with a negative term. Naturally, there has been an interest for some patent/SPC holders to receive an SPC with a negative term, since the paediatric extension can still give them a certain extension of their exclusivity.

The answer to this question was given in the *Merck and Co., Inc* case.[32] Merck handed in an application to receive the six-month paediatric extension for its diabetes pharmaceutical sitagliptin product. The important question the UKIPO had to answer was whether the SPC could in fact be of nil or negative term, in order for the medicinal product in question to qualify for the paediatric extension. The UKIPO considered that there is no concrete answer in the two Regulations (the SPC or the Paediatric Regulation), or in CJEU case law that would prevent the granting of nil or negative SPC. This was also the view of the Dutch patent office, while the Greek patent office had previously chosen to round up negative SPCs to zero.[33] The opposite view had been adopted by Germany and Portugal, concluding that a nil and negative term of SPC was excluded.[34]

In 2011, the CJEU ruled in a way that put an end to this uncertainty by stating that negative term SPCs were valid and could form the basis for a paediatric extension.[35]

---

[31] Orphan products are excluded from the six-month extension, but instead receive a two-year extension of their market exclusivity.
[32] Judgment of the Court (Second Chamber) of 8 December 2011, *Merck Sharp & Dohme Corp v Deutsches Patent- und Markenamt*, C-125/10, EU:C:2011:812.
[33] European Commission, *Study on the economic impact of supplementary protection certificates, pharmaceutical incentives and rewards in Europe*, Final report (May 2018), Copenhagen Economics.
[34] Ibid.
[35] *Merck Sharp & Dohme Corp*, C-125/10, EU:C:2011:812.

Another requirement of the regulation that has been interpreted in different ways by Member States is the requirement that the application for the six-month SPC extension must be lodged no later than two years before SPC expiry.

One of the relevant cases in this respect concerned Merck once again, in this case as the holder of an SPC for Cancidas (caspofungin). The agreed PIP was completed, and Merck obtained a positive opinion from the PDCO, confirming compliance with the agreed PIP decision. Merck then immediately applied for an SPC extension. Taking into consideration the fact that the application for SPC extension needs to be filed at the latest six months before SPC expiry, the timing of this application is very important. The central question in this case was whether the PDCO confirming compliance is sufficient in order to apply for an SPC extension. The outcome of the case was based on a combined interpretation of Articles 36(1) and 36(2) of the Paediatric Regulation and of Article 28(3), concluding that the statement of the PDCO is of crucial importance. However, in case the applicant is not able to produce this document for reasons beyond its control, an extension of the six-month deadline may be granted by the national patent office.[36]

Similar issues were considered in the *Cozaar* case. Du Pont de Nemours & Co was the holder of an SPC for Cozaar (losartan a pharmaceutical marketed by Merck & Co). The SPC entered into force on 9 July 2009 and expired on 1 September 2009. The initial MA concerned the indication of hypertension and the holder of the MA submitted another application for two new indications. Merck completed the paediatric studies in compliance with the agreed PIP and Du Pont submitted the application for the SPC extension at the UK Patent Office.

At the same time, Du Pont initiated a Mutual Recognition Procedure (MRP), with the Netherlands as the Reference Member State (RMS). However, when Du Pont handed in its application, the RMS had not approved the final version of the product information, and thus the applicant did not fulfil the requirements of Articles 36(2) and 36(3) of the Paediatric Regulation.[37] The patent office examiner granted an extension of the deadline in order for the applicant to provide evidence of compliance with the requirements of both the SPC and the Paediatric Regulation. The RMS statement was issued after the deadline had expired and thus the examiner refused the application of the SPC extension.[38] The decision was appealed to the High Court of Justice of England and Wales, which confirmed the assessment of the patent examiners.[39] In the end, the Court of Appeal reversed the decision of the High Court and allowed the granting of the SPC extension.[40]

---

[36] UK IPO, BL O/108/08, *Merck & Co Inc*, 14 April 2008.
[37] The requirements of Articles 36(2) and 36(3) were not fulfilled, as the statement of the RMS did not confirm compliance with the PIP and the product was not authorised in all Member States.
[38] UK IPO, BL O/096/09 *E I du Pont de Nemours*, 9 April 2009.
[39] *E I du Pont Nemours & Co v United Kingdom Intellectual Property Office* [2009] EWCA Civ 966.
[40] During the same period as the UK application for SPC extension, Du Pont had proceeded to further applications in the Netherlands and France, which were granted: *EI Du Pont de Nemours & Co*

Both these cases illustrate problems with the practical application of the Paediatric Regulation and also serve as proof of the interdependence of the provisions of the SPC Regulation and the Paediatric Regulation. In the aftermath of these cases, national patent offices proceeded to change their internal procedural rules, to provide greater flexibility. In its guidelines to applicants, the UK Patent Office states that the applicant has the possibility to apply for an SPC extension and then complete the application at a later time.[41]

Merck turned to the General Court in order to appeal the decision of the EMA and the European Commission, communicated by means of two letters, concerning the compliance statement for the pharmaceutical product Vfend. Merck claimed that the fact that the compliance statement could not be issued before the studies included in the agreed PIP were assessed for the purposes of the new indication was a misinterpretation of Article 28(3) of the Paediatric Regulation. Unfortunately, Merck withdrew its application and thus no ruling on the merits was provided.[42]

8. Rewards for Orphan Medicinal Products under Regulation 1901/2006

Already in Recital 29 of the Paediatric Regulation it is stated that orphan medicinal products are seldom protected by means of the patent system and thus cannot enjoy the SPC extension reward. Furthermore, Article 36(4) of the Paediatric Regulation provides that orphan drugs will not be entitled to the SPC extension even if they were patented.

On the other hand, according to Article 37 of Regulation No 1901/2006, designated orphan drugs for which the marketing authorisation application includes a complete PIP will be rewarded by means of a two-year extension of the 10-year market exclusivity.

In order for this to apply, the applicant needs to provide that (i) the application includes the results of all paediatric studies that have been conducted in accordance with the agreed PIP, and (ii) the marketing authorisation includes a statement indicating compliance of the application with the agreed and completed PIP.

As for other pharmaceuticals, there is no requirement that the orphan drug will be used for the paediatric population.

Contrary to what is the case for the SPC extension, there is no regulatory procedure to be followed when it comes to orphan drug exclusivity extension.

---

v UK Intellectual Property Office (Court of Appeal) (Ward, Jacob and Stanley Burnton LJJ): 19 August and 17 September 2009 1 [2009] EWCA Civ 966, [2010] RPC 6.

[41] UK Intellectual Property Office, *Guide to Applicants* [2013]: https://assets.publishing.service.gov.uk/government/uploads/system/uploads/attachment_data/file/309167/spctext.pdf [Accessed on 17 June 2020].

[42] Order of the General Court, *Pfizer v Commission and EMA*, T-48/14, EU:T:2014:1091.

When the compliance statement is included in the MA, with proof that the application fulfils the requirements of Article 28(3) of the Paediatric Regulation, the orphan drug will remain in the register for orphan drugs for two more years.

One question that arises relates to the scope of the orphan drug extension and Article 8 of the Paediatric Regulation. As stated in the Recital to the Regulation, orphan drugs are rarely patent-protected.[43] This would mean that Article 8 is not applicable for a new paediatric (orphan) indication of an existing orphan product which is not protected by an SPC or a patent that could lead to an SPC. That also means that the holder of the orphan drug will not be under the obligation to proceed to paediatric studies. However, this is contrary to the objectives of the Paediatric Regulation. At the same time, it is not clear whether holders of orphan drug that proceed to voluntary paediatric studies can be granted the rewards provided for under Article 37 of the Paediatric Regulation.[44]

Shire Pharmaceutical Contracts Ltd contested the decision providing that its medicinal product, marketed under the name Xagrid, was ineligible for the reward provided for under Article 37 of the Paediatric Regulation.[45] Xagrid was a non-patented orphan medicinal product authorised for the indication of essential thrombocythemia. Shire had completed paediatric studies on a voluntary basis and required the extension of the orphan drugs designation. The European Commission concluded in a communication to Shire that the company was not entitled to the extension provided for under Article 37 since voluntary paediatric studies were not included in the Paediatric Regulation. The General Court was not able to rule on the merits, since according to Article 263 TFEU a communication to a company is not to be considered an act open to legal challenge. Although no ruling from the General Court in this very important question was made, the orphan drug designation received a two-year extension after the expiration of the ten-year exclusivity.

9. Other Incentives in the System

The Paediatric Regulation includes not only an extension of an exclusive right (either an SPC or an orphan drug designation), but a series of other incentives and facilitations.

---

[43] The starting point of the Preamble to the Orphan Drugs Regulation is that pharmaceutical companies will not invest in R&D in orphan diseases without incentives, and that the most effective incentive is exclusivity (see Preamble 8 of Regulation 141/2000/EC).

[44] Research into orphan drugs is promoted and it would thus seem strange that these medicinal products would not receive the obligation and incentive to proceed to paediatric studies.

[45] Order of the General Court (Eighth Chamber) of 3 September 2014, *Shire Pharmaceutical Contracts Ltd v European Commission*, T-583/13, EU:T:2014:776.

9.1. Free Scientific Advice

Applicants for the paediatric extension can receive free scientific advice. This scientific advice may be requested during any stage of product development and may concern issues on safety and efficacy of the products. It is important to remember that the scientific advice provided by the CHMP (and the expert groups) is not binding for the EMA and for its decisions.[46]

9.2. Paediatric Use Marketing Authorisation (PUMA)

Regulation (EC) No 1901/2006 has introduced a new type of marketing authorisation, the PUMA. It was introduced as an incentive to conduct paediatric studies in respect of authorised medicinal products which do not enjoy any form of intellectual property protection. The PUMA is available for medicinal products exclusively for use in the paediatric population. A PUMA may protect a medicinal product that only includes paediatric indications, that is not protected by an SPC or by a patent that fulfils the requirements to be granted an SPC. A PUMA protects the pharmaceutical product by granting it an eight-year period of data protection, which will be combined with the 10-year period of marketing protection.[47] The product may be commercialised under the adult pharmaceutical brand name and thus benefit from consumer recognition.

There is no obligation to apply for a PUMA, but this is obviously a very favourable system in particular for small and medium-sized enterprises. PUMA applications are eligible for centralised procedure, but the national procedure is also an alternative.[48] The data submitted along with the marketing authorisation should demonstrate the safety and efficacy of the medicinal product in the paediatric population. The requirements for the collection of data and clinical trials are the same regardless of the route that is chosen. A PUMA application may be based on the data contained in the dossier of an authorised medicinal product, if the data protection exclusivity has expired.[49]

It is important to note that a PUMA application may only be submitted for medicinal products not already protected by intellectual property rights. This means that if a medicinal product is protected by patents even in just one of the Member States, it will be excluded from the PUMA procedure.[50]

---

[46] Sally Shorthose and Sarah Faircliffe, 'Paediatrics', in Sally Shorthose (ed), *Guide to Pharmaceutical Regulatory Law* (7th edn, Wolters Kluwer 2017) 239–40.

[47] This means that the exclusivity granted will be 18 years.

[48] Article 31 of the Regulation 1901/2006/EC; applications may be made in accordance with the procedure laid down in Arts 5–15 of Regulation 726/2004/EC.

[49] In the same way as in all other MA routes.

[50] See Recital 19 of Regulation 1901/2006/EC.

10. Post-approval Obligations

The Paediatric Regulation includes a built-in system of follow-up and post-approval obligations that may turn out to be rather harsh for the product holder.

10.1. Putting the Product on the Market

The pharmaceutical companies that enjoy paediatric extension have to abide by certain post-approval obligations. Article 33 of Regulation (EC) No 1901/2006 provides that the MA holder has the obligation to place the product on the market (taking into consideration the paediatric indication) within two years. Failure to comply with this obligation leads to a penalty.[51]

10.2. Pharmacovigilance

The de facto limited clinical trials conducted on the paediatric population raise an interest in continuous follow-up of the pharmacovigilance of the medicinal products with such uses. All applications for paediatric indications, paediatric line extensions, and PUMA must include details on measures to be taken to ensure the long-term follow-up of efficacy and review possible adverse reactions to the use of the medicinal product in the paediatric population. Such medicinal products may be required by the EMA to have a risk minimisation plan put into place and have specific post-marketing studies performed and reviewed by the competent authority.[52]

10.3. Paediatric Product Discontinuation

When the MA holder wishes to discontinue a paediatric product that has benefited from the rewards stipulated in provisions 36, 37 and 38 of Regulation (EC) No 1901/2006, they must give a six-month notice to the EMA and will be required to (a) transfer the MA, or (b) allow a third party that has declared its intention to place the medicinal product concerned on the market, to use the pharmaceutical as well as the preclinical and clinical information contained in the file of the medicinal product, to support a new MA application.

---

[51] Sally Shorthose and Sarah Faircliffe, 'Paediatrics', in Sally Shorthose (ed), *Guide to Pharmaceutical Regulatory Law* (7th edn, Wolters Kluwer 2017) 239–40.
[52] See Article 35 of the Regulation 1901/2006/EC.

10.4. The Paediatric Symbol

According to Article 32 of the Regulation, products authorised for a paediatric indication can use a specific symbol. The PDCO is to select an appropriate symbol and the product leaflet is to include an explanation of the meaning of the symbol.

The PDCO has held discussions concerning an appropriate symbol, stating that it was unable to recommend such a symbol, since the risks of recommendation would outweigh the benefits. The risk of misunderstanding its meaning was considered too high, since one may not count on parents reading the package leaflets, no matter how detailed and clear these are. Furthermore, the symbol would be connected to certain pharmaceuticals regardless of their dosage, strength, or formulation, something that might lead to considerable medical errors and health risks.[53]

10.5. Penalties for Breach of Regulation (EC) No 1901/2006

The penalties sanctioning the breach of regulation obligations are left to be determined by Member States. Penalties are to be effective, proportionate, and dissuasive. As a complementary measure, the EMA may ask that the Commission imposes financial penalties for infringements with regard to centrally authorised pharmaceuticals. The European Commission will make public the name of the infringer, the financial penalty to be paid, and the reasons for the penalty.[54]

10.6. Transparency

An important objective introduced by means of the Regulation is that of the transparency of the system as a whole. In fact, the Regulation imposes an obligation of publication, in the EudraCT database, of all paediatric clinical trials conducted as part of a PIP. According to Article 41, the publication must include not only completed PIPs, but also such PIPs that were prematurely terminated.

Other measures adopted to achieve the same objective are:

- the compulsory inclusion of the results of paediatric studies in the Summary of Product Characteristics and, if possible, also in the package leaflet of the medicinal product;

---

[53] European Medicines Agency, *Recommendation of the Paediatric Committee to the European Commission regarding the symbol*, London, 20 December 2007, Doc. Ref.: EMEA/498247/2007.

[54] Commission Regulation 488/2012/EU of 8 June 2012 amending Regulation 658/2007/EC concerning financial penalties for infringement of certain obligations in connection with marketing authorisations granted under Regulation 726/2004/EC of the European Parliament and of the Council [2012] OJ L 150/68.

- the publication of the decisions of the EMA following its receipt of the PDCO opinion on the PIP.[55]

The Regulation proposes further ways of promoting paediatric research, such as providing specific funds for research into medicinal products for the paediatric population from the Community budget[56] and the establishment of a European network for paediatric research. Identifying and creating an appropriate organisational structure for this network took at least eight years. However, the experience and know-how exchange at the meetings and in the collaboration and projects are deemed to be of considerable value. One of the interesting conclusions drawn through the work of the network concerns factors that delay modern pharmaceutical research and development. Therefore, part of the work of the network is focused on providing guidelines for PIP and thus assisting product developers.

10.7. Cooperation on the Basis of the Regulation

One of the important future developments in the field of paediatric research is the collaboration between the EMA and the FDA concerning the exchange of ideas and information relating to scientific, ethical, and other aspects of paediatric pharmaceutical product development.

Part of these discussions concern the development of a possibility to provide for a global development programme and thus for global PIP by harmonising the requirements of the EMA and the FDA.

11. Concluding Remarks

Since 2007, the Commission publishes a yearly report on the effects of the Paediatric Regulation, according to which the Regulation has been successful in attracting attention to research into the paediatric uses of medicinal products. A growing database of research results provides valuable knowledge in the field. However, the latest report includes a discussion of the weaknesses of the system, among which the failure of PUMA as an incentive mechanism.[57] In 2017, the Commission

---

[55] See Articles 28(1) and 25(7) of Regulation 1901/2006/EC. In fact, Article 25(7) provides for a certain control of what is being published, providing that information that is commercially confidential shall be removed from the public documents.

[56] See Article 40 of Regulation 1901/2006/EC. Furthermore, Member States are expected to collect data concerning the use of medicinal products on the paediatric population, on the basis of which the EMA and the Paediatric Working Party can provide a proposal for future research funds (based on the needs of paediatric research) under the Horizon 2020 framework.

[57] For a list of yearly reports, see https://ec.europa.eu/health/human-use/paediatric-medicines_en [Accessed on 17 June 2020]. The latest report is from 2018.

154 *The Paediatric Extension*

published an extensive report discussing the effects and impact (economic and other) of the Regulation,[58] which will be discussed in chapter eight of this book.

Already, it can be underlined that the Paediatric Regulation is directly interdependent with the SPC Regulation, the Orphan Drugs Regulation, the MA legal framework and the ATMP Regulation.[59] Needless to say, this interdependence with the other components of the regulatory system is further enhanced by the basic interdependence with the patent system. All complications originating from mismatches between the patent system and the MA system and difficulties in interpreting the scope of the basic patent and the scope of the granted SPC also become relevant for the application of the paediatric extension. This endless intertwining is interesting, but complicates the interpretation of the Regulation, since the interpretation of its provisions must be based on the interpretation of the provisions of the aforementioned Regulations. It also complicates the evaluation of the Regulation. A less expansive use of paediatric extensions does not necessarily mean that there is a problem with the Regulation itself. There might be other, exogenous factors that are of decisive influence. The pharmaceutical industry is creative and likes to test the boundaries of the system, primarily to its benefit.[60]

Naturally, testing the boundaries proves to be a rather complicated endeavour, since it might be necessary to test the boundaries in the application of several other legislative acts in order to test the scope and applicability of this specific Regulation.[61]

---

[58] On the tenth-year anniversary of the regulation.

[59] Frantzeska Papadopoulou, 'Legal Transplants and Modern Lawmaking in the Field of Pharmaceutical Patents' (2016) 47 *International Review of Intellectual Property and Competition Law*, 8, 891–911.

[60] See, for instance, negative SPCs that might constitute the bases for paediatric extensions.

[61] In the example with the negative SPCs, one must test whether an SPC could in fact have a negative duration in order to apply the paediatric extension.

6
Orphan Drugs

1. Background to the Legal Framework

Between 5,000 and 8,000 rare diseases affect 6–8 per cent of the population in Europe. The fact that these diseases affect a very small patient group is a disincentive for pharmaceutical companies, which prefer a broader potential market in order to recuperate their investments into research and product development. These rare diseases are classified as 'orphans' in the sense that they concern a very limited group of patients and as a result, it is not attractive for pharmaceutical companies to engage in the development of medicinal products aimed at treating them. In order to create a balance and support research in this particular product segment of the pharmaceutical market, Regulation (EC) No 141/2000 of the European Parliament and Council of 16 December 1999 on orphan medicinal products establishes a system of incentives for orphan drugs, stretching from the granting of exclusive right (market exclusivity) to facilitated procedures concerning MA under the European Medicines Agency (EMA).[1]

EU legislative initiatives in the field came rather late; national legislation for the support of pharmaceutical research and product development covering orphan diseases made its appearance on the international arena much earlier. In the United States, the Orphan Drugs Act was enacted in 1983; while similar legislation was introduced in Japan in 1995 and in Australia in 1998. All these different legislative initiatives provide incentives for research into orphan drugs, but these are not identical in nature and in structure.[2] These legislative predecessors introduced a mixture of 'pull' incentives (increasing the likelihood that marketing these products would be a lucrative endeavour by introducing exclusive rights) and 'push' incentives (reducing the cost and uncertainty in the development of orphan medicinal products).[3]

---

[1] Regulation 141/2000/EC of the European Parliament and of the Council of 16 December 1999 on orphan medicinal products [1999] OJ L 18/1.
[2] For the legislative history of the Orphan Drug Act, see Henry A Waxman and Joshua Green, *The Waxman Report: How Congress Really Works* (Twelve 2009); as well as Koichi Mikami, 'Orphans in the Market: The History of Orphan Drug Policy' [2017] 32 *Social History of Medicine*, 3, 609–30; see also, Matthew Herder, 'What is the Purpose of the Orphan Drug Act?' [2017] 14 *PLoS Medicine*, 1.
[3] Thus introducing both a financial and technical support for the FDA procedure, and a seven-year period of exclusivity for marketed orphan medicinal products.

156   *Orphan Drugs*

Prior to any Regulation in the field, rare diseases had been identified as a priority area in the field of public health.[4] At the same time, the Commission had proposed a programme of action including provision of information on rare diseases and support for patient organisations.[5]

In the Explanatory Memorandum of the Proposal for an Orphan Drugs Regulation,[6] the Commission reported on the unfortunate situation where a number of European patients suffering from rare diseases did not receive appropriate treatment, since there were no satisfactory market incentives in that specific pharmaceutical market segment. At the same time, the Commission referred to the US paradigm and the Orphan Drug Act of 1983,[7] as well as to the results the Orphan Drugs Act had for research being conducted into rare diseases. Thus, the Commission presented a dual perspective on the introduction of such a Regulation, an ethical one (patients suffering from rare diseases should be given the chance to access modern and effective pharmaceuticals), and a commercial one (the European pharmaceuticals industry must be given the same possibilities as its US counterpart). Referring to the consultation with stakeholders and Member States, the Commission provided that the most effective solution to the market failure of the orphan drugs market, would be market exclusivity. Thus, in order to proceed with this solution in an effective way, action had to be taken at a Community level with Article 100a of the EC Treaty serving as a legal basis.[8]

Both the subsidiarity and the proportionality principles were reviewed, and the Commission concluded that both were fulfilled, since a coherent regulation of the orphan drugs market was important for the internal market as such. Nonetheless, Member States were encouraged to participate in the process of supporting research into orphan drugs, as well as their accessibility with the means and competences they had available. In the proposal, the Commission reflected on the consistency of this particular Regulation with other Community policies and concluded that the presented proposal addressed issues that have been raised in previous and

---

[4] Commission of the European Communities, *Communication on the Framework for Action in the Field of Public Health*, COM [93] 559 final.

[5] Commission of the European Communities, *Communication from the Commission concerning a programme of Community action on rare diseases within the framework or action in the field of public health*, COM [97] 225 final.

[6] Commission of the European Communities, *Proposal for a European Parliament and Council Regulation (EC) on orphan medicinal products*, COM [1998] 450 final.

[7] Orphan Drug Act, Public Law 97-414, 9th Congress, 96 State 2049 [1983].

[8] The consultations concerning the Orphan Drugs Regulation had been ongoing since February 1995, with regular meetings between Commission officials and experts. In August 1996, the Commission circulated a preliminary draft for a Regulation to interested parties. The draft was discussed at two meetings of the Pharmaceutical Committee. It was also discussed in the broader public context of the European Parliament's Intergroup on Pharmaceutical Products, and a new amended draft was presented in December 1996. The discussions and negotiations preceding the finalisation of the draft also led to the creation of an umbrella organisation for patient groups for patients suffering from rare diseases, the EURORDIS (established March 1997).

then-current EU initiatives in the field, and that it was mutually supportive.[9] What is surprising and interesting is the fact that no reference was made to the intellectual property rights system or more specifically the patent system. The Explanatory Memorandum makes no direct reference to the implications that patent law had or might have on the orphan drugs designation system, as proposed in the Regulation, and no concrete discussion on how these might be overcome was included. While the Regulation does not target small and medium-sized enterprises, the Commission refers to the US experience, which shows that the designation system is used mainly by SMEs.

The initial Regulation (EC) No 141/2000 was amended by Regulation (EC) No 596/2009 of the European Parliament of the Council of 18 June 2009 on orphan medicinal products, also called the Orphan Drugs Regulation. The criteria for designation are specified in the implementing regulation, Commission Regulation (EC) No 847/2000 of the European Parliament and Council, enacted on 27 April 2000, a regulation focusing in particular on the provisions for the implementation of the criteria for orphan drug designation, and the definition of the terms 'similar medicinal product' and 'clinical superiority'. Apart from the Orphan Drugs Regulation, which is of central importance, the legal framework regulating orphan medicinal products includes Directive 2001/83/EC ('The Medicinal Code')[10] and Regulation 762/2004, a communication,[11] two guidelines and a Commission notice.[12]

Some 14 years after its entry into force, over 1,000 orphan drug designations have been granted. However, only 100 orphan drugs have received an EU MA. Thus, although it seems that the industry opts for this new protection scheme and finds it interesting enough to research orphan diseases, it becomes apparent that

---

[9] The other EU initiatives referred to are the Commission of the European Communities, *Communication from the Commission concerning a programme of Community action on rare diseases within the framework or action in the field of public health*, COM [97] 225 final; European Commission, *Standards, Measurements and Testing: Fourth Framework Programme for Research and Technological Development (1994-1998)*: http://aei.pitt.edu/43215/1/A7176.pdf [Accessed on 18 June 2020]; European Commission, *European Union biomedical and health research: The BIOMED I programme*, that includes a section on 'rare diseases'; as well as Commission of the European Communities, *Communication from the Commission to the Council and the European Parliament on the Outlines of an industrial policy for the pharmaceutical sector*, COM [93] 718 final.

[10] Directive 2001/83/EC of the European Parliament and of the Council of 6 November 2001 on the Community code relating to medicinal products for human use [2001] OJ L 311/67.

[11] Communication from the Commission on Regulation 141/2000/EC of the European Parliament and of the Council on orphan medicinal products [2003] OJ C 178/2.

[12] Commission of the European Communities, *Guideline on aspects of the application of Article 8(2) of Regulation 141/2000/EC of the European Parliament and of the Council: Review of the period of market exclusivity of orphan medicinal products*, C[2008] 4051 final; Commission of the European Communities, *Guideline on aspects of the application of Article 8(1) and (3) of Regulation 141/2000/EC: Assessing similarity of medicinal products versus authorised orphan medicinal products benefiting from market exclusivity and applying derogations from that market exclusivity*, C[2008] 4077 final. See also Commission notice on the application of Articles 3, 5 and 7 of Regulation 141/2000/EC on orphan medicinal products (2016/C 424/03).

158 *Orphan Drugs*

there are other challenges that need to be overcome in order for the medicinal products in question to actually reach the European pharmaceutical market and the patients.[13]

The EMA provides special arrangements for any sponsor wishing to apply for an orphan drug designation in several jurisdictions (outside the EU), as a result of a lengthy international cooperation process. It is thus possible to proceed to a common EMA/FDA application covering a parallel EU/US application. It is also possible to make a parallel application to the Japanese Ministry for Health, Labour and Welfare. Despite this combined application route, the orphan drug designation requirements are not harmonised. The cooperation does not mean that there is a common procedure of examination of applications or that the outcome of the one application influences the other.

The question of the independence of these parallel applications was tested in the *Now Pharm* case. In support of its argumentation, the applicant had provided that the medicinal product fulfilled the orphan drug designation requirements in the United States and Australia. The Court held that this was not relevant and concluded that the product in question should not be granted an orphan drug designation in the EU.[14]

2. Procedural Aspects

2.1. The Designation Process

In order to enter the designation process, the sponsor must be established in the Community. The application is to be submitted to the EMA and the EMA Committee for Orphan Medicinal Products (COMP) will review it and consider whether the product meets the requirements for an orphan drug designation. In order to qualify for an orphan drug status, the application must be submitted before an MA application is handed in.[15]

In cases where the COMP concludes that the application does not fulfil the criteria of the Orphan Drugs Regulation, it will inform the sponsor thereof. The sponsor has a period of 90 days from the receipt of the decision to provide detailed grounds of appeal to the EMA, which will submit them to the COMP. The EMA will then provide the final opinion to the Commission, which in its

---

[13] See European Medicines Agency, *Committee for Orphan Medicinal Products (COMP) meeting report on the review of applications for orphan designation*, 12 December 2014, EMA/COMP/737192/2014, Committee for Orphan Medicinal Products (COMP).

[14] Judgment of the General Court (Fifth Chamber) of 9 September 2010, *Now Pharm AG v European Commission*, T-74/08, EU:T:2010:376.

[15] See also European Commission, *Guideline on the format and content of applications for designation as orphan medicinal products and on the transfer of designations from one Sponsor to another*, Brussels, 27.03.2014, ENTR/6283/00 Rev. 4.

turn has 30 days to issue a final decision. If the designation is granted, then the orphan drug will be entered into the Community Register of Orphan Medicinal Products. In the majority of the cases, the Commission follows the proposal of the COMP, with a few exceptions, when it has 'adequate sources of information in the field in question'.[16]

During this procedure, the applicant has the possibility to withdraw the application. The applicant will be informed of the negative outcome of the COMP opinion and can proceed to a withdrawal of the application before the end of the COMP meeting. If the applicant withdraws the application before the COMP adopts a formal opinion, information concerning the application will not become public. The applicant may submit a new application at a later stage and rectify any mistakes and omissions.

The COMP's opinions, both negative and positive, are published on the EMA website together with meeting agendas, meeting reports, etc. The transparency of the procedure as a whole is prioritised in the orphan drugs system. Designated orphan drugs are listed in the Community Register of Designated Orphan Medicinal Products, which is found on the Commission's website. In the register one can find active, withdrawn, expired and refused orphan drug designations.

Article 5 of the Regulation provides the requirements for the documentation that needs to be submitted with the application. The applicant must include details on the ingredients of the product, the active ingredient, and the proposed therapeutic indication, and inform the EMA of the phase of development of the medicinal product in question.[17]

The applicant must specify whether the application is made on the basis of Article 3(1)(a) and the prevalence criterion, on paragraph 2, or on the economic criterion. Furthermore, the applicant must provide justification as to how the applicable criterion is fulfilled. Obviously, the application must also provide data from pre-clinical and clinical studies supporting the medicinal product's medical plausibility.[18] Medical plausibility is to be shown in two ways: first, with regard to the use of the medicinal product in the proposed orphan drug indication, and second, where the orphan indication refers to a specific subset of indication, evidence that supports this restriction on the basis of scientific criteria. The EMA has been very strict in this respect and evidence is required in order to prevent the artificial division of conditions that are already known into invalid subsets, or into subsets based on the stages of the disease.[19]

---

[16] Ibid.
[17] Article 4 of Regulation 141/2000/EC of the European Parliament and of the Council of 16 December 1999 on orphan medicinal products [1999] OJ L 18/1.
[18] Judgment of the General Court (Fifth Chamber) of 9 September 2010, *Now Pharm AG v European Commission*, T-74/08, EU:T:2010:376.
[19] See European Medicines Agency, *Recommendations on elements required to support the medical plausibility and the assumption of significant benefit for an orphan designation*, 2 March 2010

Furthermore, since there are provisions favourable to SMEs, the applicant should state if it belongs to this category in the application.

An important clarification made by the EMA, influencing the examination of the application, is the distinction between the 'orphan indication' for the purposes of the orphan drug designation and the 'therapeutic indication' for the purposes of the MA. With regard to the orphan drug designation, one application should be handed in for each of the following; the treatment, the prevention and the diagnosis of a condition. Thus, each of these categories is considered a separate indication. On the other hand, a sponsor may apply for orphan drug designation for a medicinal product that already enjoys an MA on condition that the orphan drug designation is made in respect of a previously non-authorised therapeutic indication. Article 7(3) of the Orphan Drugs Regulation clarifies that 'orphan' and 'non-orphan' drug designations may not be covered by the same MA and thus the sponsor holding an MA should apply for a separate MA with a different trade name for a new orphan indication. It is the orphan drug indication that will be the basis for assessment of the prevalence criterion.[20]

The application procedure is divided into the three following steps.

2.1.1. The Pre-application Meeting

This is not a mandatory step in the procedure, but, if the sponsor finds it necessary it may request a meeting with the EMA at least two months prior to the submission date. The applicant is encouraged to send preliminary documentation prior to the meetings. The objective of these meetings is often to guarantee that the application to be submitted fulfils the requirements. Such preparatory work becomes even more important when taking into consideration the rather strict timeline followed by the EMA, making it difficult for the applicant to receive deadline extensions when documentation is missing or needs to be corrected.

2.1.2. The Review of the Application

The review of the application is performed by the COMP. However, it is not the COMP, but the Commission itself, that formally grants the designation. The COMP includes a network of experts specialised in different diseases and patient groups, but they also have patient groups as full members. In order to provide further

---

EMA/COMP/15893/2009 Final Committee for Orphan Medicinal Products (COMP). This becomes even more interesting given the growing tendency for personalised medicine; see Commission notice on the application of Articles 3, 5 and 7 of Regulation 141/2000/EC on orphan medicinal products (2016/C 424/03).

[20] See also European Medicines Agency, *Procedural advice on appeal procedure for orphan medicinal product designation or review of orphan designation criteria at the time of Marketing Authorisation*, 8 May 2013, EMA/2677/01 Rev. 2.

transparency, the COMP's decisions are summarised and published. The responsibility for these summaries falls on the EMA but is also monitored by concerned sponsors and European patient group representatives.

2.1.3. Market Exclusivity Review

Article 8(2) of the Orphan Drugs Regulation provides that the 10-year market exclusivity may be reduced to six years if, at the end of the fifth year, it is established that the designated orphan drug no longer fulfils the requirements of Article 3 of the same Regulation. One example of such new evidence is that the product is sufficiently profitable, something that would make market exclusivity non-justifiable.

Guidelines issued in 2008 concerning the market exclusivity review provide that the review procedure is not automatic.[21] A mid-term review is triggered only when national authorities inform the EMA that they have sufficient information to indicate that the designation criteria are no longer met for a specific orphan drug designation. This information should ideally be submitted to the EMA at the end of the fourth year post-designation. The Member State that provides such information is also under obligation to provide evidence and a rationale for its doubts.[22]

Should the EMA decide to proceed to a review of an orphan drug designation, the criteria that will be employed are those used when the orphan drug designation was initially granted. The COMP will review the designation criteria and, if they are met, will provide an opinion according to which the period of market exclusivity will remain unchanged. If the COMP finds that the criteria are no longer met, the COMP will investigate whether any of the derogation criteria are met. If this is the case, the COMP will recommend that the market exclusivity time will not be reduced. If the criteria stipulated in Article 3(1) of the Orphan Drug Regulation are not met and no derogation is applicable, the COMP will recommend a reduction of the market exclusivity. The Commission will reach a final decision on the basis of the COMP report, and only rarely will that be contrary to the recommendation submitted by the COMP.[23]

It is important here to note that according to the initial draft of the Regulation, Article 8(2) would be formulated in a way which allows the reduction of the term of protection in cases where 'the price charged for the medicinal product

---

[21] Commission of the European Communities, *Guideline on aspects of the application of Article 8(2) of Regulation (EC) No 141/2000 of the European Parliament and of the Council: Review of the period of market exclusivity of orphan medicinal products*, C[2008] 4051 final.

[22] This is the case regardless of whether the product had previously been granted the two-year extension because of paediatric studies.

[23] See European Commission, *Guideline on the format and of content applications for designation as orphan medicinal products and on the transfer of designations from one sponsor to another*, 27.03.2014, ENTR/6283/00 Rev. 4 3 para 1 and 5.1.1.1.

162 *Orphan Drugs*

concerned is such that it allows the earning of an unreasonable profit'. The final text of the regulation provided a much more limited possibility to invoke the price/commercial value of the pharmaceutical in question, and the return of investment becomes only a criteria checked if the orphan drug has been granted on the basis of this specific criterion. Thus, in fact, an orphan drug may theoretically at the same time be a blockbuster drug with considerable commercial profits.

3. The Criteria for Orphan Drugs Designation

Naturally, in order for a product to be eligible for an orphan drug designation, it has to be a medicinal product. In practice, difficulties in interpretation occur rather often and drawing the line between, for instance, a medicinal product and a medical device can be difficult. In order to facilitate the interpretation, the European Commission has published a guidance document on this specific distinction. Medical devices and food supplements are not medicinal products and thus cannot receive an orphan drug designation in the EU.[24] Article 3 of the Orphan Drugs Regulation provides the requirements that need to be fulfilled in order for the designation to be granted.

The fact that the EU system for the designation of Orphan Drugs provides two alternative routes, namely either showing prevalence or 'insufficient return', is the result of the US experience in the field. In the United States, during the years of early operation of the Orphan Drugs Act, the FDA experienced difficulties in actually determining whether a certain drug would likely be unprofitable or not (since the two requirements were cumulatively applied). Thus, specifying a prevalence threshold under which pharmaceuticals for orphan diseases are assumed to be unprofitable seemed like a much more straightforward approach.

3.1. Article 3(1)(a): The Prevalence Criterion

An orphan drug designation presupposes that the prevalence criterion (ie insufficient return on investment), is fulfilled.

The sponsor has to prove that the medicinal product is intended to diagnose, prevent or treat a life-threatening or chronically debilitating condition that affects no more than 5 in 10,000 persons in the Community at the time when the application is handed in. The percentage of patients is calculated solely

---

[24] See Article 2 of Regulation 141/2000/EC of the European Parliament and of the Council of 16 December 1999 on orphan medicinal products [1999] OJ L 18/1, as amended (2009) OJ L188/14 Rec. 1.

on the basis of occurrence in the Community, so diseases that are common in other parts of the world could fall under the definition of orphan diseases in the EU.[25]

The sponsor needs to provide the following:[26]

(1) documentation showing that the disease for which the medicinal product would be administered does not affect more than 5 persons in 10,000 in the Community;
(2) data that provides evidence on the life-threatening or chronically debilitating nature of the condition;
(3) documentation of scientific literature available related to the specific disease or the specific treatment;
(4) information on the disease and, in particular, on whether the disease has been the subject matter of Community financed project.

Although this list may seem rather straightforward, it often proves difficult to provide the necessary documentation, mainly because of the scarcity of patients suffering from the disease in question. The scarcity of the condition also means that very few medical practitioners are informed and educated about the specific disease and a number of patients are often misdiagnosed. Other sources of complications are the different procedures concerning prevalence data in different countries of the Community. The prevalence of a certain disease could be very high in certain areas of the Community, in particular when there is a genetic link, and very low in others.[27]

An interesting question is what happens when the sponsor shows that there are no patients in the Community who would benefit from the medicinal product in question. Would that satisfy the prevalence criterion? This question became relevant in two cases. An orphan drug application for the medicinal product Tecovirimat to treat monkeypox infection was rejected by the Commission. Surprisingly, this was also one of the few Commission decisions that was contrary to the COMP proposal. Another application for the same medicament but for the treatment of variola infection (which also encompassed no patients in the EU) was submitted. In the justification for the Commission's decisions, it was stated

---

[25] In order to provide adequate documentation concerning the prevalence of the disease, the sponsor may consult EMA's guidelines, such as the European Medicines Agency, *Points to consider on the calculation and reporting of the prevalence of a condition for Orphan Designation*, 20 June 2019, EMA/COMP/436/01 Rev. 1 Committee for Orphan Medicinal Products (COMP); and European Medicines Agency, *Relevant Sources for Orphan Disease Prevalence Data*, 16 December 2014, EMA/452415/2012 Rev. 1 Human Medicines Research and Development Support.

[26] Article 2(1) of Commission Regulation 847/2000/EC of 27 April 2000 laying down the provisions for implementation of the criteria for designation of a medicinal product as an orphan medicinal product and definitions of the concepts 'similar medicinal product' and 'clinical superiority' [2000] OJ L 103/5.

[27] See European Commission, *Commission Implementing Decision of 11 January 2012 refusing the designation of 'Tecovirimat' as an orphan medicinal product under Regulation (EC) 141/2000 of the European Parliament and of the Council*, C [2011] 10128 final.

164   *Orphan Drugs*

that the requirement of prevalence was not fulfilled as there were no proven cases of patients in the Community. At the same time, the Commission specified that prevalence of the condition outside the EU or the future occurrence in the EU are not of relevance for the orphan drug designation. The Commission clarified that the sponsor has to prove that there is a patient group inside the Community at the time of the application.[28]

In the 2003 Commission Communication,[29] the European Commission addressed the issue of prevalence of the disease that the orphan drug is intended to treat. In the Communication, it was stated that if the medical product fulfilled all other requirements set out by the Regulation, an orphan drug designation was possible. During the almost 20 years that have passed since the entry into force of the Orphan Drugs Regulation, considerable data concerning prevalence of certain diseases has been collected. This information is publicly available, as a means of facilitating further applications.[30] However, this data is only to be used as guidance for applicants, which must provide their own prevalence data. Even if a disease is very rare, the applicant must refer to scientific evidence and cannot simply refer to well-known and 'obviously' rare disease.[31]

The notion of prevalence and how it is to be interpreted was one of the points discussed in the Commission notice of 2016.[32] The Commission stated that the orphan condition as specified by the sponsor would be the starting point for the scientific evaluation, but that this was not binding for the evaluation of the COMP. The notice further clarified that the prevalence calculation for medicinal products intended for the diagnosis or prevention of a condition should be made on the basis of the population to which such a product is expected to be administered on an annual basis.

3.2. The Insufficient Return on Investment Criterion

When the orphan medicinal product is to be used to diagnose, prevent, or treat a life-threatening, seriously debilitating, or serious and chronic condition, regardless

---

[28] See the Commission decision concerning medicinal product Tecovirimat. Commission Implementing Decision of 11 January 2012 refusing the designation of Tecovirimat as an orphan medicinal product under Regulation 141/2000/EC of the European Parliament and of the Council, C [2011] 10128 final.

[29] Communication from the Commission on Regulation 141/2000/EC of the European Parliament and of the Council on orphan medicinal products [2003], C 178/02.

[30] See European Medicines Agency, *Relevant Sources for Orphan Disease Prevalence Data* [2014] EMA/452415/2012 Rev. 1 Human Medicines Research and Development Support.

[31] The Committee for Orphan Medicinal Products provides guidance in this regard, see European Medicines Agency, *Points to consider on the calculation and reporting of the prevalence of a condition for Orphan Designation*, 20 June 2019, EMA/COMP/436/01 Rev. 1 Committee for Orphan Medicinal Products (COMP).

[32] Commission notice on the application of Articles 3, 5 and 7 of Regulation 141/2000/EC on orphan medicinal products [2016] C 424/03.

of disease prevalence, it has to fulfil the economic criterion. The sponsor must show that without incentives, it is not likely that the marketing of the medicinal product will in fact lead to the sufficient return of the investments necessary to develop the product in question. Applying for an orphan drug designation under the insufficient return on investment criterion presupposes that the sponsor can present all costs incurred for the research and development of the specific medicinal product, and also all future expenses expected to be incurred. The costs are to be documented according to accepted accounting principles and certified by a registered accountant.[33]

Article 2(2) of Regulation (EC) No 847/2000 provides that the sponsor is to submit specific data on: costs incurred in the development of the medicinal product, details of tax incentives (and other economic incentives) that have been available to the sponsor, future costs after the orphan drug application has been handed in, and an estimate and justification of expected revenues from the specific product. Finally, this documentation must also include data on the prevalence and incidence of the disease in the Community, which will of course have an impact on the expected revenue.

In the 2016 Commission Notice, it was specified that this criterion was to be assessed on the basis of all past and future development costs and expected revenue related to the product.[34]

Very few applications for orphan drug designations have been based on this criterion. During the years 2000–05, only two applications were received, of which one was withdrawn by the applicant.[35]

3.3. Medical Plausibility

The applicant is required to specify the medical plausibility of the medicinal product for the specific orphan drug designation. When the medicinal product is used for a specific subset of patients from a larger group, the applicant will need to prove that the medicinal product works for this specific subset of patients only. Deciding what constitutes a subset of patients is a very important part of this process. One of the roles of the COMP is to distinguish between actual subsets of patient groups and diseases and so-called 'salami-slicing' of conditions into small and artificial subset. Should the COMP consider a subset to be artificially construed, it has the possibility to proceed to an adjustment in the application and find that the medical

---

[33] European Commission, *Guideline on the format and content of applications for designation as orphan medicinal products and on the transfer of designations from one Sponsor to another* [2014] ENTR/6283/00 Rev. 4.
[34] Commission notice on the application of Articles 3, 5 and 7 of Regulation 141/2000 on orphan medicinal products [2016] C 424/03 2.
[35] European Medicines Agency, *COMP Report to the Commission in relation to art 10 of Regulation (EC) No 141/2000 on Orphan Medicinal Products*, EMA/35218/2005.

plausibility of the specific medicinal product is broader than the one initially claimed by the sponsor.

In order to provide evidence of the medicinal plausibility, the applicant is usually required to provide evidence in the form of data from clinical trials.

3.4. Article 3(1)(b) Requirements

When the application for an orphan drug fulfils either the prevalence requirement or the insufficient investment return requirement, it must also meet the conditions set out in Article 3(1)(b). Article 3(1)(b) provides that the sponsor has to show that there is no satisfactory method of diagnosis, treatment, or prevention of the condition in the Community, or if such method exists, that this new medicament will be of significant benefit to those affected by the condition.

3.4.1. Existing Satisfactory Method

The implementing Regulation (EC) 847/2000 requires that the sponsor provides details on any existing authorised medicinal product, method or medical device that is used for the same condition as the medicinal product covered by the orphan drug application.[36] In connection to this, the sponsor will have to provide information as to why the existing authorised medicinal products are not satisfactory, or why the new method (the new medicinal product) has a significant benefit.

The sponsor needs to provide evidence overturning the basic assumption that the authorised medicinal product is a satisfactory method in respect of authorised indications.[37] It is usually easier for a sponsor to provide evidence of a significant benefit, than to claim that an already authorised existing medicinal product is not satisfactory. In fact, methods of diagnosis and treatment that are commonly used are considered to constitute 'satisfactory methods'. Even those that are not subject to marketing authorisations but are often used by medical practitioners are considered to be satisfactory. An assessment of an existing method's quality and results will take into consideration experience from the use of that specific method, documented results, etc. The sponsor will be required to provide evidence, including references to scientific and medical literature.[38]

---

[36] Commission Regulation 847/2000/EC of 27 April 2000 laying down the provisions for implementation of the criteria for designation of a medicinal product as an orphan medicinal product and definitions of the concepts 'similar medicinal product' and 'clinical superiority' [2000] OJ L 103/5.

[37] The Commission announced in 2017 that it planned to review and revise the definition of 'significant benefit'.

[38] Pedro Franco, 'Orphan Drugs: The Regulatory Environment' [2013] 18 *Drug Discovery Today*, 3–4, 163–72. See also Laura Fregonese, Lesley Greene, Matthias Hofer, et al, 'Demonstrating Significant Benefit of Orphan Medicines: Analysis of 15 years of Experience in Europe' [2018] 23 *Drug Discovery Today*, 1, 90–100.

3.4.2. Significant Benefit

Proving that an already authorised medicinal product is not a satisfactory method is a difficult task. Therefore, the Commission encourages applicants to prove that their medicinal product has a significant benefit.[39]

According to Article 3(2) of the Regulation (EC) 847/2000, a significant benefit is a clinically relevant advantage or a major contribution to patient care.

Thus, when there is a satisfactory treatment for the same condition as that covered by the Orphan Drug Designation application, the sponsor will need to prove that there is a clinically relevant advantage. In practice, the sponsor will have to compare the medicinal product covered by the application with the existing (authorised or otherwise used) medicinal products. Such a comparison raises practical problems, mainly because of the scarcity of an orphan disease. Therefore, the COMP has accepted that the assessment of significant benefit may be based on certain assumptions. These assumptions could concern either improved efficacy of the medicinal product, improved safety, or 'major contribution to patient care' – for instance a much more convenient route of administration. Although the approach of the COMP provides a level of flexibility, these assumptions need to be clearly documented with practical evidence, not purely theoretical.

In the 2003 Communication of the Commission on Regulation (EC) No 141/2000, it was stated that 'significant benefit' could be based on the following elements:[40]

(a) benefits to a specific subset of patients, in particular such that are resistant to a specific method;
(b) a new source for an existing medicinal product that was previously inherent with risks;
(c) expectations of a clinically relevant improved safety profile (justified either by clinical experience or by the pharmacological properties of the substance);
(d) justification of more favourable and clinically relevant pharmacokinetic properties compared with the existing medicinal product;
(e) in cases where there are serious documented difficulties with the formulation or the route of administration of a medicinal product, a more convenient route of administration or formulation might be considered a 'significant benefit';
(f) limited availability of an existing medicinal product.

In making the assessment of whether or not a significant benefit exists, the COMP will take into consideration available data and evidence, as well as the

---

[39] See also European Medicines Agency, *Post-orphan Medicinal Product Designation Procedures. Guidance for Sponsors*, 18 March 2020, Rev. 7 EMA/469917/2018. Human Medicines Research and Development Support.
[40] Commission notice on the application of Articles 3, 5 and 7 of Regulation (EC) No 141/2000 on orphan medicinal products (2016/C 424/03).

details of the specific condition.[41] The broad discretion of the Commission to decide whether or not a significant benefit exists has been confirmed in the case T-74/08 *Now Pharm AG v European Commission*, 9 September 2010.[42] According to the Court, it could only overturn the evaluation of the Commission if the Commission had failed to follow the rules of procedure, had made an error in its assessment of the facts, or had misused its powers.

The objective of providing medicaments to patients with rare diseases in the EU has been considered such a priority that the Commission has provided for a very broad interpretation of the 'significant benefit' criterion. For instance, it has been considered to be enough that the medicament would be offered to a new market within the EU (ie that broadening the geographical scope of the availability of the medicament would entail a 'significant benefit'). Thus, if a product is authorised only in one or in very few member states, the availability of the medicinal product in all Member States would be a 'significant benefit'. However, problems in the supply of the pharmaceutical product, if these are of short duration, would only be considered if they are recurring.

Providing a transparent and stable interpretation of the term 'significant benefit' has been considered so important that a workshop was held on this topic in January 2012, at the initiative of the COMP.[43] Among the conclusions of this workshop was that there was a need to make the term more explicit and that a better definition of the scientific justifications was necessary for a 'significant benefit' to be proven. The discussions continued with the establishment of Significant Benefit Working Group, which provided input for the revision of the 2003 Communication. The Draft Notice that was published for public consultation stated that it was apparent by the text of Article 3(1)(b) of the Regulation that the 'significant benefit' should be interpreted strictly. The Draft Notice clarified that, contrary to past practices, the 'significant benefit' should not be considered on the basis of:[44]

- increased supply/quantities or extended geographical coverage (unless there was evidence of patient harm);
- enhancement of pharmaceutical quality of a product in compliance with the Committee on Medicinal Products for Human Use guidelines, which is a part of the obligation of every marketing authorisation holder;
- any other alternative mechanism.

In fact, in order to provide a 'significant benefit', there had to be a clinically relevant advantage or a major contribution to patient care.

---

[41] The specific conditions might impact on what is considered to be a significant benefit and what is not.

[42] Judgment of the General Court (Fifth Chamber) of 9 September 2010, *Now Pharm AG v European Commission*, T-74/08, EU:T:2010:376.

[43] European Medicines Agency, *Significant benefit of orphan drugs: concepts and future developments*, 12 January 2012, EMA/326061/2012, Human Medicines Development and Evaluation.

[44] Commission notice on the application of Articles 3, 5 and 7 of Regulation 141/2000/EC on orphan medicinal products [2016] C 424/03.

An interpretation of this requirement was provided in case T-724/08 *Now Pharm AG v European Commission*.[45] The Court clarified that in order to prove 'significant benefit', the applicant had to compare the effect that the specific product had on patients to that of existing, authorised medicinal products. Thus, the applicant's claim that 'significant benefit' could in fact be shown by means of presenting the intrinsic characteristics of the product itself was rejected.

Given that no clinical evidence will be available by the time the orphan drug designation application is handed in, the comparison will be based on the assumptions presented by the applicant. In order to minimise the rather high risk of subjectivity in this respect, the sponsor must provide an objective justification for the assumption presented in the application, in accordance with Article 2(3)(c) of the Orphan Drugs Regulation. The COMP will proceed to an assessment of the assumption with the assistance of relevant technical expertise, depending on the technological field. In the *Now Pharm* case, the Court considered that the decision should be a matter for the Commission's discretionary power, taking into consideration the methodological difficulties and the contradictory data in that case.

According to the Commission's Communication, the determination has to be made on a 'case-to-case basis' while in all cases the assumption of significant benefit should be justified with data that takes into consideration the specifics of patient needs, the disease and medical treatment. One example given in this respect concerns self-administration, which would be considered a 'significant benefit' if the patient is able to stay at home and live an independent life, as this would not be the case if they must be hospitalised for medical treatment.[46]

For the purposes of orphan drug designation, the ameliorated pharmaceutical quality of the product is not considered to be a 'significant benefit'.[47] In order to illustrate what may in fact constitute a 'significant benefit', the Commission has published examples, such as benefits to specific subset of patients, improved pharmacokinetics, improved safety profiles or improved route of administration.

A 2019 CJEU ruling clarified the role of the COMP and the interpretation of the term 'significant effect'.[48] Bristol Myers Squibb (BMS) was successful in its orphan drug designation application, filed in August 2012, for the medicinal product elotuzumab used in the treatment of multiple myeloma (a very serious cancer disease). In 2015, when BMS submitted an MA application for Empliciti, a medicinal product including elotuzumab, the Commission made a new examination of whether the substance in question fulfilled the criteria of the Orphan Drugs Regulation. Unfortunately (for BMS), the Commission had already granted an MA

---

[45] Judgment of the General Court (Fifth Chamber) of 9 September 2010, *Now Pharm AG v European Commission*, T-74/08, EU:T:2010:376, para 43.

[46] Commission notice on the application of Articles 3, 5 and 7 of Regulation (EC) No 141/2000 on orphan medicinal products (2016/C 424/03).

[47] Commission notice on the application of Articles 3, 5 and 7 of Regulation 141/2000/EC on orphan medicinal products [2016] C 424/03, s.A(4) para 7.

[48] Judgment of the General Court (Second Chamber) of 5 December 2018, *Bristol-Myers Squibb Pharma EEIG v European Commission and European Medicines Agency*, T-329/16, EU:T:2018:878.

for a new medicinal product, Kyprolis (carfilzomib), for treatment of the same disease. The COMP asked BMS to demonstrate the significant benefit of Empliciti over Kyprolis. In the absence of other more concrete direct comparison data, BMS submitted a scientific discussion on the significant benefit of the substance elotuzumab over that of carfilzomib. The COMP did not consider the submitted data to be satisfactory and concluded that elotuzumab's significant effect was not shown, thus leading to its removal from the Community OD register.

BMS's action for annulment of the decision was based on (i) violation of Article 5(12)(b) of the Orphan Drugs Regulation in conjunction with the principle of proportionality; (ii) violation of Article 5(12)(b) in conjunction with Article 5(8); and (iii) failure to identify the legal basis and to state reasons. The most important part of the decision concerns the violation of Article 5(12)(b) of the Orphan Drugs Regulation. In this respect, BMS presented three major arguments.

Kyprolis may not be taken into account in the review of the significant benefit, as it was authorised after the submission of the MA for Empliciti. BMS claimed that Empliciti should not have been compared with Kyprolis, as Kyprolis was authorised on 19 November 2015 (ie several months after the submission of the MA for elotuzumab). Adopting such a broad perspective would, according to BMS, call into question compliance with the principle of proportionality and run counter to the objectives of the Orphan Drugs Regulation. 'Proportionality' means that the action of the EU must be limited to what is necessary to achieve the objectives of the Treaties. Furthermore, such a comparison would be unfair, because it would mean that the applicant would not have enough time to collect all the necessary data.

The Court referred to its ruling in *Now Pharm v Commission*, T-74/08, where it held that the orphan drug in question was to be compared with all medicinal products that had been authorised in the EU (without exception), and that both Articles 5(12) and 7(3) of the Regulation provide the MA grant date, not that of the MA, as the deadline for examination of the designation criteria (ie the date on which the Commission was to determine whether the OD fulfilled the requirements of the Orphan Drugs Regulation).[49]

The Court also determined that the principle of proportionality was not breached, because the assessments concerning the significant benefit criterion were carried out objectively, from a purely scientific point of view. As such, the COMP had no scope for discretion as regards recommending to the Commission to remove the medicinal product from the Community Register of orphan medicinal products.

Conclusive evidence should show that Empliciti is no longer of significant benefit, not that it is of significant benefit. In fact, BMS claimed that according to the wording of Article 5(12)(b), at the time of MA, compelling evidence is needed

---

[49] Ibid, paras 59–75.

that the designated medicinal product is no longer of significant benefit compared with other authorised medicinal products, not that the designated medicinal product *is* of significant benefit.

In this respect, the Court repeated the obligation under 5(12)(b) to review the OD criteria before granting an MA, and that the aforementioned provision, when read together with Article 7(3), provided that the COMP must proceed to a complete re-evaluation of the designation criteria. This assessment should be new and independent of the one previously performed during the initial ODD application procedure. The Court thus concluded that there must be a positive finding – that the significant benefit criterion is met – at the time of the MA. In order to confirm its initial opinion, the COMP must satisfy itself, scientifically and objectively, that the significant benefit criterion is met.[50]

The test for the assessment of significant benefit is overly rigid. BMS claimed that the Commission applied, incorrectly, an overly rigid test to assess the significant benefit. Even though the COMP had to verify whether the available data supported the conclusion that Empliciti offered a significant benefit over Kyprolis, the COMP should not have used an overly rigid test for evidence of significant benefit. Instead, it should have (i) conducted a global assessment, focusing on all of the evidence that could substantiate the claim of significant benefit; (ii) used the general criterion of benefit for the patient; and (iii) applied a standard of proof that did not require conclusive proof and could allow for estimates and assumptions based on the available data, especially when taking into account the relevant circumstances, including the practical impossibility for the applicant to produce new comparative data.[51]

Finally, the Court considered the role of the COMP, stating that the complexity of scientific assessments in cases as the one concerned in this ruling dictated that the Commission would usually endorse the COMP's opinions. The Commission has the possibility to review the COMP in terms of its functioning, the consistency of its opinions and its statements of reasons.

3.5. Timing of the Application

There is no specific rule regarding the stage of product development at which an application for an orphan drug designation needs to be handed in. The only important aspect to consider when it comes to the timing of the application is that it should be handed in before an application for marketing authorisation of the medicament is handed in to the national authorities or centrally to the EMA. Even if the marketing authorisation is not granted, the medicinal product will not be eligible for orphan drug designation. If marketing authorisation is granted, an

---

[50] Ibid, paras 76–05.
[51] Ibid, paras 106–27.

application for an orphan drug designation may only be handled if it concerns another therapeutic indication. Article 5(1) of the Regulation provides that applications can be submitted to the EMA, without charge, at any stage of development of the medicinal product before the submission of the MA. As a result, if a sponsor has submitted an MA in any Member State before obtaining an orphan drug designation, it will not be possible to obtain an orphan drug designation for the same medicinal product and therapeutic indication.

In the case T-264/07, *CSL Behring GmbH v European Commission and the EMA*, 9 September 2010, the General Court confirmed the decisions of the EMA and the Commission providing that an orphan drug designation was invalid because of a previous marketing authorisation for the same medical indication.[52] The motivation of the ruling was that the Orphan Drugs Regulation has been introduced in order to incentivise the development of new medicinal products, not to protect already existing ones.

4. Marketing Authorisation of Orphan Drugs

The fact that a medicinal product has been designated as an orphan drug does not mean it is authorised to be sold. The same rules apply as for other medicinal products as regards the security, quality and efficacy of orphan drugs. However, procedural and other practical adjustments have been made for orphan drugs, in order to address the scarcity of clinical data (due to the limited number of patients treated for the condition). A marketing authorisation for an orphan drug covers only the orphan drug condition. In cases where the same medicinal product is used for another condition (not an orphan drug one), another marketing authorisation needs to be handed in. Orphan and non-orphan indications may not be covered under the same marketing authorisation. By means of Article 3.1 Regulation (EC) No 726/2004, all marketing authorisation applications concerning orphan drugs must be made through the centralised procedure, which also means that a single central application will lead to an EU-wide marketing authorisation.

The marketing authorisation application has to be completed with a report from the sponsor, providing that the medicinal product in question fulfils the criteria for an orphan drug designation, at the time that the marketing authorisation will be granted. Any changes or adjustments in relation to the orphan drug designation application should be reported. This report – the maintenance report – has to be handed in at the latest at the time of submission of the Committee for Medicinal Products for Human Use (CHMP) application for accelerated review or at day 121 for regular marketing authorisation procedures. Should the COMP

---

[52] The argument of the sponsor was that Articles 5(1) and 2(4)(a) of the Regulation are unlawful. See Judgment of the General Court (Fifth Chamber) of 9 September 2010, *CSL Behring GmbH v European Commission and European Medicines Agency (EMA)*, T-264/07, EU:T:2010:371.

consider it important, they can call the sponsor to an oral hearing in order to answer questions related to the maintenance report or the marketing authorisation application.

What is interesting to note is the fact that an orphan drug designation does not per se mean that the product has obtained marketing authorisation. As a result, it is theoretically possible for other applicants to submit applications for the same substance and the same therapeutic indication until one sponsor receives an MA. However, only the first successful MA sponsor will receive an MA.[53]

5. The Incentives of the Orphan Drug Designation

5.1. Market Exclusivity

Market exclusivity is the most important incentive granted by means of the Orphan Drugs Regulation. The sponsor is granted a 10-year market exclusivity, meaning that neither the Community nor the Member States will accept any other application for a marketing authorisation, grant a marketing authorisation, or accept an application to extend a marketing authorisation for the same therapeutic indication in respect of a 'similar medicinal product'. This ten-year period may be extended for another two years on condition that paediatric studies are completed.[54] Market exclusivity can be removed at six years, if the conditions for the orphan designation are no longer met.

This market exclusivity does not presuppose the granting of other intellectual property rights, such as patent rights, but could co-exist with them.

To be sure of the therapeutic indication of an orphan drug, one needs to look at the MA. There should be an identity between what is stated in the MA and what is provided for under the orphan drug designation.[55] This rather simple and straightforward rule might prove difficult to apply in practice. An orphan medicinal product may be granted for a therapeutic indication that constitutes a subset of a designated condition. An application for an MA for a second product, claiming to cover a different therapeutic condition, will have to establish the difference between the two and prove that this difference is clinically meaningful. In cases where there is an overlap between the target populations of the two medicinal products, the second sponsor will have to provide an estimate of how large this

---

[53] See also, *Medicines Law & Policy*, 'Orphan Medicinal Products in the European Union: Briefing Document', June 2019.

[54] See Article 36 of Regulation 1901/2006/EC.

[55] Commission of the European Communities, 'Guideline on aspects of the application of Article 8(1) and (3) of Regulation 141/2000/EC: *Assessing similarity of medicinal products versus authorised orphan medicinal products benefiting from market exclusivity and applying derogations from that market exclusivity*, C[2008] 4077 final 2.3, para 2.

174   *Orphan Drugs*

overlap is. On the basis thereof, the EMA will decide whether the second designation will be possible.

A similar medicinal product is one that contains an active substance similar to that covered by the orphan drug designation and that has the same therapeutic indication.[56] A similar active substance could be either an identical substance or one with the same principal molecular structural features and that works through the same mechanism.[57] The applicant will have to provide evidence concerning the structure of the proposed molecule and compare it with the orphan drug that is already designated.

The mechanism referred to above concerns the interaction of the substance with a pharmacological target (receptor or enzyme) that has a pharmacodynamic effect. Two substances will have the same mechanism if they have the same pharmacological target and the same pharmacodynamic effect. Differences relating to the route of administration, pharmacokinetics, potency or tissue distribution will not be relevant in the assessment process. Article 3(3)(c) the Regulation provides a list of examples of similar active substances.

If two substances are similar, the applicant shall submit a Similarity Report, which should include any derogations to the market exclusivity of the original sponsor under Article 8(3) and evidence supporting this. This Similarity Report should provide an overall assessment on similarity of the two substances by considering molecular structure features, mechanisms of action and therapeutic indication. The CHMP will provide an opinion on the 'similarity' of the two substances.

When a sponsor receives an MA for a subset of a designated orphan condition, the sponsor will be granted 10 years of market exclusivity. If the same sponsor decides to proceed to an MA for therapeutic indication of another subset of the orphan drug condition, the second therapeutic indication will be granted the same period of market exclusivity as the first. This means that no matter when this second application was made and approved, the second MA will expire at the same time as the first one. However, if a second sponsor obtains an MA for a therapeutic indication, a subset of the original one, this second sponsor will benefit from a full 10-year period of market exclusivity.[58]

If a sponsor for an authorised orphan medicinal product applies for a new MA for a therapeutic indication of an additional, separate orphan designation, this will entail a 10-year market exclusivity with different start and finish dates from the first one.

---

[56] Article 3(3)(b) of the Regulation 847/2000/EC.

[57] See Commission of the European Communities, 'Guideline on aspects of the application of Article 8(1) and (3) of Regulation 141/2000/EC: *Assessing similarity of medicinal products versus authorised orphan medicinal products benefiting from market exclusivity and applying derogations from that market exclusivity*', C[2008] 4077 final.

[58] See Commission of the European Communities, 'Guideline on aspects of the application of Article 8(1) and (3) of Regulation 141/2000/EC: Assessing similarity of medicinal products versus authorised orphan medicinal products benefiting from market exclusivity and applying derogations from that market exclusivity', C[2008] 4077 final s C(1) para 3.

5.2. Exceptions to Market Exclusivity

According to Article 8(3), there could be derogations to the market exclusivity provided for under Article 8(1) in certain circumstances, even in cases of similar substances. The derogations to the market exclusivity concern:

- situations where the holder of the marketing authorisation gives consent;
- when the holder of the original market authorisation is unable to provide the necessary quantities of the medicinal product;
- when the sponsor of the second medical product can prove that this product is safer, more effective, or otherwise clinically superior to the designated orphan drug.[59]

Both the EMA and national competent authorities need to consider whether there are any designated orphan drugs for which a similarity assessment would be necessary, to guarantee that the rights of the sponsor will be respected. If so, the second applicant will have to provide evidence of non-similarity, and in applicable cases will also have to submit evidence supporting one of the aforementioned derogations.

The second applicant will be required to provide the evidence on the following:

- A non-similarity report, providing for a comparison between the second medicinal product and the designated orphan drug. In the report, the applicant must address the molecular structural features, the mechanism of action and the therapeutic indication.
- In cases where a derogation according to 8(3) of the Orphan Drugs Regulation is applicable, the applicant must provide:
  (i) for a derogation under 8(3)(a), a letter from the sponsor authorising the second marketing authorisation;
  (ii) for a derogation under 8(3)(b), a report with supporting evidence as to why the supply of the authorised orphan medicinal product is considered insufficient and details as to why patients' needs are not met;
  (iii) for a derogation under 8(3)(c), a comparative report concerning the clinical superiority of the second medicinal product.

The similarity check must be repeated when the product has successfully completed the scientific assessment stage of the procedure, before receiving the marketing

---

[59] Clinical superiority means that a medicinal product is shown to provide a significant therapeutic or diagnostic advantage over and above that provided by an authorised orphan medicinal product in terms of efficacy (direct comparative clinical trials are necessary), greater safety in a substantial proportion of the patient population and, in exceptional cases, a major contribution to patient care or diagnosis.

authorisation. According to Article 3(3)(d) of the Orphan Drugs Regulation 'clinically superior' means that the medicinal product has been shown to provide a significant therapeutic or diagnostic advantage over and above that provided by an authorised orphan drug product, concerning either greater efficacy (which would in practice require the submission of clinical trial data, comparisons based on other end points may also be accepted, but the methodology used must be justified), greater efficacy in a substantial portion of the target population (direct comparative clinical trials might be required), or demonstration that the medicinal product makes a major contribution to diagnosis or patient care.

5.3. Technical Assistance/Fee Reductions

A holder of an orphan drug designation has the possibility to request protocol assistance from the EMA, a kind of scientific advice. Such requests are submitted to the Scientific Advice Working Party (SAWP) a division of the CHMP, and may be used to facilitate the sponsor's marketing authorisation application.[60]

However, protocol assistance also involves providing information and advice as to how to demonstrate significant benefit and clinical superiority.[61]

According to Article 5 of the Orphan Drugs Regulation, an ODD holder may request a reduction of all fees payable. The percentage of the reduction depends on whether the holder is an SME or whether paediatric-related assistance is being sought, and could amount to 100 per cent of the fees.

6. Post-grant Obligations of the Sponsor

The sponsor is under an obligation to submit a report on the state of development of the designated medicinal product to the EMA, on a yearly basis. In this report, the sponsor shall inform the EMA on current developments of the medicinal product, eventual problems, ongoing clinical trials and a description of the coming years' investigation plan. Sponsors holding orphan drug designations in both the EU and the United States can submit a single report to both supervisor agencies, using a shared template.

Orphan designations may be removed from the community registry in three cases: at the request of the sponsor, because of a decision of the COMP or the Commission (before the MA is granted) on the basis that the criteria of Article 3 are not fulfilled, or at the end of market exclusivity. The assessment of whether or

---

[60] See Article 9 of Regulation 141/2000/EC.
[61] See European Medicines Agency, *European Medicines Agency guidance for applicants seeking scientific advice and protocol assistance*, 30 June 2017, EMA/4260/2001 Rev. 9, Product Development Scientific Support Department.

not the medicinal product fulfils the requirements rests with the COMP, which will have to submit a report to the Commission in order for the latter to proceed to a decision.

The period of time that is required from the orphan drugs designation to the MA is usually rather long, allowing for technological developments to take place. The sponsor is thus under an obligation, when submitting its MA application, to provide information concerning the maintenance of the orphan drug designation criteria (maintenance report), and the COMP will provide a report on this regard.

Although at the time of the submission of the MA, the applicant and the sponsor must be the same, orphan drug designations are transferable. According to Article 5(11) of the Orphan Drugs Regulation, a sponsor is allowed to transfer an orphan drug designation to a new sponsor. In order for the transfer to be effective, the sponsor must submit to the EMA an electronic application that is signed by both the transferee and the transferor. Furthermore, the following documentation needs to be provided: the name and address of the transferor and the transferee, a statement certifying that a complete and up-to-date designation application has been made available to the transferee, and a document stating the date on which the proposed transfer will be implemented.[62]

The EMA will provide an opinion as to whether the transfer is admissible within 30 days from the submission of the documentation. In cases where the Commission permits the transfer, the Commission will amend the decision granting the orphan drug designation accordingly.

7. Difficulties in the Interpretation of Orphan Drugs Regulation Case Law

Key provisions of the Orphan Drugs Regulation have been considered by the CJEU and reveal difficulties in interpretation and some weaknesses of the Regulation as such.

In T-140/12 *Teva v EMA*, the Court was called to interpret core provisions of the Orphan Drugs Regulation for the first time. What was special with this specific case was that it considered the status of two orphan drugs owned by the same sponsor (Novartis).[63]

The first orphan drug was imatinib (commercialised under the name Glivec). Imatinib was granted an orphan drug designation in November 2001 to treat

---

[62] See European Commission, *Guideline on the format and content of applications for designation as orphan medicinal products and on the transfer of designations from one Sponsor to another*, ENTR/6283/00 Rev. 4.

[63] Judgment of the General Court (Sixth Chamber), 22 January 2015, *Teva Pharma BV and Teva Pharmaceuticals Europe BV v European Medicines Agency (EMA)*, T-140/12, EU:T:2015:41, para 81.

chronic myeloid leukaemia (CML). The market exclusivity of Glivec expired in November 2011, and in January 2012, Teva applied for a marketing authorisation of its generic version, with CML as one of the indications covered. The EMA refused to grant marketing authorisation for this second orphan drug for the same indication, nilotinib (commercialised under the name Tasigna). In February 2006, Novartis had applied for yet another orphan drug designation. Imatinib and Nilotinib were 'similar' medicinal products; for that reason, Novartis decided to waive its market exclusivity under Article 8(3)(a). The market exclusivity of nilotinib would expire in November 2017 and thus Teva's application would be inadmissible for the CML indication.

In its appeal to the General Court, Teva provided that Novartis had enjoyed a full-term market exclusivity of 10 years and should not be entitled to an additional term of protection for a similar substance. This would mean that Teva would enjoy a market exclusivity of 16 years in this case. The General Court rejected Teva's arguments and proceeded to some interesting interpretations of the Orphan Drugs Regulation.

The first question that the Court answered was whether an orphan drug could benefit from market exclusivity, where the marketing authorisation was initially granted based on one of the Article 8(3) derogations. The Court concluded that Tasigna, as a designated orphan drug, should be granted a 10-year market exclusivity regardless of whether or note there had previously been another similar orphan drug granted market exclusivity for the same indication. Article 8(3) poses no limitations as to the market exclusivity that will be granted as an effect of a derogation. The Court thus confirmed that Article 8(3) derogations give rise to independent market exclusivity periods, even if the sponsor of the original orphan drug designation is the same as that of the second one. The Court based its rationale on the objectives of the Orphan Drugs Regulation, providing that market exclusivity should be granted in all cases in which an orphan drug has been authorised. The Court also stated that the market exclusivity period 'cannot be regarded as equivalent to the data protection periods enjoyed by any product ... as the effects and scope of each of these mechanisms is different'.

Teva appealed the decision of the General Court, based on three different arguments. This first was that the General Court had applied an erroneous interpretation of the conditions for the grant of the 10-year market exclusivity period and that the interpretation was contrary to Article 8 of the Regulation. Teva argued that Article 8 does not address conflicting periods of market exclusivity granted under 8(1) and 8(3) of the Regulation and that the legislator had not envisaged situations like the one in this specific case. The Court of Appeal upheld the interpretation of the General Court, stating that the independent 10-year exclusivity is in line with the objectives of the Regulation of incentivising research in orphan diseases.[64]

---

[64] Judgment of the General Court (Sixth Chamber), 22 January 2015, *Teva Pharma BV and Teva Pharmaceuticals Europe BV v European Medicines Agency (EMA)*, T-140/12, EU:T:2015:41.

The second argument presented by Teva was that the General Court erred in law in its interpretation of the term of the market exclusivity period, since in the specific case the term of the market exclusivity will indirectly be prolonged. The Court of Appeal followed the line of reasoning of the General Court, the EMA and the Commission and ruled that the market exclusivity of the first orphan drug is not prolonged at least not formally, since the new market exclusivity period is in fact granted for new medicinal product.[65]

The third argument was that the General Court had failed to consider the alternative presented by Teva, that is to provide for an exception to the market exclusivity to the second medical product so as to permit the authorisation of a generic version of the first product once the period of exclusivity of the first product has expired. The Court of Appeal ruled that the General Court had in fact considered and rejected this argument. The appeal was thus dismissed in its entirety.[66]

In the T-452/14 *Laboratories CTRS v European Commission* case, the claimant (CTRS) was the holder of a market exclusivity for a designated orphan drug (Orphacol).[67] The case concerned a forthcoming marketing authorisation of a generic version sold under the tradename Kolbam. Kolbam was based on the same active ingredient as Orphacol and thus a marketing authorisation could not be granted for Orphacol's designated orphan drug uses due to Orphacol's market exclusivity. However, Kolbam was granted a marketing authorisation for three indications not covered by the orphan drug designation. Although this was welcomed by CTRS, the sponsor was concerned about the impact of the Summary of Product Characteristics (SmPC) on the market exclusivity for Orphacol, since both the SmPC and the EMA assessment of Kolbam included the therapeutic indications of Orphacol. According to CTRS, the fact that both the SmPC and the EMA concerned these therapeutic indications could be interpreted to mean that these therapeutic indications were also covered by Kolbam's marketing authorisation.

Although the Commission claimed that Orphacol's market exclusivity could not, formally, be circumvented, since Kolbam's marketing authorisation excluded the indications covered by the orphan drug designation, the General Court ruled in line with the argumentation of CTRS and provided that the Commission decision granting Kolbam marketing authorisation should be annulled.

Lastly, in T-583/13 *Shire Pharmaceutical Contracts v European Commission*, the General Court was given the opportunity to interpret Article 37 of Regulation (EC) No 1901/2006 (the Paediatric Regulation).[68] Shire, the applicant in this case,

---

[65] Judgment of the Court (Sixth Chamber) of 3 March 2016, *Teva Pharma BV and Teva Pharmaceuticals Europe BV v European Medicines Agency (EMA)*, C-138/15, EU:C:2016:136.

[66] Ibid.

[67] Judgment of the General Court (Seventh Chamber) of 11 June 2015, *Laboratoires CTRS v European Commission*, T-452/14, EU:T:2015:373.

[68] Order of the General Court (Eighth Chamber) of 3 September 2014, *Shire Pharmaceutical Contracts Ltd v European Commission*, T-583/13, EU:T:2018:165. See also judgment of the Court

brought an action to nullify the Commission's interpretation of the said provision. The application concerned the pharmaceutical Xagrid, a designated orphan drug, which enjoyed market exclusivity until November 2014.

The applicant wrote to the Commission and informed of Recital 29 and Article 37, pinpointing that the market exclusivity of an orphan product should be extended from 10 to 12 years where the requirements of Article 37 of the Paediatric Regulation are fulfilled. The applicant stated in the text sent to the Commission that Xagrid was a non-patented orphan drug, and would therefore qualify for a two-year extension as soon as the paediatric tests were completed. The Commission replied that they did not share this interpretation of Article 37 and that this provision did not constitute an entitlement for an extension of the duration of market exclusivity. The General Court found that the case was inadmissible, since the Commission letter had only expressed an 'opinion' on the application of Article 37. Therefore, it did not have any legal effects on Shire, and thus was not appealable. Although the General Court did not rule in the matter, the Commission changed its approach concerning interpretation of Article 37. Xagrid was subsequently granted the two-year paediatric extension.

In another very interesting ruling, the *Medac v Commission* case (T 549/19) the Court provided an interesting interpretation of Article 3 of the Regulation (EC) No. 141/2000, and in particular on how the evaluation of 'significant benefit' is to be performed.[69]

In the specific case, In February 2004, a treosulfan-containing drug for conditioning therapy prior to allogeneic hematopoietic stem-cell transplantation was designated as an orphan drug.

By decision of 20 June 2019, the Commission approved Treosulfan (Trecondi®) for this indication without, however, at the same time maintaining its orphan drug status. The Commission decided that Treosulfan (Trecondi®) would no longer fulfil the criteria as an orphan medicinal product according to Article 3 of Regulation (EC) No 141/2000 as Treosulfan (Trecondi®), since it could not be considered to provide significant benefit compared to medicinal products containing melphalan and cyclophosphamide. Both of these were considered to be satisfactory methods.

A very important conclusion reached by the Court is that where the medicinal product which is subject of an application for an authorisation as an orphan medicinal product is intended for the diagnosis, prevention or treatment of diseases or patient populations for which the reference medicinal products are not authorised, even if only in parts according to their respective SmPC, these reference medicinal products cannot be regarded as 'satisfactory methods' for these diseases or patient populations to that extent (paragraph 66).

(Eighth Chamber) of 29 July 2019, *European Medicines Agency v Shire Pharmaceuticals Ireland Ltd*, C-359/18 P, EU:C:2019:639.

[69] *Medac Gesellschaft für klinische Spezialpräparate v Commission*, T-549/19, EU:T:2020:444.

In recitals 67 and 68, the Court states that any other consideration would be contrary to the objectives of Regulation 141/2000 to provide incentives for the research, development and placing on the market of medicinal products for diseases that are so rare, that the pharmaceutical industry is not very inclined to develop medicinal products. It would be contrary to this objective to exclude a potential medicinal product from the benefits of Regulation 141/2000 on the sole ground that 'satisfactory methods' exist for some of the orphan diseases for which the medicinal product is intended.

Thus, in the specific case, and considering the orphan drug designation of treosulfan (Trecondi®), the Court of First Instance therefore concluded in recitals 80 and 81 that melphalan- and cyclophosphamide-based medicinal products already authorised can only be regarded as a satisfactory method in relation to conditions and populations to the extent that they are also authorised for these exact populations of patients. Since in this particular case, only a partial overlap exists, these medicinal products may not be considered to be authorised for the conditions and patients of Treosulfan and may thus not constitute 'satisfactory methods' under Article 3 of the Regulation (EC) No. 141/2000.[70]

This ruling is of course very encouraging for Orphan drug sponsors who see that the list of pharmaceuticals with which their orphan drugs are compared in order to receive or not an orphan drug designation, becomes considerably limited.

8. Concluding Remarks

The text of the Orphan Drugs Regulation is neither clear nor complete. This was already obvious at the time of the presentation of the proposal for a Regulation, where it was clarified that the Regulation should be completed with forthcoming guidelines that would clarify its provisions and facilitate its application.

Although there is not a plethora of case law concerning the Regulation, the cases that have reached the CJEU reveal that there are serious aspects of the application of the orphan drugs designation system that have not been addressed by the legislator. An illustrative example is the fact that, by making use of Article 8(3)(1), a sponsor may prolong the exclusivity for an orphan drug.

It is also obvious that the interface of the regulation with the patent system, as well as with the other regulatory rights, could have been more explicit.[71] There is no obstacle to a sponsor of an orphan drug also enjoying patent rights. However, it remains to be seen how this combination can be used and to what extent strategic

---

[70] Article 3 of Regulation 141/2000/EC.
[71] Another interface of interest is that between the Orphan Drugs Regulation and the ATMP Regulation, and the question as to whether personalised medicine could be considered to treat an orphan disease.

moves such as those noted in the *Teva* case will be allowed in the future, as well as how this will relate to competition law rules.[72] In any case, this possibility of parallel protection brings a level of uncertainty as to how the objectives of the regulation (to provide for commercial incentives where the market itself is unable to) are in fact followed up in the text of the Regulation.

Apart from issues of substance, procedural aspects of the Orphan Drugs Regulation could also benefit from further clarification. One important issue that has been considered in case law but could be clarified more is the EMA mandate when examining orphan drug designation applications.[73] In particular, whether the validation stage of an application for orphan designation is purely procedural, that is, whether the EMA is obliged to validate an application or whether it needs to assess differences between the medicinal product under application and other similar products. Although the Orphan Drugs Regulations builds upon the US model of the Orphan Drugs Act enacted in 1983, thus with numerous years of practical application, it misses bits and pieces both on a procedural and substantial level, making its *mise en oeuvre* shaky.

---

[72] Judgment of the Court (Sixth Chamber) of 3 March 2016, *Teva Pharma BV and Teva Pharmaceuticals Europe BV v European Medicines Agency (EMA)*, C-138/15, EU:C:2016:136.

[73] Judgment of the General Court (Seventh Chamber) of 22 March 2018, *Shire Pharmaceuticals Ireland Ltd v European Medicines Agency*, T-80/16, EU:T:2018:165; Judgment of the Court (Eighth Chamber) of 29 July 2019, *European Medicines Agency v Shire Pharmaceuticals Ireland Ltd*, C-359/18 P, EU:C:2019:639.

7

Advanced Therapy Medicinal Products

1. The Legal Framework

ATMPs concern cutting-edge technology in the field of pharmaceutical research. Providing genetic treatments and moving towards an increasingly personalised medicine with the benefits this has for patients (increased effectiveness of the treatment, less side effects), has for a long time now been considered the future of pharmaceutical research. While these 'new era' pharmaceuticals have been welcomed for a while now, they seem to have been more the exception than the rule, with limited accessibility and commercial viability. One of the reasons behind this limited commercialisation and expansion has been identified to be the difficulties in applying the 'traditional' regulatory regime to these very special and demanding technologies. The ATMP Regulation was thus introduced in order to address these issues and to adapt general medical law to the particularities of the ATMP applications.[1]

---

[1] The regulation of Advanced Therapy Medicinal Products by means of the Commission Directive 2009/120/EC of 14 September 2009 amending Directive 2001/83/EC of the European Parliament and of the Council on the Community code relating to medicinal products for human use as regards advanced therapy medicinal products (Text with EEA relevance) [2009] OJ L 242/3 was the first mention of such therapies in EU legislation. This Directive modified Part IV of the Annex 1 to Directive 2001/83/EC by defining the specific requirements applicable to gene therapy and somatic cell therapy medicinal products. Technological progress led to the need to regulate yet another category of ATMPs – those related to tissue-engineered products. New legislation was introduced by means of Regulation 1394/2007/EC of the European Parliament and of the Council of 13 November 2007 on advanced therapy medicinal products and amending Directive 2001/83/EC and Regulation 726/2004/EC (Text with EEA relevance) [2007] OJ L 324/121 on ATMPs, amending Directive 2001/83/EC of the European Parliament and of the Council of 6 November 2001 on the Community code relating to medicinal products for human use [2001] OJ L 311/67 as a form of *lex specialis*, with more specific provisions than those introduced by means of Directive 2001/83/EC. See Commission Directive 2009/120/EC of 14 September 2009 amending Directive 2001/83/EC of the European Parliament and of the Council on the Community code relating to medicinal products for human use as regards advanced therapy medicinal products (Text with EEA relevance) [2009] OJ L 242/3; Directive 2001/83/EC of the European Parliament and of the Council of 6 November 2001 on the Community code relating to medicinal products for human use [2001] OJ L 311/67; Regulation 1394/2007/EC of the European Parliament and of the Council of 13 November 2007 on advanced therapy medicinal products and amending Directive 2001/83/EC and Regulation 726/2004/EC (Text with EEA relevance) [2007] OJ L 324/121; Regulation 726/2004/EC of the European Parliament and of the Council of 31 March 2004 laying down Community procedures for the authorisation and supervision of medicinal products for human and veterinary use and establishing a European Medicines Agency [2004] OJ L 136/1.

The main objectives of the ATMP Regulation have been to address fundamental regulatory issues (ie the granting of marketing authorisation) related to ATMPs and to introduce incentives for SMEs to engage in research in this field. However, what is important to note is the fact that guidelines related to the implementation of the ATMP Regulation and technical requirements are not found in the Regulation itself but in other documents. The rules applied to ATMPs make up a two-level system.

The technical level concerns the technical requirements (eg concerning preclinical and clinical data requirements) are not specified in the text of the regulation. This grants the system a necessary flexibility, taking into consideration the fact that ATMP is an area of medicinal research that is evolving rapidly. The legislator has thus been faced with the challenge of creating a regulatory system that safeguards the safety and quality of such therapies while providing patients with access to these very promising therapies.[2]

Another important challenge that the legislator had to face in the final draft of the Regulation was ethical considerations, which could become rather problematic. The Regulation attempts to address ethical concerns in as simple and direct a way as possible, namely by amending Directive 2001/83 in Article 28 and adding a fourth paragraph to its Article 4. These provisions state that ethical debates concerning the use of embryonic and umbilical cord blood tissues are left to the Member States to regulate. This intention is also confirmed by the preparatory works to the ATMP Regulation.[3]

This choice of legislative structure is rather peculiar. Directives allow for a certain level of national flexibility by means of national implementation. However, the legislative choice here was that of a Regulation (ie a legislative act that is directly applicable throughout the EU). Still, the Regulation allows the Member States to proceed to rather crucial choices at a national level and with a considerable level of flexibility. This flexibility stretches so far as for Member States to prohibit research into certain forms of therapies falling under the scope of the regulation, for ethical reasons. An ATMP that has been granted marketing authorisation by means of a

---

[2] This is in fact the challenge with all regulatory rights in the field: to provide incentives for the development of medical processes and methods, while at the same time ensuring the safety and security of these methods/processes.

[3] The ATMP Regulation (Regulation 1394/2007/EC) in its Preamble 17 provides that clinical trials on advanced therapy medicinal products should be conducted in accordance with the overarching principles and ethical requirements laid out in Directive 2001/20/EC of the European Parliament and of the Council of 4 April 2001 on the approximation of the laws, regulations and administrative provisions of the Member States relating to the implementation of good clinical practice in the conduct of clinical trials on medicinal products for human use [2001] OJ L 121/34 (1). However, Commission Directive 2005/28/EC of 8 April 2005 laying down principles and detailed guidelines for good clinical practice as regards investigational medicinal products for human use, as well as the requirements for authorisation of the manufacturing or importation of such products (Text with EEA relevance) [2005] OJ L 91/13 (2) should be adapted by laying down rules tailored to consider more fully the specific technical characteristics of advanced therapy medicinal products.

centralised marketing authorisation procedure may be prohibited from commercialisation in the territory of certain Member States.[4]

The regulation establishes the sixth scientific committee of the EMA, the Committee for Advanced Therapies (the CAT), which had its first meeting in January 2009. The main role of the CAT is to provide an expert opinion to the EMA concerning ATMP marketing authorisation applications. At the request of the EMA, the CAT may provide a scientific opinion concerning ATMPs.[5]

The CAT also provides scientific advice related to the classification of ATMPs free of charge, and may be involved in matters concerning the pharmacovigilance, safety and efficacy of ATMPs.[6]

2. Definitions of Key Terms in the ATMP Regulation

The ATMP Regulation concerns pioneer technologies, with the ambition of providing a novel (or – to be more concrete – an adjusted) regulatory framework that takes their special characteristics into consideration. Thus, one of the important contributions is to provide definitions of decisive importance for the application of the system as such and for the delimitation of its scope.

2.1. Gene Therapy

A gene therapy medicinal product is a biological medicinal product composed of an active substance which contains or consists of a recombinant nucleic acid used in, or administered to, human beings with a view to regulating, repairing, replacing, adding or deleting a genetic sequence.[7] Its therapeutic, prophylactic or diagnostic effect relates directly to the recombinant nucleic acid sequence it contains, or to the product of genetic expression of this sequence.[8]

Gene therapy medicinal products expressly exclude vaccines against infectious diseases. Directive 2001/83 provides that a range of different medicinal products could fall under the scope of the definition gene therapy, such as gene therapy medicinal products based on allogeneic (coming from another human being) or xenogeneic cells, gene therapy medicinal products using autologous human

---

[4] Carolina Iglesias-López, Antonia Agustí, Mercè Obach et al, 'Regulatory Framework for Advanced Therapy Medicinal Products in Europe and United States' [2019] 10 *Frontiers in Pharmacology*, published online 30 August 2019.

[5] See Articles 20–23 of Regulation 1394/2007/EC.

[6] See also, with respect to the way different forms of medicinal products are to be regulated in the EU, European Parliament, *Medicinal Products in the European Union: The legal framework for medicines for human use*, April 2015, PE 554.174.

[7] See Section 2.1, Part IV, Annex 1 to Directive 2001/83/EC.

[8] Ibid.

cells (emanating from the patient him- or herself), and administration of ready-prepared vectors with inserted (prophylactic, diagnostic or therapeutic) genetic material.[9]

2.2. Somatic Cell Therapy Medicinal Products

A somatic cell therapy medicinal product is a biological product which has the following characteristics:[10]

(a) It contains or consists of cells or tissues that have been subject to substantial manipulation so that the biological characteristics, physiological functions, or structural properties relevant for the intended clinical use have been altered, or of cells or tissues that are not intended to be used for the same essential functions in the recipient and the donor.
(b) It is presented as having properties for, or is used in or administered to human beings with a view of treating, preventing, or diagnosing a disease through the pharmacological, immunological, or metabolic action of its cells or tissues.

In Annex 1 of the ATMP Regulation, there is a list of genetic manipulations which are not considered to be substantial enough to fall under the scope of the aforementioned definition. Such manipulations include cutting, grinding, shaping, centrifugation, soaking in antibiotics, antimicrobial solutions, sterilisation, irradiation, cell separation, concentration or purification, filtering, lyophilisation, freezing, cryopreservation and vitrification.

According to Part IV, somatic cell therapy medicinal products include cells manipulated to modify their immunological metabolic or other functional properties in qualitative or quantitative aspects, cell sorted, selected, manipulated, and subsequently undergoing a manufacturing process in order to obtain a finished medicinal product, cells manipulated, combined with non-cellular components, and exerting the principal intended action in the finished product, autologous cell derivatives expressed in vitro under specific culture conditions, and cells genetically modified or otherwise manipulated to express previously unexpressed or non-homologous functional properties. In the same Annex, it is stated that the entire manufacturing process, from the collection of materials from the patient to the re-injection into the patient, shall be considered a single intervention.[11]

---

[9] Section 2.1, Part IV Annex 1 to Directive 2001/83/EC attempts to provide a definition of what gene therapy is. Reading the definition makes it clear that the scope of what may be included under this concept is broad and rather uncertain.

[10] See Section 2.2. Part IV, Annex 1 to Directive 2001/83/EC.

[11] Carolina Iglesias-López, Antonia Agustí, Mercè Obach et al, 'Regulatory Framework for Advanced Therapy Medicinal Products in Europe and United States' [2019] 10 *Frontiers in Pharmacology*, published online 30 August 2019.

For other medicinal products, the following three results of the manufacturing process are identified:

- starting materials: materials from which the active substance is manufactured (ie organs, tissues, bodily fluids, or cells);
- active substances: manipulated cells, cell lysates, proliferating cells and cells used in conjunction with inert matrices and medical devices;
- finished medicinal products: the active substance in the form of its final container for the intended medical use.

2.3. Tissue-engineered Products (Article 2(b) of the ATMP Regulation)

A tissue-engineered product may contain cells or tissues of human or animal origin, or both. The cells may be viable or non-viable, and may contain additional substances such as cellular products, biomolecules, biomaterials, chemical substances, scaffolds, or matrices. However, products which contain or consist solely of non-viable human or animal cells and/or tissues, which do not contain any viable cells or tissues and which do not act principally by pharmacological, immunological, or metabolic action, are excluded from the scope of the regulation.

A cell or tissue is considered to be 'engineered' if it fulfils one of the following conditions:

- the cells or tissues have been subject to substantial manipulation, for achievement of the biological characteristics, physiological functions, or structural properties relevant for the intended regeneration, repair, or replacement (note that the list of manipulations cited as not substantial enough is only relevant for the determination of the scope of the specific provision);
- the cells or tissues are not intended to be used for the same essential function or functions in the recipient as in the donor.

2.4. Combined ATMPs

According to Article 2(1)(d) of the ATMP Regulation, 'a combined advanced therapy medicinal product' is an advanced therapy medicinal product given that:

(i) it incorporates, as an integral part of the product, one or more medical devices within the meaning of Article 1(2)(a) Directive 93/42/EEC or one or more active implantable devices with the meaning of Article 1(2)(c) of Directive 90/385/EEC, and

(ii) its cellular or tissue part contains viable cells or tissues or its cellular or tissue part containing non-viable cells or tissues must be liable to act upon the human body with action that can be considered as primary to that of the devices referred to.

Where the two conditions are fulfilled, the combined ATMPs are treated as ATMPs and fall under the same legal framework, meaning that they are also subject to the centralised marketing authorisation procedure. Article 6 of the ATMP Regulation provides that medical devices and implantable medical devices forming part of a combined ATMP must comply with the essential requirements of Directive 93/42/EEC and Directive 90/385/EEC, respectively.[12]

A public consultation that has been conducted by the European Commission has shown that separate assessment of the medical device and the medicinal product is regarded as excessive in the cases where the device is not marketed separately. It has been demonstrated that this requirement promotes marketing authorisation of existing devices more than development of new devices.

2.5. Rules of Classification

Articles 2(3) to 5 of the ATMP Regulation define a hierarchy of ATMP categories:

- An ATMP containing both autologous and allogeneic cells or tissues will be considered to be an ATMP for allogeneic use.
- A product that falls both within the definition of 'tissue-engineered product' and within the definition of 'somatic cell therapy medicinal product' will be considered to be a 'tissue-engineered product'.
- A product which falls within the definitions of a 'somatic cell therapy medicinal product', a 'tissue engineered product', and a 'gene therapy medicinal product' shall be considered to be a 'gene therapy medicinal product'.

Article 17 of the ATMP Regulation gives applicants the possibility to receive scientific assistance in determining whether a product based on genes, cells, or tissues meets the scientific criteria for an ATMP classification. The objective is to address questions which arise with regard to the classification issues, as early as possible in the product development process. The Committee for Advanced Therapies (CAT) delivers scientific information on ATMP classification within 60 days from the date of the receipt of a request from the therapy developer.[13] A summary of the assessments of the CAT is available on the EMA website.

---

[12] Furthermore, the Commission has drafted specific guidelines with respect to the evaluation of combined ATMPs.
[13] It does so after consultation with the European Commission.

The classification of ATMPs creates one of the major difficulties in the application of the ATMP Regulation.[14] The difficulties concern several issues, such as whether or not manipulation of living materials is considered substantial, and classification of products that could potentially be categorised as medicines, medical devices, cosmetics, or tissues and cells. It is important to increase clarity in the field, since product developers would benefit from knowing which regulatory framework applies to their products, as early as possible in product development process. CAT assessments provide a guideline, but are not binding; harmonisation through the role is thus not possible. Despite the existence of the CAT guidelines, Member States' authorities interpret the classification principles in different ways, leading to a rather divergent application of the ATMP Regulation.

3. The ATMP Regulation and Other European Legislation

The legal framework concerning ATMPs is rather fragmented. It consists of a number of Directives, concerning medicinal products for human use, medical devices, quality and safety standards for human tissues and cells, and implantable medical devices, as well as the Regulation concerning the centralised marketing authorisation procedure.[15]

There is an important link between the ATMP Regulation and the Directive 2004/23/EC concerning standards of quality and safety for human tissues and cells intended for human applications. ATMPs are derived and/or produced from human tissues and cells. A specific set of rules apply to those products, whereby not all phases of the manufacturing process of an ATMP fall within the scope of the ATMP Regulations. These rules are found in Article 2(1) of the Directive and Article 3 of the ATMP Regulation. According to these two provisions, the donation, procurement and testing of human tissue and cells involved in the manufacture of ATMPs remain governed by the provisions of the Directive 2004/23/EC and its national implementing instruments.[16]

---

[14] According to the Commission report.

[15] Regulation 726/2004/EC of the European Parliament and of the Council of 31 March 2004 laying down Community procedures for the authorisation and supervision of medicinal products for human and veterinary use and establishing a European Medicines Agency (Text with EEA relevance) [2004] OJ L 136/1.

[16] See Directive 2001/83/EC of the European Parliament and of the Council of 6 November 2001 on the Community code relating to medicinal products for human use [2001] OJ L 311/67; Directive 2004/23/EC of the European Parliament and of the Council of 31 March 2004 on setting standards of quality and safety for the donation, procurement, testing, processing, preservation, storage and distribution of human tissues and cells [2004] OJ L 102/48; Council Directive 93/42/EEC of 14 June 1993 concerning medical devices [1993] OJ L 169/1; Council Directive 90/385/EEC of 20 June 1990 on the approximation of the laws of the Member States relating to active implantable medical devices [1990] OJ L 189/17. Regulation 726/2004/EC of the European Parliament and of the Council of 31 March 2004 laying down Community procedures for the authorisation and supervision of medicinal products for human and veterinary use and establishing a European Medicines Agency [2004] OJ L 136/1.

Directive 2004/23 stipulates the obligations of Member States, which include designating a competent authority for implementing requirements for accrediting, designating, authorising, or licensing the conditions in which procurement is taking place.[17] However, the way in which these provisions are formulated leaves room for national interpretation.[18]

On the other hand, Directives 2015/565[19] and 2015/566[20] include detailed rules concerning the coding of human cells and tissues intended for human application.[21]

Member States may include exemptions on condition that the traceability from donor to recipient is ensured in some other way and that the imported tissues are not used by anyone but the intended recipient. Tissues and cells that are intended for industrial use will most likely not fall under any such exemption, although that remains unclear.[22]

The definition of a 'one-off import' is as follows:

> the import of any specific type of tissue or cell which is intended for recipients known to the importing tissue establishment and the third country supplier before the importation occurs. Such an import of any specific type of tissue or cell shall normally not occur more than once for any given recipient. Imports from the same third country supplier taking place on a regular or repented basis shall not be considered to be 'one-off imports'.[23]

The provisions of the Directive provide also for an extended control possibility of the importing establishment's suppliers. Competent authorities will have the right to review the activities and facilities of any third country supplier during the duration of the written cooperation agreement and for a period of two years after its expiration.[24]

---

[17] See Article 6(1) of the Directive 2004/23/EC.

[18] European Medicines Agency, *Guideline on Safety and Efficacy Follow-up Risk management of ATMPS*, London, 20 November 2008, Doc. Ref. EMEA/149995/2008.

[19] Commission Directive 2015/565/EU of 8 April 2015 amending Directive 2006/86/EC as regards certain technical requirements for the coding of human tissues and cells (Text with EEA relevance) [2015] OJ L 93/43.

[20] Commission Directive 2015/566/EU of 8 April 2015 implementing Directive 2004/23/EC as regards the procedures for verifying the equivalent standards of quality and safety of imported tissues and cells (Text with EEA relevance) [2015] OJ L 93/56.

[21] These Directives should have been implemented by the Member States at the latest on 26 October 2016 and start to apply by 26 April 2017.

[22] See Recital 2 in the Preamble of Directive 2015/566/EU, 'Exchanges of tissues and cells increasingly take place on a worldwide basis and Directive 2004/23/EC therefore requires that imports of tissues and cells are undertaken by tissue establishments accredited, designated, authorised or licensed by Member States for that purpose. Exceptions to that requirement are laid down in Article 9(3) of Directive 2004/23/EC allowing competent authorities to directly authorise the import of specific tissues and cells under the conditions laid down in Article 6 of Commission Directive 2006/17/EC (2) or in case of emergency. These exceptions are regularly used, but not limited to, allowing the import of hematopoietic stem cells from bone marrow, peripheral blood or cord blood which is used in the treatment of a number of life-threatening conditions'.

[23] European Commission, *Inspection of Tissue and Cell Procurement and Tissue Establishment, Operational Guidelines*, Ref. Ares[2015]1822725 – 29 April 2015.

[24] See Article 7 of the Commission Directive 2015/566/EU.

4. Marketing Authorisation for ATMPs

In order for ATMPs to be placed on the market, they have to undergo the centralised marketing authorisation procedure. However, there is an exemption, the 'hospital exemption', that is applicable under certain circumstances and means there is no need for the ATMP to undergo a MA procedure in order to be used in clinical practice.[25]

4.1. The Main Procedure: The Centralised MA

The marketing authorisation procedure under Regulation 726/2004 is used in the case of ATMPs and combined ATMPs. The only difference is the role of the CAT. According to Article 8 of the ATMP Regulation, the CHMP is obliged to consult with the CAT for any scientific assessment concerning ATMPs. The same obligation also applies when an applicant requests re-examination of an opinion.

4.2. The Hospital Exemption

According to Article 28(2) of Regulation 1394/2007, a new paragraph 7 is included in Article 3 of Directive 2001/83/EC, providing an exemption from the scope of the harmonised pharmaceutical legislation is applicable where certain criteria are fulfilled.[26]

The hospital exemption provides ATMPs that are prepared on a non-routine basis according to specific quality standards, and used within the same Member State in a hospital under the exclusive professional responsibility of a medical practitioner, in order to comply with an individual medical prescription for a custom-made product for an individual patient, do not fall under the European pharmaceutical legislation. Such products will instead be regulated by national legislation.[27]

This provision gives Member States the possibility to authorise the use of ATMPs in hospitals for individual patients when these in fact lack marketing authorisation. The possible 'side effects' of this exemption were discussed in the public consultation launched by the DG Health and Consumers concerning the application of the ATMP Regulation and scientific advice on any other initiative in the Community related to ATMPs.

---

[25] Article 28(2) of Regulation 1394/2007/EC.
[26] Article 28(2) of Regulation 1394/2007/EC which, in turn, amended Article 3 of Directive 2001/83.
[27] European Medicines Agency, 'Guideline on Safety and Efficacy Follow-up Risk management of ATMPs' London, 20 November 2008, Doc. Ref. EMEA/149995/2008.

The report of the public consultation pinpointed, among other things, an overly lenient marketing authorisation. According to the Commission this could have detrimental effects on public health. Making use of the hospital exemption means that the legislation on clinical trials is not applicable, which results in a lack of data on the safety and efficacy of the method. It also gives Member States the discretionary power to treat these methods in differing ways.[28]

The possibility of taking advantage of the 'hospital exemption' might be the reason why so few ATMPs are put on the market through the centralised marketing authorisation procedure.[29] Among the ATMPs that were on the market at the time of the entry into force of the ATMP Regulation, very few were subsequently subject to a MA. Thus, the statistics on ATMPs in the EU do not correspond to the actual ATMP market.

The Commission report (the result of the open consultation) stated that further clarifications of the 'hospital exemption' and the requirements linked to this exemption were needed.

4.3. The Marketing Authorisation Procedure for ATMPs

The requirements for marketing authorisation of ATMPs are regulated in Part IV of Annex I to Directive 2001/83/EC. Apart from the general requirements applicable to other medicinal products, ATMPs must comply with specific additional criteria.

In order to assess the product's quality, non-clinical and clinical data are to be submitted on the basis of a risk-based analysis. This risk-based analysis must comply with the scientific guidelines relating to the quality, safety and efficacy of medicinal products.[30]

This risk analysis should encompass the entire product development process. The Annex lists a number of risk factors that could be relevant, such as the origin of the cells (autologous, allogeneic, xenogeneic), the ability to proliferate and/or differentiate and to initiate an immune response, the level of cell manipulation, the combination of cells with bioactive molecules or structural materials, the nature of the gene therapy medicinal products, the extent of replication competence of viruses or microorganisms used in vivo, the level of integration of nucleic acids sequences or genes into the genome, the long-term functionality, and the risk of oncogenicity, as well as the route of administration and use.

The applicant must provide scientific justifications if it wished to deviate from any of the requirements of the Annex.

---

[28] European Commission, *Regulation (EC) 1394/2007 on Advanced Therapy Medicinal Products: Summary of Responses to the Public Consultation*, Brussels, SANCO/D5/RSR/iv [2013] ddg1.d5.

[29] Twelve applications have been submitted to CAT and only four have been placed on the market through the marketing authorisation procedure.

[30] See also the website of the EMA, www.ema.europa.eu/en.

The consultation report of 2014 revealed that developers of ATMPs wished for greater flexibility with regard to the requirements, taking into consideration the fact that not all ATMPs are the same or have the same characteristics.[31]

4.4. Incentives for Small- and Medium-sized Enterprises

SMEs can be given significant reduction of the fees (90 per cent) for scientific advice and the possibility to defer the part of the amount that is payable until the date when the marketing authorisation is granted.[32] Non-SMEs may also benefit from a fee reduction of 65 per cent. However, there are no post-grant economic incentives and no further facilitations for entering the market for companies active in the field of ATMPs.

4.5. Other Requirements Related to ATMPs

The ATMP Regulation provides a list of derogations from Directive 2001/83 related to the contents of the Summary of Product Characteristics, the labelling and the package leaflet.[33]

The regulation also requires that the Commission develops guidelines concerning Good Manufacturing Practices (GMP) for ATMPs. In order to provide for the necessary information – and thus the necessary starting point for drafting GMPs – a public consultation was initiated in 2015.[34] The consultation document reveals that blood and tissue establishments authorised and supervised under the Directive 2004/23 do not require additional audits by the ATMP manufacturer regarding compliance with the requirements on donation, procurement and testing.[35]

---

[31] European Commission, *Report from the Commission to the European Parliament and the Council in accordance with Article 25 of Regulation (EC) 1394/2007 of the European Parliament and of the Council on advanced therapy medicinal products and amending Directive 2001/83/EC and Regulation (EC) 726/2004*, COM [2014] 188 final.

[32] This fee may be reduced by 50 per cent and may not be payable if the marketing authorisation is not granted, if the ATMP is for a special public health interest. See also European Commission, 'Targeted stakeholder consultation on the development of Good Manufacturing Practice for Advanced Therapy Medicinal Products pursuant to Article 5 of Regulation 1394/2007', https://ec.europa.eu/health/human-use/advanced-therapies/developments/2015_11_pc_gmp_atmp_en [Accessed on 18 June 2020].

[33] See Article 10, Chapter 4: 'By way of derogation from Article 11 of Directive 2001/83/EC, the summary of the product characteristics for advanced therapy medicinal products shall contain the information listed in Annex II to this Regulation, in the order indicated therein.'

[34] European Commission, *Guidelines of 22.11.2017 Good Manufacturing Practice for Advanced Therapy Medicinal Products*, C (2017) 7694 final.

[35] Directive 2004/23/EC of the European Parliament and of the Council of 31 March 2004 on setting standards of quality and safety for the donation, procurement, testing, processing, preservation, storage and distribution of human tissues and cells [2004] OJ L 102/48.

5. Post-authorisation Requirements

Article 14 of the ATMP Regulation states that in addition to fulfilling the requirements on pharmacovigilance provided for under Articles 21–29 of Regulation 726/2004, the applicant must also take measures to follow up on the efficacy and adverse reactions to ATMPs. In cases where there is reason for concern, the European Commission may, on the advice of EMA, include in the marketing authorisation the obligation to put in place a risk management system to identify, characterise, prevent, or minimise risks related to ATMPs including to evaluate the effectiveness of that system and/or carry out, and submit to the EMA, specific marketing studies.[36]

The EMA may also request the MA holder to provide additional reports evaluating the effectiveness of any risk management system and the results of any studies performed. Any evaluation of studies performed should also be included in the periodic safety update reports (PSURs) provided for by Regulation 726/2004.[37]

If serious adverse effects are noted, the EMA will inform the national competent authorities that are responsible for implementation of Directives 90/385/EEC, 93/42/EEC and 2004/23/EC.

Another important requirement for the marketing authorisation holder is to provide for the traceability of ATMPs. According to Recital 22 of the ATMP Regulation, it is essential to monitor the safety of the ATMPs through a system for the traceability of the patient and the product, including its starting materials. Furthermore, this system must be compliant with the requirements laid out in Directives 95/46,[38] 2004/23[39] and 2002/98.[40] According to Article 15 of the ATMP Regulation, a system needs to be put in place in order to allow that all substances that come in contact with the product's constituent cells or tissues can be traced through sourcing, manufacturing, packaging storage, transport and delivery to the hospital institution or private practice. The marketing authorisation holder must keep the information for a period of 30 years from the expiry of the product or for a longer period of time, if this is one of the requirements for the granting of marketing authorisation. Furthermore, in case of bankruptcy or liquidation and

---

[36] European Medicines Agency, *Guideline on Safety and Efficacy Follow-up Risk management of ATMPs*, London, 20 November 2008, Doc. Ref. EMEA/149995/2008.

[37] See, in this respect, Aniello Santoro, Georgy Genov, Almath Spooner, et al, 'Promoting and Protecting Public Health: How the European Union Pharmacovigilance System Works' (2017) 40 *Drug Safety*, 10, 855–69.

[38] Directive 95/46/EC of the European Parliament and of the Council of 24 October 1995 on the protection of individuals with regard to the processing of personal data and on the free movement of such data [1995] OJ L 281/31.

[39] Directive 2004/23/EC of the European Parliament and of the Council of 31 March 2004 on setting standards of quality and safety for the donation, procurement, testing, processing, preservation, storage and distribution of human tissues and cells [2004] OJ L 102/48.

[40] Directive 2002/98/EC of the European Parliament and of the Council of 27 January 2003 setting standards of quality and safety for the collection, testing, processing, storage and distribution of human blood and blood components and amending Directive 2001/83/EC [2003] OJ L 33/30.

where this know-how is not transferred to a third party, the information is to be transferred to the EMA. Even if the marketing authorisation is suspended or withdrawn, the holder of the marketing authorisation is still bound by the traceability obligations.

6. Concluding Remarks

There is no doubt that the ATMP Regulation is different from the other Regulations discussed in this book. It is a Regulation that serves to provide a regulatory framework for what may be considered pioneering gene therapies. The starting point for this Regulation is the fact that the special characteristics of these therapeutic methods make it difficult to apply the general regulatory framework.[41] At the same time, this Regulation shares the common objective of boosting the European industry in the field. In the specific case of ATMPs, research and commercialisation are predominantly left to SMEs, public hospitals and universities. Although this objective is similar, if not identical, to that of other Regulations, the target group in this case is so different that the way in which the objective is applied and evaluated must necessarily be different.[42]

There seem to be two major sources of concern with this specific regulation. The first is the level of flexibility left to Member States and the effect this has in harmonising the regulatory framework for ATMPs. The other is the scope and application of the hospital exemption. The degree of flexibility given to national legislation and national authorities applying the regulation has been feared to have effects contrary to what which the Regulation is supposed to achieve: a harmonised approach that will also support the European ATMP R&D. Public consultations have also been clear on the negative effects that the divergent application of the hospital exemption has. This lack of predictability hampers investments in this specific research field.[43]

Another factor that undoubtedly influences the application of the ATMP Regulation and the development of the ATMP market in general is of course the character of the stakeholders involved. Public research institutions and hospitals are not characterised by strategic behaviour and business agility, and this might be an important aspect to consider when justifying whether the regulation has not been tested and debated in the same way as others.

---

[41] In particular the Medicinal Code (Directive 2001/83/EC).
[42] In this case, the European industry consists of SMEs and research institutes, while in the other Regulations what is considered when referring to European industry and R&D is pharmaceutical industries, in terms of non-negligible commercial entities.
[43] The public consultation of 2016 is clear in this respect, see n 36.

8
How Effective is the Effectiveness Test in the Field of Regulatory Rights?

There is no doubt that the Regulations that have been discussed and analysed in this book are part of a broader system. They share a number of common characteristics and objectives and are based on the same parameters, with other legislative acts, such as the Medicinal Code,[1] Guidelines, procedural rules and national legislation – in the field of both marketing authorisation and intellectual property rights – being of central importance.[2] Thus, the MA procedure, the EMA and the various Committees are relevant for all these regulations. Lastly, data protection is most certainly another parameter of relevance and importance to take into consideration in the analysis of the system as a whole, and of each regulation separately.

This final chapter of the book is structured based on the steps in the application of the effectiveness test.[3] Thus, it will present and analyse the objectives, contents, context and results of these Regulations separately, and as components of a single system. It attempts to illustrate how the different regulatory rights interact and intertwine and how other – seemingly exogenous – factors, such as the IP system, interfere with and influence their application and interpretation.

1. The Objectives

A common denominator for all of these Regulations is the objective to support and protect the European pharmaceuticals industry. The starting point for all these regulatory rights is that the European industry needs strong protection in Europe in order to develop and thrive, as well as of course that of patient safety.[4]

---

[1] Directive 2001/83/EC of the European Parliament and of the Council of 6 November 2001 on the Community code relating to medicinal products for human use [2001] OJ L 311/67.
[2] See, for instance, the European Patent Convention [2001], OJ EPO 2001, Special edition No 4, 55. This Convention has become an integral part of the Revision Act of 29 November 2000 under Article 3(2), second sentence, of that Act.
[3] Maria Mousmouti, *Designing Effective Legislation* (Edward Elgar Publishing 2019).
[4] See, for instance, paragraph 2 in the Orphan Drugs Regulation (Regulation 141/2000/EC) or paragraph 3 in the SPC Regulation (Regulation 469/2009/EC).

However, the regulatory system developed in Europe will apply equally to European and US pharmaceutical companies operating in the EU.

The viability of the aforementioned starting point and the objective of EU regulatory rights depends on a basic assumption: that domestic markets are of utmost importance for the development of the domestic industry. But is this really the case? Naturally, the conditions of the domestic market have an impact on the development of the industry. The question is how decisive this impact is.

Pharmaceutical companies have global markets and seek to sell their products in many different countries. At the same time, it is not a given that the most valuable markets are those where they are established. On the contrary, the important markets are those where a company sells most of its products. Furthermore, there is no clear link between domestic rights and the level of domestic innovation.[5] On the other hand, taking into consideration how expensive it is to bring a medicinal product from R&D to the market (US$648 million to US$2.6 billion),[6] pharmaceutical companies need straightforward commercial incentives in order to invest. They need reassurance that they will be able to recoup their strategic investments. That means that they have an expectation that they will sell products either to a few patients, but at a high price, or to a large group of patients.

According to studies on the structure of the pharmaceutical industry, home markets constitute only a small part of the pharmaceutical market's total share.[7] A good example is Novo Nordisk, a pharmaceutical company situated in Denmark. The Danish market represents only 0.4 per cent of its sales worldwide. Thus, changes in the regulatory rights in Denmark would probably have little impact on the total sales of the company. On the other hand, the protection in the countries with which Novo Nordisk trades most is important and has an impact on the company's R&D choices.

Furthermore, according to the Copenhagen Economics report, the wealth of the EU countries with which a given company trades most seems to have a positive effect on domestic spending on pharmaceutical R&D.[8] However, the report notes that when these variables are applied to the United States, it becomes obvious that the domestic market is important. This is due to the facts that the US market represents over 54 per cent of the total sales of the pharmaceuticals market and that R&D takes place in the United States, something that means that changes in domestic protection will have an impact on domestic R&D choices.[9]

---

[5] See Nikolaus Thumm, *Intellectual Property Rights: National Systems and Harmonization in Europe* (Springer 2000).
[6] Joseph A DiMasi, Henry G Grabowski and Ronald W Hansen, 'Innovation in the Pharmaceutical Industry: New Estimates of R&D Costs' [2016] 47 *Journal of Health Economics*, 20–33.
[7] European Commission, *Study on the economic impact of supplementary protection certificates, pharmaceutical incentives and rewards in Europe*, Final report [2018], Copenhagen Economics 100.
[8] Ibid.
[9] However, this is only documented as regards US companies and changes in US legislation.

An important and interesting conclusion to be drawn from these studies is that this basic assumption, expressed in the objectives and in the accompanying Commission Communications of all regulations analysed in this book, is flawed.[10] There does not seem to be clear data showing that by providing a regulatory system that in principle copies its US counterpart, the European pharmaceuticals industry will be supported in the same way as the US pharmaceutical industry in the United States.

There is another basic assumption that has been decisive for the legislative architecture and legislative choices of regulatory rights, namely that the US and EU pharmaceuticals market and industry, as such, are comparable. The fact that this assumption has had a central role in the legislative activity in the specific field, does not come as a surprise, since the EU Regulations are legal transplants that attempt to transfer the US legal framework to the EU.[11]

While the Commission has been transparent about the fact that the Regulations are legal transplants from the United States, the legislative choices and the drafting do not seem to take into consideration the need for any adjustments or the importance of noting the differences between the respective pharmaceutical markets.[12] In the Communications preceding the Regulations as originally proposed, clear references are made to the origins of the Regulations and to the need to provide the same support to the European pharmaceuticals industry as that provided to its counterpart in the United States. However, no reference or discussion is provided with regard to any differences between the two jurisdictions that need to be taken into consideration and should influence the adaptation of the legal regulatory framework.[13] There is, for instance, no reference regarding interplay with the intellectual property rights system or regarding the difference in the US approach, with federal legislation in the field, on the one hand, and the lack of EU harmonisation, on the other.[14]

Another strong position of the legislator is that medicinal products will not be developed in Europe if there is no exclusivity. The Preamble of the SPC Regulation provides a very interesting illustration of this approach:

> Medicinal products, especially those that are the result of long, costly research will not continue to be developed in the Community and in Europe unless they are covered by favourable rules that provide for sufficient protection to encourage such research.

---

[10] The main argument being that in order to support the European pharmaceuticals industry, a beneficial regulatory system must be provided in Europe.

[11] This is stated in the Commission Communications as well as in the Preambles of the Regulations, see, for instance, paragraph 2 in the Orphan Drugs Regulation or paragraph 3 in the SPC Regulation.

[12] In the preparatory works and in the sources used by the author in this book.

[13] The legal transplant assumes that the US pharmaceutical industry is granted exclusivities and prerogatives that the European pharmaceutical industry does not enjoy, making it important to introduce similar exclusivities and rights in Europe.

[14] Patent law is not harmonised at an EU level, with the exception of the Directive 98/44/EC of the European Parliament and of the Council of 6 July 1998 on the legal protection of biotechnological inventions [1998] OJ L 213/13.

A relevant aspect to consider in this respect is that framing the objectives of these Regulations under the need to protect the European pharmaceutical industry from US and Japanese competition, has also been a necessity from a legislative architecture perspective. This was required in order for the Regulations to be considered measures boosting the internal market, which could have Article 100A of the EEC Treaty as a legal basis. As has been previously stated in this book, the competence of the EU in matters related to public health is very limited and under the continuous scrutiny of Member States.

Another aspect that seems to obstruct a transparent and straightforward evaluation of these Regulations is the terminology used, and how this has evolved alongside changes in technology, health politics and markets. The 'pharmaceutical industry' was, at the time the first SPC Regulation was negotiated, a term used to describe the originators, the part of the industry that invested in R&D and placed new medicinal products on the market. Several years later, at the latest revision of the SPC Regulation, introducing the stockpiling moratorium, the same term was used, but its meaning had changed. The objective was to support the pharmaceutical industry in Europe, as previously, but this term is now seen in a new light, covering (or even focusing on) the important role of the generics industry.[15]

This shift in the terminology is most certainly of value for the evaluation of regulatory rights. The generics industry has traditionally been seen as something that the European pharmaceuticals industry needs to be protected from. Recently, and as a result of economic constraints, healthcare budget issues and political pressure, it is the interests of the generics industry (as part of the pharmaceutical industry), that need to be prioritised and protected.

Thus, when the objective of a regulation is to 'protect the interests of the European pharmaceuticals industry', it is vital to know what this term includes. Is it only the 'originators' or both the originators and the generics? The outcome of such an evaluation could differ greatly depending on the exact scope and meaning of the term.

This evolution of the content and spirit of legislative acts is interesting, while also acting as a factor that blurs the evaluation process and raises questions as to how to apply the effectiveness test on these specific legislative acts.

In order to look into the objectives of these four Regulations, it has not been enough to look into the objectives stipulated in the Preambles or Articles. It has been of interest to look into the negotiating history, the different drafts made, and the priorities that were promoted by different stakeholders. Although this book has as a goal to treat the different Regulations on an equal basis, the SPC Regulation has in the past years received much more attention from the legislator, courts and commentators, and will thus have to be discussed more extensively.

---

[15] See European Commission, *Proposal for a Regulation of the European Parliament and of the Council amending Regulation (EC) 469/2009 concerning the supplementary protection certificate for medicinal products*, COM [2018] 317 final, 2018/0161 (COD).

1.1. The SPC Regulation

1.1.1. The Objectives through the Lens of Negotiating History

Taking into consideration the important impact that SPCs have on the pharmaceutical industry, and the rather controversial issues that arise with regard to their granting and enforcement, it is easy to understand why drafting the first SPC Regulation was a complicated matter.

As early as in the 1980s, an extensive campaign was initiated by the European pharmaceutical industry lobbying for extension of the patent terms for pharmaceutical products. During this time, both the United States (1984) and Japan (1988) were in the process of introducing similar legislation, with the objective of compensating pharmaceutical innovators for their lengthy research processes and the time-consuming pre-market clinical trials and MA procedures.[16] The industry claimed that with the number of novel chemical substances with medicinal properties diminishing, the length of research and registration procedures was increasing, and that this had a clear negative effect on the competitiveness of the European industry. In its 1998 report, the Commission provided statistics on R&D intensities, having developed from 7–8 per cent in the 1980s to 10–12 per cent in the 1990s.[17] The main reasons were identified as being the increasing regulatory requirements combined with the difficulty of testing pharmaceuticals for chronic diseases, and the impact this had on the total turnover of drug discovery.[18]

Politicians expressed concern that the European pharmaceutical industry was losing its position on the international pharmaceuticals market and that research-intensive companies would move from Europe to the United States.[19]

The European Federation of Pharmaceutical Industries and Associations (EFPIA) obviously had a strong interest in a new system and in 1988 began lobbying for a patent prolongation regime.[20,21]

---

[16] Office of Technology Assessment, 'Patent-Term Extension and the Pharmaceutical Industry' (August 1981).

[17] Commission of the European Communities, *Communication on the Single Market in Pharmaceuticals*, COM [1998] 588 final.

[18] Ibid.

[19] Here we find again the basic assumption of the central role of the domestic market. Although the concerns were noted and discussed at an EU level, it was the Member States (especially those with strong pharmaceutical industries) that reacted first. Italy and France introduced a patent extension system in 1991 that entailed an effective term of protection of 17 years in France and 18 years in Italy. Naturally, the growing interest of nations to provide adequate protection for the pharmaceutical industry increased the pressure on the Commission, since fragmented national regulations would have an adverse impact to the internal market.

[20] This is the association that has represented the interests of the pharmaceutical industry since 1978. The role of the EFPIA is to protect the interests of the European pharmaceutical industry, to monitor and try to influence the Community politics of relevance for this specific industry, and to negotiate with the EC institutions.

[21] The first official contacts were made with Berthold Schwab, the Head of the Competition Directorate General (DG)'s Unit for Intellectual and Industrial Property, in order to discuss the possibility to provide for a patent extension. According to the EFPIA Director General at the time

The EFPIA had to review its strategy and find a way to present this proposal as a matter for EU competence. The most attractive option was promoting it as an issue of industrial policy. In order to do so, it had to be shown that the lack of a patent extension term system had an impact on innovation and the competitiveness of the Community. Thus, the issue had to be handled by the DGIII (Industrial Affairs) and by Fernand Sauer, the head of the Unit for Pharmaceuticals and Cosmetics (DGIII/E/F). This contact appears to have been more fruitful and after negotiations an agreement was reached according to which the DGIII would support the patent extension term. In exchange, the industry would support the Commission's initiatives concerning pricing, in particular the Transparency Directive (what would later become Directive89/105/EEC).[22]

This exchange of mutual support with the industry was not something that Mr Sauer was open about.[23] With this support as a starting point, the EFPIA continued by seeking support from other Commission bodies and national associations. The growing support meant that a complete, elaborate proposal had to be prepared. The patent extension had to be presented as necessary and it seemed obvious that in order to be successful in this regard, solid evidence was required.[24]

Within the EFPIA, an expert group was set up in order to prepare the necessary documentation. The group gathered information on shortened patent periods for several hundred products within specific product categories. This work was facilitated by the contributions of the Association of British Pharmaceutical Industry (ABPI) which had previously highlighted the need for measures at a national level and had gathered relevant data. The ABPI had data demonstrating declining exports and growing imports in Europe.[25]

In Germany, the effective term of protection was eight years, while it was often only six years in the United Kingdom. Supporting arguments also included information on legislation in Japan and the United States concerning patent

---

(Nelly Baudrihaye), the DG did not consider this to be a matter for the Commission to act upon. In fact, matters related to pharmaceuticals were placed under the mandate of the Industrial Affairs DG, and the Commission could act only when industrial policy issues were considered. According to DG Schwab, patents on medicines were considered to have a direct and indirect impact on national healthcare and thus neither the Commission nor the DGIV would have the mandate to act in this respect. See Munir Pirmohamed and Graham Lewis, 'The Implications of Pharmacogenetics and Pharmacogenomics for Drug Development and Health Care', in Elias Mossialos, Monique Mrazek and Tom Walley (eds), *Regulating Pharmaceuticals in Europe: Striving For Efficiency, Equity and Quality* (Open University Press, 2004).

[22] Council Directive 89/105/EEC of 21 December 1988 relating to the transparency of measures regulating the prices of medicinal products for human use and their inclusion in the scope of national health insurance systems [1988] OJ L 40/8.

[23] See EFPIA, 'Completing the Internal Market for Pharmaceuticals' (Brussels 1998).

[24] Ibid.

[25] At the same time, information concerning the effective term of patent protection was gathered by several companies. These companies referred to the lengthy registration procedure, which often extends over more than six years which, when subtracted from the 20 years of patent protection yields a very short effective protection term compared with other products and technological fields.

restoration and the effect this would have in the development of their domestic industries and their competition with Europe. Lastly, national initiatives providing for patent extension terms were presented as proof of the need for action at a Community level. The results of the work of the expert group were published as 'Memorandum of the Need of the European Pharmaceutical Industry for Restoration of Effective Patent Term for Pharmaceuticals' covering the period of 1960–1988.[26] The report was published in 1988, after which the Commission drafted a 'Proposal for a Council Regulation Concerning the Creation of a Supplementary Protection Certificate (SPC) for Medicinal Products'.[27] The proposal was presented for the consideration of the European Parliament, the Council of Ministers and the Economic and Social Committee in April 1990.[28]

It seemed that the proposal was drafted with the demands of the industry as a starting point. The Commission's initial approach would have guaranteed a 30-year effective patent protection period. This proposal was beyond the approaches adopted in both the United States and Japan, which provided 25-year protection. On the other hand, the Hatch-Waxman Act introduced a 'fast-track' procedure for the registration of generic pharmaceuticals.[29] It seemed that the Commission was proceeding towards stronger protection of the pharmaceutical industry, without providing any counterbalance guaranteeing competition on the pharmaceutical market. In this regard, the Commission adopted a much more radical position than its counterparts in the United States and Japan.

The side effect of this clear pro-industry approach was a growing reaction to it and the development of a generics lobby group. While the first Commission proposal was the result of closed-door discussions, the proposal was then spread, read by a broader public, and subject to comments and proposals for amendments. The Parliament's reading procedures require that the text under adoption be read by a number of committees and other groups of stakeholders. Furthermore, the Council of Ministers must report on the position of Member States, which requires that the document is read and discussed on a broad basis.[30]

The next step in the process would be the agreement of the ministers. The proposal was assigned to the Internal Market Council. Getting the support of Member States was not an easy endeavour. Extending the term of protection also meant that generic pharmaceuticals would be delayed in entering the market. This would mean that public health expenditures for pharmaceuticals would be high for a longer period of time. Not all EU countries had the same interests as France

---

[26] For an extensive review of the negotiating history of the SPC Regulation, see Govin Permanand, *EU Pharmaceutical Regulation: The Politics of Policy-Making* (European Policy Research Unit Series, Manchester University Press 2006) 92–117.

[27] Council Regulation 1768/92/EEC of 18 June 1992 concerning the creation of a supplementary protection certificate for medicinal products [1992] OJ L 182/1.

[28] Permanand (n 13), 92–117.

[29] Ibid.

[30] Ibid.

and Italy. Countries such as Greece, Spain and Portugal – with strong generics industries – were worried about the potential effects of this regulation on their domestic industries. Interestingly, even countries such as the United Kingdom and Germany, initiators of the process for a patent term extension, expressed their strong concerns when it came to the actual text of the proposal. For these countries, cost-effective public health was a priority that seemed to be contravened by the proposal at hand.

The Commission had based the proposal on Article 100(a) (free movement and single-market legislation). The EFPIA was aware that Portugal, Spain and Greece would most likely not support the proposal, making it even more important to gain the support of the Parliament. Although this was a clear objective, it was obvious that it would be difficult to achieve, given the first reactions of the MEPs. In 1990, the proposal was assigned to the Parliament's Committee on Legal Affairs and Citizens' Rights. A number of other committees were consulted: the Committee on Monetary Affairs and Industrial Policy, the Committee on Energy, Research and Technology, and the Committee on the Environment, Public Health and Consumer Protection. The results of the deliberations in the Committees were very interesting. The Committee on the Environment, Public Health and Consumer Protection stated that the conclusions, or rather the starting points, of the proposal of the Commission were not solid. The Committee questioned whether there was really a risk of relocation of investment and above all whether the proposal would in fact benefit the European patient. One of the interesting conclusions of the Committee was that the pharmaceutical industry was not in a position to guarantee that the introduction of a patent extension term would mean more medicines would be invented. The Committee thus questioned the very basis of the SPC initiative. On the other hand, the Economic and Social Committee (ESC) published a series of interesting comments in its Opinion.[31] The first fundamental question concerned the legal basis of the proposal. The objection of the ESC concerned the fact that the proposal was based on Article 100A of the EEC Treaty, whereas the correct legal basis should have been that of Community health policy or, to be more specific, of the internal market for medicinal products. The ESC chose to approach the issue of patent term extension for pharmaceutical products from a public health perspective, although the report was in agreement regarding the fact that it was important to 'align on US and Japanese patent protection laws so as to safeguard the competitive position of the Community's pharmaceutical industry'.

The ESC required the Commission to provide data on how this new proposed system of patent term extension would influence the generics industry. Another important perspective to consider, according to the Committee, was how prices in pharmaceutical products would be influenced by the new system. Although the

[31] Ibid.

Committee expressed a critique against the proposal, it still granted its approval, based on public health concerns (accessibility of pharmaceuticals, research incentives) instead of referring to the interests of the pharmaceutical industry, as put forward by the Commission.

Lastly, the Parliamentary Committee on Legal Affairs, and Citizens' Rights expressed the view that the same protection should be provided to plant protection research, since this was also a research-intensive industry decisive for public health.[32]

In parallel with these preparatory discussions, concerns were expressed on the compatibility of the system with the European Patent Convention. According to Article 63(1) of the EPC, a patent was granted for a period of 20 years from the date when the patent application was handed in. The question was how it would be possible to circumvent this specific patent term. Proceeding to any changes in the text of the EPC would require the agreement of three-quarters of the signatories of the EPC, several of which were not even members of the EU. Furthermore, it would not be possible to grant an extra five-year period, since it would be granted for all technological areas, irrespective of the need of marketing authorisation.[33]

Member States pressured the Commission to call a meeting to discuss this issue. The result of this meeting was agreement regarding an addition to Article 63. According to the amended provision, Member States would be able to extend the term of a patent automatically after expiration. This extension would be applicable as long as the product or process was under an obligation to undergo an administrative procedure in order to be placed on the market in that Member State. This was a satisfactory compromise for all parties, and the negotiations for the introduction of the SPC Regulation could continue without its relation to the text of the EPC being addressed.

With that major issue out of the way, the Parliament agreed to support the text of the Regulation on condition that some minor changes were made. For example, Member States were granted different implementation dates.[34] Although this was

---

[32] Opinion (29 November 1990 EP 1990b).
[33] See Permanand, n 25.
[34] Countries like Greece, Portugal and Spain (opponents to the SPC regulation), with large generics industries, were granted until January 1998 to implement the SPC, in order to give time to the national industries to adjust to the new rules. The second amendment proposed by the Parliament was that the date of first authorisation, after which the term of the SPC would be decided, would be different in different Member States. According to the proposed text of the Regulation, marketing authorisations that could be taken into consideration for the granting of SPC were those granted as of 1 January 1985. However, some special solutions were necessary here as well. Germany had introduced a new pharmaceutical pricing system that would be influenced by the SPC Regulation and for German marketing authorisations the date was 1 January 1988. Belgium and Italy pushed the date back to 1 January 1982, in order for more pharmaceuticals to be eligible for protection. A final and non-minor amendment concerned the term of the SPC protection, which was reduced from 10 years (in the Commission's proposal) to five.

a success for the pharmaceutical industry, the EFPIA was not completely satisfied; it preferred the 'imaginative and creative' proposal of the Commission.[35]

There was significant reaction to the final text. Generic manufacturers were faced with a new reality that had a direct impact on their business model, with longer and more expensive R&D times.[36]

The opponents of the regulation included patient and consumers groups, which expressed concerns regarding the extension of the exclusive rights and the impact this might have on the accessibility of pharmaceuticals as well as pricing.[37] The European Consumer Organisation published a statement in 1991 stating that the Regulation constituted 'carte blanche' for the pharmaceutical industry. Like the generics companies, the UK National Consumer Council stated that the expiry of patent protection did not mean that the industry would lose its central role in the market,[38] and that increasing the patent term in the way suggested by the text of the Regulation would mean greater costs for consumers and taxpayers. Thus, at the time of the introduction of the regulation, not only consumer organisations and representatives of the generics industry expressed a concern in this regard. Industry experts also warned that prices could increase.

The reactions to the Regulation did not cease after agreement on the proposed text. The Consumers in the European Community Group expressed the view that the extension should only be applicable to new molecular entities which represented a genuine therapeutic gain. This was also argued by the generics industry and the Parliament after the first reading of the text.[39]

It seems that opposition to the text of the Regulation was not as successful in its reactions and proposals for adjustments to the text of the Commission. One of the reasons for this was that the critique came too late in the process and not in a coordinated manner. The association of generics companies in the EU was established only in 1992, the same year that the Regulation was adopted.[40] The consumer organisations were also a bit too late in the process, publishing their opinions at a time when a final text was almost adopted.[41]

---

[35] EFPIA, *EFPIA Comments on the New Proposals Contained in Preliminary Draft Rev. 5*, (Brussels 1992a); EFPIA, *Memorandum on an Industrial Policy for the European Pharmaceutical Industry* (EFPIA III3485/92) (Brussels 1992b).

[36] Generic companies collected data in order to inform the Commission about the challenges faced by the generics industry and to reject some of the pharmaceutical industry's claims. One important factor that was highlighted was that the exclusivity enjoyed by pharmaceutical companies in practice (innovators) was in fact longer than the term of patent protection.

[37] Pricing and reimbursement of pharmaceutical products was another sensitive area of EU competence.

[38] HoL [1991] Patent Protection for Medicinal Products. UK House of Lords Select Committee on the European Communities, Session 1991–1992; 1st Report: HMSO.

[39] See Permanand, n 25.

[40] The European Generic and Biosimilar Medicines Association is now Medicines for Europe. The fact that the generics industry lacked a coordinated approach was naturally detrimental to their lobbying activities.

[41] See Permanand, n 25.

In September 1989, a first preliminary draft proposal was presented, replaced by the official version in April 1990. After some revisions that were partially based on the first reading of the Parliament,[42] the Council Common Position was published in February 1992 and, with minor modifications, adopted as Regulation (EEC) 1768/92 in July 1992.[43]

1.1.2. The Objectives of the SPC Regulation in its Text

The Preamble of the SPC Regulation lists a series of basic assumptions underlining the importance of the Regulation or impacting on its wording. These include that medicinal products will not be developed in Europe if there is no exclusivity, that there is a risk of relocation of pharmaceutical research from Europe to other jurisdictions, that disparities at the national level should be avoided, and that the total protection term shall not exceed 15 years. Apart from these basic principles, the text of the Regulation does not provide any concrete list of objectives. Furthermore, there is no guidance as to how a future monitoring of the Regulation should measure and evaluate its effects.

The indirectly expressed objectives that the regulation is introduced to fulfil could be classified into three categories: supply-side objectives, demand-side objectives and market impact objectives.[44]

The first aspect of the supply-side objective is the attraction of pharmaceutical innovation to the EU. Naturally, given the time and costs necessary for the development of new pharmaceuticals, the effective protection period provided by an exclusive right is of relevance when proceeding to strategic R&D decisions. Although there is no clear data on the link between patent protection and domestic R&D, one might assume that an increase in the general effective protection period in the EU would lead to an increase in R&D in the EU, and that as SPCs increase, they lead to increased innovative activity in the individual Member States.

Although there must be a connection between the SPC and R&D investments, the existence of SPCs is not the decisive factor. There are other issues that contribute to the choice of where to locate R&D facilities, such as level of education, infrastructure and political stability. An overview on which countries have the highest levels of R&D investment in pharmaceuticals shows China at the top, with 21.5 per cent, followed by the United States, with 7 per cent.[45]

---

[42] European Parliament, 'Legislative Resolution (Cooperation Procedure: First Reading) Embodying the Opinion of the European Parliament on the Commission Proposal for a Council Regulation Concerning the Creation of a Supplementary Protection Certificate for Medicinal Products', [1991] OJ CO, 19, 28 January 1991: 95.

[43] Council Regulation 1768/92/EC of 18 June 1992 concerning the creation of a supplementary protection certificate for medicinal products [1992] OJ L 182/1.

[44] European Commission, *Study on the economic impact of supplementary protection certificates, pharmaceutical incentives and rewards in Europe*, Final report [May 2018], Copenhagen Economics.

[45] Ibid.

With regard to the second part of the objective, to prevent delocalisation of pharmaceutical innovation and manufacturing, one could conclude that pharmaceutical companies (like companies from other industries) could readily proceed to relocation of low value-adding activities (such as manufacturing), while relocating R&D would be a more difficult strategic decision.

The third aspect of the supply-side objective is ensuring that research-based industry has market protection for a sufficient period of time. This is an important and difficult objective to assess. Providing adequate, but not excessive, protection is a precise and difficult balancing act. SPCs provide for a longer term of exclusivity, meaning that competitors are excluded from the market for a longer period of time. Given that the effective protection time has been getting shorter in the past few years, one might draw the conclusion that SPCs play a very important role. The fourth perspective of the supply-side objective is that it should contribute to a fall in medicine prices following SPC expiry. While it is natural that the prices of a pharmaceutical will fall after (or even shortly before) an SPC expires (which is usually the last exclusive right covering a pharmaceutical product), this could hardly be considered to be the achievement of the SPC, rather a side-effect thereof. Furthermore, the Regulation serves to promote competition through innovation. SPC protection would, according to the objectives of the Regulation, promote further innovation, by 'forcing' competitors to innovate around a protected medicinal product.

The sixth parameter of the supply-side objective is to encourage innovation demanded and needed by customers, patients and stakeholders. As has been discussed above, the decision to place a pharmaceutical product on the market will largely depend on the profitability on that specific market. Of course, there might be other factors influencing such decisions, such as price-referencing and reimbursement systems. On average, 10 per cent of pharmaceutical products receive SPC protection, and the protection received is 2.6 years on average.

What remains interesting is the fact that the objective is based on the therapeutic properties of the medicinal product, which have no relevance for the application of the Regulation. SPC protection is granted in order to compensate for development times, not to meet any specific therapeutic need. Although decisions made by pharmaceutical companies are based on their profit-maximising strategies, one could assume that granting an exclusive right for pharmaceutical products will boost research in the industry as a whole. If one were to attempt to find a more concrete link between the two (the granting of SPC and the specific objective), one would need to prove that the pharmaceuticals that are most needed take more than five years to develop.

The objectives as expressed in the text of the SPC Regulation also concern the demand-side perspective. The first focuses on the accessibility and spread of innovative products across the internal market. Although the possibility to apply for a centralised marketing authorisation provides a clear objective for a pharmaceutical company to place the pharmaceutical on the entire internal market, this 'internal market' approach only works for the marketing authorisation as such. Both patents and SPCs are national rights. Thus, pharmaceutical companies may have reasons not to proceed to an EU launch of the product, such as the costs connected to applying for and preserving patents and SPCs and the fact that the outcome is uncertain because of the fragmentation of rules (and how they are applied) across EU Member States. This also means that pharmaceutical companies will be faced with the choice of applying for protection or not, on the basis of how attractive a specific market is. This could mean that a potential launch would be protected by a shorter period of exclusivity. A unitary SPC gives protection on the entire internal market, including on national markets that are not very attractive. This increases the chances of having pharmaceutical products launched in those jurisdictions. The second sub-objective in the Regulation is to prevent supply shortages and missed or deferred market launches. Naturally, supply shortages have considerable effects on both the individual patient and the healthcare system as a whole.

One reason for supply shortages is low profit margins, which in turn could be due to many different factors, including competition from generics. When generics enter the market, prices on pharmaceuticals become so low that the profit margins are nil.[46] This is a rather weak argument; although profit margins might be lower, there is more competition, which in itself should lead to a price reduction. It seems that the fragmented system of SPC protection that is available today is not in a position to guarantee an early launch of pharmaceuticals in all jurisdictions: important markets will get them first.[47] Although the protection granted by SPCs is not currently optimal, according to Kyle, the lag between international launch and EU launch is slowly but steadily shrinking.[48] There is, on the other hand, no evidence that a longer term of protection will guarantee an earlier product launch.[49]

On the demand side of the SPC objectives, the third objective provided is the availability of generics. According to the rationale of the Regulation, it is by means of the disclosure in the patent applications of the original pharmaceuticals that generics are developed. The Copenhagen study claims that there must be a positive correlation between the number of originator medicinal products and the number of generic pharmaceuticals. One could doubt the credibility of this argument, taking into consideration the fact that reverse-engineering is a very effective way of acquiring technological knowledge, thus making disclosure less important. However, in the field of pharmaceuticals, the effects from an efficiency and patient safety perspective are most crucial. In this respect, the role of the originators is far

---

[46] Ibid.
[47] This is expected to change by means of the introduction of unitary SPC.
[48] Margaret Kyle, 'Economic Analysis of Supplementary Protection Certificates in Europe', January 30, 2017 https://ec.europa.eu/info/publications/economic-analysis-supplementary-protection-certificates-europe_en [Accessed on 20 January 2020].
[49] European Commission, *Study on the economic impact of supplementary protection certificates, pharmaceutical incentives and rewards in Europe*, Final report [May 2018], Copenhagen Economics.

more important. Generics companies often base their own marketing authorisations on the clinical trial dossiers submitted by originators. Thus, these materials and documentation save the generics manufacturers from considerable costs and time-consuming clinical trials. Although the Regulation may have many positive aspects, SPCs undoubtedly delay the entry of generics on the market.

The fourth objective on the demand side is preventing limitations in the availability of innovative products through industry pricing strategies. This objective is formulated in a way that makes it rather difficult to understand. If the objective is meant to state that SPCs will limit the strategic choices behind the decisions to place a certain pharmaceutical on the market (or not) and when to do so, it seems very naïve. In a complicated setting, like the pharmaceutical market, strategic decisions are the combined result of many factors, such as tender periods, pricing, corporate structure of competitors, number of competitors, market shares and length of average patient treatment to just name a few.[50] It seems only natural that pharmaceutical companies will charge monopoly prices when they can, and that longer periods of exclusivity give them space to dictate market conditions for a longer period of time.[51]

The Regulation also includes market impact objectives, as it serves to develop the European pharmaceutical industry by protecting originators and thus guaranteeing improved accessibility of pharmaceuticals to patients. On the other hand, this should not mean that originators receive excessive protection that would lead to pharmaceuticals being sold at exorbitant prices.[52]

An objective of the Regulation was thus a decrease in the prices of SPC-protected products relative to products without SPCs. As has been discussed earlier in this book, the rationale behind this objective is rather difficult to comprehend. Pharmaceutical companies are profit-driven entities that operate on a highly competitive international market. They will seek to maximise profits and to charge prices that guarantee the highest turnover possible, even if that exceeds the investments made for the development of this product. Linking the granting of an exclusive right, like the SPC, to a lowering of the prices would presuppose that when launching a product on the market, pharmaceutical companies seek compensation amounting to a specified amount of money during the period of exclusivity. By increasing the exclusivity period, they will be able to divide the expected profits over a longer period of time. This conclusion (and its starting point) does not seem supported by the real market conditions under which the

---

[50] Ibid.

[51] It has been claimed that in the United States and for certain pharmaceuticals, expiry of exclusive rights has led to higher, rather than lower, prices. See Richard Frank and David Salkever, 'Pricing, Patent Loss and the Market for Pharmaceuticals' [1993] 59 *Southern Economic Journal*, 2, NBER Working Paper No w3803.

[52] It may appear paradoxical that exclusivity would increase accessibility. It could of course increase R&D, since there is a 'promise' of compensation due to the grant of exclusivity. However, that does not mean that medicines are also accessible.

pharmaceutical industry operates. The second perspective added to the market impact objective of the Regulation concerns the fact that extended protection is justified by the revenues and profits for the different categories of eligible medicinal and plant protection products. Naturally, the SPC system enhances the value of medicinal products. There is a big difference between having 10 years and 15 years of effective protection and a longer term of exclusivity will give pharmaceutical companies a better chance to make a profit. That said, it should be clarified that SPC protection is granted irrespective of the investments made and the revenues and profits from a specific product. The SPC is based only on the time that has elapsed between the granting of a patent and the granting of marketing authorisation. There is no reference to the costs or profits when deciding whether or not to grant an SPC, or how long this exclusive right would apply.

Lastly, the Regulation is intended to contribute to closing the gap between the European pharmaceutical industry and major competitors on the international market. In the early 1990s, the Commission in its memorandum preceding the SPC Regulation, provided that there had been a notable decrease in the number of molecules developed by European manufacturers, as well as an erosion of their respective market shares in an international market share overview.[53] While there is no economic data indicating a link between investments into pharmaceutical research and the exclusive rights granted in the home country of the pharmaceutical company, the Regulation could be considered to contribute to promoting investment. A longer term of the exclusive right granted for a medicinal product is certainly a positive factor when discussing potential further investments into research. That said, there are a number of other factors at a national level that influence the statuses of the specific products on the market and how these translate into commercial gains.

Regulatory exclusivities are becoming more and more relevant and valuable. Although a company may in theory circumvent data and market exclusivity by developing its own clinical data, this happens very rarely in practice, likely as a result of the time and investments required.

Personalised medicine[54] might have unique needs in this respect, and thus a new approach might be needed to cover such pharmaceutical products.[55] Such pharmaceuticals will have a very limited market, meaning that intellectual property rights might not constitute an adequate form of protection. In the work of Burk, the example of Myriad Genetics is used to show that by using patent rights as a shield and blocking all potential competitors from research in the same area for a number of years, the patent holder manages to collect very important data

---

[53] See Commission of the European Communities, 'Proposal for a Council Regulation (EEC) concerning the creation of a supplementary protection certificate for medicinal products', COM (90) 101 final – SYN 255.

[54] See EU Health Ministers' Council conclusions on personalised medicines for patients (2015/C 421/03).

[55] See Dan L Burk, 'Patents as Data Aggregators in Personalized Medicine' [2015] 21 *Boston University Journal of Science and Technology Law*, 2, UC Irvine School of Law Research Paper No 2015-47.

that might have a number of applications. These include the field of personalised medicine and securing first-entrant status on a new market, an advantage that in a rapidly changing technological field like modern pharmaceuticals is equivalent to, or better than, intellectual property rights as such. Needless to say, when patents do not constitute an incentive, neither will SPCs.

1.2. The Orphan Drugs Regulation

1.2.1. The Objectives through the Lens of the Negotiation History

The intention of the EU to provide solutions and motivation for the Regulation of orphan drugs was featured in the Commission's work programme from 1997. Already in the Council Resolution of 20 December 1995 on orphan medicinal products, it was provided that a common approach to rare diseases and orphan medicinal products would have advantages in epidemiological, public health and economic terms.

An interesting source of information with regard to the negotiating history of the Regulation is found in the transcripts of the workshop in Brussels on 5 May 1998 organised by the European Foundation for the Advancement of Medicine in cooperation with the Commission.[56] The purpose of the workshop was to discuss the forthcoming Orphan Drugs Regulation. The transcripts of the workshop are representative of the views on the proposed Regulation since the participants came from the Commission and the EMA, as well as industry and patient groups, such as the European Organization for Rare Disorders, Médecins Sans Frontières, etc.

Patrik Deboyser, the Head of Pharmaceuticals & Cosmetics in DG III, presented the draft Regulation and confirmed that this was modelled on the US Orphan Drugs Act.[57] The US experience influenced the Commission and contributed to it focusing more on prevalence as a criterion for orphan designation than on the economic criteria that were initially considered.[58]

Concerning the Committee that would be responsible for examining orphan drug applications, Deboyser stated that it should have representatives from Member States and from patient organisations, a novelty in the system, since this would be a Committee with a decision mandate, not solely a consulting role to the Commission.[59]

---

[56] Transcripts of the workshop are available at https://ec.europa.eu/health/sites/health/files/files/orphanmp/doc/proc5598_en.pdf [Accessed on 18 June 2020].

[57] e-CFR 21 PART 316 Orphan Drugs & the Orphan Drugs Act 1983. For an overview of the legislative history of the Orphan Drugs Act, see Henry Waxman and Joshua Green, *The Waxman Report: How Congress Really Works* (Grand Central Publishing, 2009).

[58] The EU prevalence requirement lies between those in the United States and Japan. For life-threatening and seriously debilitating diseases, an orphan drug designation is possible even if the prevalence is over 5/10,000.

[59] The first time that patient groups would have a mandate to participate in binding decisions.

In the proposal, it was stipulated that orphan drugs would be granted a 10-year period of exclusivity (unlike in the United States, where the period was seven years), and that there would be a requirement that MA for orphan drugs must be granted under the centralised procedure. Deboyser also referred to the possibility to withdraw a designation if the criteria were no longer met or if excessive prices were charged. DGVII and DGV based the proposal on shared experiences from research programmes on orphan diseases that had been financed by the Commission and previous and current Community actions on rare diseases and experiences from these.

The EMA representative Patrick Le Courtois presented the regulatory arrangements that would accommodate the special needs of the orphan drugs system, namely the annex of Directive 75/318/EEC point G, according to which it would be possible to grant marketing authorisation even when it is not possible to produce comprehensive data because the indication for which the product is intended is rare.[60] Furthermore, these regulatory measures provide for pre-submission advice and meetings, as well as a possibility to resort to an accelerated process for the granting of marketing authorisation.[61]

The EMA referred to the US experience and the advice the EMA might receive from the FDA for the overall functioning of the system. It is clear from the EMA intervention that the priority of the agency was to place the mandate of orphan drugs designation on the CPMP, which according to the EMA already had considerable experience with the specific product segment. At the workshop, the Commission presented the establishment of the EU Committee of Experts on Rare Diseases[62] which was later replaced by the Commission expert group on rare diseases.

Patient group representatives limited themselves to regretting the delays in the negotiations and preparations to the Regulation, urging the Commission to complete the work as soon as possible, without commenting on the specific provisions and the system design as a whole.[63] The industry also limited itself to very general comments. An interesting point made was that a very important factor that influenced the accessibility of orphan drugs and incentives to the industry was the pricing of pharmaceuticals, something that is not addressed in the Regulation. The organisation Médecins Sans Frontières concluded that the Regulation was designed for western world diseases, not tropical ones.[64]

---

[60] A necessary adjustment in order for MA to be possible to grant to orphan drugs.
[61] See transcripts of the workshop: https://ec.europa.eu/health/sites/health/files/files/orphanmp/doc/proc5598_en.pdf [Accessed on 19 June 2020].
[62] The Committee is introduced already in the Preamble, see paragraph 6 of the Preamble to Commission Decision of 30 November 2009 establishing a European Union Committee of Experts on Rare Diseases [2009].
[63] Such as Abbey S. Meyers from the National Organization for Rare Disorders NORD, USA and Stephanie Korsia from the European Organization for Rare Disorders.
[64] See *Drug Development For Neglected Diseases: A Deficient Market And A Public-Health Policy Failure* (12 July 2002) https://www.doctorswithoutborders.org/what-we-do/news-stories/research/drug-development-neglected-diseases-deficient-market-and-public.

The words of Patrick Deboyser are of utmost interest: 'I think it is explained in the explanatory memorandum that the protection by the market exclusivity as an orphan drug is in fact a new intellectual property right which we are creating.' Deboyser considered this new right to be weaker than patent rights, but stronger than data exclusivity, since this does not protect against an entity developing its own data and submitting an MA application.[65] For some reason, this statement is not in any way reflected in the text, preamble, or Commission Communication related to the Regulation. In fact, no further reference is made to the status of the orphan drugs designation or its interrelation to the IP system.

The Orphan Drugs Regulation was complemented with other initiatives concerning public health and healthcare issues such as codification of orphan diseases (the International Classification of Diseases ICD-9 or ICD-10 systems), in which most orphan drug diseases were absent.[66] Some Member States started using ORPHA codes (from the ORPHANET project) to improve their health statistics systems.[67] Pressure was put on WHO ICD-I to ensure that rare diseases were included in international nomenclatures.[68]

Furthermore, some provisions of Directive 2011/24/EU actually concern patients of rare diseases.[69] Other important factors in addressing orphan drugs issues have included the collection and availability of information, such as the Rare Best Practices project (co-funded by the FP7), and the empowerment of patient organisations by consulting them in relation to EU policies in the field of rare diseases and promoting their activities.[70]

One might wonder why the transcript of this workshop is so important, and how this differs from the Communication of the Commission. Although no revolutionary information is presented, it provides a rare opportunity to almost hear the representatives of the legislator express views on the proposed legislative act

---

[65] See p. 36 in the workshop transcripts: https://ec.europa.eu/health/sites/health/files/files/orphanmp/doc/proc5598_en.pdf [Accessed on 19 June 2020].

[66] Orphanet Joint Action is an initiative under the EU Health Programme, involving all Member States. It is a relational database available in seven languages and aiming to link information on over 6,000 diseases. The EU funded 120 collaborative research projects relevant to rare diseases through the Seventh Framework Programme for Innovation and Technological Development (FP7), with a total budget of 620 million euros.

[67] Another interesting question raised was whether the different initiatives on the part of the Commission, such as action programmes, research funds etc, would be better coordinated through the new Regulation.

[68] Despite financing projects and research programmes encompassing 34 projects with a cost of 26.8 ECU, and with 21 companies participating, the desired effects were still not experienced. There was a need to provide for a more coordinated way of networking, as well as a need for speed and transparency. Also, while more was spent on orphan drugs, the definition of what constitutes an orphan drug would be important, and this was unclear.

[69] Consolidated text: Directive 2011/24/EU of the European Parliament and of the Council of 9 March 2011 on the application of patients' rights in cross-border healthcare [2011] OJ L 88/45 (current consolidated version 01/01/2014).

[70] Patient organisations have received operating funds through the EU Health Programme.

214 *How Effective is the Effectiveness Test in the Field of Regulatory Rights?*

and discuss its origins and prospects. Even major stakeholders, like the pharmaceutical industry and patient organisations, come to life in this discussion on the text of the proposed Regulation. It is also interesting that, in presenting the proposed Regulation, the Commission also gave an increased mandate and enhanced role to patient organisations. However, these organisations did not fully avail of this opportunity and were involved in, and contributed to the discussions of the workshop, only to a limited degree. One would, for example, have expected reactions to the statement of Deboyser on the status of the orphan drugs designation as equivalent to a *sui generis* IP right, and its reference to the patent system.

1.2.2. *The Objectives of the Orphan Drugs Regulation in its Text*

The legal basis for the Regulation is Article 100a, while the major objective that was expressed in the proposal was to establish a Community procedure for designating orphan medicinal products and to introduce incentives for orphan medicinal products research, development and marketing, in particular by granting exclusive marketing rights for a 10-year period.[71]

The starting point of the Regulation is stipulated in paragraph 1 of the Preamble and it is very clear: the pharmaceutical industry would not be willing to invest in R&D for orphan diseases under normal market conditions. Thus, a regulatory intervention was necessary.[72] The most appropriate means of addressing the reported market failure was considered to be introducing a new exclusivity, which took the form of market exclusivity.[73]

In its first article, the Regulation provides that:

> The purpose of this Regulation is to lay down a Community procedure for the designation of medicinal products as orphan medicinal products and to provide incentives for the research, development and placing on the market of designated orphan medicinal products.[74]

The Regulation provides harmonised criteria and a centralised procedure for the designation and marketing authorisation of orphan drugs.[75]

---

[71] Explanatory Memorandum of Regulation 141/2000/EC.

[72] In paragraph 1 of the Preamble, the definition of orphan drugs is oversimplified, stating that orphan drugs are such medicinal products where the cost of R&D cannot be covered due to limited prevalence. A more concrete definition of what constitutes an orphan drug is provided for in paragraph 3 of the Preamble, where prevalence and economic criteria are discussed.

[73] See paragraph 8 of the Preamble, referring to the US experience and the broader regulatory framework that this new Regulation must take into consideration.

[74] Article 1 Consolidated text: Regulation 141/2000/EC.

[75] Introducing national measures would be contrary to Directive 65/65/EEC and uncoordinated measures would also entail obstacles to intra-Community trade in the long run. The choice of using a Regulation instead of a Directive contributes to legislative simplicity since Member States do not have to implement the EU legislative act, by introducing or amending national legislation. Thus, a higher degree of harmonisation could be possible.

The importance of market exclusivity had previously been confirmed in the United States and Japan, and paragraph 2 of the Preamble makes it clear that these two international paradigms were important driving forces for the introduction of the EU regulation.[76]

The objective of the Regulation, to boost the R&D of orphan drugs by means of the market exclusivity, is balanced by introducing the possibility to withdraw market exclusivity if the requirements stipulated in the Orphan Drugs Regulation are no longer fulfilled after the sixth year of the designation.[77] However, as has been previously discussed in this book, this is not a mandatory or regular control that the EMA proceeds to *ex officio*. In fact, there are very few orphan drugs whose designations have been withdrawn.[78]

The Preamble and the text of the Regulation, as well as the Communication that accompanied its introduction, have a surprising and complete lack of any reference to intellectual property rights in general and patent rights in particular. The definition of orphan drugs and the specification of criteria for orphan drug designation remain silent as to the possibilities or complications that may arise when an orphan drug is also patent-protected and how this influences its orphan drug designation. No reference is made to the patent system with regard to its balancing mechanism and the possibility to withdraw an orphan drug designation. A pending patent application (or a granted patent for that matter) might constitute an indication of expected future, non-negligible commercial returns of the medicinal product in question, yet this is not mentioned.[79] It remains unclear to the author why this is the case and whether this is a mere omission or a conscious choice on the part of the legislator. In any case, it is odd and a factor that needs to be taken into consideration when discussing the objectives and the results of the Orphan Drugs Regulation.

Further, although – as previously seen – one of the primary initiators of the orphan drugs designation system proclaimed that this is a *sui generis* IP right,[80] no further reference to its status as such is mentioned in the text of the Regulation.

---

[76] See paragraph 2 of the Preamble. Reference to the US paradigm was very extensive in the Communication concerning the proposal to the regulation, with particular reference to the economic criteria, since it was very difficult to cover sales and R&D costs in the United States. During the years 1983–92, orphan drugs designations were granted only on the basis of epidemiological criteria.

[77] Paragraph 11 of the Preamble states that rare diseases have been identified as a priority area for Community action within the framework for action in the field of public health. The Commission, in its communication concerning a programme of Community action on rare diseases within the framework for action in the field of public health decided to give rare diseases priority within the public health framework. The European Parliament and the Council adopted Decision 1295/1999/EC of 29 April 1999, adopting a programme of Community action on rare diseases within the framework for action in the field of public health (1999 to 2003) (2), including actions to provide information, to deal with clusters of rare diseases in a population, and to support relevant patient organisations. This Regulation implements one of the priorities laid down in this programme of action.

[78] However, it can be stated that the intention of the legislator is to provide a balanced right.

[79] The prospect of considerable commercial returns is what would motivate a pharmaceutical company to proceed with a lengthy and costly patent application procedure.

[80] See Patrick Deboyser's opinion in the Commission workshop on the Orphan Drugs Regulation (n 57).

1.3. The Paediatric Regulation

1.3.1. The Objectives through the Lens of the History of the Negotiations

The Paediatric Regulation is based on two very important starting points, namely the fact that there are too few pharmaceuticals developed particularly for the paediatric population, and the fact that only half of the pharmaceuticals actually used on children had been tested for use on the paediatric population and thus had known properties and side effects for this patient group.[81] The unfortunate lack of suitable authorised medicinal products to treat conditions in children results from the fact that pharmaceutical companies do not perform the R&D necessary to adapt medicinal products to the needs of the paediatric population. This leaves no alternative for prescribers other than using adult products 'off-label' and using unauthorised (unlicensed) products, with the associated risks of inefficacy and/or adverse reactions. In addition, existing data which could provide useful and important information is frequently not made available to health practitioners.[82]

Thus, as in the case of the Orphan Drugs Regulation, the starting point for the objectives and the introduction of the Regulation is that there is a medicinal risk for the paediatric population and that this risk will not be addressed by the industry without regulatory intervention. The reason why this market failure occurs is not as explicitly specified as in the case of orphan drugs, but depends on the fact that research into paediatric applications is not considered commercially attractive or viable.[83] Contrary to the approach adopted in the Orphan Drugs Regulation, the Paediatric Regulation includes a combination of obligations and rights for the industry. Thus, the Regulation introduces a number of obligations that the pharmaceutical industry has to fulfil when developing a new pharmaceutical, while at the same time granting the possibility to enjoy benefits, in terms of extension of SPCs or orphan drugs designations.[84]

The interest of the Commission in addressing the lack of effectiveness and safety of medicines for the paediatric population was initially expressed by initiating discussions, workshops, and research programmes both in the EU and at the international level. Already in 1997, the European Commission organised a round table of experts to discuss paediatric medicines at the EMA. One of the

---

[81] S Turner, A J Nunn, K Fielding, et al, 'Adverse Drug Reactions to Unlicensed and Off-label Drugs on Paediatric Awards: A Prospective Study' [1999] 88 *Acta Paediatrica*, 9, 965–68.

[82] Ibid.

[83] In fact, the paediatric population is not limited, as in the case of orphan diseases. However, R&D in this patient segment presents risks and very high costs.

[84] See European Medicines Agency, *The European Paediatric Initiative: History of the Paediatric Regulation* Doc Ref: EMEA/17967/04 Rev 1. [2007]. See also, as part of the background to the regulation, The European Agency for the Evaluation of Medicinal Products, 'Report on the expert round table on the difficulties related to the use of new medicinal products in children held on 18 December 1997' London, 30 July 1998, EMEA/27164/98 Rev. 1.

conclusions at that time was that there was a need to strengthen the legislation, in particular by introducing a system including both incentives and obligations. In 1998, the Commission supported international discussion on the performance of clinical trials in children in the context of the International Conference on Harmonisation (ICH).[85] An ICH guideline was agreed upon, with the main goals being to encourage and facilitate timely paediatric medicinal product development internationally, and to provide an outline of critical issues in paediatric drug development and approaches to the safe, efficient and ethical study of medicinal products for children. Subsequently, the ICH guideline was presented as the European guideline.[86] Furthermore, the Directive (2001/20/EC) on Good Clinical Practice for Clinical Trials was adopted in April 2001, expressing some specific concerns about performing clinical trials on children and setting our rules for the protection of children during clinical trials.

In October 2006, the European Commission (DG Enterprise and Industry) released a draft document on 'Ethical considerations for clinical trials performed in children – Recommendations of the Ad Hoc Group for the development of implementing guidelines for Directive 2001/20/EC relating to good clinical practice in the conduct of clinical trials on medicinal products for human use'.[87] This document aimed to provide recommendations on various ethical aspects of clinical trials performed on children, intending to contribute to protection of children as the subjects of clinical trials and to facilitate a harmonised approach to clinical trials across the EU Member States. This was a further step towards EU harmonisation, since detailed rules on clinical trials were traditionally a matter of national competence.

The legislative process for a paediatric regulation was initiated by a discussion on a memorandum presented under the French EU presidency. Subsequently, the Council of (Health) Ministers adopted a Resolution on 14 December 2000 asking the European Commission to draw up a legislative proposal (Regulation) on this topic, which was considered a public health priority. In February 2002, the European Commission published a consultation paper on 'Better medicines for children – proposed regulatory actions in paediatric medicinal products'.[88] This paper represented one of the first steps of the Commission to address the problem. As a result of the Commission's Better Regulation Action Plan,[89] the proposed

---

[85] This is an organisation working on the harmonisation of pharmaceutical regulatory requirements between the EU, Japan and the United States.

[86] European Medicines Agency, *ICH E11(R1) guideline on clinical investigation of medicinal products in the paediatric population*, [2017] EMA/CPMP/ICH/2711/1999.

[87] European Commission, *Ethical Considerations for Clinical Trials on Medicinal Products Conducted with the Paediatric Population: Recommendations of the ad hoc group for the development of implementing guidelines for Directive 2001/20/EC relating to good clinical practice in the conduct of clinical trials on medicinal products for human use (2006)*, Final text published 2008.

[88] European Commission, *Better Medicines for Children from Concept to Reality: Progress Report on the Paediatric Regulation (EC) 1901/2006* COM [2013] 443 Final.

[89] Commission of the European Communities, 'Communication from the Commission, Action plan "Simplifying and improving the regulatory environment"', COM (2002) 278 final, Brussels, 5.6.2002.

Regulation on medicinal products for paediatric use was subject to an extended impact assessment. It aimed to analyse all the economic, social and environmental consequences of any major Regulation. In March 2004, the European Commission consulted on a draft Regulation on medicinal products for paediatric use, and in September 2004, the European Commission released the first proposal for a Regulation on medicinal products for paediatric use, together with an explanatory memorandum, the extended impact assessment, and a question and answer document.[90]

The text of the Regulation was agreed upon by the European Parliament on 1 June 2006.[91] The paediatric legislation comprises Regulation (EC) No 1901/2006 and the amending Regulation (EC) No 1902/2006.[92]

1.3.2. The Objectives of the Paediatric Regulation in its Text

The overall policy objective of the regulation was to improve the health of European children by increasing the research, development and regulated authorisation of medicines for use in children, with as few safety risks as possible.

The Preamble of the Regulation presents the problematic situation that the Regulation serves to remedy, namely that medicines given to children have not been tested for paediatric use. Already in the Preamble, the Regulation states its main objectives, namely to increase the development of medicines for use in children, to ensure that medicines used to treat children are subject to high-quality research, and appropriately authorised for use in children, to improve the information available on the use of medicines in children, and to achieve these objectives without subjecting children to unnecessary clinical trials, while in full compliance with the EU Clinical Trials Directive.[93]

Article 1 provides the objectives and purpose of the regulation:

> This Regulation lays down rules concerning the development of medicinal products for human use in order to meet the specific therapeutic needs of the paediatric population, without subjecting the paediatric population to unnecessary clinical or other trials and in compliance with Directive 2001/20/EC.

---

[90] Draft European Parliament and Council Regulation (EC) on medicinal products for paediatric use, https://ec.europa.eu/health//sites/health/files/files/paediatrics/docs/extended_impact_assessment_final_3_september_en.pdf [Accessed on 19 June 2020] (text of the Communication). The proposal for a Regulation on medicinal products for paediatric use went into a second reading in the European Parliament.

[91] On 27 December 2006, the Regulation was published in the Official Journal of the European Union. It entered into force on 26 January 2007.

[92] Regulation 1902/2006/EC of the European Parliament and of the Council of 20 December 2006 amending Regulation 1901/2006 on medicinal products for paediatric use (Text with EEA relevance) [2006] OJ L 378/20.

[93] Directive 2001/20/EC of the European Parliament and of the Council of 4 April 2001 on the approximation of the laws, regulations and administrative provisions of the Member States relating to the implementation of good clinical practice in the conduct of clinical trials on medicinal products for human use [2001] OJ L 121/34.

To ensure that all the medicines needed by children fall within the scope of the proposal and to fully understand the measures proposed, it is necessary to break medicinal products down into three groups: products in development (not yet authorised), authorised products still covered by patents or supplementary protection certificates, and authorised products no longer covered by such instruments. The Regulation contained a package of measures to achieve its objectives, in terms of both procedural aspects and regulatory and technical requirements.

In order to provide the incentives for compliance with this specific system, a pharmaceutical company is granted a six-month extension of its SPC protection or a two-year extension of the exclusivity granted through an orphan drug designation. The average costs for testing medicines for children are estimated to be four million euros per product. Testing medicines on children involves additional costs, such as administrative costs and costs for clinical trials. According to the Rand study, such an extension has a value of 0.8 to 9.1 million euros per product.[94] The same report stated that the six-month SPC extension would result in only a very modest increase in spending on medicines, totalling 0.06–0.25 per cent of European pharmaceutical expenditure. The costs for the generics industry would be 4–51 million euros.[95]

1.4. The ATMP Regulation

1.4.1. The Objectives through the Lens of the History of the Negotiations

The negotiation history of the ATMP Regulation reveals that the core objectives expressed in the text of the Regulation, namely, to provide a harmonised and tailored regulatory environment for new gene and cell therapies, were also the driving forces behind the legislative initiative.

Both industry representatives and policymakers were clear on the fact that there was an urgent need for EU legislation in the ATMP field to safeguard interests of public health and patient rights. Matters of competence were naturally an issue in this case too, with the industry claiming that the internal market for ATMPs was seriously endangered by the lack of EU legislation. In this specific case, the 'common safety concerns in public health' were the central focus and thus the Commission had to navigate the rather stormy waters of shared competence. The Commission was able to proceed on the basis of the proportionality and subsidiarity principles, claiming that existing EU legislation and national measures in the field had proven to be insufficient.

---

[94] Wija J Oortwijn, Edwin Horlings, Silvia Anton, et al, *Extended Impact Assessment of a Draft EC Regulation on Medicinal Products for Paediatric Use* (Rand 2004).
[95] ibid.

Industry representatives, such as EuropaBio, considered an EU Regulation in the field to be a positive development that would increase predictability and investments, while also increasing patient benefits.[96]

The first meeting at which the European regulatory regime was in focus was that of a working group of experts, convened in June 2000.[97] The working group discussed the questionnaire, collecting responses from all Member States, which revealed fundamental disagreements in important aspects of the ATMP Regulation and the lack of regulation in several Member States.[98]

In a 2003 report by DG Sanco, it was recognised that tissue-engineered products (TEPs) differed considerably from medical devices and pharmaceuticals and thus were not appropriately covered by the then-current EU pharmaceutical regulation framework. In the drafting of the Regulation, stakeholders expressed their concerns as to terminological issues and in particular the terms 'substantial manipulation', and 'engineered'. They proposed more specific definitions, in order to avoid future distinction issues in relation to other cell technologies. While the Commission had not previously considered the US paradigm, as in the other three Regulations, in this rather controversial terminological issue it chose to adopt the FDA definition.[99]

The fragmented national regulatory requirements that apply to ATMPs and the impediments these entail for the free movement of such products, patient access to innovative therapies, and the EU competitiveness in this important technological area, were considered central drivers of EU harmonisation.

In the Executive Summary of the Commission Staff Working Document, it was clarified that the success of the proposal would depend on attention being paid to certain categories of stakeholders, in particular hospitals and small and medium-sized enterprises. The Commission stated that the subsequent establishment of technical requirements for tissue-engineered products and related scientific guidelines would be important to ensure that the overall regulatory framework was balanced.[100]

It should be noted that two important stakeholder groups –academia and public establishments – were not actively involved in the negotiation of the regulation. The outcome of the public consultations, led by the DG Enterprise in 2002

---

[96] See for instance EuropaBIO White Paper: *EuropaBio Position & Policy Recommendations to support EU ATMP Innovation*, 9 March 2020 https://atmpsweden.se/wp-content/uploads/2020/03/EuropaBio-ATMP-Whitepaper_09032020.pdf.

[97] See also Jean-Paul Pirnay, Alain Vanderkelen, et al, 'Business Oriented EU Human Cell and Tissue Product Legislation will Adversely Impact MS' Health Care Systems' [2013] 14 *Cell Tissue Bank*, 4, 525–60. See also Juli Mansnérus, 'Encountering Challenges with the EU Regulation on Advance Therapy Medical Products' [2015] 22 *European Journal of Health Law*, 5, 426–61.

[98] See also Juli Mansnérus, 'Commercialisation of Advanced Therapies. A Study of the EU Regulation on Advanced Medical Products' [2016] Academic Dissertation, University of Helsinki.

[99] Stating that certain manipulations are not to be defined as substantial, see Annex 1 of the ATMP Regulation. It is also important to note that the decision was made, during the negotiation process of the ATMP Regulation, to leave TEPs outside the scope of the Clinical Trials Directive (Directive 2001/20/EC) and instead include them in the ATMP Regulation.

[100] In the Public Consultation, it was clarified that this was not done.

and 2004, revealed that while the participation of tissue engineering companies was overwhelming, public institutions, hospitals and research groups were silent.

The Regulation was subject to an extensive debate in the Parliament, in particular with regard to issues of commercialisation of altruistic cell and tissue donations, and concerns related to the integrity and inviolability of human dignity. Indeed, the European Parliament Committee on Legal Affairs (JURI) attempted to exclude hESCs-based ATMPs from the scope of the ATMP Regulation.[101] However, this amendment was not accepted, as there was considered to be a need to regulate such categories of ATMPs as well. Thus, the text of the Regulation that entered into force on 30 December 2008 remained ethically neutral.[102]

1.4.2. The Objectives of the ATMP Regulation in its Text

The aim of the ATMP Regulation is to offer a consolidated regulatory framework for these innovative medicines and it was designed to 'ensure the free movement of these medicines within the EU, to facilitate their access to the EU market, and to foster the competitiveness of European pharmaceutical companies in the field, while guaranteeing the highest level of health protection for patients.'[103]

The Articles of the Regulation are rather silent on its concrete objectives, while the Preamble provides a detailed overview of the background and legislative objectives.[104]

The Regulation as, its title reveals, amends Directive 2001/83 and Regulation 726/2004. It provides clarifications as to how ATMPs are to be regulated and how the overall regulatory framework is to be applied to this specific category of medicinal products, along with clarification and definition of important terms related to the central objective of the Regulation. The application of Directive 2001/83/EC is discussed in several paragraphs of the Preamble.[105]

---

[101] The reasoning behind this proposal was: 'Legislation in force in Member States concerning the use of certain types of cells, such as embryonic stem cells, varies considerably. The regulation of advanced therapy medicinal products at Community level should not interfere with decisions made by Member States on whether to allow the use of any specific type of cells. It should also not affect the application of national legislation prohibiting or restricting the sale, supply or use of medicinal products containing, consisting of or derived from these cells. Moreover, it is impossible to assess when, if ever, research on these cells will reach the stage at which commercial products made from these cells could be placed on the market. In order to respect the basic principles and the proper functioning of the internal market and to ensure legal certainty.' See Miroslav Mikolášik, 'Report on the proposal for a regulation of the European Parliament and of the Council on advanced therapy medicinal products and amending Directive 2001/83/EC and Regulation (EC) 726/2004' COM [2005] 0567 – C6-0401/2005–2005/0227(COD), Committee on the Environment, Public Health and Food Safety, see amendment 3.
[102] Juli Mansnérus, 'Commercialisation of Advanced Therapies. A study of the EU Regulation on Advanced Medical Products' (2016) Academic Dissertation, University of Helsinki 93–99.
[103] See EMA website, www.ema.europa.eu/en/human-regulatory/overview/advanced-therapies/legal-framework-advanced-therapies [Accessed on 21 June 2020].
[104] The Preamble of the ATMP Regulation includes 31 paragraphs.
[105] Paragraphs 2, 3, 4, 6, 20 and 31 of the Preamble. The Preamble refers to the relation of the specific Regulation to a number of other legislative acts, including the Charter of Fundamental Rights of the European Union, the Convention on Human Rights and Biomedicine, and Directive 2004/23/EC.

Paragraph 5 of the Preamble provides the reasons that justify special treatment of ATMPs from a regulatory perspective, namely their complexity and novelty. The same paragraph includes the expression of a concern that justifies a legislative intervention: the fact that without specially tailored and harmonised rules, the free movement of these products within the Community and the effective operation of the internal market in the biotechnological field would be hindered.[106]

In addition to this clear market perspective, the Regulation has a strong public health objective, to guarantee the efficacy and safety of these medicinal products by introducing follow-up and monitoring obligations.[107]

While the Preambles of the other three regulations discussed in this book provide overviews of the background of the respective legislative acts and presentations of the objectives motivating their introduction, the Preamble of the ATMP Regulation includes a set of detailed provisions as to how ATMPs are to be regulated, what principles and rules are to be applied, and which adjustments to the overall regulatory system are needed for these specific medicinal products. The objectives of the Regulation are interspersed in a long list of other detailed provisions that could very well have been included in the core text of the Regulation.

2. The Contents

The contents of the four regulations have been discussed extensively in the previous chapters of the book. A short review of the main characteristics of the respective regulations is included below, with a particular focus on more problematic and ambiguous aspects that have an impact on their effectiveness or that influence their interaction.

When evaluating the effectiveness of a Regulation, the contents are naturally of major importance. Lack of clarity in the contents, or contents that do not match the objectives of the Regulation will have a directly negative effect on its overall effectiveness.

2.1. The SPC Regulation

Stipulating the contents of the SPC Regulation has been one of the most important and interesting challenges for practitioners, academics and judges engaged in the field of pharmaceutical law.[108] CJEU rulings concerning the

---

[106] Paragraph 5 of the Preamble.
[107] According to paragraph 20 of the Preamble, the applicant might be required to provide a suitable risk-management system to address risks related to ATMPs.
[108] See ch 3 of this book for a review of relevant case law concerning the interpretation of core provisions in the SPC Regulation.

provisions of the SPC Regulation have increased dramatically since 2010 and a number of interesting clarifications have been required by national courts. Some fluctuations in the CJEU case law and the vague language in other cases have led to a rather fragmented interpretation and application of the Regulation at a national level.

One of the major problematic aspects of the SPC Regulation has been defining what the subject matter of the protection actually is. The fact that the Regulation is dependent on both specific terminology in, and interpretation of the patent system and the MA system, makes the SPC provisions vulnerable to fluctuations in these interpretations. The question of the extent to which fluctuations in the patent system should influence the granting of SPCs has become central in relation to the protection of second medical indications. While the patent system has evolved to facilitate and promote the patentability of second medical indications, recent CJEU case law seems to restrict the margins of protection, opting for a stricter interpretation of the text of the Regulation.

The contents of the SPC Regulation still appear somewhat unstable, creating a degree of uncertainty in how it is (or should be) applied.

2.2. The Orphan Drugs Regulation

In the case of the Orphan Drugs Regulation, the need to supplement and clarify its contents was obvious already on the day it was negotiated. In the drafting of the Orphan Drugs Regulation, the Commission warned that the Regulation provides only for the basic legal framework and that the administrative procedures would need to be complemented by means of Guidelines.[109]

Since the entry into force of the Regulation, the Commission had attempted to clarify its contents by regularly publishing Guidelines concerning the interpretation and practical application of its key provisions, such as Articles 8(1) and 8(3).[110] Still, the provisions of the Regulation remain rather unclear and its application and interaction with other Regulations is not unproblematic, as has been discussed in this book.

2.3. The Paediatric Regulation

The Paediatric Regulation provides for a six-month extension of an SPC term (or a two-year extension of an orphan drug designation).

---

[109] See ch 4 of this book.
[110] See Commission of the European Communities, 'Guideline on aspects of the application of Article 8(1) and (3) of Regulation 141/2000/EC: Assessing similarity of medicinal products versus authorised orphan medicinal products benefiting from market exclusivity and applying derogations from that market exclusivity', C(2008) 4077 final, Brussels, 19.9.2008.

The Regulation encompasses a combination of incentives and obligations. Pharmaceutical companies are under an obligation to proceed to PIPs. In return, they can receive an extension of exclusivity, under the overall legal framework of SPCs or orphan drug designations, depending on how the medicinal product is classified and originally protected.

One could say that the contents of the Paediatric Regulation are not independent since its application and interpretation are directly dependent on the application and interpretation of the SPC Regulation and the Orphan Drugs Regulation, of which it indirectly becomes an integral part.[111]

Furthermore, the Regulation introduces a new MA procedure (PUMA) for medicinal products with paediatric use, having as an objective to facilitate MA for such products. This part of the Regulation has a different scope than the rest, since it concerns only medicinal products that have a paediatric application.[112] The paediatric extension is interesting in that it provides incentives for conducting clinical studies, while the term of protection granted is completely unrelated to the time needed to proceed to completion of the PIP.

In the Preamble of the Paediatric Regulation there is no mention of the time lost while the product owner proceeds with the PIP. On the contrary, the extension period of six months is used as an incentive for conducting the studies necessary. In fact, SPC prolongation is not limited to paediatric uses, but applies to all uses of the medicinal product that is the subject matter to an SPC. Given the precise focus of the incentive, it has been important to limit the possibility of being granted multiple incentives for the same cause.

According to Article 36(5) of Regulation 1901/2006, the applicant may not receive a paediatric extension of the SPC term in cases where a one-year extension of data exclusivity has been granted for a paediatric indication. According to certain interpretations of this Article, this limitation only applies in cases where the extension of data exclusivity has been granted for new paediatric indications. If the extension has been granted for non-paediatric indications, the SPC holder can be granted a six-month extension. Although Recital 28 of the Paediatric Regulation provides that extension is a reward for performing clinical trials in the paediatric population, the rest of the Articles do not specify whether the SPC holder must perform these trials or whether they could be performed by a third party not related to the SPC holder.

2.4. The ATMP Regulation

The ATMP Regulation provides a support system for innovation in the field of personalised medicine and personalised therapies. It introduces tailored

---

[111] The Paediatric Regulation introduces a system of incentives that works only under the framework of the application of these two other Regulations.

[112] The extension of the exclusivity is granted irrespective of whether or not the medicinal product has a paediatric use.

regulatory principles for evaluation, for the mandatory centralised marketing authorisation procedure for ATMPs, for post-authorisation follow-up, and for traceability.

This particular Regulation is a *lex specialis* introduced in order to guarantee the efficacy, safety, and – indirectly – the commercial viability of ATMPs. The regulation includes in its scope a number of categories of medicinal products for human use that are 'complex, heterogeneous class of innovative therapies that combine features of medicine, cell biology, science and engineering to regenerate, repair or replace damaged tissues or cells'.[113] Determining what is included in the scope of the regulation requires a profound scientific analysis, making this one of the problematic aspects of the content of the Regulation.[114]

This regulation also includes a number of provisions tailored to support SMEs, academia and non-profit organisations. The special focus on these categories of stakeholders was justified on the basis on the fact that core ATMP research is performed by such research centres.

3. The Context

In the process of presenting the elements that together constitute important aspects of the regulatory system, and the regulations as such, it has become obvious that one of the most important aspects is the context in which they operate, which also constitutes a decisive factor in their effectiveness. It is interesting to note how one Regulation constitutes a relevant context for another and how all four of them relate to the MA system, the data protection system, and the patent system. While these interactions operate on different levels, they are all relevant and impact on the Regulations' respective effectiveness. Interestingly, this aspect is often overlooked by the Commission.

Although there are clearly points of interdependence between the Regulations, between the Regulations and the patent system, and between the Regulations and the MA system, little reference is made to these in the Explanatory memorandums, in their respective negotiating history, or in the Preambles and provisions. Most alarmingly, not only was context not expressly discussed or mentioned, it was not even taken into consideration in the drafting of the Regulations.

---

[113] European Medicines Agency, *Reflection paper on classification of advanced therapy medicinal products*, 21 May 2015, EMA/CAT/600280/2010 rev. 1, Committee for Advanced Therapies (CAT); Anne-Katrin Bock, Emilio Rodriguez-Cerezo, Bärbel Hüsing et al, 'Human tissue-engineered products: Potential socio-economic impacts of a new European regulatory framework for authorisation, supervision and vigilance' [2005] Synthesis report Eur 21838 EN, Institute for Prospective Technology Studies, https://ec.europa.eu/health/sites/health/files/files/advtherapies/docs/adopted_amendments_20070130_en.pdf [Accessed on 20 June 2020].

[114] One problematic provision is Article 2(1) (c) of the Regulation.

As has been discussed previously in this book, context has been of relevance for the courts, both the CJEU and national courts, when interpreting the provisions of the Regulations. The practical implications of the lacking consideration of context have been noticeable in certain unfortunate situations that counteract the objectives and effectiveness of the Regulations.

3.1. Other Regulatory Rights

3.1.1. Combination of Protection

Pharmaceutical companies interact on a complicated multilayered market where each day of exclusivity matters, in terms of both recouping investments and further development of research in the technological area. It is thus not surprising that these companies look into as many complementary protection possibilities as they can. The broader and lengthier the protection, the better. Here, regulatory rights rule supreme. They provide a more diversified and, in some cases, lengthier protection than was originally conceived of.

The MA procedure, which is required in order to place a medicinal product on the market, is also the source of a form of exclusivity that works parallel to patent rights, SPCs, and other regulatory rights. At the same time, the 8 + 2 + 1 years of data and market exclusivity are completely independent of patent rights and SPCs. There is of course a difference in the level of protection granted since medicinal products are only partially protected by means of data and market exclusivity. In theory, a competitor could enter the market by developing and submitting its own clinical data.[115] Taking into consideration how strictly regulated clinical trials are, the costs they entail, and the time required to provide a full documentation dossier for an MA application, this possibility remains largely theoretical. Generics companies build their business models on market entrance after these forms of exclusivities expire.

Data and market exclusivity provide for a minimum protection term of 10 years, which can lapse when patent protection has already expired. It is interesting that these two systems (and the SPC) lead separate parallel lives, with different protection terms and potentially different starting points. Since 2005, the importance and duration of data and market exclusivity have increased. According to data, during the past few years, this form of protection has meant that originators were able to keep generics companies out of the market for an additional 2.4 years.[116] Furthermore, for 39 per cent of all pharmaceuticals included in the data, data and market exclusivity was the last right to expire.

---

[115] Thyra De Jongh, Alfred Radauer, Sven Bostyn and Joost Poort, 'Effects of supplementary protection mechanisms for pharmaceutical products' (Technopolis Group) Final report, May 2018.
[116] Ibid.

However, this is not the case for pharmaceuticals with a second medical indication. In such cases, the one-year extension of the market exclusivity will have expired before the SPC. SPCs were previously extensively granted for second medical indication patents, but after the *Abraxis* case, this situation seems to have changed and market exclusivity might be the last to expire in these product categories too.[117]

In one of the scientific reports related to the Commission's evaluation of the SPC system, a list of medicinal products was based on the different exclusive rights that they enjoyed. In this report, the ways in which pharmaceutical companies, both originators and generics companies, approached and handled the exclusive rights covering their pharmaceutical products became obvious. It was clear that they adopted a holistic perspective, where the interaction between IP rights and regulatory rights was a rule rather than an exception.[118]

What makes this report interesting is the variety on the list of medicines considered: blockbuster drugs, paediatric applications, orphan drugs and generics. One interesting case presented is that of Humira, a pharmaceutical with several applications for instance in the field of juvenile arthritis, paediatric psoriasis etc. The first patent was filed in 1997 and the MA application in 2003. When all the patents (SPCs and paediatric extensions) expired in 2018, the product had enjoyed a total 28.2 years of effective protection across countries in the EU. Humira has been protected by no less than 100 patents in total. The EMA approved three different PIPs for Humira. It enjoys six different orphan drug designations in the United States, with protection extended until 2023. According to Humira's own estimates, when its SPC expired in the EU, the international sales of the drug had decreased by 15 per cent per year.[119] Several biosimilar versions of Humira had already been granted an MA but were not able to enter the market before the expiry of the Humira SPC.[120]

Sovaldi, another interesting pharmaceutical, with a documented development time of six years, will have enjoyed a total of 18.8 years of effective protection by the time its patent or SPC expires. Sovaldi is covered by a total of 14 different patent families. While the product has no orphan designations in the EU, it was granted one in the United States in 2016. Sovaldi patents have been challenged several times by organisations such as Doctors of the World, claiming that the technology behind this pharmaceutical is not new.

---

[117] Judgment of the Court (Fourth Chamber) of 21 March 2019, *Abraxis Bioscience LLC v Comptroller General of Patents*, C-443/17, EU:C:2019:238.
[118] European Commission, *Study on the economic impact of supplementary protection certificates, pharmaceutical incentives and rewards in Europe*, Final report [May 2018], Copenhagen Economics.
[119] Ibid.
[120] AbbVie, the owner of Humira, has been accused of intentionally blocking and delaying procedures when patent rights to their product have been challenged, while later voluntarily offering to invalidate the patents in question. By doing so, it created costs and practical issues for competitors that meant they often found it hard to litigate.

3.1.2. The Protection of the One is the Basis for the Other

3.1.2.1. Negative SPCs

As has previously been discussed in this book, an SPC may be granted with a negative (or nil) term of protection. As a result, a negative SPC may constitute the mere basis for the granting of a paediatric extension. This solution leads to the rather unfortunate situation where the patent owner has to proceed to a cumbersome and expensive SPC application, not for the SPC as such, but for the extension that the Paediatric Regulation offers, for which an SPC is necessary. This trend increases the workload of national patent authorities, which must examine the SPC application, even though it is known that an SPC positive term is not possible. To address this, Switzerland introduced the Therapeutic Product Act. In combination with the Swiss Patent Act, this resulted in the introduction of a new form of SPC: the 'paediatric supplementary certificate'.[121]

This certificate provides the same protection as an SPC from the expiration date of the patent. In order to be granted a paediatric supplementary certificate, the product cannot have been granted any previous SPCs. In other words, the patent owner is faced with two possibilities, either to apply for a standard SPC and on the basis of that also receive the extension of six months, if the product fulfils the requirements of the Paediatric Regulation (up to five years and six months protection in total), or to apply for a paediatric SPC that has a total duration of six months.[122]

In this solution, negative SPCs would be of no interest for medicinal products with a paediatric application. At the same time, all pharmaceuticals for which the agreed PIP has been completed would be granted the six-month extension in accordance with the requirements of the Paediatric Regulation. It is important to note that the only party that can receive the paediatric supplementary certificate is the patent holder. If clinical trials have been performed by a third party, the consent of this third party must be submitted in the application. In this way, Swiss Patent Law has been able to address the so called *Medeva* cliff. The *Medeva* test is applied even in this novel form of paediatric extension, meaning that 'it is essential that the product is detailed in the patent claims in a form recognisable for a person skilled in the art'.[123]

3.1.2.2. Orphan Drugs/Paediatric Extension

A paediatric extension of two years is granted to medicinal products that enjoy orphan drug designation. However, the Orphan Drugs Regulation has not

---

[121] Federal Act on Medicinal Products and Medical Devices (Therapeutic Products Act, TPA) of 15 December 2000 (Status as of 1 January 2020) The Federal Assembly of the Swiss Confederation.

[122] Judgment of the Court (Second Chamber) of 8 December 2011, *Merck Sharp & Dohme Corp v Deutsches Patent- und Markenamt*, C-125/10, EU:C:2011:812.

[123] The provisions relating to paediatric extensions refer explicitly to the requirements for granting a 'traditional' SPC, and thus the *Medeva* case law is also applied to paediatric extensions.

considered and addressed the situation where an orphan drug is covered by patent rights. Taking into consideration that this situation is not addressed, and thus not excluded either, orphan drugs are not in any way prevented from applying for a patent in parallel to an orphan drug designation. However, the question is whether this also allows that the same medicinal product would be granted both the two-year extension of its orphan drug designation and the six-month extension of its SPC term, for completion of the same PIP. Granting a double extension for the same medicinal product would appear to contradict the objectives of the regulation.

At the same time, excluding a 'double' incentive presupposes an identity in the populations on which clinical trials have been performed. This is not necessarily the case. The orphan drug designation will be limited to the orphan disease, while the patented invention might have a broader scope of application. This issue is not finally settled since it has not been addressed as an overall question of principle in recent CJEU case law. What has been raised in case law is a more technical question: if it is possible to remove a medicinal product from the orphan drug registry and in that way be granted a six-month extension to its SPC protection.[124]

This question was posed in two national court cases that received considerable attention at an EU level, one from the Court of Milan[125] and the other from the Court of the Hague.[126]

In both cases, the question was whether the removal of a designation by the patent holder for a product that was previously registered in the orphan drugs registry (and at the same time patented) would lead to it being granted a six-month extension of its SPC. In the Court of Milan case, the important factor was that the patent holder chose not to use the two-year extension of the orphan designation. The Court refers to Article 37 of the Paediatric Regulation, which explicitly prohibits use of both incentives. In the ruling of the Court of the Hague, the court concluded that the decisive moment is the moment of application for the paediatric extension. Still, no clarity was brought by these two rulings as to the deadline for when the patent holder can remove the medicinal product from the orphan drugs registry to acquire the six-month SPC extension.[127]

There are different approaches in the literature concerning the appropriate dates for the removal from the orphan drug registry. However, both commentators and case law seem to agree that to be eligible for the SPC extension, the patent

---

[124] Judgment of the Court (Sixth Chamber) of 3 March 2016, *Teva Pharma BV and Teva Pharmaceuticals Europe BV v European Medicines Agency (EMA)*, C-138/15, EU:C:2016:136.

[125] Tribunal of Milan, Decision of 23 February 2016, *Teva Italia SRL et al v Novartis AG et al*, Case 52274-1/2015.

[126] District Court of the Hague, *Novartis AG v Teva BV et al*, Decision of 30 March 2016, C/09/500844/KG ZA 15-1829.

[127] The question answered is whether it is possible in the specific case. Thus, it is difficult to draw general conclusions.

holder cannot previously have enjoyed the two-year paediatric extension of the orphan drug market exclusivity.[128]

The application for an extension should be filed at the latest two years before the expiration of the SPC, which can be difficult for patent holders and may lead to practical concerns in cases where the MA is not yet granted at that time. Two alternative approaches have been presented as solutions to this problem in relation to the timeline requirements of the paediatric extension.

One alternative is to require that the application for extension is made before the deadline, but permit supplementation of the application with the statement referred to in Article 28(3) of Regulation 469/2009. Another way of tackling this is by providing for an expedited form of MA in cases where an application of paediatric extension is pending. However, this second option does not address the time needed to complete paediatric studies and acquire the statement required by Article 28(3) of the Paediatric Regulation.[129]

3.2. The Patent System

Although the patent system is not explicitly named in any of these Regulations,[130] it is always there in the background, creating both possibilities and interpretational challenges. In some cases, such as in the SPC and Paediatric Regulations, the patent rights are a *sine qua non*, and the necessary basis upon which these regulatory rights are based. Orphan drugs and ATMPs, meanwhile, seem to live parallel lives. However, these parallel lives are not uncomplicated and often intersect with the patent rights.[131]

The patent system constitutes a necessary context for the SPC Regulation since the exclusivity granted thereby is based on the patent system. However, even this is not an uncomplicated relation. The SPC is not an extension of the patent term, and the scope of the SPC is not the same as that of the patent it is based on. That being said, patent-related rules are relevant for the SPC application as well as for the validity and enforcement of the SPC rights. This is an important source of complications. SPCs are regulated by means of an EU Regulation, while the patent system is not harmonised at the EU level.[132] This creates a disturbing paradox, since one of the most central parts in the examination of an SPC application is determining the scope of the basic patent. In CJEU case law, an increasing number of references are made to the patent system, in particular to the interpretation of the scope of patent rights. Lacking EU principles of interpretation, the Court

---

[128] See Shorthose (2017) § 6.04.
[129] It seems that this is a central requirement, not something that can be satisfied à posteriori.
[130] With the exception of the Paediatric Regulation explicitly excluding patented pharmaceuticals from the PUMA procedure.
[131] See, for instance, the question of whether a medicinal product covered by both an orphan drug designation and a patent may receive a paediatric extension and under what circumstances.
[132] With the exception of the Biotech Directive (Directive 98/44/EC).

has resorted to Article 69 of the EPC and its Protocol. In the end, deciding how Article 69 will be interpreted and applied is a matter for the national courts.[133]

The Unitary Patent was considered to be an attractive way of tackling these issues, since it would constitute a unified platform upon which to base the granting and enforcement of SPCs.[134]

The SPC is usually granted before the patent lapses and thus the pharmaceutical is under current protection. However, there are situations where the patent expires before an SPC is granted.[135] Even in such cases, generics companies refrain from entering the market in order to avoid costs and legal risks. This reluctance on the part of generics companies probably explains why there are no cases covering this specific scenario.

The problematic aspects of the interrelation between patent rights and the SPC system also contaminate the application of the Paediatric Regulation, since this provides a further extension to the granted SPC term, and thus obscurities as to the scope of the SPC or its validity and enforcement will most likely also be relevant during the term of the paediatric extension.

Medicinal products may be covered by both a patent (or SPC) and an orphan drug designation at the same time. This is something of a paradox, as proceeding with the cumbersome, costly, and time-consuming procedure of patent application presupposes that there is a commercial interest in the specific pharmaceutical product and an expectation of financial returns. Thus, the basic assumption of the Orphan Drugs Regulation – that under normal market conditions and without the regulatory intervention, there will be no investments in the specific area of research – would not stand. This is not addressed in the text of the Regulation or in its negotiation history.

The Paediatric Regulation does not include any extensive reference to the patent system, with the exception of the part concerning the alternative MA route introduced by the regulation, the PUMA. It is important to note that a PUMA application may only be submitted for medicinal products not already protected by intellectual property rights. This means that if a medicinal product is protected by patents, even in just one of the Member States, it will be excluded from the PUMA procedure.[136]

---

[133] On the differences in interpreting Article 69 EPC and the role of the Protocol, see Karen Walsh, 'Promoting Harmonization Across the European Patent System Through Judicial Dialogue and Cooperation' [2019] 50 *International Review of Intellectual Property and Competition Law*, 408–40.

[134] For information as to how the SPC was expected to function under the Unitary Patent Package, see https://ec.europa.eu/growth/industry/policy/intellectual-property/patents/supplementary-protection-certificates_en [Accessed on 20 June 2020].

[135] See also Miguel Vidal-Quadras, 'Analysis of EU Regulation 2019/933 on the SPC Manufacturing Waiver Exception' [2019] 50 *International Review of Intellectual Property and Competition Law*, 971–1005.

[136] See Recital 19 of the Paediatric Regulation (Regulation 1901/2006/EC of the European Parliament and of the Council of 12 December 2006 on medicinal products for paediatric use and amending Regulation 1768/92/EEC, Directive 2001/20/EC, Directive 2001/83/EC and Regulation 726/2004 / EC[2006] OJ L 378/1.

ATMPs and patent law seem to live separate lives. Naturally an ATMP may be protected by a patent. However, neither the preamble nor the text of the ATMP Regulation makes mention of the patent system. When looking into the legislative history of the ATMP Regulation, we find a proposed amendment to the text that would introduce a morality exception in line with the debate that took place in relation to the Biotechnology Directive, namely the exclusion of embryonic stem cells. This exception was not introduced into the final text of the Regulation, which chose to remain neutral from a morality perspective.[137]

3.3. The MA System

The dependence of the SPC system on the MA system is obvious. No MA means no SPC.[138]

However, in what ways and to what extent this relation influences the SPC system is not entirely clear. Naturally, the terminology, scope and application of the MA framework are of direct relevance, and a continuous source of complications, as case law reveals.[139]

One area that is debated concerns who is to be granted the SPC, the patent holder or the MA holder. Another question is what happens when the former acts without the authorisation of the latter.

As has previously been stated, an MA granted to a third party may in fact allow a patent holder to receive an SPC if the latter is able to show that they contributed in the product development. Making use of third-party MAs, so-called SPC squatting, is a very important question, and yet not settled in CJEU case law.

The fact that the MA procedure has become even more demanding and lengthy than before also means that the relevance and strategic importance of SPCs for the pharmaceutical industry has considerably increased. The question is what this is due to. If it is a result of increasingly complex rules, compensation by means of the SPC makes sense. However, if it is the result of the industry's own sabotage, delays and tactics then the system does not work as it should and counteracts its own objectives.

The Paediatric Regulation, as well as the Orphan Drugs Regulation and the ATMP Regulation, provide for amendments to the MA legal framework by introducing exceptions encompassing the special characteristics of the categories of medicinal products they concern.

---

[137] See ch 4 of this book.
[138] This is one of the prerequisites of the SPC system and also the reason for the existence of the SPC as such, since it serves to compensate for the effective patent protection time lost due to the MA procedure.
[139] A question brought to the CJEU for instance in *Eli Lilly and Co v Genentech Inc* [2019] EWHC 388 (Pat), but that remained unanswered in the Order of the Court (Ninth Chamber) of 5 September 2019, *Eli Lilly and Company v Genentech Inc*, C-239/19, EU:C:2019:687.

Another point of intersection concerns the situation when the MA holder wishes to discontinue a paediatric product that has benefited from the rewards stipulated in Provisions 36, 37 and 38 of Regulation (EC) No 1901/2006. In this case, the MA holder will have to give a six-month notice to the EMA and will be required to (a) transfer the marketing authorisation or (b) allow a third party, that has declared its intention to place the medicinal product concerned on the market, to use the pharmaceutical as well as the preclinical and clinical information contained in the file of the medicinal product to support a new marketing authorisation application. This means that these provisions of the Paediatric Regulation provide for a circumvention of the data exclusivity. The MA holder is thus under certain pressure to continue manufacturing such a pharmaceutical. Making clinical data available to third parties could have an impact on the MA of other medicinal products and contribute to a weakening of the product exclusivity portfolio as a whole.

4. The Results

4.1. The SPC Regulation

4.1.1. From Objectives to Results?

An evaluation of the SPC Regulation requires a review of its objectives.

One of the central objectives of the SPC Regulations was to make R&D of medicinal products more attractive by extending the term of exclusivity. Offering a longer term of exclusivity in the EU would also mean that pharmaceutical companies not established in the EU would find it attractive to move their activities, while companies already situated in the EU would have no interest in moving elsewhere. In the negotiating history of the SPC Regulation, we find a direct comparison to the benefits offered to the US pharmaceuticals industry by means of the patent extension system. Although the imbalances between the regulatory environment in the United States and that in the EU were considered to be of fundamental importance for the introduction of the SPC Regulation, no reliable data indicated that there was a gap between the European industry and the US industry, nor does any data indicate that any such gap is now closed.

What can be confirmed is that MA approval times have grown longer, even though applications are handled much faster. The clinical trials required nowadays are much more demanding and increasingly time-consuming (lengthening from 466 to 780 days during the period 1999 to 2005).

The SPC system was expected to serve as a means of promoting the development of a broader variety of innovative pharmaceuticals. It was also hoped to work as a means of addressing supply shortages. How this would be achieved is rather unclear, as supply shortages often occur while a pharmaceutical is covered by an exclusive right. There is no evidence of broader accessibility. On the contrary, it seems that SPCs create further room for strategic decisions concerning when and where product launch is to take place, pricing, etc. On the other hand, SPCs are becoming increasingly relevant, more applications are being submitted and more case law related to them is being produced both by the CJEU and by national courts. If the evaluation were purely numerical, the SPC Regulation would appear very effective.

The SPC Regulation seems to be something of a 'living' organism, evolving considerably during the past 20 years. There has been a very intensive dialogue between national courts, and between the national courts and the CJEU. The CJEU has been very productive and has appeared eager to contribute decisively in how the Regulation is to be interpreted (and not).

This extensive CJEU case law and the interpretation of the Regulation has entailed looking at the text of the Regulation from completely different perspectives. Interpreting the will of the legislator in different ways makes it difficult to actually trace the text back to the objectives of the legislator and thus proceed to an application of the effectiveness test. Even the legislator, when presenting the proposal for a moratorium in 2018, seemed to adopt a new perspective and proceed to a further interpretation of the objectives of the Regulation.[140] The question of whether second medical indications may enjoy SPC protection has forced the CJEU to go back to the objectives of the Regulation, as well as to consider the principles of interpretation that are to be employed. Interestingly, in this process of revealing what the legislator intended with regard to medicinal products with second medical indications, courts and commentators resorted to the objectives of the patent system. It has been claimed that the patent system endorses innovations in any forms possible and that patents for second medical indications should be promoted. In fact, the patent system has been adjusted in order to promote the patentability of second medical indications. As a result, a similar development should be expected for SPCs on second medical indications. This is an interesting argument, but disregards the fact that the patent system rewards inventiveness, while the SPC is a remedy to the effective patent protection time lost due to the MA procedure.

Thus, explaining that a certain provision of the SPC regulation is to be interpreted by invoking patent law-related objectives is, if not wrong, at very least misleading.

It seems that both the CJEU and national courts are in agreement that the SPC Regulation includes a number of unfortunate formulations and provisions that are difficult to interpret or adjust to the new technological developments in pharmaceutical research. CJEU case law clearly shows that several important points of the

---

[140] European Commission, *Proposal for a Regulation of the European Parliament and of the Council amending Regulation (EC) 469/2009 concerning the supplementary protection certificate for medicinal products*, COM [2018] 317 final, 2018/0161 (COD).

Regulation, in particular, those related to the interface with the patent system and the MA system, have been overlooked.[141]

The interpretations of the Regulation by the national courts and the CJEU seem in some cases to be rather independent of the original text. Thereby, a somewhat new Regulation text than that which the legislator initially envisioned is created. The Regulation is of course part of a broader framework, in which evolution occurs of the balance between the right to public health, the right of patients and the need for support to the pharmaceutical industry that was created at the time the regulation was introduced, and in which a new approach and in some ways even a new set of objectives are promoted.

While the Moratorium Regulation amends only specific parts of the SPC regulation, concerning the enforcement of rights, its preparatory works revealed a new approach as to what is important in the pharmaceutical industry and who is to receive the support of the legislator. The question is of course whether this was really the intention and, if so, whether it should be. How is an effectiveness test to proceed when the objectives are unclear, or even worse, when the objectives have been modified? Which objectives are we to employ as a starting point to make this evaluation? Is it the original text of the regulation that will be the basis of our evaluation, or the objectives as reiterated in CJEU case law, or the latest review of the legislator – in this case in the latest amendments to the SPC regulation?

In a US case, *Fisons*, the US Supreme Court stated, with regard to a second medical indication and patent extension, that although it would make sense to protect and promote research into second medical indication products, providing for patent extension was not the intention of the legislator.[142] As a result, amending this initial perspective is not left to the court, but to the legislator.[143]

The CJEU has several times stated that it is not entitled to assume the role of the community legislature and interpret a provision in a manner contrary to the express wording of legislation.[144] It has also stated that it may deviate from the text of a provision in order to close a gap that would otherwise imply unequal treatment, in order to avoid a conflict with primary law, or in order to consider new legal or technical developments.[145]

The question of whether SPCs protect medicinal products, and whether the subject matter of an SPC is really based on where the focus of pharmaceutical R&D lies is of course important in assessing the effectiveness of the regulation.

---

[141] See ch 4 of this book for an overview of case law.
[142] See *Fisons plc v Quigg*, 876 F.2d 99, 101 (Fed. Cir. 1989).
[143] See also the mention of the case, and its importance in the European Commission, 'Study on the Legal Aspects of Supplementary Protection Certificates in the EU', Final Report [2018] Max Planck Institute for Innovation and Competition, Annex II.
[144] Judgment of the Court (Fifth Chamber) of 23 March 2000, *Hauptzollamt Neubrandenburg v Leszek Labis and Sagpol SC Transport Miedzynarodowy i Spedycja*, C-310/98 and C-406/98, EU:C:2000:154
[145] Margaret Kyle, 'Economic Analysis of Supplementary Protection Certificates in Europe', January 30, 2017.

How can we assess if the regulation supports the pharmaceutical industry and provides compensation for the lengthy MA process if the products that the pharmaceutical R&D focuses on and develops are excluded from the scope of the Regulation?

One can note a large increase (49 per cent) in the number of employees in the pharmaceutical industry in the EU during the past few years. However, it remains unclear whether this is related to the SPC Regulation.[146] In this regard, the conclusions reached by Kyle are both interesting and important.[147] There is undoubtedly a positive correlation between the number of SPCs and the number of generic products on the market. However, this might be due to the simple fact that valuable medicinal products will be protected by originators using SPCs, and it is with these products that generics companies will want to be the first to enter the market. The Copenhagen study drew the conclusion that SPCs might lead to increased, but delayed, generics entry. On the other hand, delayed generics entry could have the negative effect that generics are produced for pharmaceuticals that are in fact outdated. The second conclusion seems more credible than the first. According to the Copenhagen Economics report, data from the pharmaceutical market proves that an increased share of the total pharmaceutical market share is represented by generics. It is impossible to tell if this is a positive effect of the SPC Regulation, but it can at least be concluded that the Regulation has not had a negative effect.[148]

The Copenhagen Economics report provides data presenting the development of new chemical entities (NCEs) during two time periods: 1982–92 and 1993–2002. These data show that the share of NCEs discovered in Europe has decreased by 6 per cent during the second period, while the share discovered in the United States has increased by 10 per cent.[149]

In general, one could conclude that, the fact that SPC protection is granted without any reference to investments and returns leads to it being disconnected from some of the incentives of the regulation. Thus, the extended exclusive right does not correspond to anything other than to a development term that is longer than five years. Naturally, providing for requirements for the granting of the SPC that entail a review of costs and benefits could cause considerable difficulties and an increased risk of manipulation on the part of originators. It is only the company itself that knows the real costs and returns of a certain product. However, the term of exclusivity seems to be disconnected from the objective. One interesting example is that of the paediatric extension. A six-month period is added to the term of the

---

[146] European Commission, *Study on the economic impact of supplementary protection certificates, pharmaceutical incentives and rewards in Europe*, Final report [2018], Copenhagen Economics.
[147] See n 142.
[148] See OECD, '*Improving Forecasting of Pharmaceutical Spending Insights from 23 OECD and EU Countries: Analytical Report*' [2019].
[149] In the same report, a correlation between NCE discovery and R&D spending is presented, but the model appears to have some weaknesses in terms of how the two perspectives are combined and juxtaposed, preventing the drawing of any conclusions.

SPC in cases where the pharmaceutical company has drafted an agreed Paediatric Investigation Plan (PIP). Even if the pharmaceutical in question has no uses for the paediatric population, the pharmaceutical is granted an extended six-month period that applies to all uses of the product. The paediatric extension could in fact be most valuable for a pharmaceutical with a considerable adult patient group. In this sense, the incentive is decoupled or disconnected from the effect.

Another perspective that is not taken into consideration in the SPC Regulation objectives involves the research models in the pharmaceutical industry or, to be more concrete, the factors that have an impact on these models. Today, pharmaceutical research is to a large extent based on big data technology. Such technology holds considerable value for pharma innovation and exists off the radar of modern IP rights but constitutes a considerable threshold for new entrants.

There is no doubt that SPC is a trade-off, between delaying generics entrance and boosting pharmaceutical innovation. However, the question is whether this trade-off is economic or purely political.

Furthermore, it seems that an important part of the SPC Regulation objectives will not be achieved until a unitary SPC right can be introduced.[150] The fragmentation that is noted today is detrimental to several of the objectives of the Regulation and to the creation of a European pharmaceutical products market. Although data prove that the use of SPCs is increasing over time, national fragmentation has a persistent and annoying negative impact on the effectiveness of the system as a whole. This is, of course, related to the lack of a harmonised EU patent system. Pharmaceutical companies will choose to file SPC applications only in Member States that they consider to be strategically attractive, not in all Member States. There is also considerable uncertainty regarding how the SPC Regulation is to be implemented and interpreted; thus, the outcome of identical SPC applications might differ from one Member State to another.[151]

4.1.2. Objectives and Results in a State of Flux?

As has previously been stated, the amended Regulation introduced a new production moratorium.[152]

The preparatory works to the proposed amendment revealed that the purpose of a legislative act may also be seen in a new light depending on what is meant by the terms employed in the legislative act at a given time. In this specific case, it becomes obvious that the legislator has taken into consideration how priorities change and how the internal hierarchy of these priorities might be adjusted to

---

[150] Given the latest developments concerning the Unitary Patent Package, it seems that this is not an option, at least in the short term.
[151] As has been shown previously in the book, even the case law of the CJEU fluctuates.
[152] Regulation 2019/933/EU of the European Parliament and of the Council of 20 May 2019 amending Regulation 469/2009/EC concerning the supplementary protection certificate for medicinal products (Text with EEA relevance) [2019] OJ L 153/1.

new societal needs, economic factors and technological advancements. While the purposes of the new SPC Regulation might appear unchanged, in particular in cases of commercial and economic incentives, it is inevitable that they will most probably take on different meanings over time; markets do not stay the same over the course of 30 years.

Negotiations preceding the amendments to the Regulation bring valuable insights as to how the Commission perceived the purpose of the Regulation as a whole at that time, how the content was interpreted, and how the Regulation worked within the broader legal system (ie the general 'context' of the regulation).[153]

In the proposal, the Commission states that the purpose of the amendments are of pure commercial character, 'to boost investment and job creation in the manufacturing of generics and biosimilars in the Union by restoring a level playing field between EU-based manufacturing and manufacturing in non-EU countries'.[154] In other words, the proposal lacks any form of public health perspective or consideration. It is further stated that the proposal serves to remedy certain unintended consequences resulting from the SPC system.

Referring to the purpose of the SPC Regulation as such, the Commission clearly indicates that it was also of a purely commercial character with a central focus on the internal market, 'aimed to provide the pharmaceutical industry with sufficient incentives to innovate and to promote, within the Union, the investment in research and innovation needed to develop medicinal products and to prevent the relocation of pharmaceutical research outside the Union'. What is rather striking is the fact that the Commission concludes that there is a need for clarity in the provisions of the Regulation, while it also states that any further guidance on how the SPC Regulation is to be applied should await the rulings of the CJEU.[155]

Thus, the Commission Communication accompanying the proposed Regulation provides very interesting insights into the effects of the SPC Regulation and, more interestingly, its side effects.

As has been shown previously in this book, the main purpose of the original Regulation was also to support the pharmaceutical industry. The Commission stated that Europe had traditionally been the hub of pharmaceutical research and that this competitive position was under threat as EU-based manufacturers could not produce pharmaceuticals protected by SPCs. The Commission concluded that EU-based manufacturers did not have the same possibilities of entering the market as non-EU ones, as an effect of the SPC Regulation. A side-effect, or even a direct effect of the Regulation, is the extension of the exclusivity protecting

---

[153] European Commission, 'Proposal for a Regulation of the European Parliament and of the Council amending Regulation (EC) No 469/2009 concerning the supplementary protection certificate for medicinal products', COM [2018] 317 final, 2018/0161 (COD).

[154] Ibid.

[155] At the time, several cases for which we now have a ruling were pending, such as *Abraxis Bioscience*, C-443/17, EU:C:2019:238; and *Eli Lilly and Company v Genentech Inc*, C-239/19, EU:C:2019:687.

pharmaceutical products. In the late 1980s, this was considered to be crucial for research in the pharmaceutical sector; now, it is considered to be a major impediment.

One can conclude that there has been a considerable shift in what constitutes a priority. In both the 1992 and 2009 SPC Regulation, the EU pharmaceutical industry that was to be supported encompassed the originators (the pharmaceutical companies engaged in R&D). In 2019, the important markets identified by the Commission were those of generics and biosimilars. Boosting the pharmaceutical industry in this case does not necessarily mean boosting the R&D pharmaceutical industry (the originators), but rather the manufacturing pharmaceutical industry (including or even prioritising the generics).

What is both interesting and surprising is that the Commission reflected on future commercial opportunities that will become available to the pharmaceutical industry when a number of medicinal products will enter the public domain. This phenomenon, referred to as a 'patent cliff', and the commercial opportunities this may provide for the European (manufacturing) pharmaceutical industry were the starting point for the Commission's proposed amendment, as opposed to the previous objective of diminishing the 'patent cliff' by providing for an extension to the term of patent protection. In a short sentence, the Commission reflected on the impact this would have on the accessibility of previously patented pharmaceuticals as well as the impact on national public health budgets. Issues of health and product safety are referred to under the impact assessment, stating that consumers prefer generics that originate in the EU, not in third countries.[156] The Commission also stated that the proposal would be positive for the entire EU pharmaceutical industrial ecosystem, since many SPC holders have outsourced branches of their activities to non-EU countries, where they develop generics and biosimilars. This is an interesting point, though parts of it are rather unclear. If it means that the originators choose to outsource activities pertaining to the development of the generic and biosimilar versions of their own products, the question is why. However, if this means that originators are making generic versions of other companies' pharmaceuticals, this is decidedly a development in the structure of the industry. Still, the Commission failed to explain how any of these aforementioned scenarios would be impacted by the proposal. One can also question the viability of the Commission's argument that the new exception would make it easier for SPC holders to enforce their rights in the long run. How or why this would be the case is not further developed.

In the discussion on consistency with other Union policies, what strikes the reader is that there is no reference to the paediatric extension or the Orphan Drugs Regulation, although it is obvious that these are interrelated and of relevance for the overall discussion and for the achievement of the objectives of the specific

---

[156] The Commission's proposal also includes a review of safeguards for the protection of pharmaceutical companies (originators) and introduces transparency and labelling measures.

amendments. Thus, even in these latest amendments to the SPC Regulation, very little (if any) attention is paid to the context in which this Regulation is to operate.

With regard to the legal basis for the amendment to the SPC Regulation, the Commission is content to refer to the fact that the infringement of a right originating in Community legislation may only be alleviated by means of another Community Regulation. At the same time, reference is made to the fact that any diverging national implementation would be contrary to the principles of the internal market.[157]

The Commission has proceeded with both an impact assessment and a three-month public consultation, and supplemented its underlying work with a number of relevant studies.[158] Still, central aspects of importance for the effectiveness of the regulation have been overlooked, as previously shown in this book.

The proposal also includes interesting input as regards the future evaluation of the amendment, making results as quantifiable as possible. The effectiveness of the Regulation will thus be monitored by the Commission on the basis of the following elements:

(i) the number of EU manufacturing sites for generics and biosimilars producing products covered by the Regulation;
(ii) the number of entries of EU manufactured products into export markets;
(iii) the time of entry after expiry of the certificate in Member States for products covered by Regulation; and
(iv) the amount of R&D activities in the EU by innovators and by generics and biosimilars companies.

In order to minimise the input of pharmaceutical companies, which would create a risk of subjectivity, the Commission will primarily use indicators from available objective data sources.

Although the Commission has done its utmost to introduce quantifiable objectives, very little is stated as to how data will be collected and prioritised. Some of the data could easily be considered to be trade secrets, while other data will be difficult to find. Even if relevant data are made available to the Commission, it is questionable whether it would be possible to evaluate the results of the amendments in the way proposed. Establishing a link between the number of EU generics and biosimilars manufacturing sites and the amendments to the Regulation seems difficult.

---

[157] According to the Commission, proportionality is guaranteed by making the amendment available only to such SPCs that are granted after its entry into force, not those that have already been granted. By limiting the applicability of the SPC moratorium, the Commission has guaranteed that it will not impact on the legitimate expectations of the SPC holders.

[158] See European Commission, *Summary of the replies to the public consultation on Supplementary Protection Certificates and patent research exemptions for sectors whose products are subject to regulated market authorisation*, SWD [2018] 242 final.

In the amendment to the SPC Regulation, it is made clear that the objectives of the Regulation have to be seen under new light. Furthermore, it is clear that the results of the Regulation (in its form previous to the 2019 amendment) had side effects that the new amended Regulation serves to address. The rather simplistic approach that exclusive rights will lead to increased innovation is thus seriously questioned.

4.2. The Orphan Drugs Regulation

A numerical evaluation of the Orphan Drugs Regulation is overwhelming. In 2000 only nine orphan drugs were marketed. In 2018 there was a total of 3,210 applications, out of which 2,121 were granted an orphan designation. Out of these 2,121 designations, 524 concerned a new condition while 89 per cent concerned diseases with a prevalence of three or fewer patients per 10,000. MA has been granted for 164 of these orphan drugs.[159]

Although the special characteristics of orphan drugs seem to be accommodated under the framework of the EU marketing authorisation procedure, this procedure is not equivalent or in any way auxiliary to the evaluation of clinical effectiveness that is to be made for the purposes of pricing, reimbursement, or inclusion under a national public health system. In fact, the criteria employed during that evaluation are not necessarily adapted to the special characteristics and needs of orphan medicines, and it might prove to be more restrictive than the CHMP procedure. In France, medical products have to show clinical added value, not clinical effectiveness as such. This means that the French system promotes a form of subjective system, where the product's effectiveness is not tested against objective criteria but against a relative standard set by other available medicines.[160]

In order to further illustrate the difference between the two systems, one could say that the marketing authorisation is an all-or-nothing procedure (the MA is either granted or not) and that the decision on effectiveness is based on the benefit of the doubt, while the control performed for pricing and reimbursement purposes is subject to much greater scrutiny, and the level of evidence required is usually higher.[161]

---

[159] EMA, 'Orphan medicines figures 2000–2018' (Europa 2018) www.ema.europa.eu/en/documents/report/annual-report-use-special-contribution-orphan-medicinal-products-2018_en.pdf [Accessed on 20 July 2020]. See also a very interesting report (though commissioned by Shire and thus with a biased perspective), Pugatch Consilium, 'Benchmarking Success: Evaluating the Orphan Regulation and Its impact on Patients and Rare Disease, R&D in the European Union' [2019] www.pugatch-consilium.com/reports/Benchmarking_success.pdf [Accessed on 20 July 2020].

[160] European Commission, *Study on the Legal Aspects of Supplementary Protection Certificates in the EU*, Final Report [2018] Max Planck Institute for Innovation and Competition, Annex III.

[161] Wills Hughes-Wilson, Ana Palma, Ad Schuurman, et al, 'Paying for the Orphan Drug System: Break Or Bend? Is it Time for a New Evaluation System for Payers in Europe to Take Account of New Rare Disease Treatments?' [2012] 7 *Orphanet Journal of Rare Diseases*, 74.

Another aspect that has restricted the accessibility of orphan drugs is that they are very expensive. They tend to be much more expensive than non-orphan drugs, but very innovative, pharmaceuticals that treat severe, life-threatening conditions. The question is whether they could be financed through a normal national public health system. EURORDIS claims that with the exception of two specific pharmaceuticals, imatinib and enzyme replacement therapies, orphan drugs do not represent an important part of the public health budget. One factor that reduces the total cost for orphan drugs is low prevalence; with a low number of patients the costs are also limited. Furthermore, not all patients suffering from an orphan disease can access a given medicine (due to the lack of necessary facilities or because not all individuals can be treated by the pharmaceutical in question). It seems that the price of a pharmaceutical does not increase with the rarity of the disease it treats.

The Commission has stated that pricing and reimbursement systems are the bottleneck in access to orphan drugs. Even if incentives are given to pharmaceutical companies in order to invest in R&D of orphan drugs, patient access requires a pricing and reimbursement system that supports such pharmaceuticals and that guarantees that these reach the patients that need them. Although the EU has limited competence and thus limited possibility to influence the national obstacles to accessibility, there are some ways in which it could contribute to providing broader accessibility at the national level.[162]

The EU could provide more extensive and detailed data on the actual prices of orphan drugs and how they impact on public health budgets. It is in a position to do so, as it could collate information on pricing and reimbursement from all Member States. Such data could counteract what seems to be a misunderstanding relating to the prices and economic effects of orphan drugs.

With regard to the costs for the development of orphan drugs, the only audited public statement is that of the Genzyme Corporation, suggesting that development costs are substantial, but somewhat lower than the costs for mainstream pharmaceuticals (this is the case mainly because the clinical development programme involves smaller numbers).

Reimbursement of orphan drugs has been presented as one of the major issues in the accessibility of pharmaceuticals. Most countries have lower requirements with regard to effectiveness for orphan drugs than for other categories of pharmaceuticals and the requirement of clinical evidence can be fulfilled with literature reviews and data from manufacturers.[163]

In order to increase accessibility and taking into consideration the limitations that certain countries place on reimbursement of orphan drugs, a new

---

[162] Commission of the European Communities, *Commission Staff Working Document on the experience acquired as a result of the application of Regulation (EC) No 141/2000 on orphan medicinal products and account of the public health benefits obtained*, SEC [2006] 832.

[163] It is thus easier to get reimbursement for an orphan drug than for a usual pharmaceutical.

scheme of cooperation between national public health systems and orphan drug donors is increasingly being used, namely Managed Entry Agreements (MEAs). Such agreements are becoming increasingly common worldwide, as 'innovative reimbursement approaches' to fund high-cost drugs. The manufacturer has to enter into a negotiation with the payer and include considerations of the expectable health improvements in the pricing and reimbursement scheme. Finance-based MEAs may take on a variety of forms, such as cost capping (beyond a certain cost threshold, the drug is provided at a discount or at zero cost), utilisation capping (any number of doses beyond an agreed amount has financial consequences), price volume agreements and free or discounted initiation (treatment is free or discounted up to a specified number of doses). Some EU Member States, including Italy, the Netherlands and Sweden use this new system.[164]

The question that arises (and also constitutes a difficult dilemma in relation to the objectives and the results of the Orphan Drugs Regulation) is whether it is better that research in orphan diseases is being performed even if it leads to pharmaceuticals that are not accessible to patients. In other words, the question is, is the regulation a successful one if pharmaceutical companies choose to invest in research into such diseases or alternatively, is its success dependent on the results of the research actually reaching patients of orphan diseases?

Answering the question of whether the Orphan Drugs Regulation actually fulfils its objectives is not easy. It does succeed in creating an objective for innovation. However, the lack of consideration as to how this objective relates to the general context in which it is expected to operate makes it difficult to provide a clear conclusion. Is the exclusivity granted really the best incentive and how much has it (in isolation) actually contributed to orphan drug research? As has previously been shown in this chapter, the objectives of the Orphan Drugs Regulation are based on two (flawed) starting points, namely (i) that pharmaceutical companies will not invest in research into orphan drugs without a new form of exclusivity, even though it is clear that they often do so and choose to apply for patent protection, and (ii) that the orphan drugs market is not attractive for pharmaceutical companies, even though it has been proven that it is and even though this is not affected by the Orphan Drugs Regulation, but by national pricing and reimbursement decisions.

In this respect, it is also paramount to note that the orphan drugs system is unfortunately structured in such a way that actually allows for abuses which counteract its objectives and thus have an impact on its results.[165] It has been shown that orphan drugs designations have been used as a basis upon which to promote a pricing strategy that is otherwise unjustifiable. An illustration of such practices

---

[164] Trevor Jozef Piatkiewicz, Janine Marie Traulsen and Tove Holm-Larsen, 'Risk-Sharing Agreements in the EU: A Systematic Review of Major Trends' [2017] 2 *PharmacoEconomics Open*, 2, 109–23.
[165] See *Medicines Law & Policy*, 'Orphan Medicinal Products in the European Union: Briefing Document', June 2019.

is the case of *Laediant Biosciences*. Cerebrotendinous xanthomatosis (CTX) is a rare genetic disease, whereby patients are unable to produce sufficient quantities of the primary bile acid chenodeoxycholic acid (CDCA). In the Netherlands, CDCA was marketed from 1976 to 2008 for the treatment of gallstones, at a price of €0.28 per capsule. Since 1999 the same substance was also prescribed, off-label, for the treatment of CTX. Leadiant Biosciences, a pharmaceutical firm, managed to acquire the marketing rights to Chenofalk, the medicinal product containing CDCA for the gallstones indication, and then (a) withdraw that product from the market for the gallstones indication and (b) received orphan drug designation and marketing authorisation in 2017 for CDCA (Leadiant) as an orphan medicinal product for CTX. With the orphan drug designation at hand, they set a price of €140 per capsule, representing a 500-fold rise over the previously available CDCA medicinal product, and raising the patient treatment price from €300 to €150,000 per year.[166]

The fact that an orphan drugs designation provides exclusivity which translates into undeniable market value also explains the tendency of the industry to exploit and abuse the system. In particular, by attempting to define the prevalence of the disease with as limited a scope as possible, a practice of so-called '*salami slicing*', pharmaceutical companies attempt to artificially create orphan diseases in order to be able to make extensive use of the system. In an era where we are moving towards increasingly personalised medicine, it seems only natural that diseases could in fact be defined in a way as to cover only one patient. This practice has been noted extensively in the field of oncology but seems to be gradually expanding to other fields. In this respect, the interaction of the Orphan Drugs Regulation with the ATMP remains rather unexplored.

Strategic exploitation of the Regulation is, as it has previously been noted, almost encouraged in the text of the Regulation. Article 8(3) allows a sponsor to prolong a first orphan designation with a new independent 10-year exclusivity period. Surprisingly enough, this can repeat an unlimited number of times provided that the other requirements of the Regulation are fulfilled.[167] Thus, evergreening is in fact much more limited and regulated in the field of patents than in orphan drugs.

The orphan drugs market is a commercially interesting playing field and what better a way to confirm that than by looking into the stakeholders engaged in it? Statistics reveal that the orphan drugs market is not a market for SMEs, but for powerful multinational pharmaceutical industries such as Novartis (with orphan drug sales of US$12.9 billion), Roche (with orphan drugs sales US$10 billion), Celgene (US$9.1 billion) and Bristol-Myers Squibb (US$6.6 billion).

Finally, another aspect of the results of the Orphan Drugs Regulation that is rarely discussed is the fact that in cases of public health emergencies, a pharmaceutical protected by a patent or SPC is subject to a legal framework of exceptions

---

[166] See also, Matthew Newman, *Leadiant Given Pause for Thought by Dutch View of 'Orphan Drug' Price Hikes* (MLex Market Insight, 14 November 2018).
[167] See Article 3 of the Orphan Drugs Regulation.

and compulsory licensing that provides for its accessibility. This is not the case with orphan drugs, where such a system does not exist. Of course, one could question whether an orphan disease may in fact constitute a public health crisis but as has been shown previously in this book, the prevalence of orphan diseases is not particularly limited.[168]

4.3. The Paediatric Regulation

The Paediatric Regulation was expected to lead to an improvement in the health of the children of Europe, through ensuring the generation of robust, evidence-based information on the use of medicines for children; greater availability of such information, and greater availability of authorised medicines for children.[169] Ineffective treatment of children, incorrect dosing for children and adverse drug reactions in children would thus be minimised. This should lead, as far as children were concerned, to a reduced number of hospital days, fewer deaths, and increased quality of life and thus bring our society the economic benefits associated with these savings and benefits. It should also be noted that research, development and authorisation of medicines in the EU could also benefit children outside the EU, including in less developed countries.[170]

The industry can benefit from the Paediatric Regulation in various ways. The six-month SPC extension would allow the industry to recover the costs of paediatric testing of new products and make a profit estimated at between 0.8 and 9.1 million euros per product marketed. This would, in turn, constitute an incentive for further research. Furthermore, the data generated to satisfy EU requirements could be used to support MA applications outside the EU. Increased research and development of paediatric medicines in the EU could help generate high-quality, skilled jobs, and investment in the EU, as has been the case in the United States. New business opportunities would be created through the PUMA, through capitalisation of niche markets that were as yet unexploited, and through the need for clinical trials and support services and for consultancy services.[171]

The requirements for phase III clinical trials in children were in the proposal to the Regulation estimated to cost the industry an average of four million euros per product, yielding a total across the entire industry of 160–360 million euros

---

[168] With a population of 500 million in the EU, a prevalence of 5/10,000 is equivalent to a maximum of approximately 250,000 patients for a particular orphan disease.
[169] European Commission, '*Better Medicines for Children from Concept to Reality: Progress Report on the Paediatric Regulation (EC) 1901/2006*' COM [2013] 443 Final.
[170] Oortwijn (n 93).
[171] European Medicines Agency, *5-year Report to the European Commission. General report on the experience acquired as a result of the application of the Paediatric Regulation*, 8 July 2012, EMA/428172/2012. See also European Medicines Agency, *Report to the European Commission on companies and products that have benefited from any of the rewards and incentives in the Paediatric Regulation and on companies that have failed to comply with any of the obligations in this regulation*, 9 September 2014, EMA/24516/2014 Corr.3.

after the first year. This corresponds to a 1–2.5 per cent increase in total European expenditure on drug development after the first year. If the innovation industry were to allocate a fixed amount of revenue to all research and development, the resources allocated to meet the requirement for paediatric testing would likely be cut from other research and development projects.

However, the effect is inevitably modest, due to the real costs associated with the requirements. Because the industry is likely to want to access the rewards and incentives of SPC extension (or extended market exclusivity for orphan medicines), the proposal is likely to stimulate innovation, particularly for products already authorised. Such innovation may also benefit adults. Other costs for the innovation industry include administrative costs incurred to meet regulatory requirements, manufacturing costs if a specific child formulation is required and marketing costs. Overall, the costs of clinical trials in children, if added to the costs of medicines, would add less than 0.5 per cent to the price of an individual medicine.

In addition, the six-month extension of SPCs, leading to delayed entry of generics onto the market, could add between 0.06 and 0.25 per cent to European expenditure on pharmaceuticals over time. However, this is likely to be balanced by reduced healthcare costs from the supply of safer and more effective medicines for children. A six-month SPC extension could also incur the generics sector a one-time loss of between 86 and 342 million euros in lost opportunity costs.[172] This loss would not be at the expense of generics already on the market. It would represent a decline in market opportunities. In addition, a large proportion of off-patent products are produced by innovator manufacturers, so the estimated loss represents a maximum. It should be noted that these estimates are based on a number of assumptions. It should also be noted that the first SPC extensions will not occur for many years (considering the time to entry into force of the Paediatric Regulation and the fact that the extension is at the end of the patent or SPC life). Lastly, SPC extensions will occur gradually over time, when the requirements in the draft Paediatric Regulation are met and subsequently rewarded. The use of deferrals from the requirements in the proposal will prevent the requirements from delaying the authorisation of medicines for adults. In the first few years after coming into force, the proposal will lead to a significant increase in work for regulators and put pressure on the currently limited resources for conducting clinical trials in children. This initial pressure in conducting clinical trials will be relieved through the increased capacity for paediatric research already available in the United States. The proposal has no significant environmental or sustainability impacts. It is difficult to judge the balance of benefits and costs of the Paediatric Regulation. This is due to the fact that while it is possible to make an estimate of the costs resulting from the proposal, robust data are not available to allow estimation of the value, both economic and social, of the lives of children that will be saved and the improvements in the quality of life of the children of Europe.

---

[172] See Copenhagen report.

The proposal aims to meet its objective of improved EU child health through stimulating research, development and authorisation of medicines for children and to provide the various stakeholders with as many gains as possible. When adopted, the Regulation should not only improve the health of the children of Europe, but may also stimulate innovation for existing pharmaceuticals.

Evaluating the effectiveness of the Paediatric Regulation as such is difficult in practice, as the Regulation is expected to be applied in symbiosis with the SPC Regulation and the Orphan Drugs Regulation. Thus, if one is to consider the part of the Paediatric Regulation that concerns exclusivity,[173] one needs to look into the system as a whole. Furthermore, it is equally important to analyse the impact of the Regulation on MA procedures and the impacts these have on stakeholders in the pharmaceutical industry.

4.4. The ATMP Regulation

There is an increasing number of companies in this specific field of medicinal research and an increasing investment trend, but only 15 marketing authorisation applications have been submitted and only six MAs have been granted to ATMPs.[174]

At the time of writing, only four ATMPs have valid MAs. These include treatments for prostate cancer, cartilage defects, and metastatic defects of the knee. Almost 70 per cent of sponsors for clinical trials on ATMPs are non-profits or SMEs, which means that they continue to be the principal stakeholders in the developments of the ATMP Regulation.[175]

The EMA has authorised only nine ATMPs from 2009 to 2017: three gene therapy products, two somatic cell products, and four tissue-engineered products. Five of them have given rise to an SPC and none of them seem to have been considered in case law. What seems clear that there are some difficulties with the description and classification of ATMPs. Unlike biologically active substances, which can be described as amino acid sequences, ATMPs must be described in a more functional language, which has created several problems for both stakeholders and authorities.[176]

The expectation at the introduction of the Regulation was that the Clinical Trials Regulation Reg 536/2004 would contribute to several ATMPs entering the European market.

However, the main question is whether the ATMP Regulation serves its purpose and has facilitated the access of ATMPs in the EU market, while at the same time guaranteeing the highest level of protection for EU patients.

---

[173] Six months of SPC extension or two years of orphan drug designation extension.
[174] Until January 2020.
[175] As was the case at the introduction of the ATMP Regulation.
[176] European Commission, *Regulation (EC) 1394/2007 on Advanced Therapy Medicinal Products: Summary of Responses to the Public Consultation*, Brussels, SANCO/D5/RSR/iv [2013] ddg1.d5.

What has been discussed, even more than the impact of the ATMP Regulation as a whole, is the impact of the hospital exemption. Reading the impact assessment of the UK's proposed national arrangements under the hospital exemption laid down in Regulation (EC) No 1394/2007 reveals that this exemption was the most problematic aspect of the Regulation, and thus also the most interesting aspect from an evaluation perspective. The exemption was introduced in order to create flexibility in the strict requirements of the centralised MA for small-scale activities carried out at hospitals. The Regulation does not contain detailed provisions on how the hospital exemption will work in practice; it is the responsibility of Member States to put in place, at the national level, a number of safeguards related to certain parameters in order to protect public health.[177]

In the Public Consultation launched on 20 December 2012, 25 per cent of the participants expressed a negative view of the ATMP Regulation as a whole and some disappointment regarding how it has worked in practice. The Regulation's high requirements were considered to be responsible for the disappearance of some innovative products from the market, and also seemed to have discouraged new developments in the specific technological field. According to stakeholders in the ATMP market, the effect of the Regulation was limited to the 'hospital exemption'. Although the starting point of the Regulation is to take into consideration the special characteristics of the ATMP products,[178] it seems that the requirements have failed to address these.

In particular, it has been noted that it is difficult to apply the requirement of the concept of 'active substance' to these specific products, considering the high variability of living materials. Furthermore, the requirement of pre-clinical data is contested as a non-appropriate means of testing the safety of cell-based and gene therapy medicinal products.[179]

The MA procedure provided for under the ATMP Regulation should, according to stakeholders, be streamlined further.[180]

The 'hospital exemption' has been considered to be of central importance, as a means of providing patients with new revolutionary medical methods. Although this has been identified as an important provision, the fact that it is interpreted and thus applied in a fragmented way at the national level has been

---

[177] See also Alex Faulkner, 'Regulatory Policy as Innovation: Constructing Rules of Engagement of a Technological Zone for Tissue Engineering in the European Union' [2009] 38 *Research Policy*, 4, 637–46.

[178] Some of the special characteristics of ATMP products are the high degree of variability of the starting materials and the tailor-made products, making standardisation impossible.

[179] For examples of national practices see Matthias Renner, Brigitte Anliker, Ralf Sanzenbacher, et al, 'Regulation of Clinical Trials with Advanced Therapy Medicinal Products in Germany' [2015] 871 *Advances in Experimental Medicine and Biology*, 87–101.

[180] Stakeholders stated that the current system of validation of the device part by notified bodies was not appropriate if the intended use of the device in the ATMP was not the same as the device manufacturer's intended use. Stakeholders also stated that interaction between the CAT and the notified bodies was necessary.

considered problematic. Furthermore, this exemption has created an anti-incentive to the pharmaceutical industry, which in its turn believes that it is often used to circumvent the MA requirements. A way to address this would be by limiting the use of the hospital exemption to the cases where there are no other authorised products. Furthermore, it would be of interest to have more information on the uses made under the 'hospital exemption'. Lastly, technical progress in the field of ATMP applications could dictate the flexibility in the scope of the Regulation and the broad mandate to the CAT to determine which products fall under the scope of the ATMP Regulation.

The boundaries between the application of the ATMP Regulation, the Directive on Human Tissues and Cells, and the Clinical Trials Directive are rather blurry. According to some stakeholders, it might be necessary to have special rules developed for clinical trials with ATMPs.[181]

As has been previously stated, major stakeholders in the field of ATMP research are the SMEs, universities and state hospitals. Thus, ATMP trials very often remain in the academic field and have, for various reasons, not moved forward to industrial development. Potential reasons include that they are in early trials and have no clear objective of commercialisation, that they have encountered difficulties in attracting investment, or that they are having difficulties in acquiring clinical trials authorisation.[182] In other words, while the ATMP Regulation as such might be successful, the objectives would require a broader overview of the regulatory system, one not possible by means of an EU Regulation.

What is equally apparent is the fact that the hospital exemption, intended to bring a level of flexibility into the system, potentially leads to a weakening of the system and a trend promoting its circumvention. If the major stakeholders of the system are also those that are able to make use of the hospital exemption, the ATMP Regulation seems to be falling short of its set objectives. If stakeholders can avoid a cumbersome MA procedure, even if this is adjusted to the ATMP products' special characteristics, they will do so.

5. General Conclusions

Applying the effectiveness test in a complicated regulatory environment like that of pharmaceutical regulation involves certain challenges.

It requires that objectives are identified and observing how the contents of the Regulations are applied and interpreted to achieve those. Needless to say, this is not a simple endeavour; it means following the specific application of each Regulation to see how this influences stakeholders and the functioning of the

---

[181] EUTCD is made up of three Directives, the parent Directive (2004/23/EC), which provides the framework legislation, and two technical Directives (2006/17/EC and 2006/86/EC).
[182] Juli Mansnérus, 'Commercialisation of Advanced Therapies. A study of the EU Regulation on Advanced Medical Products' [2016] Academic Dissertation, University of Helsinki 173–76.

pharmaceutical market in general, as well as how it fulfils its objectives. This in its turn presupposes looking into how national courts implement, interpret and apply the respective Regulations and how they define and interpret the interface between them.[183]

All four Regulations in focus in this book were introduced in an attempt to provide the European pharmaceutical industry with similar regulatory conditions to those in the United States, by directly or indirectly referring to the positive results these regulatory rights have had for the US pharmaceutical industry. Given that this was done without any discussion on the differences between the industries in the respective jurisdictions or the differences in the markets and in the broader regulatory context in which these regulatory systems operate, the evaluation of these regulations turns into a complicated endeavour.[184] If the overarching objectives are to boost the European pharmaceutical industry and provide similar conditions to guarantee that it is competitive at an international level and in particular in relation to its US counterpart. Substantial data would be required to confirm that the US and European pharmaceutical industry are similar with regard to size, product focus, R&D status etc, and that the only difference between them is created by the regulatory systems under which they operate. Even without engaging in the process of collecting data, we know that this is not the case. There is one central factor that is characteristic of the different conditions under which the regulatory rights operate in the respective jurisdictions. The United States, on the one hand, has a federal patent law and specialised patent courts. In Europe, meanwhile, pharmaceutical companies have to relate to fragmented national patent laws, with patent rights that might be valid in one Member States and invalid in another, and where the scope of protection may vary subject to national interpretation.[185]

The differences in the legislative architecture of regulatory rights between the country of origin (or country of inspiration) and the recipient region extend beyond patent law. In the Explanatory Memorandum on the Regulations,[186] it is plainly stated that the legislative choice of a Regulation provides the simplicity necessary and paves the way for a direct and undisturbed application of the legislative act, without a need for national implementation, with the risks of diverging outcomes that this might entail. Opting for a Regulation was without a doubt a good idea, but it has been proven in practice that the desired total harmonisation has not been possible. In the case of the SPC Regulation, it is the national

---

[183] It thus means that the model developed by Mousmouti needs to be further developed and adjusted in order to be applied to these specific regulations.

[184] Antón L García, 'Is the Copy Better than the Original? The Regulation of Orphan Drugs: A US–EU Comparative Perspective' [2004] Academic Thesis, Harvard Law School.

[185] In the United States, patent law is federal law, in the EU it is a matter for national legislation and national courts, with the exception of the Biotech Directive (Directive 98/44/EC).

[186] ECORYS, 'How well does regulation work? The cases of paediatric medicines, orphan drugs and advanced therapies', Final report, Client: Ministry of Health, Welfare and Sport Rotterdam, 9 November 2015.

authorities that examine SPC applications and grant rights. This leaves space for national approaches. Furthermore, procedural rules concerning the application of the SPC Regulation are to be decided at a national level, bringing a certain fragmentation to the system. The same situation applies with regard to the invalidity and enforcement of rights, and although the CJEU has produced a series of interesting rulings interpreting the provisions of the SPC Regulation, national courts tend to apply and interpret both the text of the Regulation and the CJEU rulings in divergent ways.

Another source of national divergences in the case of the SPC Regulation is variations in its translations. An illustrative example of this is Article 3(b), providing that the MA needs to be in force when the SPC is granted. In the French, Spanish and Italian texts this is presented as a requirement, whereas in the English text other interpretations are possible.[187]

The national divergences related to SPCs affect the application of the paediatric extension as well.[188]

National diversification is also due to the fact that the legislative framework of the MA procedure is based on a Directive, not a Regulation. Therefore, the involvement and thus also the impact of national legislation in the MA field plays a very important role, except for the categories of pharmaceuticals falling under the scope of the centralised procedure.

In all four of the Regulations analysed in this book, one of the major objectives is the accessibility of pharmaceuticals: the accessibility of medicines for orphan diseases, the accessibility of medicines for the paediatric population (and related know-how), the accessibility of ATMPs, or the accessibility of innovative medicines in general. However, assuming that this major objective may be fulfilled by means of the measures provided for under the Regulations presupposes a rather simplistic view of the structure and the factors of decisive importance in the pharmaceutical market. As has been discussed previously in this book, the pharmaceutical market is anything but simple.

Pricing and reimbursement systems play a major role in the accessibility of medicinal products. Product launch in specific jurisdictions is partly dependent on the national pricing and reimbursement systems available, as well as on the decisions of national authorities concerning specific medical products. Thus, accessibility is dependent on factors that are not limited to the application of the Regulations as such. Therefore, testing their effectiveness on the basis of this central objective would most certainly lead to a negative result. National price-referencing policies are decisive. When a high-price country references the prices of a low-price country, it will be more profitable for the pharmaceutical company to delay the launch of the product in the low-price country. Price referencing and the risk of parallel import are of central importance for the strategic choices of

---

[187] In the English text, this is not a requirement for being granted an MA.
[188] Since the application of the Paediatric Regulation is partly based on the SPC Regulation.

pharmaceutical companies. Although these two factors are clearly very important, their exact impact is very difficult to measure. Thus, it is difficult to provide an estimate of the interrelation between the two.

The issue of accessibility of pharmaceuticals and the factors that influence it have been the subject of several studies. The study of Kyle and Qian looked into how changes in IP rights affected the speed of medicinal product launches. However, the authors focused on patents and refrained from looking into the role of other rights, such as regulatory rights, which are at least equally important to pharmaceutical research.[189]

Danzon and Epstein studied the effect of price regulation and competition on medicinal product launches in 15 countries during the period 1992–2003.[190] They confirmed that the availability of a pharmaceutical in a low-price country would depend on price referencing in a high-price country. Cockburn et al studied the timing of the launch of new innovative medicine using information on 642 medicinal products from 76 countries for the years 1983–2002.[191] Some interesting results of the report include the fact that certain medicinal products are delayed in their market entry in some countries by as much as 10 years from the date of the first launch, while in other countries, they are never launched.[192]

While the EU Regulations are valid and apply in the same way in all EU countries, there are considerable divergences between different jurisdictions. There are in fact EU Member States where not even 50 per cent of the internationally launched pharmaceuticals ever enter the market. Taking into consideration the fact that the incentives for launching a product decrease with time, as the term of IP protection grows shorter, many products may never be launched in these jurisdictions. Europe and the United States have different pricing trends; in the United States, the older the pharmaceutical, the more expensive it is, while the trend is the opposite in Europe.[193]

Pricing and reimbursement issues are to be regulated at a national level and have for a long time constituted a no-go zone for EU competence.[194] They are at the same time of central importance for the effectiveness of all four Regulations.

---

[189] Margaret Kyle and Yi Qian, 'Intellectual Property Rights and Access to Innovation: Evidence from Trips' [2014]. NBER Working Paper No w20799.

[190] Patricia M Danzon, Andrew Epstein, Sean Nicholson, 'Mergers and Acquisitions in the Pharmaceutical and Biotech Industries' [2007] 28 *Managerial and Decision Economics*, 4–5, 307–28.

[191] Iain M Cockburn, Jean O Lanjouw and Mark Schankerman, 'Patents and the Global Diffusion of New Drugs' [2016] 106 *American Economic Review*, 1, 136–64.

[192] The reasons for that are of course strategic, depending on the national pricing and reimbursement policies.

[193] Patricia M Danzon, Andrew Epstein, Sean Nicholson, 'Mergers and Acquisitions in the Pharmaceutical and Biotech Industries' [2007] 28 *Managerial and Decision Economics*, 4–5, 307–28.

[194] The EU has attempted to harmonise pricing and reimbursement of medicines, mainly through the Transparency Directive Council Directive 89/105/EEC of 21 December 1988 relating to the transparency of measures regulating the prices of medicinal products for human use and their inclusion in the scope of national health insurance systems [1988] OJ L 40/8; however, these initiatives had a limited impact.

Pharmaceutical companies will not proceed to investments (even if these would be protected by some form of exclusivity, be it core IP or not), if they do not know that there is a market for their products. A market, in the field of pharmaceuticals, is decided in the pricing and reimbursement decisions taken by national healthcare systems. Thus, it would be rather naïve to draw any conclusions as to whether the Orphan Drugs Regulation actually achieves the objective of allowing patients of orphan diseases to access medicinal products, when the national pricing and reimbursement systems do not allow for the available pharmaceuticals to reach them. On the other hand, it is difficult to discuss the commercial viability of an orphan drug, since there are situations the reimbursement conditions are such that the pharmaceutical company is more than reimbursed for the R&D costs undertaken, even though the patient group is very limited.

Interestingly enough, the Orphan Drugs Regulation is also the only regulation that has attempted to link a reward to the commercial success (or simply commercial viability) of a pharmaceutical. The economic criterion according to which the product developer of an orphan drug may receive exclusivity when shown that without incentives, it is not likely that the marketing of the medicinal product will in fact lead to a sufficient return of the investments necessary to develop the product in question has failed miserably. Out of hundreds of orphan drugs designations since the introduction of the Regulation, only one was granted on the basis of the economic return criterion. This experience might also work as a good argument as to why introducing economic and commercial success criteria in any of the regulatory rights (SPCs, paediatric extensions etc) is a bad idea. In fact, it is very difficult to provide the necessary evidence for the application of such a criterion, and it is equally difficult for national authorities (or for the EMA for that matter) to control and question the evidence submitted.

The fact that prices of pharmaceuticals are not, as in other sectors, the result of market forces, but to a large extent the result of deals (and deal-breaking) between the pharmaceutical industry and national governments, is an important factor in the evaluation of the effectiveness both of the Regulations as such and of the regulatory system as a whole. These deals are very rarely limited to pricing and reimbursement and may also involve issues such as investments in R&D or production facilities. Thus, such decisions are very difficult to separate from other national policy decisions.[195]

The uncertainties related to EU competence in the field of public health have a considerable impact on the effectiveness of these regulations. This is partly because of the fact that they induce the Commission to formulate the objectives of the Regulations in ways that would limit competence objections to the greatest

---

[195] Another source of complication is the fact that the pricing and reimbursement decisions are made by different authorities/offices in different Member States and this has as an effect that they are part of different policy frameworks. In Portugal, it is the Directorate General for Trade and Competition, in Germany, it is the Federal Standing Committee of Physicians and Sickness Funds, and in Austria the Federal Ministry for Social Security and Generations, for example.

degree possible. As has been previously discussed in this book,[196] this will also mean that the Commission will formulate Preambles and objectives with relevant CJEU case law as a starting point.[197] The side-effect of these strategic choices in legislative drafting is that the texts of the Regulations (as well as the Explanatory Memorandums) might be only remotely connected to their real objectives, while the objectives included in the text might seem vague and not directly connected to the needs which the Regulation seeks to address.

The gap between the blackletter text and the reality of the application of the Regulations has been noted several times in previous chapters of this book, in particular with regard to the SPC Regulation.[198] The interpretation of the provisions of the Regulation by the CJEU has been called into question as a means of rewriting the Regulation through interpretation.[199] Although the CJEU has recently seemed much more reluctant in proceeding to generous interpretations,[200] there is reason to discuss whether a lack of effectiveness of a Regulation can be addressed and remedied by means of CJEU case law. If this is the case, one should then also consider how far this post-legislative drafting re-balancing might go and when it would become too much. When is the CJEU to compensate for a less successful legislative architecture, and when does this constitute re-writing legislation? It seems that a counterbalancing mechanism is necessary and expecting this role to be played solely by the CJEU seems overoptimistic, if not naïve. There is a clear need to consider the role of competition law in this respect and to explore its potential in achieving a well-functioning and truly balanced market.[201]

In any case, it seems that the increasing number of CJEU cases, at least for the SPC Regulation, manifests the weaknesses of the legislative acts as such, and the uncertainties that stakeholders face in their implementation. At the same time, the rising number of cases that concern the objectives of the Regulations and how these are to be interpreted in the rest of the provisions creates some problems in the application of the effectiveness test. The first step of the test consists of defining the objectives of a legislative act, and thus the questions that arise are what objectives are we to look into in this respect, how much could the 'fresh' approach of the CJEU deviate from the objectives of the legislator, and how will that impact on its application? The struggles related to legislative objective 'hunting' and when this takes place (at the time of the introduction of the legislation or at the time of the evaluation) may be further complicated when the legislation is

---

[196] See ch 1 of this book with regard to EU competence.
[197] See Judgment of the Court of 10 December 2002, *The Queen v Secretary of State for Health, ex parte British American Tobacco (Investments) Ltd and Imperial Tobacco Ltd*, C-491/01, EU:C:2002:741.
[198] But also with regard to Orphan Drugs.
[199] See Judgment of the Court (Fourth Chamber) of 19 July 2012, *Neurim Pharmaceuticals (1991) Ltd v Comptroller-General of Patents*, C-130/11, EU:C:2012:489.
[200] See Judgment of the Court (Fourth Chamber) of 21 March 2019, *Abraxis Bioscience LLC v Comptroller General of Patents*, C-443/17, EU:C:2019:238.
[201] Duncan Matthews, 'Patenting Strategies and Competition Law in the Pharmaceutical Sector: Implications for Access to Medicines' [2016] 38 *European Review of Intellectual Property*, 11, 661–67.

borrowed or transplanted from another jurisdiction or is disguised for purposes of contested competence such as in the case of the Regulation at hand.[202]

The effectiveness of these Regulations is of course also dependent on the work of the authorities vested with their application and interpretation. In this respect, the role of the EMA is of course of central importance. The close cooperation of the EMA and the FDA, combined with the fact that the European legal framework has its legislative origins in the United States, is an important aspect to consider when looking into the evaluation of the system as a whole. This informal institutional alignment will have an impact on how regulatory rights are to be interpreted (if it has not already had such an impact).

Applying the effectiveness test to these four Regulations has made at least one thing very clear: the objectives of these legislative acts are very often based on simplistic (or even naïve) assumptions, and very rarely supported by data. The fundamental assumption that has constituted the starting point of all four Regulations is that there is a simple trigger for directing innovation in a specific direction, and that is by regulatory intervention and in particular by the granting of exclusive rights. Exclusivity is promoted as a panacea, with no consideration paid to the already existing forms of exclusivity that this would interact with, and without reflecting on the particularities of the pharmaceutical industry, which do not allow for overly simplistic solutions.

What I find very interesting is that when looking into the negotiating history of these Regulations, serious concerns are expressed as to the viability and stability of the objectives – and the means to achieve them – that are presented as their drivers. In particular with regard to the SPC Regulation, major issues of weaknesses from an effectiveness perspective had already been discussed in the early 1990s, with regard to whether the patent extension term would in fact mean that more medicines would be introduced in the long run,[203] and the lack of satisfactory ways to address the relation with the patent system.[204] The question is why these concerns were not addressed by the legislator at the time of the drafting of the Regulation, and why they have been allowed to constitute the Achilles' heel of the Regulation as such and of the entire regulatory system as such.[205]

The evaluation of these four regulations by means of the effectiveness test gives the impression that the legislator has missed a very important aspect, one that constituted the starting point of this book, namely that these Regulations are part of broader system. This means that the legislative drafting of one Regulation should take into account the legislative history, context and effects of the others. Furthermore, all four Regulations are related – directly or indirectly – to the

---

[202] As is the case in the Regulations discussed here.
[203] The Committee on the Environment, Public Health and Consumer Protection when discussing the draft regulation.
[204] Parliamentary Committee on Legal Affairs Opinion on the draft SPC Regulation.
[205] European Commission, *Study on the economic impact of supplementary protection certificates, pharmaceutical incentives and rewards in Europe*, Final report [May 2018], Copenhagen Economics.

patent and MA legal framework. The choice of keeping these four Regulations, and the two major legal frameworks with which they interact, as isolated as possible, is the Trojan horse of the system. The interfaces are there, and – when not regulated – they allow for strategic behaviour, open up to generous judicial interpretations, and produce side-effects that clearly counteract the objectives of the Regulations.[206]

Equally fascinating is the fact that the regulations evolve in different directions even when they concern very similar interpretational challenges and when the instance dealing with them is the same (ie the CJEU). Two recent CJEU cases, *Shire* and *Abraxis* are illustrative of a very interesting juxtaposition. The *Abraxis* and *Santen* cases concern the SPC Regulation and in particular the question of whether an SPC may be granted to a second medical indication patent. The Court concluded that where there is an identity in the active substance between the MA submitted for the purposes of the SPC application and that which was submitted previously (for the other medical indication), then this identity will be prohibitive for the grant of an SPC.[207] In this regard, the Court is of the opinion that the therapeutic indication as such is not of relevance for the determination of whether a second SPC is to be granted. The fact that the active substance in the two MAs is the same is enough to exclude it from protection. In the *Shire* case,[208] the Court reasons in a different way. In this case it elevates the role of the therapeutic indication stating that the differences in this respect support the view that these are two different products and thus that the second medicinal product is to be granted protection (although its active substance is identical to a previous orphan drug designation). Thus, according to the Court a 'medicinal product' is different from an 'active substance' and the latter is a component of the former. Furthermore, a reference is made to Directive 2001/83/EC according to which the identity between two medicinal products has to be established on the basis of other relevant factors (than only the active substance), such as the medical product's excipients. Certainly, the Court was called to interpret two different regulations with different requirements of protection in these two cases. Nevertheless, the differences in the reasoning are striking. The SPC regulation refers to a medicinal product, at the same time choosing to define 'product' as the 'active ingredient or combination of active ingredients'.[209] The Orphan Drugs Regulation on the other hand defines a medicinal product as a medicinal product for human use, as defined in Article 2 of Directive 65/65/EEC.

The term is however the same; a 'medicinal product' needs to have the same stable definition in regulatory law, irrespective of whether it concerns SPCs or

---

[206] An example of this is, for instance, Article 8(3)(1) of the Orphan Drugs Regulation, giving the sponsor the possibility to actually register further new versions of the same orphan drug and receive a new term of exclusivity.
[207] *Abraxis Bioscience LLC*, C-443/17, EU:C:2019:238.
[208] *Shire Pharmaceuticals Ireland Ltd*, C-359/18 P, EU:C:2019:639.
[209] Article 1(a) and Article 3 SPC Regulation.

orphan drugs. In the end, the basis of the definition is the medical code (Directives 65/65/EEC and 2001/83/EC), and the reason for that must be the need to share a common base and regulatory uniformity. From *Shire's* perception that a medicinal product is not only the active ingredient but also the methods of administration, the therapeutic effect,[210] to the very limited *Abraxis* and *Santen* view of a product as an active ingredient. Naturally, this difference in approach has enormous effects, in the *Shire* case opening up broader protection possibilities in orphan designations, while in the *Abraxis* and *Santen* closing the door to second medical indication SPCs.

In this regard, it is also interesting to note the recent *Medac* T549/19 case, where the General Court delimits the scope of substances that could constitute 'satisfactory methods', thus also extending the possibilities for an orphan drug designation.[211] Once more, off-label use of pharmaceuticals seems to have a limited (if any) effect on the protection granted by an orphan drug designation, strengthening thus its protection. The strengthened protection of orphan drugs vis-à-vis off-label use, also constitutes an example of cases where orphan drugs may in fact enjoy a broader protection than patented pharmaceuticals.

The interchangeable terms and concepts, deviations in definitions and a lack of coherence in the system have unfortunately not ended with the drafting of these regulations. The CJEU, vested with the task of vital importance for the future of the system as whole, perceives these different regulations as isolated islands rather than parts of a whole, of a system that operates on one market and where stakeholders in one most probably have a strategic interest in the other.

The roles of objectives, their flaws or misrepresentations and their tendency to mutate naturally have a decisive impact on the outcome of the effectiveness test. There is no better way to express this than with the following quote:

> The doctrine of the law then is this: that precedents and rules must be followed, unless flatly absurd or unjust: for though their reason be not obvious at first view, yet we owe such a deference to former times as not to suppose they acted wholly without consideration.
>
> William Blackstone, *Commentaries on the Laws of England*

---

[210] See n 201, paras 30–31.
[211] Judgment of the General Court (Tenth Chamber) of 23 September 2020, *Medac Gesellschaft für klinische Spezialpräparate v Commission*, T-549/19, EU:T:2020:444.

BIBLIOGRAPHY

Official Publications

Abbott Laboratories' SPC Application, Patent Office (Mr R J Walker): 25 July 2002 [2004] RPC 20

Bock A-K, Rodriguez-Cerezo E, Hüsing B, et al, '*Human tissue-engineered products: Potential socio-economic impacts of a new European regulatory framework for authorisation, supervision and vigilance*', Synthesis report Eur 21838 EN, Institute for Prospective Technology Studies (Seville) [2005] 1–58

Checchini P, 'The Cost of Non-Agencies with Relevance to the Internal Market' (EU Parliament 2016)

Commission of the European Communities, '*Guideline on aspects of the application of Article 8(2) of Regulation (EC) No 141/2000 of the European Parliament and of the Council: Review of the period of market exclusivity of orphan medicinal products*', COM [2008] 4051 final

Commission of the European Communities, '*Guideline on aspects of the application of Article 8(1) and (3) of Regulation (EC) No 141/2000: Assessing similarity of medicinal products versus authorised orphan medicinal products benefiting from market exclusivity and applying derogations from that market exclusivity*', COM [2008] 4077 final

Commission of the European Communities, *An industrial competitiveness policy for the European chemical industry: an example. Communication from the Commission to the Council, the European Parliament and the Economic and Social Committee*, COM [96] 187 final

Commission of the European Communities, *Commission Communication to the Council and the Parliament on the Outlines of an Industrial Policy for the Pharmaceutical Sector in the European Community* COM [93] 718

Commission of the European Communities, *Commission Staff Working Document on the experience acquired as a result of the application of Regulation (EC) No 141/2000 on orphan medicinal products and account of the public health benefits obtained* SEC [2006] 832

Commission of the European Communities, *Communication from the Commission concerning a programme of Community action on rare diseases within the framework or action in the field of public health*, COM [97] 225 final

Commission of the European Communities, *Communication from the Commission to the Council and the European Parliament on the Outlines of an industrial policy for the pharmaceutical sector*, COM [93] 718 final

Commission of the European Communities, *Communication from the Commission, Action plan 'Simplifying and improving the regulatory environment*', COM (2002) 278 final

Commission of the European Communities, *Communication on the Framework for Action in the Field of Public Health*, COM [93] 559 final

Commission of the European Communities, *Communication on the Single Market in Pharmaceuticals*, COM [1998] 588 final

Commission of the European Communities, *Pharmaceuticals in the European Union, Commission of the European Communities, Enterprise Directorate-General*, Brussels, 2000

Commission of the European Communities, *Proposal for a Council Regulation (EEC) concerning the creation of a supplementary protection certificate for medicinal products*, COM [90] 101 final – SYN 255

Commission of the European Communities, *Proposal for a European Parliament and Council Regulation (EC) on orphan medicinal products* COM [1998] 450 final

Commission of the European Communities, *Proposal for a Regulation of the European Parliament and of the Council laying down Community procedures for the authorisation and supervision of medicinal products for human and veterinary use and establishing a European Agency for the Evaluation of Medicinal Products* COM (2001) 404 final

Committee on Legal Affairs, *Compromise amendments on the draft report on supplementary protection certificate for medicinal products* [2019] 2018/0161(COD)

Completing the Internal Market: White Paper from the Commission to the European Council (Milan, 28–29 June 1985), COM (85) 310, Vol 1985/0130

Consumer's Consultative Commission, *Resolution of the Consumers' Consultative Commission Concerning the European Agency for the Evaluation of Medicinal Products* [1991] Brussels

De Jongh T, Radauer A, Bostyn S and Poort J, *Effects of supplementary protection mechanisms for pharmaceutical products* (Technopolis Group) Final report, May 2018

Economic and Social Committee, '*Opinion on the Proposal for a Council Regulation (EEC) Laying Down Community Procedures for the Authorisation and Supervision of Medicinal Products for Human Veterinary Use and Establishing a European Agency for the Evaluation of Medicinal Products*', Official Journal of the European Communities [1991] 91/C 269/84

ECORYS, *How well does regulation work? The cases of paediatric medicines*

EFPIA, *Completing the Internal Market for Pharmaceuticals* (Brussels 1998)

EFPIA, *Delivering High Quality Health Care in the European Union – Policy Concerns for the Pharmaceuticals industry* (Brussels 1996)

EFPIA, *EFPIA Comments on the New Proposals Contained in Preliminary Draft Rev 5* (Brussels 1992a)

EFPIA, *Memorandum on an Industrial Policy for the European Pharmaceutical Industry* (EFPIA III3485/92) (Brussels 1992b)

European Agency for the Evaluation of Medicinal Products, *Report on the expert round table on the difficulties related to the use of new medicinal products in children held on 18 December 1997* [1998] EMEA/27164/98 Rev 1

European Association of Euro-Pharmaceutical Companies, *Response to Consultation Paper by European Association of Euro-Pharmaceutical Companies (EAEPC)*, Brussels, 2001 COM [2015] 216 final

European Commission, *A Guideline on Changing the Classification for the Supply of a Medicinal Product for Human Use* (Revision January 2006)

European Commission, *A Guideline on Summary of Product Characteristics* (SmPC), September 2009

European Commission, *An evaluation of the European Medicines Agency*, January 2010

European Commission, *Assessing the economic impacts of changing exemption provisions during patent and SPC protection in Europe*, Charles River Associates, February 2016

European Commission, *Better Medicines for Children from Concept to Reality: Progress Report on the Paediatric Regulation (EC) N°1901/2006* COM (2013) 443 Final

European Commission, *Commission Guideline – Guidance on posting and publication of result-related information on clinical trials in relation to the implementation of Article 57(2) of Regulation (EC) No 726/2004* [2012] C/302/03

European Commission, *Commission Implementing Decision of 11 January 2012 refusing the designation of 'Tecovirimat' as an orphan medicinal product under Regulation (EC) No 141/2000 of the European Parliament and of the Council*, COM [2011] 10128 final

European Commission, *Commission notice on the application of Articles 3, 5 and 7 of Regulation (EC) No 141/2000 on orphan medicinal products* [2016] OJ C 424/03

European Commission, *Commission Staff Working Document: Better Regulation Guidelines* SWD [2017] 350

European Commission, *Commission Staff Working Document: Investing in health: Social investment package* SWD [2013] 43 final

European Commission, *Communication from the Commission on Regulation (EC) No 141/2000 of the European Parliament and of the Council on orphan medicinal products* [2003] OJ C 178/02

European Commission, *Communication from the Commission to the European Parliament and the Council: Proposal for an Interinstitutional Agreement on Better Regulation*

260 Bibliography

European Commission, *Communication from the Commission to the European Parliament, the Council, the European Economic and Social Committee and the Committee of the Regions: Completing the Better Regulation Agenda: Better solutions for better results* COM [2017] 651 final

European Commission, *Communication from the Commission to the European Parliament, the Council, the European Economic and Social Committee and the Committee of the Regions: The principles of subsidiarity and proportionality: Strengthening their role in the EU's policymaking* COM [2018] 703

European Commission, *Communication from the Commission to the European Parliament, the European Council and the Council, Better Regulation: Delivering better results for a stronger Union* [2016] 615 final

European Commission, *Communication from the Commission to the European Parliament, the Council, the European Economic and Social Committee and the Committee of the Regions: Better regulation for better results – An EU agenda* COM [2015] 215 final

European Commission, *Communication from the Commission: Guideline on the format and content of applications for agreement or modification of a paediatric investigation plan and requests for waivers or deferrals and concerning the operation of the compliance check and on criteria for assessing significant studies (Text with EEA relevance)* [2014] OJ C-338/1

European Commission, *Communication to the European Parliament, the Council, the European Economic and Social Committee and the committee of the Regions, Upgrading the Single Market: more opportunities for people and business*, COM [2015] 550 final

European Commission, *Ethical Considerations for Clinical Trials on Medicinal Products Conducted with the Paediatric Population: Recommendations of the ad hoc group for the development of implementing guidelines for Directive 2001/20/EC relating to good clinical practice in the conduct of clinical trials on medicinal products for human use (2006)*, Final text published [2008]

European Commission, *Final Report of the Pharmaceutical Sector Inquiry*, 8 July 2009

European Commission, *Guide to the Case Law of the European Court of Justice, on Articles 56 et seq TFEU: Freedom to Provide Services*

European Commission, *Guide to the Comprehensive Economic and Trade Agreement (CETA)* [2017]

European Commission, *Guideline on the format and content of applications for designation as orphan medicinal products and on the transfer of designations from one Sponsor to another* [2014] ENTR/6283/00 Rev 4

European Commission, *Guidelines of 22.11.2017 Good Manufacturing Practice for Advanced Therapy Medicinal Products*, COM [2017] 7694 final

European Commission, *Guidelines relating to the application of the Council Directive 90/385/EEC on Active Implantable Medical Devices, the Council Directive 93/42/EEC on Medical Devices*, MEDDEV 2. 1/3 rev 3

European Commission, *Impact assessment accompanying the document 'Proposal for a Regulation of the European Parliament and of the Council establishing a Health for Growth Programme, the third programme of EU action in the field of health for the period 2014–2020'* (Commission Staff Working Paper) SEC [2011] 1322

European Commission, *Inauguration of the European Agency for the Evaluation of Medicinal Products* (Press Release) 26 January 1995

European Commission, *Inspection of Tissue and Cell Procurement and Tissue Establishment, Operational Guidelines* Ref. Ares [2015] 1822725

European Commission, *Joint practical guide of the European Parliament, the Council and the Commission for persons involved in the drafting of European Union legislation* (EU publication, Publications Office of the European Union, Luxembourg 2015)

European Commission, *Notice to Applicants: Volume 2A Procedures for marketing authorisation Chapter 1 Marketing Authorisation* [2013]

European Commission, *Notice to applicants: Volume 2A Procedures for marketing Chapter 1 Marketing Authorisation*, November 2005

European Commission, *Proposal for a Regulation of the European Parliament and of the Council amending Regulation (EC) No 469/2009 concerning the supplementary protection certificate for medicinal products*, COM [2018] 317 final, 2018/0161 (COD)

European Commission, *Regulation (EC) No 1394/2007 on Advanced Therapy Medicinal Products: Summary of Responses to the Public Consultation* [2013] SANCO/D5/RSR/iv ddg1.d5

European Commission, *Report from the Commission to the Council on the Activities of the Committee for Proprietary Medicinal Products* COM [88] 143 final

European Commission, *Report from the Commission to the European Parliament and the Council in accordance with Article 59(4) of Directive 2001/83/EC of the European Parliament and of the Council of 6 November 2001 on the Community code relating to medicinal products for human use*, COM [2017] 135 final

European Commission, *Report from the Commission to the European Parliament and the Council in accordance with Article 25 of Regulation (EC) No 1394/2007 of the European Parliament and of the Council on advanced therapy medicinal products and amending Directive 2001/83/EC and Regulation (EC) No 726/2004*, COM [2014] 188

European Commission, *Report from the Commission: Annual Report 2017 on the Application of the Principles of Subsidiarity and Proportionality* COM [2018] 490 final

European Commission, *Standards, Measurements and Testing: Fourth Framework Programme for Research and Technological Development (1994-1998)*

European Commission, *Study on the economic impact of supplementary protection certificates, pharmaceutical incentives and rewards in Europe*, Final report (May 2018), Copenhagen Economics

European Commission, *Study on the Legal Aspects of Supplementary Protection Certificates in the EU*, Final Report [2018] Max Planck Institute for Innovation and Competition

European Commission, *Targeted stakeholder consultation on the development of Good Manufacturing Practice for Advanced Therapy Medicinal Products pursuant to Article 5 of Regulation 1394/2007*

European Commission, *Together for Health: A Strategic Approach for the EU 2008-2013* (White Paper) IP/07/1571

European Commission, *Volume 2A, Procedures for marketing authorisation Chapter 2 Mutual Recognition February 2007*, Brussels, ENTR/F2/ SM

European Medical Agency, *Committee for Advanced Therapies (CAT) Rules of Procedure* [2020] EMA/CAT/454446/2008 rev. 3, Committee for Advanced Therapies

European Medical Agency, *Committee for Advanced Therapies (CAT) Rules of Procedure* [2020] EMA/CAT/454446/2008 rev. 3 Committee for Advanced Therapies

European Medical Agency, *Pharmacovigilance Risk Assessment Committee Rules of Procedure* [2020] EMA/PRAC/567515/2012 Rev.2

European Medicine Agency, *ICH Topic M 4 Common Technical Document for the Registration of Pharmaceuticals for Human Use – Organisation CTD, ICH Topic M 4 Common Technical Document for the Registration of Pharmaceuticals for Human Use – Organisation CTD* [2004] (CPMP/ICH/2887/99)

European Medicines Agency, *5-year Report to the European Commission. General report on the experience acquired as a result of the application of the Paediatric Regulation* [2012] EMA/428172/2012

European Medicines Agency, *Committee for Medicinal Products for Veterinary Use: Rules of Procedure* [2020] EMA/CVMP/422/04 Rev 2 EMA/MB/47098/2007

European Medicines Agency, *Committee for Medicinal Products for Veterinary Use (CVMP) Work Plan 2020* [2019] EMA/CVMP/505315/2019

European Medicines Agency, *Committee for Orphan Medicinal Products (COMP): Work Plan 2020 Adopted by the Committee on 22 January 2020* [2020] EMA/COMP/478696/2019 Inspections, Human Medicines Pharmacovigilance and Committees Division

European Medicines Agency, *Committee for Orphan Medicinal Products (COMP) meeting report on the review of applications for orphan designation* [2014], EMA/COMP/737192/2014, Committee for Orphan Medicinal Products (COMP)

European Medicines Agency, *COMP Report to the Commission in relation to art 10 of Regulation (EC) No 141/2000 on Orphan Medicinal Products* [2005] EMA/35218/2005

European Medicines Agency, *EMA action plan related to the European Commission's recommendations on product information* [2017] EMA/680018/2017

European Medicines Agency, *European Medicines Agency guidance for applicants seeking scientific advice and protocol assistance* [2017], EMA/4260/2001 Rev 9, Product Development Scientific Support Department

European Medicines Agency, *European Medicines Agency policy on publication of clinical data for medicinal products for human use*, EMA/144064/2019

European Medicines Agency, *Guideline on Safety and Efficacy Follow-up Risk management of ATMPS* [2008] Doc Ref EMEA/149995/2008

European Medicines Agency, *How to better apply the Paediatric Regulation to boost development of medicines for children: Report on a multi-stakeholder workshop held at EMA on 20 March 2018*

European Medicines Agency, *Human Medicines Evaluation Division European Medicines Agency pre-authorisation procedural advice for users of the centralised procedure* [2020] EMA/821278/2015

European Medicines Agency, *ICH E11(R1) guideline on clinical investigation of medicinal products in the pediatric population* [2017], EMA/CPMP/ICH/2711/1999

European Medicines Agency, *Paediatric Gaucher disease: A strategic collaborative approach from EMA and FDA* [2017], EMA/237265/2017

European Medicines Agency, *Points to consider on the calculation and reporting of the prevalence of a condition for Orphan Designation* [2019], EMA/COMP/436/01 Rev. 1 Committee for Orphan Medicinal Products (COMP)

European Medicines Agency, *Post-orphan Medicinal Product Designation Procedures. Guidance for sponsors* [2020], Rev.7 EMA/469917/2018. Human Medicines Research and Development Support

European Medicines Agency, *Procedural advice on appeal procedure for orphan medicinal product designation or review of orphan designation criteria at the time of Marketing Authorisation* [2013] EMA/2677/01 Rev. 2

European Medicines Agency, *Questions and answers on the European Medicines Agency policy on publication of clinical data for medicinal products for human use* [2019] EMA/357536/2014, Rev. 2

European Medicines Agency, *Recommendation of the Pediatric Committee to the European Commission regarding the symbol* [2007], Doc Ref: EMEA/498247/2007

European Medicines Agency, *Recommendations on elements required to support the medical plausibility and the assumption of significant benefit for an orphan designation* [2010] EMA/COMP/15893/2009 Final Committee for Orphan Medicinal Products (COMP)

European Medicines Agency, *Reflection paper on classification of advanced therapy medicinal products* [2015] EMA/CAT/600280/2010 rev. 1, Committee for Advanced Therapies (CAT)

European Medicines Agency, *Relevant sources for Orphan Disease Prevalence Data* [2014], EMA/452415/2012 Rev. 1 Human Medicines Research and Development Support

European Medicines Agency, *Report to the European Commission on companies and products that have benefited from any of the rewards and incentives in the Paediatric Regulation and on companies that have failed to comply with any of the obligations in this regulation* [2014], EMA/24516/2014 Corr. 3

European Medicines Agency, *Rules of procedure of the Paediatric Committee (PDCO)* [2020] EMA/348440/2008 Rev.2 Paediatric Committee (PDCO)

European Medicines Agency, *Significant benefit of orphan drugs: concepts and future developments* [2012], EMA/326061/2012, Human Medicines Development and Evaluation

European Medicines Agency, *Summary of Opinion (initial authorisation): Aubagio* [2013] EMA/379992/2013 Committee for Medicinal Products for Human Use (CHMP)

European Medicines Agency, *Summary of Opinion (initial authorisation) Tecfidera DImethyl fumarate* [2013] EMA/167897/2013/Rev 2 Committee for Medicinal Products for Human Use (CHMP)

European Medicines Agency, *The European paediatric initiative: History of the Paediatric Regulation* [2007] Doc. Ref:EMEA/17967/04 Rev 1

European Medicines Agency, *Working Group on Clinical Trials conducted outside of the EU/EEA Reflection paper on ethical and GCP aspects of clinical trials of medicinal products for human use conducted outside of the EU/EEA and submitted in marketing authorisation applications to the EU Regulatory Authorities* 16 April 2012 EMA/121340/2011

European Parliament, *Legislative Resolution (Cooperation Procedure: First Reading) Embodying the Opinion of the European Parliament on the Commission Proposal for a Council Regulation Concerning the Creation of a Supplementary Protection Certificate for Medicinal Products* [1991a] OJ CO, 19 28 January 1991:95

European Parliament, *Medicinal Products in the European Union: The legal framework for medicines for human use* [2015], PE 554.174

Guide de Légistique de France (3e Edition, La Documentation française, Paris 2017)

IMS Institute for Healthcare Informatics, *Declining Medicine Use and Costs: For Better or Worse? A Review of the Use of Medicines in the United States in 2012*, May 2013

Medical Device Coordination Group, *Guidance on the renewal of designation and monitoring of notified bodies under Directives 90/385/EEC and 93/42/EEC to be performed in accordance with Commission Implementing Regulation (EU) 2020/666 amending Commission Implementing Regulation (EU) 920/2013*, MDCG 2020-11, May 2020

Medicines for Europe, *Comparison of expiry dates of protection worldwide*

Medicines Law & Policy, 'Orphan Medicinal Products in the European Union: Briefing Document', June 2019

Mestre-Ferrandiz J, Sussex J and Adrian and Towse, *The R&D cost of a new medicine* (Office of Health Economics 2012)

Mikolášik M, 'Report on the on the proposal for a regulation of the European Parliament and of the Council on advanced therapy medicinal products and amending Directive 2001/83/EC and Regulation (EC) No 726/2004' COM [2005] 0567 – OJ C6-0401/2005–2005/0227(COD), Committee on the Environment, Public Health and Food Safety

NCC, *Balancing Acts – Conflict of Interest in the Regulation of Medicine. London: National Consumer Office* [1993]

OECD, *Improving Forecasting of Pharmaceutical Spending Insights from 23 OECD and EU Countries: Analytical Report* [2019]

OECD, *Improving Policy Instruments through Impact Assessment* [2001] SIGMA Papers, No 31, OECD Publishing, Paris

Office of Technology Assessment, *Patent-Term Extension and the Pharmaceutical Industry* [August 1981]

'*Orphan drugs and advanced therapies*', Final report, Client: Ministry of Health, Welfare and Sport Rotterdam [2015]

Principles of Interactions between EMA and FDA Pediatric Therapeutics [June 2007]

Pugatch Consilium, *Benchmarking Success: Evaluating the Orphan Regulation and Its impact on Patients and Rare Disease, R&D in the European Union* [2019]

UK Intellectual Property Office, '*Applicant: Cerus Corporation Issue: Whether applications SPC/GB/07/043 and SPC/GB/07/044 meet the requirements of Article 2 and Article 3(b) of the Regulation*', BL O/14/14

Books

Abbott F M and Dukes G, *Global Pharmaceutical Policy* (Edward Elgar 2009)

Barral P E, *Ten Years of Results in Pharmaceutical Research Throughout the World (1975–1984)* (Prospective et Sante Publique 1985)

Brückner C, *Supplementary Protection Certificates with Paediatric Extension of Duration* (2nd ed, Heymanns 2015)

Flear M L, Farrell A, Hervey T K, and Murphy T, *European Law and New Health Technologies* (Oxford University Press 2013)

Hartley T, *The Foundations of European Community Law: An Introduction to the Constitutional and Administrative Law of the European Community* (Clarendon Press 1994)

Hervey T K and McHale J V, *Law in Context: Health Law and the European Union* (Cambridge University Press 2004)
Howells G, *The Tobacco Challenge: Legal Policy and Consumer Protection* (Ashgate Publishing 2011)
Jørgensen K E (ed), *Reflective Approaches to European Governance* (Palgrave Macmillan 1997)
Klaassen C D, Casarett and Doull's Toxicology: *The Basic Science of Poisons* (8th ed, McGraw-Hill Education 2013)
Manley M I and Vickers M, *Navigating European Pharmaceutical Law* (Oxford University Press 2015)
Meuwese A C M, *Impact Assessment in EU Lawmaking* (Wolters Kluwer 2008)
Mosialos E, Mrazek M M and Walley T (eds), *Regulating Pharmaceuticals in Europe: Striving for Efficiency, Equity and Quality* (European Observatory on Health Systems and Policies Series Maidenhead, Open University Press 2004)
Mossialos E et al, *Health Systems Governance in Europe: The Role of EU Law and Policy* (Cambridge University Press 2010)
Mousmouti M, *Designing Effective Legislation* (Edward Elgar Publishing 2019)
Oortwijn W J, Horlings E, Anton S, et al, *Extended Impact Assessment of a Draft EC Regulation on Medicinal Products for Paediatric Use* (Rand 2004)
Permanand G, *EU Pharmaceutical Regulation: The Politics of Policy-Making* (European Policy Research Unit Series, Manchester University Press 2006)
Scherer F M, *Industry Structure, Strategy, and Public Policy* (Prentice Hall 1996)
Shorthose S, *Guide to EU Pharmaceutical Regulatory Law* (7th ed, Wolters Kluwer 2017)
Thumm N, *Intellectual Property Rights: National Systems and Harmonisation in Europe* (Springer 2000)
Waxman H A and Green J, *The Waxman Report: How Congress Really Works* (Twelve 2009)

Journal Articles and Other Sources

Abraham J and Lewis G, 'Secrecy and Transparency of Medicines Licensing in the EU' [1998] *The Lancet*, 352 (9126), 480–82
Albrecht H, 'Experiences with PIPs and their required revisions on the critical path of the development of medicines in indications for adult patients', Master of Drugs Regulatory Affairs, Bonn [2013] Available at https://dgra.de/media/pdf/studium/masterthesis/master_albrecht_h.pdf [last accessed on 20 January 2021]
Annon A, 'A Drug Tzar is Born', *The Economist*, 7 May 1994, 74
Armitage R A, 'The Hatch-Waxman Act: A Path Forward for Making it More Modern' [2014] 40 *William Mitchell Law Review*, 4, 1200–58
Arunasalam V C and De Corte F, 'Supplementary Protection Certificates for Plant Protection Products: The Story of "The Ugly Duckling"' [2016] 11 *Journal of Intellectual Property Law & Practice*, 11, 833–40
Banzi R, Bertele V, Demotes-Mainard J et al, 'Fostering EMA's Transparency Policy' [2014] 25 *European Journal of Internal Medicine*, 8, 681–84
Bowmann G, 'Legislation and Explanation' [2000], *Loophole* 5
Brougher J T, 'The Biosimilars Act: Promoting or Discouraging the Development of Generic Biologics?' [2010] 7 *Biotechnology Healthcare*, Winter, 10, 22–23
Burk D L, 'Patents as Data Aggregators in Personalized Medicine' [2015] 21 *Boston University Journal of Science and Technology Law*, 2, UC Irvine School of Law Research Paper No 2015–47
Cockburn I M, Jean O Lanjouw and Mark Schankerman, 'Patents and the Global Diffusion of New Drugs' [2016] 106 *American Economic Review*, 1, 136–64
Coen J P V L and Xanthaki H, 'Legal Transplants and Comparative Concepts: Eclecticism Defeated?' [2013] 34 *Statute Law Review*, 2, 128–37
Crosby S, 'The New Tobacco Control Directive: An Illiberal and Illegal Disdain for the Law' [2002] 27 *European Law Review*, 2, 177–93

Dagg N, Baldwin S and Rollins Dr T, 'From Takeda to Teva v Merck: Are we Treading the Right Path on Combination Product SPCs? (Part 2)' [2017] 39 *European Intellectual Property Review*, 11, 697–704

Danzon P M, Epstein A, Nicholson S, 'Mergers and Acquisitions in the Pharmaceutical and Biotech Industries' [2007] 28 *Managerial and Decision Economics*, 4–5, 307–28

Danzon P M, Wang Y R and Wang L, 'The Impact of Price Regulation on the Launch Delay of New Drugs – Evidence from Twenty-Five Major Markets in the 1990s' [2005] 14 *Health Economics*, 269–92

De Benedetto M, 'Effective Law from a Regulatory and Administrative Law Perspective' [2018] 9 *European Journal of Risk Regulation*, 3, 391–415

Dehousse R, 'Regulation by Networks in the European Community: The Role of European Agencies' [1997] 4 *Journal of European Public Policy*, 2, 246–61

Dickson M and Gagnon J P, 'Key Factors in the Rising Cost of New Drug Discovery and Development' [2004] 3 *Nature Reviews Drug Discovery*, 5, 417–29

DiMasi J A, Grabowski H G and Hansen R W, 'Innovation in the Pharmaceutical Industry: New Estimates of R&D Costs' [2016] 47 *Journal of Health Economics*, 20–33

DiMasi J A, Grabowski H G and Hansen R W, 'The Price of Innovation: New Estimates of Drug Development Costs' [2003] 22 *Journal of Health Economics*, 151–85

DiMasi J A, Kim J, Getz K A, 'The Impact of Collaborative and Risk-Sharing Innovation Approaches on Clinical and Regulatory Cycle Times' [2014] 48 *Therapeutic Innovation and Regulatory Science* (SAGE Journals), 4, 482–87

Faulkner A, 'Regulatory Policy as Innovation: Constructing Rules of Engagement of a Technological Zone for Tissue Engineering in the European Union' [2009] 38 *Research Policy*, 4, 637–46

Franco P, 'Orphan Drugs: The Regulatory Environment' [2013] 18 *Drug Discovery Today*, 163–72

Fregonese L, Greene L, Hofer M, et al, 'Demonstrating Significant Benefit of Orphan Medicines: Analysis of 15 Years of Experience in Europe' [2018] 23 *Drug Discovery Today*, 1, 90–100

García A L, 'Is the Copy Better than the Original? The Regulation of Orphan Drugs: a US–EU Comparative Perspective' [2004] Academic Thesis, Harvard Law School

Griffin T D, 'Policies on Drugs in the New Europe' [1990] *British Medical Journal* 1536

H Berlin and Bengt Jönsson, 'International Dissemination of New Drugs: A Comparative Study of Six Countries' [1986] 7 *Managerial and Decision Economics*, 4, 235–42

Herder M, 'What is the Purpose of the Orphan Drug Act?' [2017] 14 *PLoS Medicine*, 1, 1–4

Hervey T, 'Up in Smoke? Community (Anti) Tobacco Law and Policy' [2001] 26 *European Law Review*, 2, 101–25

Hughes-Wilson W, Palma A, Schuurman A, et al, 'Paying for the Orphan Drug System: Break or Bend? Is it Time for a New Evaluation System for Payers in Europe to Take Account of New Rare Disease Treatments?' [2012] 7 *Orphanet Journal of Rare Diseases*, 74

Iglesias-López C, Agustí A, Obach M et al, 'Regulatory Framework for Advanced Therapy Medicinal Products in Europe and United States' [2019] 10 *Frontiers in Pharmacology*, available at www.frontiersin.org/articles/10.3389/fphar.2019.00921/pdf [last accessed on 20 January 2021]

Jones E, 'On the Relevance of Supplementary Plant Protection Certificates on the Basis of Marketing Authorisations for Combination Products' [2011] *GRUR International* 1017

Kidd D, 'The International Conference on Harmonization of Pharmaceutical Regulations, the European Medicines Evaluation Agency, and the FDA: Who's Zooming Who?' [1996] 4 *Indiana Journal of Global Legal Studies*, 1, 183–206

Kingham R F, Bogaert P W L, Eddy P S, 'The New European Medicines Agency' [1994] 49 *Food and Drug Law Journal*, 2, 301–22

Kumm M, 'Constitutionalising Subsidiarity in Integrated Markets: The Case of Tobacco Regulation in the European Union' [2006] 12 *European Law Journal*, 4, 503–33

Kyle M and Qian Y, 'Intellectual Property Rights and Access to Innovation: Evidence from Trips' [2014] NBER Working Paper No w20799

Kyle M, 'Economic Analysis of Supplementary Protection Certificates in Europe', 30 January 2017, available at https://ec.europa.eu/info/publications/economic-analysis-supplementary-protection-certificates-europe_en [last accessed on 20 January 2021]

Laeken Declaration on the Future of the European Union, adopted by the Heads of State and Government at the Laeken Summit, 14–15 December 2001, Bulletin of the European Union. 2001, No 12. Luxembourg: Office for Official Publications of the European Communities. 'Presidency Conclusions of the Laeken European Council (14 and 15 December 2001)' 19–23

Liu H-W, 'Harmonizing the Internal Market, or Public Health? – Revisiting Case C-491/01 (British American Tobacco) and Case C-380/03 (Tobacco Advertising II)' [2009] 15 *Columbia Journal European Law Online*, 41

Lundberg E and Hysing E, 'The Value of Participation: Exploring the Role of Public Consultations from the Vantage Point of Interest Groups' [2015] 39 *Scandinavian Political Studies*, 1, 1–21

Luzzatto L, Hyry H I, Schieppati A, et al 'Outrageous Prices of Orphan Drugs: A Call for Collaboration' [2018], 392 *Lancet*,10149, 791–94

MacNaughton G and Forman L, 'The Value of Mainstreaming Human Rights into Health Impact Assessment' [2014] 11 *International Journal of Environmental Research and Public Health*, 10, 10076–90

Mansnérus J, 'Commercialisation of Advanced Therapies. A Study of the EU Regulation on Advanced Medical Products' [2016] Academic Dissertation, University of Helsinki

Mansnérus J, 'Encountering Challenges with the EU Regulation on Advance Therapy Medical Products' [2015] 22 *European Journal of Health Law*, 5, 426–61

Marketletter, 'EC Drugs Move: Recipe for Disaster' [1989] 2 July, p 6

Matthews D, 'Patenting Strategies and Competition Law in the Pharmaceutical Sector: Implications for Access to Medicines' [2016] 38 *European Review of Intellectual Property*, 11, 661–67

Mazer E H, 'Supplementary Protection Certificates in the European Economic Community' [1993], 48 *Food & Drug Law Journal*, 4, 571–74

Mikami K, 'Orphans in the Market: The History of Orphan Drug Policy' [2017] 32 *Social History of Medicine*, 3, 609–30

Miller H I, 'Sick Process' [1999] *Hoover Digest*, No 1

Miller J, 'A Typology of Legal Transplants: Using Sociology, Legal History and Argentine Examples to Explain the Transplant Process' [2013] 51 *The American Journal of Comparative Law*, 4, 839–85

Mossialos E and McKee M, 'Is a European Healthcare Policy Emerging?' [2001] 323 *BMJ* (Clinical research ed), 7307, 248

Mousmouti M, 'Effectiveness as an Aspect of Quality of EU Legislation: Is It Feasible?' [2014] 2 *The Theory and Practice of Legislation*, 3, 309–27

Mousmouti M, 'Making Legislative Effectiveness an Operational Concept: Unfolding the Effectiveness Test as a Conceptual Tool for Lawmaking' [2018] 9 *European Journal of Risk Regulation*, 3, 445–64

Mousmouti M, 'Operationalising Quality of Legislation through the Effectiveness Test' [2012] 6 *Legisprudence*, 2, 192–105

Papadopoulou F, 'Supplementary Protection Certificates: Still a Grey Area?' [2016] 11 *Journal of Intellectual Property Law and Practice*, 5, 372–81

Papadopoulou F, 'Legal Transplants and Modern Lawmaking in the Field of Pharmaceutical Patents' [2016] 47 *International Review of Intellectual Property and Competition Law*, 8, 891–911

Piatkiewicz T J, Traulsen J M and Holm-Larsen T, 'Risk-Sharing Agreements in the EU: A Systematic Review of Major Trends' [2017] 2 *PharmacoEconomics Open*, 2, 109–23

Pirnay J-P, Vanderkelen A, et al, 'Business Oriented EU Human Cell and Tissue Product Legislation will Adversely Impact Member States' Health Care Systems' [2013] 14 *Cell Tissue Bank*, 4, 525–605

Pugatch M, 'Measuring the Strength of National Pharmaceutical Intellectual Property Regimes: Creating a New Pharmaceutical IP Index' [2006] 9 *Journal of World Intellectual Property*, 4, 373–91

Renner M, Anliker B, Sanzenbacher R, et al, 'Regulation of Clinical Trials with Advanced Therapy Medicinal Products in Germany' [2015] 871 *Advances in Experimental Medicine and Biology*, 87–101

Ross W, 'It's no FDA – Maybe it Even Works a Little Better, an Interview with Brian P Ager, Director General of the European Federation of Pharmaceutical Industries and Associations' [2000] 35 *Medical Marketing and Media*, 8, 61–67

Santoro A, Genov G, Spooner A, et al, 'Promoting and Protecting Public Health: How the European Union Pharmacovigilance System Works' [2017] 40 *Drug Safety*, 10, 855–69

Sauner-Leroy J-B, 'The impact of the implementation of the Single Market Programme on productive efficiency and on mark-ups in the European Union manufacturing industry' [2003] *European Economy-Economic Papers 2008-2015*, 192, Directorate General Economic and Financial Affairs (DG ECFIN), European Commission

Schell J, 'Neurim: A New Definition of "Product" in Supplementary Protection Certificates?' [2013] 8 *Journal of Intellectual Property Law & Practice*, 9, 723–28

Spamann H, 'Contemporary Legal Transplants. Legal Families and the Diffusion of (Corporate) Law' [2009] Harvard Law School, Discussion Paper No 28

Toebes B and Herrmann J R, 'The European Union and Health and Human Rights' [2011] *European Human Rights Law Review*, No 4, 419–36

Tuominen N, 'An IP Perspective on Defensive Patenting Strategies of the EU Pharmaceutical Industry' [2012] 34 *European Intellectual Property Review*, 8, 541–51

Turner S, Nunn A J, Fielding K, et al, 'Adverse Drug Reactions to Unlicensed and Off-label Drugs on Paediatric Awards: A Prospective Study' [1999] 88 *Acta Paediatrica*, 9, 965–68

Van der Brink M, 'Justice, Legitimacy and the Authority of Legislation within the European Union' [2019] 82 *Modern Law Review*, 2, 293–318

Vidal-Quadras M, 'Analysis of EU Regulation 2019/933 on the SPC Manufacturing Waiver Exception' [2019] 50 *International Review of Intellectual Property and Competition Law*, 1, 971–1005

Vogel D, 'The Globalization of Pharmaceutical Regulation' [1998] 11 *Governance; An International Journal of Policy and Administration*, 1, 1–22

Walsh K, 'Promoting Harmonisation Across the European Patent System Through Judicial Dialogue and Cooperation' [2019] 50 *International Review of Intellectual Property and Competition Law*, 408–40

Watson A, 'Legal Transplants and European Private Law' [2000] 4 *Electronic Journal of Comparative Law*, 4

Weatherill S, 'The Limits of Legislative Harmonization Ten Years after Tobacco Advertising: How the Court's Case Law has become a "Drafting Guide"' [2011] 12 *German Law Journal* 03, 827–64

Wertheimer A, 'Off-label Prescribing of Drugs for Children' [2011] 6 *Current Drug Safety*, 1, 46–48

Wyatt D, 'Community Competence to Regulate the Internal Market' [2007] Oxford Legal Studies Research Paper, No 9/2007

Xanthaki H, 'An Enlightened Approach to Legislative Scrutiny: Focusing on Effectiveness' 9 *European Journal of Risk Regulation* [2019] 3, 431–44

Ydreskog M, 'Opting Out of the Unified Patent Court and "Opting In". Reflections from a Patent Attorney Perspective' [2014] *Nordiskt Immateriellt Rättsskydd* 104–06

Yüksel K and Tuğlular I, 'Critical Review of European Medicines Agency (EMA) Assessment Report and Related Literature on Domperidone' [2019] 41 *International Journal of Clinical Pharmacy*, 387–90

Zamboni M, 'Legislative Policy and Effectiveness: A (Small) Contribution from Legal Theory' [2018] 9 *European Journal of Risk Regulation*, 3, 416–30

INDEX

active ingredients:
    active substance as, 112–13 (case law)
    basic patent protects, 121–2 (case law)
    definition, 88
    medicinal products and, identical, 113, 132
    patent protection certificate for, 108–9 (case law)
    SPC application granted for, 112 (case law)
active substances:
    active ingredient as, 112–13 (case law)
    definition, 88
    medical products, different from, 256, 257 (case law)
    similarities between, 174
advanced therapy medicinal products (ATMPs), 50, 183–95
    authorisation of, 247
    classification of, 188–9
    combined, 187–8
    GMPs and, 193
    legislation covering, 189–90
    MA for, 193–4, 194–5
    patent law and, 232
    product labelling and, 193
    small- and medium-sized enterprises and, 193
    traceability of, 194–5
application dossier, 55–7
Association of British Pharmaceutical Industry (ABPI), 201
    1988 policy paper, 45
ATMP Regulation (2009), 183–5, 219–22
    amendment of previous regulations in, 221
    contents of, 224–5
    DG Sanco report (2003) and, 220
    ethical concerns covered in, 184
    evaluation of, 247–9
    hospital exemption and, 248–9
    negotiations for, 219–21
    objectives of, 184, 221–2
    stakeholders' interests in, 220–1, 247, 249
authorisation procedures:
    drugs, requirement for, 2
    300-day maximum limit for, 41

basic patents:
    active ingredients protected by, 108, 121–2 (case law)
    scope of and SPC Regulation, 110–11
    two, designated for six SPC applications, 109 (case law)
Better medicines for children – proposed regulatory actions in paediatric medicinal products (2002 consultation paper), 217
Better Regulation Action Plan (EC, 2002), 217–18
Better Regulation Guidelines, 25
biotechnological pharmaceutical products, applications submitted to CPMP, 5
centralised procedures (CP), 58–60
    applications, process for, 59
    pharmaceutical products, used for, 59
Certificate of Conformity, 114
certificates of suitability (CEPs), 56
Charles Rivers Associates study (2017) (impact of exceptions to patent and SPC rights), 126
children:
    clinical trials in, 245–6
    SPC extensions' effect on costs, 246
clinical data, collection of, 66–7
clinical trials, 66–8
    children, in, 245–6
    transparency in paediatric clinical trials, 152–3
Clinical Trials Directive (2001), 137, 218, 249
combination products:
    patent extension and, 112
    SPC for, 95
Committee for Advanced Therapies (CAT), 50, 185
Committee for Medicinal Products for Human Use (CHMP), 47–8, 73, 140, 141
Committee for Medicinal Products for Veterinary Use (CVMP), 45, 48
Committee for Orphan Medicinal Products (COMP), 48–9, 160–1

market exclusivity review and, 161–2
medical plausibility and, 165–6
orphan medicinal products designation process and, 158–9
role of and interpretation of significant effect, 169–71 (case law)
significant benefit and, 167–71
Committee for Proprietary Medicinal Products (CPMP) (1988):
biotechnological and high-tech pharmaceutical products' MA applications, 5
EMA, establishment of and, 38
role and mandate of, 3
Committee on Herbal Medicinal Products (HMPC), 45, 50
Common Technical Document (CTD), 55
Community Register of Orphan Medicinal Products, 159, 170
orphan drug designations' removal from, 176–7, 177–8
competence:
public health measures and, 15–16
Regulations and Directives in, 16–18 (case law)
TFEU Article 114 and, 16–18 (case law)
compliance, 30
control and PIPs, 142–4
principle of proportionality and, 170–1 (case law)
Comprehensive Economic and Trade Agreement (CETA), 125–6
conferral principle and public health competence, 15
confidentiality, presumption of, 62–3 (case law)
Consumer's Consultative Committee's (CCC) views on MA system, 40
Coordination Group for Mutual Recognition and Decentralised Procedures: Human (CMDh), 52
Copenhagen Economics report, 197, 236
core inventive test, 111–12 (case law)
Court of Justice of the European Union (CJEU) and SPC Regulation, 234–5, 254–5

data exclusivity, 65–82, 226–7
generics and, 70–6
legal framework of, 65–7
minimum term of, 72–3
pre-clinical and clinical studies, for, 78
protection granted under, 76–7
Rx-to-OTC switches, of, 79–80
variations of original pharmaceutical products and, 78–9

data protection, 66–7
medicinal products, for, 72
decentralised procedure (DCP), 41, 47, 57, 61, 107
demand-side objective (SPC), 207–9
device-drug products and SPC Regulation, 116–17 (case law)
'disclosure test' (patents), 109
diseases:
development of and pharmaceutical product research, 10
rare, Community action programme on, 19

Economic and Social Committee (ESC) comments on SPC proposal, 203–4
effectiveness, 23–4
legislation and, 30
test, 24, 196–249, 255–6
'Ethical considerations for clinical trials performed in children' (European Commission, 2006), 217
European Commission (EC):
paediatric medicine, on, 216–17
significant benefit criterion and, 167–8 (case law)
European Consumers Organisation (BEUC) views on EMA, 40
European Directorate for the Quality of Medicines (EDQM), 52, 56
European Federation of Pharmaceutical Industries and Associations (EFPIA), 200–1
pharmaceutical companies' recognition of MA, 39
European Medicines Agency (EMA), 5–6, 37–51, 140, 255
background of, 37–41
BEUC's views on, 40
criticism of, 39
establishment of and CPMP report (1988), 38
FDA and collaboration over paediatric research, 153, 255
financing of, 43, 44
International Society of Drug Bulletins, criticism of, 44
justification for, 37
legal basis of, 41–5
MA, 46
mandate and role of, 45–7
MS views on, 40
patients' interests, 43
PDCO waiver, 143–4 (case law)
pharmaceutical companies' support for, 37–8

Index   271

pharmaceutical products, considered by, 46
post-authorisation control of medicinal products by, 47
publications of, 43–4
revised proposal for (1991), 42–3
safety of medicines, responsibility for, 45
scientific committees, operation of under, 44–5
transparency in, 43
European Patent Convention compatibility with SPC Regulation, 204–5
European pharmaceutical industry:
international market and, gap between, 210
regulation of, 196–9
European Public Assessment Reports (EPARS) (EMA publication), 44, 47
European Union (EU):
documents, right of access to, 62–3
Health Strategy (2007), 20
legal order and internal market, 13
MA procedure, orphan drugs under, 241
patent system, vi
pharmaceutical markets compared with US, 198
pharmaceutical sector, need for regulation of, 1–8
US and, 31–3
exceptions to market exclusivity, 175–6
conditions for, 175
second applicant's evidence, 175
exclusivity:
market *see* market exclusivity
medicinal products and, 198
orphan drugs designation of as market value, 244
existing satisfactory method (orphan medical products), 166

Final Report of the Pharmaceutical Sector Inquiry (2009), 8–9
Food and Drug Administration (FDA) (US), 2, 44, 163
EMA and, collaboration over paediatric research, 153, 255
formula magistralis and officinalis, 64
France, treatment of orphan drugs in, 241
functional definition (patent), 96, 97

gene therapy, 185–6
generic products:
definition, 69
MA for, 69–80

medicinal, not classified as medicinal products, 75
SPC protection, expiry of and, 127–8
generics (pharmaceutical), 10
data exclusivity and, 70–6
dossier, 75
generic defined, 71
manufacturers' function and role of, 70–2
SPC and, 208–9
global health (health strategy), 20
Good Manufacturing Practices (GMPs), 58
ATMP and, 193
goods, free movement of, 13

Heads of Medicines Agencies (HMA), 51
health care and subsidiarity principle, 14–15
health law, 6–7
evolution of and internal market, 7
regulative factors for, 7
health services, cross-border, 18
Health 2020 (WHO), 21
high-risk devices, control regimes for, 114
high-tech pharmaceutical products, CPMP, applications submitted to, 5
hospital exemption (ATMP), 64, 195, 248–9
ATMP Regulation and, 248–9
MA and, 191–2
Human Genome Science (HGS), 96–7
human tissue and cells, Directives for, 189–90

impact assessment, 25, 26–8
criticism and overview of, 27–8
Mousmouti on, 27
questions codifying, 26–7
industry pricing strategies, 209
infringement test (patents), 109
intellectual property:
action plan (COM (2020) 760 final), vi–vii
orphan drugs and, 215
intellectual property rights (IPR) and legislative drafting, 33
internal market:
EU legal order, in, 13
European pharmaceutical industry and, gap between, 210
health law, evolution of and, 7
public health policies and, 14
International Conference on Harmonisation of Technical Requirements for Registration of Pharmaceuticals for Human Use (ICH) (2017), 52, 137
paediatric medicine, guideline on, 217

international non-proprietary name (INN), 61
International Society of Drug Bulletins, EMA
    criticism of, 44
investment criterion, insufficient return on
    (orphan medicinal products), 164–5

legal transplantation, 31–2
legislation and effectiveness, 30
legislative drafters, skills of, 33–4
legislative drafting, 32–4
    IPR and, 33
licensees and licensors, MA holders,
    can be, 130–1
Lisbon Treaty, public health protection in, 12
low profit margins and SPC, 208

Maastricht Treaty, public health
    protection in, 12
Managed Entry Agreements (MEAs), 243
market exclusivity (orphan drugs),
    72, 173–4, 226–7
    exceptions to *see* exceptions to market
        exclusivity
    Medicinal Code and, 77
    orphan drugs and, 213, 215
    Orphan Drugs Regulation, under, 8
    period (Orphan Drugs Regulation), 177–80
        (case law)
market exclusivity (orphan drugs) review:
    COMP and, 161–2
    orphan medicinal products application
        procedure and, 161–2
market impact objectives, 209
marketing authorisation applications, 55
    protection levels in, 226
marketing authorisation holders, 73–4
    licensors and licensees, can be,
        130–1 (case law)
    patent holder is not, 129 (case law)
marketing authorisation procedures, 53–63,
    192–3
    acquisition of patents in, 106–8
    alternative, 57–63
    application dossier for, 55–7
    choice of for pharmaceutical products, 69
    Directives for, 54, 68–9
    European Union, orphan drugs under, 241
    legal framework of, 54–5
    regulatory agencies and, 36–64
    transparency of, 62–3 (case law)
marketing authorisation system:
    CCC's views on, 40
    conditional, 60

objective of, 133–4
overview of, 232–3
marketing authorisations (MA), 141–2
    agency for, 5–6
    ATMP and, 191–3, 194–5
    centralised, 191
    'compassionate use' option, 59–60
    Directive, terminology used in, 133
    EMA processing of, 46
    first and grant of SPC, 90–1 (case law)
    generic products, for, 69–80
    German regulatory authority (BfArM),
        from, 80–1 (case law)
    global, concept of, and Medicinal Code, 72
    hospital exemption and, 191–2
    medicines, new, for, 141–2
    MS recognition of, 39
    orphan drugs, of, 54, 172–3
    paediatric pharmaceuticals, of, 54, 233
    patent application and, time elapsed between,
        117–19 (case law)
    post-authorisation requirements, 194–5
    risk analysis for, 192–3
    SPC applications and, 87, 91–2 (case law)
    third-party, 129–30 (case law)
    validity, renewal and termination of, 59, 61–2
    withdrawal of, 76 (case law)
Medeva ruling, 92, 94, 110–11 (case law), 228
medical devices, 114–17
    regulatory framework for, 114
    SPC protection denied for, 114–15
medical plausibility (orphan medical
    products) and COMP, 165–6
Medicinal Code:
    generic application of, 75
    global MA concept in, 72
    market exclusivity and, 77
    medicinal product definition in, 87–8
    Part II, Annex I, 74
    reference pharmaceutical role of product
        authorised under, 79
    well-established use and, 80
medicinal products:
    accessibility of, pricing and reimbursement
        system role in, 251–3
    active ingredient and absolute
        identity, 113, 132
    active substances, different from, 256, 257
        (case law)
    authorisation for, 4
    commercialisation of, 3
    data protection for, 72
    definition of, 3, 88

dossiers of, 70
exclusive rights of, maximisation of, 227
exclusivity and, 198
generic medicinal products, not
    classified as, 75
guidelines for, 54–5
legal interpretation of, 106–13 (case law)
post-authorisation control of by EMA, 47
results of manufacturing process, 187
somatic cell therapy and, 186
SPC and, 119–20, 120–1 (case law)
Member States (MS):
EMA, views on, 40–2
MA, recognition of by, 39
SPC applications, rules for, 92–3
mixed devices and substances, classification and treatment of, 115–16 (case law)
Moratorium Regulation, 235
Mousmouti, Maria, 23–4
impact assessment, on, 27
mutual recognition procedure (MRP), 38, 39, 40, 57, 60, 69

national competent authorities of European Member States, 51–2
national procedure, 46, 57, 61, 150
Neurim **ruling,** 102–4 (case law)
'new active substance', 74 (case law)
'no generic of a generic' principle, 75
'non-European' pharmaceutical market, investigation of, 4–5
non-orphan medicinal products, six-month extension of SPC protection, for, 145–6 (case law)
non-similarity report, 175
Notice to Applicants (NTA), 54–5
Novo Nordisk (Danish pharmaceutical company)), 197

'one-off import' (human tissue and cells) defined, 190
original pharmaceutical products, data exclusivity of variation of, 78–9
orphan drugs, 155–82
codification of and Orphan Drugs
    Regulation, 213
Community patients benefit from, 163–4
cost of considered, 242–3
France, treatment of in, 241
intellectual property and, 215
MA of, 54, 172–3
market, stakeholders in, 244
market exclusivity and, 213, 215

marketing of, 241
removal of designation, 229 (case law)
SPC extension, eligibility for, 229–30
orphan drugs designation, 157–8
criteria for, 162–72
exclusivity of as market value, 244
fee reduction for, 176
MA and, 173–4
prevalence criterion for, 162–4
removal from community register, 176–7
sponsor's post-grant obligations, 176–7
technical assistance for, 176
timing of application, 171–2 (case law)
transfer to new sponsor, 177
two years paediatric extension, 228–9
Orphan Drugs Regulation (2009), 155–7, 211–15
codification of orphan diseases and, 213
content of, 233
enactment of, 157
evaluation of, 243–4
interpretation of, 177–81 (case law)
market exclusivity under, 8
negotiations for, 211–14
objective of, 214
proposal for, discussions on, 156–7, 212
workshop on (1998), 211
'orphan indication' and' therapeutic indication' distinguished, 160
orphan medicinal products:
designation, procedure for, and COMP, 158–60
documentation required for application, 159
extension periods for, 148–9 (case law)
legislation for and overview of, 155
withdrawal of application, 159
orphan medicinal products application procedure:
market exclusivity review, 161–2
pre-application meeting, 160
review of application, 160–1

Paediatric Committee (PDCO), 49, 140–1
EMA and waiver, 143–4 (case law)
exemptions and waivers under, 143–5 (case law)
paediatric extension, 137–54
scope of, 122
two-year and orphan drug designation, 228–9
Paediatric Investigation Plans (PIPs), 49, 138–9, 141–2

compliance control, 142–4
deadlines for, 143
deferral of initiation or completion of, 145
ethical concerns about, 143
modification of, 142
trial details in, 142
paediatric medicine:
European Commission on, 216–17
ICH guideline on, 217
lack of, 216
testing, costs of, 219
paediatric products:
development, free scientific advice during, 150
discontinuation of, 151
MA and, 233
pharmacovigilance for, 151
putting on the market within two years, 151
Paediatric Regulation, 216–19
Articles 7 and 8, 139–40
background to, 137–8
basis of, 8
contents of, 223–4
evaluation of, 245–7
industry benefits of, 245
legal framework of, 139–40
legislative process for, 217–18
negotiations for, 216–18
objective of, 218–19
patent system's not referred to, 231
text of agreed, 218
paediatric research:
clinical trials, transparency in and, 152–3
FDA and EMA's collaboration over, 153, 255
Paediatric Use Marketing Authorisation (PUMA) (2006), 81, 140, 150
parallel trade (pharmaceutical markets), 4 (case law)
patent claims, antibody structure mentioned in, 111
patent holders:
MA, are not holders of, 129 (case law)
patent term lost, compensation for, 5
several for one product, 128–9 (case law)
SPC rights of, 89–90
patent law and ATMP, 232
patent protection:
certificate, active ingredient for, 108–9 (case law)
expired patents, for, 108–9 (case law)
pharmaceutical products, of, 96–100 (case law)
patent rights:
exceptions to, 126–8
SPC Regulation and, 84–5
patent system:
Paediatric Regulation, and, 231
SPC Regulation and, 230–1
patent terms:
patent holders' compensation for shortened, 5
extension of for pharmaceutical products, 200
protection of, comparison of, 201–2
patents:
acquisition of, 106–8
application for and MA, interval between, 117–19 (case law)
basic see basic patents
extension of and combination products, 112
interpretation by person skilled in the art, 98–9
'patent cliff', 239
post-grant claims, 95
protection under see patent protection
second medical indication, SPC granted to, 256, 257 (case law)
SPCs, relationship to, 93–6
subject of the invention, 95
unitary, 231
patients' interests and EMA, 43
personalised medicine, 210–11
pharmaceutical companies:
EMA, support for, 37–8
European, global and home markets of, 197
MA, recognition of, 39
pharmaceutical industry:
business models of, 10
change of priorities, 239
European see European pharmaceutical industry
product development, 9
structure of, 8–10
pharmaceutical markets regulation, 6
European, comparison with US pharmaceutical markets, 198
regulation of products and, 6
pharmaceutical research:
remuneration or compensation for, 104
SPC Regulation and, 237
pharmaceutical sector:
acquisition of patents in, 106–8
effective legislation for, 22–3

Index   275

pharmaceutical strategy for Europe
        (COM (2020) 761 final), vii
pharmaceuticals:
    clinical benefits added to, 77–8
    complex, 93–6 (case law)
    cost of (2003 and 2019), 66
    CP used for, 59
    improvements to, 77–80
    MA of, 5–6, 38–9
    manufacturing of, regulation of, 125
    names of, 61
    need of, EMA's consideration of, 46
    new active ingredients, 55–6
    new medical indication of and SPC
        application, 104–6 (case law)
    old, second medical use for, 100–6
        (case law)
    one SPC only, subject to, 87
    original, 68–9
    over-the-counter (OTC), 79
    packaging, details of, 56
    paediatric, MA of, 54
    paediatric symbol for, 152
    patent protection of, 96–100 (case law)
    patent terms' extension of, 200
    pricing of, 6
    regulation of, US system of, 2
    research and development of diseases, 10
    see also medicinal products
pharmacovigilance:
    paediatric products, of, 151
    Risk Assessment Committee
        (PRAC), 45, 51
plant protection:
    action, 113
    products, 9, 210
    Regulation, 85, 91
    research, protection for, 204
Plavix case (2008), 80–1
pre-clinical and clinical studies,
        data exclusivity for, 78
prevalence criterion:
    information required for, 163
    orphan drugs designation, for, 162–4
    scarcity of Community patients,
        and, 163–4
products:
    definition, 88
    development, 65–6
    interpretation of term, 88–9 (case law),
        101–4 (case law)
    labelling and ATMP, 193

regulation of and regulation of
        pharmaceutical market, 6
    SPC protection of, 88
proportionality principle and compliance,
        170–1 (case law)
Proposal for a Council Regulation Concerning
        the Creation of a Supplementary
        Protection Certificate for Medicinal
        Products, 202
Proposal for a Regulation laying down
        Community Procedures for the
        Authorization and Supervision of
        Medicinal Products for Human and
        Veterinary Use and Establishing a
        European Agency for the Evaluation
        of Medicinal Products (1990), 40–1
protection:
    combination of methods for, 226–7
    data exclusivity, granted under, 76–7
    levels, MA applications, in, 226
    patent terms', comparison of, 201–2
    plant see plant protection
public consultations, 25, 28–9
public health:
    policies and internal market, 14
    protection, treaty references to, 12–13
public health competence, 10–18
    conferral principle and, 15
    legal basis of, 10–14
public health programmes, 19–21
    first (2003– 2008), objectives of, 19
    Health Strategy (2008–2013), 20
    third (2014–2020), objectives of, 20–1

reference:
    dossier, 75
    products, 70
Regulation (EC) No 1901/2006, penalties for
        breach of, 152
regulations, changes in terminology of, 199
regulatory agencies and MA procedure, 36–64
regulatory rights, 82
    European system of, v
    legislative character of, 31
replacement compounding, 64
risk:
    analysis, MA's, 192–3
    management system, 194
    Pharmacovigilance Risk Assessment
        Committee, 45, 51
Rx-to-OTC switches, data exclusivity
        of, 79–80

safety of medicines, EMA's responsibility for, 45
Sanco, DG (2003 report), 220
'satisfactory methods':
   existing satisfactory method (orphan medical products), 166
   orphan drugs and, 180–1 (case law)
   scope of substances as, 257 (case law)
significant benefit (orphan medicinal products), 167–71, 180–1 (case law)
   COMP and, 167
   criterion and European Commission, 167–9 (case law)
   elements of, 167
   interpretation of, 168
   practices not considered to be of, 168
   provision of, justification for, 168–9 (case law)
   test for, 171
Significant Benefit Working Group, 168
'significant effect', interpretation of and COMP's role, 169–71
similar active substance, 174
'similar medicinal product', 173–4
Similarity Report, 174
Single Market Programme, regulation of pharmaceutical market under, 6
small- and medium-sized enterprises:
   ATMP and, 193
   office of, 45–6
social security systems (EU), 13
somatic cell therapy medicinal products, 186
specific market, 30
specific mechanism (SPC), 123–4 (case law)
structural formula in patent, 96, 97
subject matter excluded, 113–17
subsidiarity principle and health care, 14–15
Summaries of Product Characteristics (EMA publication), 43–4
Summary of Product Characteristics (SmPC), 55
   medicinal products' properties listed in, 56
Supplementary Protection Certificate (SPC), 5, 83–136
   case, 14
   combination products, for, 95
   duration of, 84
   explanatory memorandum, 85
   first MA, and grant of, 90–1
   infringement, 119–20, 120–1 (case law), 127
   interpretation of, 85
   invalidity of, 121
   legal framework, 86–93
   low profit margins and, 208
   negative or nil term, 85, 119, 146, 228
   patents, relationship to, 93–6
   proposal, ESC comments on, 203–4
   regulation of, 84
   second medical indication patent, granted to, 256, 257 (case law)
   SPC Regulation, and grant of, 131 (case law)
   terms, extension of, 223–4
Supplementary Protection Certificate applications, 89–91
   active ingredient, granted for, 112 (case law)
   applicants, 89
   complex pharmaceuticals, for, 93–6 (case law)
   granting of and new medical indication, 104–6 (case law)
   MA and, 87, 91–2 (case law)
   MS rules for, 92–3
   six, two basic patents designated for, 109 (case law)
Supplementary Protection Certificate extensions, 84
   application time limit for, 147 (case law)
   children's medicine, effect on, 246
   non-orphan medicinal products, six-month extension for, 145–6 (case law)
   orphan drugs' eligibility for, 229–30
Supplementary Protection Certificate manufacturing waiver, 124–8
   justification for, 124
   lack of, consequences of, 124–5
Supplementary Protection Certificate protected products, 88
   pricing of and SPC Regulation, 209–10
Supplementary Protection Certificate protection, 236–7
   calculation of, 117
   duration of, 117–28
   expiry of and generic products, 127–8
   medical devices, denial of for, 114–15
   medicinal products, for, 119–20
   nil or negative, 119
   non-orphan medicinal products, six-month extension for, 145–6 (case law)
   patent application and MA, time elapsed between, 117–19 (case law)
   products, of, 88
   scope of, 122–3 (case law)
Supplementary Protection Certificate protection requirements, 86–9
   six-month deadline, start date of, 86–7 (case law)

Supplementary Protection Certificate Regulation, 200–11
  amendment to, necessity for, 237–9
  application of, 84–5
  Article 3, 64, 87, 91–6 (case law), 100–3 (case law), 106–10, 166–71
  basic assumptions in, 206
  basic patents, scope of, 110–11
  CJEU and, 234–5, 254–5
  content of, 222–3
  device-drug products and, 116–17 (case law)
  effectiveness of, 235–6
  European Patent Convention, compatibility with, 204–5
  grant of SPC precluded by, 131 (case law)
  internal hierarchy of, 103–4 (case law)
  national interpretation of, 250–1
  negotiating history of, 200–6
  objectives of, 233
  opposition to, 205
  patent rights and, 84–5
  patent system and, 230–1
  pharmaceutical research and, 237
  SPC-protected products, pricing of and, 209–10
  terminology used in, 133
Supplementary Protection Certificate rights:
  exceptions to, 126–8
  patent holders', 89–90
Supplementary Protection Certificate system, 133–4, 233–4
  UPP's impact on, 85–6
stakeholders, 6, 25, 28, 41, 156, 195, 225
  ATMP Regulation and, 220–1, 247, 249
substances, scope of as 'satisfactory methods', 257 (case law)
supply-side objective (SPC), 206–7

Takeda **test,** 109 (case law)
'therapeutic indication' and 'orphan indication' distinguished, 160
tissue-engineered products (TEPs), 187, 220
'Together for Health' (2007), 20
transparency:
  EMA, in, 43
  MA procedure, of, 62–3 (case law)
  paediatric research and clinical trials, in, 152–3
Treaty on the Functioning of the European Union (TFEU):
  Article 114 and competence, 16–18 (case law)
  public health protection in, 12–13

Unitary Patent Package (UPP), 134
  SPC system, impact on, 85–6
United Kingdom Intellectual Property Office (UKIPO), 86, 87, 102, 107
  medicinal product definitions, on, 87–8 (case law)
United States (US):
  EU and, 31–3
  pharmaceutical markets compared with EU, 198
  pharmaceutical products, regulation of, 2

'well established substance', new indication for, 78
Well Established Use (WEU):
  Medicinal Code and, 80
  medicinal products and, 79–80 (case law)
WHO Conference of Drug Regulatory Authorities (ICDRA) (1989), 53